J. A. Lorimer
1989

FORTRAN 77

FORTRAN 77

Hart C. Bezner

Wilfrid Laurier University
Waterloo, Ontario

Prentice Hall, Englewood Cliffs, New Jersey 07632

Library of Congress Cataloging-in-Publication Data

Bezner, Hart C.
FORTRAN 77.

Includes index.
1. FORTRAN (Computer program language) I. Title.
QA76.73.F25B493 1989 005.13'3 87-32795
ISBN 0-13-329509-5

Editorial/production supervision and
interior design: *TKM Productions*
Cover design: *Diane Saxe*
Manufacturing buyer: *Mary Noonan*

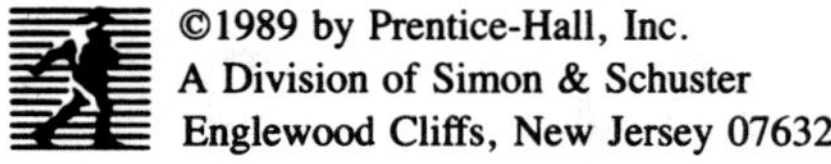

A Division of Simon & Schuster
Englewood Cliffs, New Jersey 07632

LIMITS OF LIABILITY AND DISCLAIMER OF WARRANTY

The author and publisher of this book have used their best efforts in preparing this book. These efforts include the development, research, and testing of the theories and programs to determine their effectiveness. The author and publisher make no warranty of any kind, expressed or implied, with regard to these programs or the documentation contained in this book. The author and publisher shall not be liable in any event for incidental or consequential damages in connection with, or arising out of, the furnishing, performance, or use of these programs.

Printed in the United States of America

10 9 8 7 6 5 4 3 2 1

ISBN 0-13-329509-5

PRENTICE-HALL INTERNATIONAL (UK) LIMITED, *London*
PRENTICE-HALL OF AUSTRALIA PTY, LIMITED, *Sydney*
PRENTICE-HALL CANADA INC., *Toronto*
PRENTICE-HALL HISPANOAMERICANA, S.A., *Mexico*
PRENTICE-HALL OF INDIA PRIVATE LIMITED, *New Delhi*
PRENTICE-HALL OF JAPAN, INC., *Tokyo*
SIMON & SCHUSTER ASIA PTE. LTD., *Singapore*
EDITORA PRENTICE-HALL DO BRASIL, LTDA., *Rio de Janeiro*

A.G.D.

Contents

8 FILE INPUT/OUTPUT 124

9 TRANSFER OF CONTROL AND SELECTION CONTROL STRUCTURES 139

Preface

Students arriving for their first year at colleges and universities bring with them surprisingly varied backgrounds in computing, ranging from no previous exposure to fairly extensive familiarity.

This great diversity is a relatively recent phenomenon and is the direct consequence of elementary and secondary school systems attempting to discover their own roles and scope in a field new to many.

The task of defining the focus of a first course in computing at the postsecondary level has become correspondingly difficult. If the instructor assumes that the students have no previous background, the classes will be uninteresting and possibly offensive to many. Conversely, should the instructor assume a certain level of background, the aim may be far too high for some and still fall short for others. It is a difficult situation at best, made even more critical by the fact that the introductory course is frequently the keystone to subsequent computing courses.

This book is the author's response to this difficult situation. It is designed to provide the student with a highly logical and linear progression from first principles to advanced concepts. A conscious effort is made throughout to make the material highly readable and filled with well-focused examples. It is designed to stimulate rewarding experimentation, and the problems are intended to be realistic, without fostering unnecessary frustration.

Students with previous computing experience will find sufficient new and worthwhile material, but those who lack prior exposure will also consider the concepts readily understandable, although a much greater investment of their time is required.

Experience has taught that unless there is definite understanding of the various data types and their internal representations, beginning FORTRAN programmers never join the circle of insiders and never feel entirely at ease with the language. The book, therefore, starts by introducing this critically important area. The instructor is free to determine the degree of emphasis, which might range from light to intense, but the topic should most certainly be covered for the sake of the better understanding it opens.

One of the more important features of *FORTRAN 77* is file handling and this area deserves considerably better treatment than generally found. The importance of file processing stems from the growing use of the computer as an information machine rather than just a numeric problem solver. This book introduces file handling relatively early and it is one of the major threads running throughout. In order to use files effectively, record-oriented I/O must be understood, and again that topic is introduced early, along with the list-directed features offered by the language.

Many feel that the most important goal in a computing course is to get students to write simple but complete programs as early as possible so as to make the course relevant. The author feels that before that can happen, a strong foundation must be established. Programs are not developed until they can be placed on a secure foundation.

The book is intended for serious introductory computing courses. It is less suitable for lighter offerings in computer literacy. The material can be covered in a single term or semester, and it is designed to foster considerable growth in depth and breadth of understanding.

It is the author's experience that it usually becomes obvious during the first week which students will succeed, who will just get by, and who should be advised to drop the course. Many years of experience have also made it obvious that we must never assume that any student can become a computing star through the investment of sufficient effort. Such stardom seems to demand special talent, a talent not often found in the general population, but a goodly number of those, through patience and hard work, do achieve exceptional levels and become valuable contributors.

FORTRAN Is the language chosen here because full implementations of FORTRAN 77 (ANSI FORTRAN X3.9–1978) are readily available on many large, medium, and small computers, and because the standard incorporates file handling.

FORTRAN was not conceived in academic isolation, but has firm roots in the real world. It is no longer the sole domain of scientists and mathematicians but, because of its elegant and effective file-manipulation abilities, is finding its way into the broader world of business applications.

Computers were new in 1957 when FORTRAN made its public debut. It has since grown considerably.

I would like to express gratitude to my many students, past and present, who inspired this book, and for whom it was written. They have strained out many a gnat and camel, and pointed out gaps in the roadway that needed to be bridged. Special thanks to the following individuals for their reviews of my manuscript: Keith Olson, Montana College of Mineral Science & Technology, Butte, Montana; Michael Gonzales, Beaver College, Glenside, Pennsylvania; and Douglas Kerley, Florida Junior College, Jacksonville, Florida

I also wish to thank Professor Burr Cartwrignt Brundage for his kindness in permitting me to borrow, for Chapter 14, a paragraph from his remarkable book, *A Rain of Darts, The Mexica Aztecs*, copyright © 1972, the University of Texas Press, Austin.

Hart C. Bezner

FORTRAN 77

1

Number Systems

The ability to count is probably the earliest acquired mathematical skill. So early in fact that as we grow older we spend little time meditating on the nature of this remarkable ability. Counting involves the concept of adding yet another one many times, until all of the items have been counted. The count at each stage is given a name, symbolically called the *total*. It does not take long after first becoming conscious of the concept of counting to realize that the process leads in the direction of infinity and that along the way an infinite number of totals is encountered. Because each total is a distinct entity, it must have its own name.

Obviously, it is not practical to attempt to learn an infinite number of distinct names, one for each total encountered during the counting process, and yet each such entity *must* have a distinct name. Different cultures have dealt with this problem in differing ways. In some cultures, only the first 11 totals are given distinct names, for example: none, one, two, three, four, five, six, seven, eight, nine, and ten. Other cultures go a little further and add two more, say eleven and twelve. Some cultures have 21 distinct names, one each for the totals from none to twenty. Twenty appears to be a natural barrier beyond which it becomes awkward to invent new names. As a matter of fact, we find that the emerging human consciousness encounters its first real barrier at about the total of ten. Many young children will proudly inform us that they can count up to ten, but display problems with the quantities eleven, twelve, and beyond. When learning a foreign language, we are reminded that we probably experienced that same obstacle in our own childhood when we realize that counting in the new language seems most difficult from about eleven to fifteen.

1.1 THE ICOSAL NUMBER SYSTEM

The problem of an infinite number of entities requiring an infinite number of distinct names is solved by invoking yet another unique human talent, the ability to impose order and structure. As an example, consider a society in which the basic counting system recognizes quantities from none to twenty as distinct entities. To count a small heap of beans, a market vendor will count off a group of twenty. The group cannot be made larger because no unique name exists to designate the number of beans in a larger group. The vendor then starts a new group, counting twenty beans into it, and then creates a third group of twenty. A fourth group of twenty is then started, but all the beans have been counted when the vendor reaches ten. The total number of beans is then reported as three groups of twenty and ten. Because of clever grouping, it becomes possible to count considerably beyond twenty. In our particular example, the group of twenty is a definite concept and as such ought to be given a simple name. English speakers call it a *score*. Many other languages also recognize a group of twenty as a distinct entity and assign a name to it. In the Bible, the human lifespan is said to be three score and ten, or 70 years. French-speaking people refer to a certain quantity as *quatre-vingt*, which you will recognize as four groups of twenty.

Twenty such groups of twenty would also be an important concept and should probably be given a unique name, such as *score-score*, containing 400 items. Twenty such score-scores might be called one score-score-score, containing 8000 items. Twenty of these might be called a score-score-score-score, containing 160,000. A load of beans might thus be found to contain 17 score-score-score-score and 8 score-score and 3 score and 15, which is 17 times 160,000 plus 8 times 400 plus 3 times 20 plus 15, which adds up to 2,723,275. A number system based on twenty may be called *icosal*, after the Greek word *eikosi*, meaning twenty.

1.2 THE DECIMAL NUMBER SYSTEM

In our own counting system, the basic group contains 10 items, and for this reason it is called the *decimal* system. The system is also called the *Arabic* system, although its early roots can be traced to India, where we find evidence that the Hindus used some of its symbols as early as the third century before the common era. The system was introduced into the Arab world about A.D. 700, and its first recorded use in Europe occurred in 976. The Arabs modified the system extensively, adding to it positional notation, and they formalized the concept of "none" by inventing a symbol for it, namely, 0. The system has remained essentially unchanged since its introduction to Europe and shines with elegant simplicity. The system is based on ten, using the 10 symbols 0, 1, 2, 3, 4, 5, 6, 7, 8, and 9. The basic group in the system contains 10 items, but there is no special symbol to denote this quantity.

Instead, positional notation is used and the quantity is shown as 10. The position of the 1 tells us that we are dealing with one group of 10 items and the zero tells us that there are no more individual items. 75 conveys seven groups of 10 and five individual items. The basic group of 10 items does have a special name; it is called *ten*. The word thus conveys not only a count but also a basic group. Ten such groups form a larger group, important enough to be assigned the special name *hundred*. Again, positional notation is used to indicate such groups of hundreds. The notation 704 conveys seven groups of hundred, no groups of ten, and four individual items. We are so accustomed to the Arabic positional notation that we do not frequently pause to dwell on the human genius mirrored in it.

As implied earlier, groupings of ten are as significant to the decimal system as are the groupings of twenty to the icosal system. The basic group of ten items is called ten. Ten such groups of ten items are called one hundred. Ten groups of a hundred form a new group called one thousand. Ten groups of a thousand might have easily been given another special name, but ten thousand was the obvious choice. Ten groups of ten thousand form a new group called hundred thousand. A group of ten hundred thousands is given the special name million, followed by ten million, then hundred million. A group of ten of these is also considered to be important enough to deserve its own name, but the world does not agree on that name. In North America, one thousand million is usually called one billion, whereas many other countries refer to it as one milliard. In some countries, notably Britain and Germany, the name billion refers to one million million and not to one thousand million. The special names for groupings of ten, in other words, become vague as the quantities thus conveyed fall outside our common experiences.

You might be interested to learn that some people refer to the quantity represented by 1 followed by 100 zeros as 1 *googol*. Similarly, 1 followed by 1 googol of zeros is called 1 *googolplex*.

Why is our number system based on 10? The reason appears to be because we have 10 fingers. Because we also have 10 toes, we might expect to find systems based on 20, which we do, of course. We even find systems based on both 5 and 20 in which the basic group contains five items and four of these basic groups constitute another basic group containing 20 items.

1.3 THE OCTAL NUMBER SYSTEM

It should be obvious by now that the base of a number system is completely arbitrary and to emphasize this fact, we will examine a system based on 8. This particular system is called the *octal* system and uses eight Arabic symbols 0, 1, 2, 3, 4, 5, 6, 7 along with positional notation. Counting follows the same pattern as in the decimal system, except that no digit larger than 7 can appear in any of the positions. Counting in the octal system is shown in Fig. 1.1.

You will do well to go through this sequence carefully, understanding all the entries. Again, 10 represents one basic group, consisting of eight items in this case and no individual items. The quantity symbolized by 10 in the octal system is represented by 8 in the decimal system, i.e., $10_8 = 8_{10}$, where the subscripts 8

0	17	71	777
1	20	72	1000
2	21	73	1001
3	22	74	. . .
4	. . .	75	. . .
5	. . .	76	1776
6	. . .	77	1777
7	27	100	2000
10	30	101	. . .
11	31	102	. . .
12	. . .	. . .	2777
13	. . .	. . .	3000
14	66	. . .	3001
15	67	775	3002
16	70	776	3003

Figure 1.1 Counting in the octal system.

and 10 are decimal references to the respective bases. A problem is that we have no name for 10 in the octal system, and so we simply call it ten octal. A number such as 37 octal (i.e., 37_8) tells us that we have 3 groups of 8 items plus 7 more individual items, which is equivalent to 31_{10}. Similarly, 100_8 denotes 1 group of 8 groups of 8, which is 64_{10}. 231_8 implies 2 groups of 8 groups of 8 plus 3 groups of 8 plus 1 individual item, making 231_8 equivalent to 153_{10}.

1.4 THE HEXADECIMAL NUMBER SYSTEM

Because the base of a number system is so clearly arbitrary, we might investigate a system based on 16. Such a system is called *hexadecimal* and requires 16 unique symbols to represent the possible digits. Rather than invent 16 new symbols, it has become customary to borrow the 10 Arabic symbols from the decimal system and to supplement these with the first six letters from the Roman alphabet, giving us the following 16 digits: 0, 1, 2, 3, 4, 5, 6, 7, 8, 9, A, B, C, D, E, and F. Note

0	12	33	201	20B4
1	13	. . .	202	20B5
2	. . .	. . .	. . .	20B6
3	. . .	97	. . .	20B7
4	19	98	9FE	20B8
5	1A	99	9FF	20B9
6	1B	9A	A00	20BA
7	1C	9B	A01	20BB
8	1D	9C	. . .	20BC
9	1E	9D	1FFF	20BD
A	1F	9E	2000	20BE
B	20	9F	2001	20BF
C	. . .	A0	. . .	20C0
D	. . .	A1	20AF	20C1
E	2F	. . .	20B0	20C2
F	30	FF	20B1	20C3
10	31	100	20B2	20C4
11	32	. . .	20B3	. . .

Figure 1.2 Counting in the hexadecimal system.

that the additional digits A to F give us six more fundamental symbols for expressing totals before it becomes necessary to invoke positional notation. Needless to say, $A_{16} = 10_{10}$ and $F_{16} = 15_{10}$.

Counting in the hexadecimal system is also very simple, as shown in Fig. 1.2. Again, you are encouraged to study the sequence carefully, understanding it in detail. A number like 2A looks strange because it contains a letter from the alphabet to which we suddenly attach numeric significance. Some find this to be an obstacle and never quite come to terms with the hexadecimal number system. Being aware of the nature of this obstacle, however, makes it much easier to overcome. Taking a closer look at $2A_{16}$, we recognize from our understanding of positional notation that 2 groups of 16 are involved to which A_{16} individual items are added, giving us $(32 + 10)_{10} = 42_{10}$.

1.5 THE BINARY NUMBER SYSTEM

To emphasize once again that the base of a number system is arbitrary, we will look at a system based on 2, called the *binary* system. In this system, only two digits are available, namely 0 and 1. ''No'' item is represented by 0. A single item is represented by 1. If we now add another single item, we form one basic group of 2 items, and we represent that count by 10_2, which denotes 1 group of 2 items with 0 additional items. Adding one more item would give us 1 group of 2 with 1 individual item, or 11_2. If we then add another item, we get 1 group of 2 groups of 2, no remaining single group of 2, and no remaining individual items, or 100_2.

Counting in the binary system is also delightfully simple. Study Fig. 1.3 and the pattern will become clear. The binary system does not appear very useful at first until it is recognized that many electronic circuits and devices exhibit two stable states and could thus be used to remember either a 0 or a 1. Six such bistable circuits placed side by side could thus be configured to store a binary number such as 110010, which has a decimal equivalent of 50. A current pulse, a voltage pulse,

0	10001	100010
1	10010	100011
10	10011	100100
11	10100	100101
100	10101	100110
101	10110	100111
110	10111	101000
111	11000	101001
1000	11001	101010
1001	11010	101011
1010	11011	101100
1011	11100	101101
1100	11101	101110
1101	11110	101111
1110	11111	110000
1111	100000	110001
10000	100001	110010

Figure 1.3 Counting in the binary system.

or even a magnetic pulse might then be allowed to act on the third circuit, changing its state from 0 to 1. The array of six binary digits would then contain 111010, which is equivalent to decimal 58. To illustrate further, each circuit in the array could receive a pulse causing it to flip to its opposite state, leaving the array with 000101, which has the modest decimal equivalent of 5. Circuitry could be designed to shift all the binary digits in the array to the left by one position to yield 001010, the decimal equivalent of which is 10. Notice that the simple act of shifting the binary digits to the left had the effect of multiplying the binary number by 2. You can see that bistable circuits and bistable devices, arranged as arrays of suitable width, permit the storage and manipulation of numeric quantities inside the computer, provided that such quantities be expressed in binary form.

1.6 CONVERSIONS BETWEEN THE BINARY, OCTAL, AND HEXADECIMAL SYSTEMS

We looked at five different number systems, namely those based on 20, 16, 10, 8, and 2, and you might feel somewhat uneasy that you will be required to convert back and forth among these systems, but this is hardly the intent of a book on FORTRAN, especially since a more general and formal treatment is usually encountered in other courses. There is, however, a very special relationship between 2, 8, and 16, which are all powers of 2. Because of this, we might really expect the octal and hexadecimal number systems to be condensed versions of the binary system. This is indeed true, making it very easy to convert from any one of these three systems to either of the other two, and you will be able to do this readily. Figure 1.4 lists the first 16 numbers in each of these three systems, and it makes such conversions very simple. You will find it most rewarding to memorize the first 16 hex numbers and their binary equivalents, but until you have memorized these, you can always generate the table and look up the equivalents. The octal column is used only as far as 7 when you convert either from octal or to octal, and it

Hex	Octal	Binary
0	00	0000
1	01	0001
2	02	0010
3	03	0011
4	04	0100
5	05	0101
6	06	0110
7	07	0111
8	10	1000
9	11	1001
A	12	1010
B	13	1011
C	14	1100
D	15	1101
E	16	1110
F	17	1111

Figure 1.4 The first 16 hex numbers and their octal and binary equivalents.

agrees with the hexadecimal column between 0 and 7, making the memory work easier. Let's look at several conversion examples.

As our first example, we convert the binary number 11001101001010 to hexadecimal. To accomplish the conversion, simply break the binary number into groups of four digits, starting from the right. Then, write the hexadecimal equivalent of each group below it, preferably from memory, but you may wish to use the table until you feel completely at home.

```
11 0011 0100 1010
 3    3    4    A
```

or $11001101001010_2 = 334A_{16}$, which is the desired conversion.

The next illustration involves converting the binary number 11001101001010 to octal. This time the binary number is broken into groups of three, again from the right. The octal equivalent of each group of three is then written below it.

```
11 001 101 001 010
 3   1   5   1   2
```

or $11001101001010_2 = 31512_8$.

To convert a hexadecimal number to binary is just as simple. The hex digits are written and the corresponding four binary digits are written below these. Hex 1F3BA3 demonstrates the procedure:

```
   1    F    3    B    A    3
0001 1111 0011 1011 1010 0011
```

or $1F3BA3_{16} = 111110011101110100011_2$. Notice that the leading zeros can be omitted.

An octal-to-binary conversion is shown next. The octal digits are written and the three binary digits corresponding to each octal digit are written below that digit. We practice on octal 137401:

```
  1   3   7   4   0   1
001 011 111 100 000 001
```

or $137401_8 = 1011111100000001_2$.

Changing a number from octal to hex is a simple two-step process. The octal number is first converted to binary and the resulting binary digits are then divided into groups of four and converted to the corresponding hex digits. Octal 14057 is converted to hex to illustrate the method:

```
  1   4   0   5   7
001 100 000 101 111
0001 1000 0010 1111
   1    8    2    F
```

or $14057_8 = 182F_{16}$.

The last example involves the conversion of a hex number to octal, 1F34B to be specific. The pattern should be clear to you by now. We first write the hex number and then convert each hex digit to the corresponding group of four binary digits. The resulting binary string is then divided into groups of three digits, starting from the right as always. The groups of three binary digits are then expressed as octal digits:

```
     1    F    3    4    B
   0001 1111 0011 0100 1011
  00 011 111 001 101 001 011
  0   3   7   1   5   1   3
```

or $1F34B_{16} = 371513_8$.

1.7 EXAMPLES

Example 1.1

Convert 111_{16} to decimal.

Solution The number 111_{16} represents, starting with the rightmost digit, 1 item plus 1 group of 16_{10} items plus 1 group of $(16 \times 16)_{10}$ items, i.e., $(1 + 16 + 256)_{10} = 273_{10}$. Thus, $111_{16} = 273_{10}$.

Example 1.2

Convert 123_{16} to decimal.

Solution The number 123_{16} represents 3 items plus 2 groups of 16_{10} plus one group of 256_{10}. Thus, $123_{16} = 291_{10}$.

Example 1.3

Convert 247_8 to decimal.

Solution

$$247_8 = (7 \times 1 + 4 \times 8 + 2 \times 64)_{10} = 167_{10}.$$

Example 1.4

Convert 342_8 to decimal.

Solution

$$342_8 = (2 \times 1 + 4 \times 8 + 3 \times 64)_{10} = 226_{10}.$$

Example 1.5

Convert 12132_4 to decimal.

Solution

$$12132_4 = (2 \times 1 + 3 \times 4 + 1 \times 16 + 2 \times 64 + 1 \times 256)_{10} = 414_{10}.$$

Example 1.6

Convert 31042_4 to decimal.

Solution The given number is obviously not based on 4 because it contains a 4. A number based on 4 must not contain digits larger than 3. The problem statement is in error.

Example 1.7

Convert 20011210_3 to decimal.

Solution

$$20011210_3 = (0 \times 1 + 1 \times 3 + 2 \times 9 + 1 \times 27 + 1 \times 81 + 0 \times 243 + 0 \times 729 + 2 \times 2187)_{10} = 4503_{10}.$$

Example 1.8

Convert 33_{10} to hex.

Solution In hexadecimal positional notation, the first digit on the right has a weight of 1. The second digit from the right has a weight of 16_{10}, while the third, fourth, and fifth digits from the right have weights of 256_{10}, 4096_{10}, and 65536_{10}, respectively. 33_{10} is obviously composed of 2 groups of 16 plus 1, which is represented as 21_{16} in positional notation.

Example 1.9

Convert 121_{10} to hex.

Solution 121_{10} is composed of 7 groups of 16, which is 112_{10}, with 9 left over. This quantity is represented by 79_{16} in hexadecimal positional notation. Thus, $121_{10} = 79_{16}$.

Example 1.10

Convert 125_{10} to hex.

Solution 125_{10} consists of 7 groups of 16_{10} with 13_{10} left over. 13_{10} is D_{16}. Therefore, $125_{10} = 7D_{16}$.

Example 1.11

Convert 3927_{10} to hex.

Solution

$$3927_{10} = (3840 + 80 + 7)_{10} = (15 \times 256 + 5 \times 16 + 7)_{10} = F57_{16}.$$

(Recall that $15_{10} = F_{16}$.)

Example 1.12

Convert 29_{10} to octal.

Solution In octal positional notation, the first digit on the right has a weight of 1. The second digit from the right has a weight of 8, whereas the third, fourth, and fifth digits from the right have weights of 64_{10}, 512_{10}, and 4096_{10}, respectively. 29_{10} obviously consists of 3 groups of 8 with 5 left over. In other words, $29_{10} = 35_8$.

Example 1.13

Convert 391_{10} to octal.

Solution 391_{10} consists of 6 groups of 64, plus 0 groups of 8, with 7 left over. Therefore, $391_{10} = 607_8$.

Example 1.14

Convert $13579BDF_{16}$ to binary.

Solution From memory, or using Fig. 1.4, convert each hex digit into the equivalent group of four binary digits. Therefore,

$$13579BDF_{16} = 00010011010101111001101111011111_2.$$

The leading zeros can be omitted.

1.8 PROBLEMS

1.1. Convert 1532_{16} to decimal. *Answer*: 5426_{10}.

1.2. Convert $12F_{16}$ to decimal. *Answer*: 303_{10}.

1.3. Convert $82F_{16}$ to decimal. *Answer*: 2095_{10}.

1.4. Convert $A2F_{16}$ to decimal. *Answer*: 2607_{10}.

1.5. Convert $F2F_{16}$ to decimal. *Answer*: 3887_{10}.

1.6. Convert 111_8 to decimal. *Answer*: 73_{10}.

1.7. Convert 117_8 to decimal. *Answer*: 79_{10}.

1.8. Convert 177_8 to decimal. *Answer*: 127_{10}.

1.9. Convert 577_8 to decimal. *Answer*: 383_{10}.

1.10. Convert 777_8 to decimal. *Answer*: 511_{10}.

1.11. Convert 1000_8 to decimal. *Answer*: 512_{10}.

1.12. Convert 1234_5 to decimal. *Answer*: 194_{10}.

1.13. Convert $1AB_{12}$ to decimal. *Answer*: 275_{10}.

1.14. Convert $1AB_{13}$ to decimal. *Answer*: 310_{10}.

1.15. Convert $1AB_{14}$ to decimal. *Answer*: 347_{10}.

1.16. Convert $1AB_{15}$ to decimal. *Answer*: 386_{10}.

1.17. Convert $1AB_{16}$ to decimal. *Answer*: 427_{10}.

1.18. Convert $1AB_{11}$ to decimal. *Answer*: Error in notation.

1.19. Convert 429_{10} to hex. *Answer*: $1AD_{16}$.

1.20. Convert 429_{10} to base 15. *Answer*: $1D9_{15}$.

1.21. Convert 429_{10} to base 14. *Answer*: 229_{14}.

1.22. Convert 429_{10} to base 12. *Answer*: $2B9_{12}$.

1.23. Convert 429_{10} to base 9. *Answer*: 526_{9}.

1.24. Convert 429_{10} to base 8. *Answer*: 655_{8}.

1.25. Convert 429_{10} to base 5. *Answer*: 3204_{5}.

1.26. Convert 429_{10} to base 4. *Answer*: 12231_{4}.

1.27. Convert 429_{10} to base 3. *Answer*: 120220_{3}.

1.28. Convert 429_{10} to base 2. *Answer*: 110101101_{2}.

1.29. Convert 429_{10} to base 1. *Answer*: 111111111111 . . . —429 of them. This takes us back to the cave wall.

1.30. Convert $AF301_{16}$ to binary. *Answer*: 10101111001100000001_{2}.

1.31. Convert 741732_{8} to binary. *Answer*: 111100001111011010_{2}.

1.32. Convert $1011011101011100001011011 1_{2}$ to octal. *Answer*: 267270267_{8}.

1.33. Convert $10110111010111000010110111_{2}$ to hex. *Answer*: $2DD70B7_{16}$.

1.34. Convert 7214730152_{8} to hex. *Answer*: $3A33B06A_{16}$.

1.35. Convert $7214A_{16}$ to octal. *Answer*: 1620512_{8}.

2

Internal Storage Concepts

In Chapter 1, we discussed number systems and stated that some electronic circuits and devices exhibit two stable states, making them ideal for storing binary digits inside the computer. We now take a closer look at numeric storage in binary form.

2.1 BINARY NUMBER STORAGE INSIDE THE COMPUTER

The only two digits used in the binary system are 0 and 1, and any mechanical or electronic device with two stable states can be used to store such binary digits. Devices or circuits possessing two stable states are said to be *bistable*. One of these stable states can be used to store the digit 0 whereas the opposite state denotes 1. To make the issue more graphic, consider an ordinary wall-mounted light switch. The switch is a mechanical bistable device, possessing the two stable states *up* and *down*. We could now arbitrarily declare that up represents the binary digit 1 and down corresponds to the binary digit 0 and then use the light switch as a memory device for storing numeric information. The largest number that could be stored, however, is 1 unless we placed several such switches side by side with positional notation in mind. Figure 2.1 illustrates all eight possible settings if we were to build a memory array consisting of three switches placed side by side.

Figure 2.2 shows the eight binary numeric equivalents of these switch settings, if we agree that *down* represents 0 and that *up* represents 1. The eight binary numbers in Fig. 2.2 have the decimal equivalents 0, 1, 2, 3, 4, 5, 6, and 7. If now a

Down	Down	Down
Down	Down	Up
Down	Up	Down
Down	Up	Up
Up	Down	Down
Up	Down	Up
Up	Up	Down
Up	Up	Up

Figure 2.1 The eight possible configurations of an array of three light switches.

0	0	0
0	0	1
0	1	0
0	1	1
1	0	0
1	0	1
1	1	0
1	1	1

Figure 2.2 The binary number equivalents of the eight switchsettings.

fourth switch were added to this array of three switches, numbers from 0 to 15 could be stored, whereas an array of five switches provides 32 different possibilities. If the array were broadened to eight switches, 256 unique configurations would become possible. An array of 16 switches can hold 65,536 different settings, and 32 switches placed side by side have a capacity of 4,294,967,296 distinct combinations.

In general, if a storage array is n binary digits wide, 2^n different quantities can be stored in that array in binary form. You should convince yourself that this is so, by considering storage arrays with a width of two digits, three digits, four digits, etc. If this simple point is not clear to you, you will trip over some of the subsequent material.

2.2 ACCOMMODATING NEGATIVE NUMBERS

Getting back to the computer, if the machine were to provide arrays, each composed of, say, 32 bistable elements, we could store 4,294,967,296 different binary numbers in each such array, covering the full range from 00000000000000000000000000000000 to 11111111111111111111111111111111, and it might be felt that a computer with the ability to store such large numbers could be of practical value.

Further thought makes us realize, however, that we have not yet confronted the necessity of also being able to store negative numbers. It is obvious that we must develop some scheme for dividing the range of possible representations into a negative group and into a positive group, with a special slot for zero. There are various ways of doing this, and an obvious way might be to treat the first element of the storage array as a sign. If the first element were zero, the array could be assumed to contain a positive number, and if the first element contained a 1, negative storage would be signaled. This type of scheme is actually used in some systems, but the logical design of the arithmetic unit is considerably simpler when a somewhat different approach is used. Needless to say, whatever scheme is devised, half of the representation range must be assigned to negative numbers and the other half to positive numbers and zero. This approach would permit our 32-element storage array to store decimal equivalents ranging from −2,147,483,648 to +2,147,483,647. The positive range includes zero, explaining why the largest positive number is 1 less than might be expected.

Again, we can generalize and say that if a storage array is n binary digits wide, 2^n different binary numbers can be stored there. Now, half of 2^n is 2^{n-1}, as will become obvious to you when you compare 2^4 with 2^3, for example. This means that an n-digit array can store 2^{n-1} different negative numbers and 2^{n-1} positive numbers, including zero. This means, of course, that the most negative possible number is -2^{n-1}, whereas the largest possible positive number is $+2^{n-1} - 1$.

It was implied previously that there are potentially better ways of storing negative numbers than simply preceding the magnitude of the number with a 1, and to illustrate just how simple the most commonly used alternative scheme is, we will again look at the $2^3 = 8$ possible configurations of a three-digit storage array, as shown in Fig. 2.3. 2^{3-1}, or 4, of these 8 configurations must be reserved for negative numbers, the most negative of which is −4. The other 2^{3-1} are reserved for the positive numbers and zero, limiting the largest positive number to +3.

000
001
010
011
100
101
110
111

Figure 2.3 The three-digit storage array.

Now the questions are: Which of these eight available patterns are reserved for the four negative numbers? Which three are assigned to the positive numbers? Which pattern is used to store zero? It seems that the choices are relatively arbitrary, but they should make sense. Figure 2.4 shows how the assignments are generally made. At first glance, you might feel that these assignments are not as sensible as they ought to be, but they will be justified after we discuss Fig. 2.5. Before moving on to that example though, you should take another good look at Fig. 2.4.

Binary content	Decimal equivalent
000	0
001	1
010	2
011	3
100	−4
101	−3
110	−2
111	−1

Figure 2.4 Assigning zero and positive and negative numbers.

Binary content	Decimal equivalent	Binary content	Decimal equivalent
00000	0	10000	−16
00001	1	10001	−15
00010	2	10010	−14
00011	3	10011	−13
00100	4	10100	−12
00101	5	10101	−11
00110	6	10110	−10
00111	7	10111	−9
01000	8	11000	−8
01001	9	11001	−7
01010	10	11010	−6
01011	11	11011	−5
01100	12	11100	−4
01101	13	11101	−3
01110	14	11110	−2
01111	15	11111	−1

Figure 2.5 Numeric storage in a five-digit memory array.

Figure 2.5 illustrates a five-digit memory array. The array can store 2^5, or 32 different combinations, 2^4, or 16, of which are reserved for the positive numbers and zero, whereas the remaining 16 are used for the negative numbers. The assignment of the negative numbers follows precisely the scheme illustrated in Fig. 2.4. You will benefit from a careful comparison of these two examples because a clear pattern is obvious. In particular, you should compare the binary representations of zero, the largest positive numbers, the most negative numbers in the two tables, and you should compare the binary representations of −1. After the comparison, you will be able to predict the binary representations of zero, −1, the largest positive number, and the most negative number in any *n*-digit binary storage array.

Although you are probably quite willing to accept the division of the binary representations into positive and negative ranges, you may still be wondering why this particular representation scheme was chosen. But the reason is a good one, for if you take the binary pattern corresponding to a particular positive number and add to it the binary pattern assigned to its negative counterpart in Fig. 2.5, the sum will be 00000 with a carry digit of 1. This carry digit drops off the left end because the array is not wide enough to accommodate it. This is another way of saying that positive and negative numbers are represented such that when a positive number is added to its negative counterpart, the resulting sum is zero. This interesting phenomenon is now illustrated by Fig. 2.6, where the binary representation of −8 is added to that of +8. (Keep in mind that in the binary system $0 + 0 = 0$, $1 + 0 = 1$, $0 + 1 = 1$, and $1 + 1 = 0$ with a carry of 1.)

As a further illustration, study Fig. 2.7, where the binary representation of −10 is added to that of +10.

```
 01000   (+8)
+11000   (−8)
------
100000   (leaving 00000 because the 1 overflows)
```

Figure 2.6 The internal representation of +8 and its negative counterpart.

```
 01010   (+10)
+10110   (-10)
------
100000   (leaving 00000 after overflow)
```

Figure 2.7 The internal representation of +10 and its negative counterpart.

2.3 THE TWO'S COMPLEMENT OF A BINARY NUMBER

In the previous section, we considered a scheme in which the binary representation of a positive number and the binary representation of its negative counterpart add to zero with an overflowing carry digit. Two binary numbers that add to zero in this manner are said to be each other's *two's complement.* It is easy to deduce the two's complement of a binary number because this involves a simple two-step process. The procedure will not be justified theoretically. Instead, we simply demonstrate that it works and consider this to be sufficient.

The first step in finding the two's complement of a given binary number requires that you first invert it by turning every 1 into a 0 and every 0 into a 1. The resulting binary number is called the *one's complement.* We then add 1 to the least significant digit of this one's complement, giving us the desired two's complement.

As always, a picture is worth many convoluted sentences, and we therefore illustrate the process of two's complementing in Fig. 2.8. In this illustration, the internal representation of -12_{10} is deduced from our knowledge that the internal representation of $+12_{10}$ is 01100 in a five-bit memory array. If you now return to Fig. 2.5, you will find that 10100 is indeed the internal representation of -12_{10}. Before moving on, it is emphasized again that the representation of a negative number as the two's complement of its positive counterpart, and vice versa, of course, makes the logical design of the computer's arithmetic unit much simpler.

This is a good place to introduce the technical term *bit,* which is simply a contraction of *binary digit.* In studying Figs. 2.4 and 2.5, you will notice that all the negative numbers have the first bit set to 1, whereas the positive numbers and zero have a 0 first bit. For this reason, the first bit is frequently referred to as the *sign bit.* Note that we did not set the first bit to 1 to flag a negative number. Instead, the sign bit was turned on as an automatic consequence of the complementing process.

Looking at Figs. 2.4 and 2.5 once again, you will notice that the numbers progress in the positive direction from zero to the maximum positive number. At this point, a discontinuity occurs as we suddenly jump to the most negative number. Notice, however, that the progression continues in the same positive direction because the numbers become less negative as we continue to move down the tables.

```
01100   (binary representation of +12)

10011   (the one's complement of 01100)
   +1   (adding 1 to get the two's complement)
-----
10100   (the two's complement of 01100, representing -12)
```

Figure 2.8 Deducing the two's complement of +12.

We have seen enough now to understand the following readily: Suppose that someone tells you that the basic storage array in a certain computer is 12 bits wide and that the machine employs two's complemented internal storage. Based on your observations, you can now safely predict that 0_{10} is stored as 000000000000, that the largest positive number is stored as 011111111111 and that this is equal to $2^{11} - 1 = 2047$, and that the most negative number is $100000000000 = -2^{11} = -2048$, and that -1 is stored internally as 111111111111. If this is not abundantly clear, take another thorough look at Figs. 2.4 and 2.5.

It is obvious now that storing numeric quantities inside the computer is not only possible, but can be accomplished in a surprisingly simple manner. If you have come to terms with the basic concepts, then you are probably wondering how fractions and alphabetic characters can be stored. These questions are addressed in the following chapter, but before getting into more detail, we should review our travels to this point by being reminded that on the most fundamental level only bits can be stored in memory arrays. It was easy to see that the ability to store bits permits us to store numeric quantities, provided we express these in binary form. We soon recognized, however, that provisions must be made for negative numbers. To that end, we decided that the capacity of a storage array should be divided into two ranges, half reserved for negative numbers and the other half for zero and the positive numbers.

As a little exercise, let's assume that you open the front panel on a computer, locate the first array of memory, which might happen to consist of 16 bits, and find the binary pattern 1111111111111111 stored there. If someone asked you for the bit pattern in the array, you could simply read out the bits as 1111111111111111. You would find it much simpler though, to report the bit pattern in hex as FFFF or in octal as 177777. You are conveying the same information, but in a more compact and manageable manner. Note that you converted only the bit pattern in the storage array to hex and octal, and not necessarily the magnitude of the number stored there. For that matter, you cannot even be sure that a number is stored in the array. For all you know, it could be some other sort of data. If you were now asked to assume that the array did indeed contain a number and to assume that the number were stored in two's complement form, you would conclude that the array contained -1!

Anyway, do not be unduly worried if some of the details have not taken firm root yet. The intent of all this is to prepare you for greater things by laying a specific foundation.

2.4 BITS, NIBBLES, BYTES, WORDS, AND PAGES

Mechanical calculators are based on the decimal system. They contain gears, each with 10 teeth, and every tooth defines a stable state. Whenever a particular gear undergoes 10 clicks, it makes one complete revolution and causes its neighbor to the left to advance by one click, exactly as you have often observed on the odometer of a car. If all the gears in the calculator were replaced with 16-tooth gears, the calculator would automatically turn into a hexadecimal device, performing the four basic arithmetic operations flawlessly. If eight-tooth gears were used, an octal calculator would be born. Mechanical calculators are slow but their simplicity exerts a strong attraction. It is not surprising that during the early years of the computer's evolution, people sought mechanical or electronic devices with 10 stable states. One such mechanical device is the telephone stepping relay, and early attempts were made to incorporate that technology into computers. Unacceptably low speeds proved to be the downfall, and before long it became apparent that if the computer were to operate at electronic rather than mechanical speeds, the designers had to shift their attention to electronic circuits.

It would be a happy event indeed if a simple circuit or elementary electronic device were found to possess 10 stable states, but nature favors two stable states. It is very easy, for example, to design small so-called *flip-flop* circuits, which exhibit two identifiable and stable states. Pulses injected into such flip-flop circuits cause them to flip to the opposite state, which they maintain until another external pulse causes a transition to the former state. Flip-flop circuits can be designed with extremely low switching times, in the nanosecond range, where one nanosecond is 10^{-9} seconds. If such devices are to constitute the basic building blocks of the computer, then we are forced to design the computer around the binary number system. We must also be prepared to expend considerable effort in the design of interface equipment to allow us to work in the decimal system externally while the computer operates in the binary system internally. Understanding how a computer works is largely a matter of understanding and accepting the choice of the binary system inside the machine and understanding how the machine stores and manipulates such binary data.

The most elementary storage element in the computer then is some form of flip-flop circuit. This circuit, by virtue of its bistable nature, is able to store a single binary digit, either 0 or 1. As mentioned earlier, the contraction of binary digit is bit, but the meaning of the word bit has broadened somewhat to include not only the binary digit stored in a circuit, but also the circuit itself. A storage array composed of six flip-flop circuits, for example, is simply referred to as a six-bit register.

A grouping of four bits turns out to be a useful entity and is called a *nibble*. The term nibble is of fairly recent origin and not yet fully accepted, but is gaining adherents.

Another useful grouping of bits is called a *byte*. A byte can contain six, eight, or nine bits, depending on the manufacturer of the hardware. The eight-bit byte is by far the most common, but a strong case could be made for larger bytes. The reasons will be discussed in the following chapter, in connection with character data.

Another useful grouping of bits is the *word*. A word of memory can be as small as four bits, in which case it would be the same size as a nibble, or it might be as large as 64 bits. Some machines have eight-bit words, including many of the older microcomputers. Other machines use 12-, 16-, 18-, 24-, 32-, 36-, 48-, 60-, or 64-bit words. Eight-bit word microcomputers were succeeded by 16-bit micros and these, in turn, are yielding to the new wave of 32-bit microprocessors.

Words are conveniently grouped into *pages*. A page can contain as few as 128 words or as many as 2048, or more, again depending on the manufacturer.

The relationship between bits, nibbles, bytes, words, and pages varies considerably as you look at the broad spectrum of available computers, but is well established within any one family of machines. What appears to be the emerging trend is shown in Fig. 2.9.

From the perspective of the FORTRAN user, the byte is generally associated with character data, involving the storage of textual information, whereas the word is associated with numeric data, but all this will become considerably clearer in the following chapter.

In the early days, computers had small memories, composed of a few dozen words. By the midsixties, a 16,384-byte (16-kilobyte) memory was considered respectable, and by the midseventies, people with 1,048,576-byte (1-megabyte) machines were the object of great envy. It is now quite common to encounter machines with 32 or even 64 megabytes, and it is felt that we will soon find computers with several gigabytes of main memory (one gigabyte is 1,000 megabytes, or 1,000,000,000 bytes).

A 32-megabyte memory actually consists of 33,554,432 bytes, or 268,435,456 bits, on the assumption that eight-bit bytes are involved. Each bit involves a flip-flop circuit, or similar structure, and it is difficult to picture 268 million flip-flops functioning flawlessly day after day. The flip-flops are so small that nearby cosmic ray events occasionally induce a change of state, causing a bit to be picked or dropped, corrupting the data in the affected word of memory. Such data corruption would normally force a machine to "crash" itself, rather than produce incorrect results. During such a crash, all users might be dropped from the machine to permit it to reinitialize or boot itself. To minimize such upheavals, many machines attach about six extra bits to each double word of memory. These additional bits are transparent to the user, but store enough redundant information to permit the machine to detect bit corruptions in double words of memory. If a single bit is in error, the machine can actually tell which bit is involved, allowing it to flip that bit to repair the problem. Such single-bit repairs occur on the fly, unseen by the user. The machine records each repaired bit in its error log, telling the customer engineer precisely which circuit chip on which board was involved. If the same chip is reported repeatedly, it is simply replaced. The extra watchdog bits are often called EDAC bits, where EDAC stands for error detection and correction. EDAC bits usually detect and correct only single-bit failures within a double word of memory, but this covers most cases because multiple-bit failures within the same double word are quite rare. Should multiple bits fail within such a double word, the problem

1 bit	–	The basic element of storage
1 nibble	–	4 bits
1 byte	–	8 bits = 2 nibbles
1 word	–	32 bits = 4 bytes
1 page	–	128, 512, or 1024 words

Figure 2.9 The relationship between bits, nibbles, bytes, words, and pages.

would still be detected, but it could not be corrected. The machine would then be required to crash itself to preserve its integrity.

In addition to the main memories just discussed, machines are usually also equipped with slower external memories residing on spinning disks, with capacities ranging from 64 kilobytes to hundreds of gigabytes. It is possible to store bits, bytes, words, and pages on these disks, with data transfers between the main memory and the disk occurring one or more pages at a time.

2.5 EXAMPLES

Example 2.1

A 32-bit word of memory contains the bit settings FFFFFE95. The word is known to contain numeric information stored in two's complement form. Is the stored number positive or negative?

Solution The word contains 11111111111111111111111010010101, which is simply the expansion of the above hex abbreviation. Because the first bit is turned on, and because we know that the word contains numeric information stored in two's complement form, the quantity is obviously negative.

Example 2.2

Deduce the actual numeric content of the word in the previous problem.

Solution The word contains a negative number. To find the positive counterpart of that number, two's complementing is performed:

11111111111111111111111010010101	(content of word)
00000000000000000000000101101010	(one's complement of content)
+1	
00000000000000000000000101101011	(two's complement)

This two's complement obviously represents a positive number because the first bit is turned off. The positive number is $16B_{16} = 363_{10}$. We therefore conclude that the word of memory with the bit pattern FFFFFE95 contains the negative number $-16B_{16} = -363_{10}$.

Example 2.3

How many different numbers can be stored in a 10-bit word?

Solution The word can hold 2^{10} different quantities. $2^{10} = 2 \times 2 \times 2 \times 2 \times 2 \times 2 \times 2 \times 2 \times 2 \times 2 = 1024$. The possibilities range from -512 through $+511$ if two's complementing is used.

Example 2.4

Assuming a 12-bit word and two's complement storage, what is the largest positive number, the most negative number, the representation of -1, and the representation of zero?

Solution The largest positive number is $+2^{11} - 1 = +2047$. The most negative number is $-2^{11} = -2048$. The internal representation of -1 is 111111111111 (i.e., hex FFF, or oct 7777). The internal representation of zero is 0000000000 (i.e., hex 000, or oct 0000).

2.6 PROBLEMS

2.1. If the representation of 30654_{10} in a 16-bit word is 0111011110111110, deduce the internal representation of -30654_{10}. Assume that two's complemented storage is involved. *Answer*: 1000100001000010, or hex 8842.

2.2 Show the hex-abbreviated internal 32-bit representation of $+100_{10}$. *Answer*: 00000064.

2.3. Show the hex-abbreviated internal 32-bit representation of -100_{10}. Assume two's complement storage. *Answer*: FFFFFF9C.

2.4. Show the hex-abbreviated internal 32-bit representation of $32{,}767_{10}$. *Answer*: 00007FFF.

2.5. Show the hex-abbreviated internal 32-bit representation of $-32{,}768_{10}$. Assume two's complement storage. *Answer*: FFFF8000.

2.6. Show the hex-abbreviated internal 32-bit representation of $2{,}147{,}483{,}647_{10}$. *Answer*: 7FFFFFFF.

2.7. Show the hex-abbreviated internal 32-bit representation of $-2{,}147{,}483{,}648_{10}$. Assume two's complement storage. *Answer*: 80000000.

2.7 SUGGESTED RESEARCH

Discuss with your instructor the type of hardware you will be using for your work. Ask about the number of bits/byte and the number of bytes/word. Ask about the memory size and try to get some information about automatic error detection and correction (EDAC.)

3

Internal Representations and Data Types

In Chapter 2, we saw that it is easy to store numbers in words of memory. It was shown that an n-bit word can store 2^n different bit patterns, and hence 2^n different binary numbers. The need to accommodate negative numbers led to the concept of two's complementing. By the time we reached the end of the chapter, we knew how to store positive and negative whole numbers, and it is hoped that now you are curious about the various schemes used to represent numbers with fractional components.

Although the storage method discussed in Chapter 2 cannot accommodate fractions, it turns out that some mathematical problems involve only whole numbers, usually referred to as *integers*. For this reason, FORTRAN provides access to this storage method, and any datum stored in this way is said to be of type *integer*. A number with a fractional component obviously needs a different internal representation and is said to be of type *real*. The FORTRAN programmer differentiates between these two numeric data types and is always conscious of the way they interact. A programmer is also interested in nonnumeric data storage to accommodate character and logical data items. This chapter examines various data types and their internal representations.

3.1 DATA TYPES

As just mentioned, a programmer requires three basic data types, namely numeric, character, and logical. Numeric data, as seen, can be integer or real. Character data are used to store text strings such as English sentences, and logical data permit the storing of the two truth values, true and false.

3.2 NUMERIC DATA

Numeric data constitute one of the three basic data types, and FORTRAN programmers categorize such data as either integer or real. Numeric data can be represented in three fundamentally different modes internally, however, depending on the needs of the programmer. The three modes are known as *fixed-point*, *floating-point*, and *binary-coded decimal* (BCD). Lest these terms cause confusion, it is emphasized that they apply to internal representations rather than data types. Integer and real are FORTRAN data types, whereas the terms fixed-point, floating-point, and BCD refer to internal representations. The next three sections take a preliminary look at these internal representations followed by a much more detailed examination. All this will bring the FORTRAN terms integer and real into focus.

3.3 PRELIMINARY LOOK AT INTERNAL FIXED-POINT STORAGE

The standard positional representation of a quantity allows you to express whole numbers or fractions of any magnitude, provided there is enough physical space in which to write the quantity. This space consideration is important because the representations become wider the larger the integer portion of the quantity, or the smaller its fractional component. This is obvious when you look at the four numbers in Fig. 3.1, the first of which is very large whereas the second is very small. The third and fourth are less extreme. This standard positional representation can also be called fixed-point because the weight of each of the digits is determined by its fixed distance from the decimal point. If the digit is two positions to the left of the point, it has a weight of 100. If it is two positions to the right of the decimal point, its weight is 1/100.

The four numbers are added in Fig. 3.2, where digits of similar weight are placed underneath each other, and the resulting columns are added. This is another way of saying that the decimal points must be aligned before the addition is performed.

The addition is completely accurate, but requires an adding machine with a very wide register. A wide register is required whenever very large and very small numbers are added or subtracted. You can also sense that the physical location of the decimal point in the adding machine is critical. It was located just right in our example, permitting us to enter the smallest and the largest numbers without losing digits. Had the decimal point been located a single digit position to the right of the current position, it would have meant the sacrifice of the last digit of the small

```
834000000000000000000000.0
0.000000000000000000000834
                    22.18
                     3.1415926
```

Figure 3.1 Fixed-point representation.

```
834000000000000000000000.0
                       0.000000000000000000000834
                      22.18
                       3.1415926
-------------------------------------------------
834000000000000000000025.321592600000000000000834
```

Figure 3.2 Aligning the decimal points before the addition is performed.

number. It would have been no great loss, but some of the precision would have been compromised. Had the decimal point been located a single position to the left of the current position, it would have meant the loss of the first digit of the large number, the most significant digit, which we can never afford to lose. A good adding machine, however, permits the position of the decimal point to be adjusted to accommodate extremes. All this is not really new, but you might be surprised by the suggestion that our conventional way of writing numbers may be called fixed-point.

3.4 PRELIMINARY LOOK AT INTERNAL FLOATING-POINT STORAGE

Those who deal with very large or very small numbers find the standard positional notation, which we just called fixed-point, awkward. Not only does it require a great deal of space, but when many digits are involved, the notation does not readily convey the magnitude of the number. To improve on this weakness, it has become customary to group the digits by threes, but even then it is often necessary to count the number of groups of threes to get a feeling for the magnitude. A more radical attempt to improve on this dual weakness involves the shift to so-called *scientific notation*. In this notation, the number is expressed as a factor multiplied by an appropriate power of 10. Figure 3.3 illustrates the previous four numbers expressed in scientific notation, also known as *floating-point*.

Floating-point representation proved to be quite helpful for the first two numbers. Not only did it reduce the space requirements, but it also readily conveyed their magnitudes. The two smaller numbers did not become more readable in this form, perhaps somewhat less so, and they required more space than before. Looking at these four floating-point numbers, you will notice a lack of standardization as to the location of the decimal point; it would be better if that location were determined by some convention. There is such a convention, giving us so-called normalized floating-point representation, in which the factor of the power of 10, also known as the *mantissa*, is a number less than 1 and greater than or equal to 0.1. The normalized floating-point representations of the four numbers are shown in Fig.

$$834.0 \times 10^{21}$$
$$0.834 \times 10^{-20}$$
$$22.18 \times 10^{0}$$
$$3.1415926 \times 10^{0}$$

Figure 3.3 Scientific notation or floating-point.

$$0.834 \times 10^{24}$$
$$0.834 \times 10^{-20}$$
$$0.2218 \times 10^{2}$$
$$0.31415926 \times 10^{1}$$

Figure 3.4 Normalized floating-point.

3.4. All this is familiar territory for you, and the only new terms were probably floating-point, normalized floating-point, and mantissa.

3.5 PRELIMINARY LOOK AT INTERNAL BINARY-CODED DECIMAL STORAGE

Binary-coded decimal storage, also known as BCD, is very easy to understand although you might not see much use for it initially. Imagine that you have a typewriter without Arabic numerals, and you have decided to invent a special code for each missing digit. The codes shown in Fig. 3.5 are as good as any.

0	–	0000
1	–	0001
2	–	0010
3	–	0011
4	–	0100
5	–	0101
6	–	0110
7	–	0111
8	–	1000
9	–	1001

Figure 3.5 Encoding the 10 decimal digits.

If you were now typing a letter in which you had to quote a dollar amount of $19.25, you could type it in code, as illustrated in Fig. 3.6.

$ 0001 1001 0010 0101

Figure 3.6 The encoded dollar amount.

Yes, we did encode each decimal digit, choosing the binary equivalent of each digit as the code. Our encoded decimal number could thus be called a BCD, or binary-coded decimal number. It's as simple as that.

A much closer look will now be taken at these three internal numeric representations. There will be considerable overlap between the preceding and the following material, but this is intentional.

3.6 INTERNAL FIXED-POINT REPRESENTATION REVISITED

In Chapter 2, we saw how easily whole numbers can be stored in words of memory. The numbers are simply converted to binary equivalent form and stored in the available bits. This equivalent representation works only for positive numbers, however, and the concept of two's complementing was introduced to permit the storage of negative numbers. The problem of storing fractions was alluded to but never resolved.

It was also mentioned that FORTRAN programmers refer to whole numbers as integers and they refer to numbers with fractional components as real. A FORTRAN programmer is always conscious of the differences between real numbers and integers for reasons that will become obvious.

One sensible way of storing real numbers in a word of memory is to superimpose on that word an imaginary dividing line and decreeing that all the bits to the left of this line shall represent the integer component of the number to be stored and all the bits to the right of the line constitute the fraction. It is obvious that the decimal analog to this imaginary dividing line is the decimal point. We interpret the number 3.14159_{10}, for example, as being composed of the integer component 3 and the fractional component .14159. In the octal system, the dividing line is called the *octal point*, and *hexadecimal point* in the hex system. In the binary system, it is referred to as the *binary point*, but its general name is *radix point*. (*Radix* is the Latin word for *root* and in mathematical usage refers to the base of a number system. Hence, 10 is referred to as the radix of the decimal system.)

It is important to understand that a binary point cannot be stored within a word of memory because the word will accommodate only bits. Instead, its position is understood to lie between a certain pair of bits, and any number stored in a word of memory in two's complement form, with an implied binary point, is said to be stored in fixed-point form. In some programming languages, the user controls the implied position of the binary point, whereas in others, the position is imposed by the hardware or software. These very simple concepts are illustrated in Fig. 3.7, where real numbers are stored in fixed-point form in 32-bit words of memory. The binary point is assumed to lie between the sixteenth and seventeenth bits.

You will find it profitable to work through these examples, especially the negative ones. Keep in mind the brute-force rule for finding the two's complement of a binary number. You invert all the bits to get the one's complement and then you add 1 to the least significant bit, which is always the last bit, regardless of the position of the binary point. Figure 3.8 will help you understand how decimal

Decimal number	Binary equivalent	Fixed-point storage
5.0	101.0	00000000000001010000000000000000
5.5	101.1	00000000000001011000000000000000
5.75	101.11	00000000000001011100000000000000
5.875	101.111	00000000000001011110000000000000
50.9375	110010.1111	00000000001100101111 000000000000
500.875	111110100.111	00000001111101001110000000000000
5000.875	1001110001000.111	00010011100010001110000000000000
32767.6640625	111111111111111.1010101	01111111111111111010101000000000
−1.0	−1.0	11111111111111110000000000000000
−1.5	−1.1	11111111111111101000000000000000
−500.875	−111110100.111	11111110000010110010000000000000

Figure 3.7 Internal fixed-point representations of numbers with fractional components.

0.1_2	=	$1/2_{10}$	=	0.5_{10}
0.01_2	=	$1/4_{10}$	=	0.25_{10}
0.001_2	=	$1/8_{10}$	=	0.125_{10}
0.0001_2	=	$1/16_{10}$	=	0.0625_{10}
0.11_2	=	$(1/2 + 1/4)_{10}$	=	0.75_{10}
0.111_2	=	$(1/2 + 1/4 + 1/8)_{10}$	=	0.875_{10}

Figure 3.8 The decimal equivalents of some binary fractions.

fractions can be converted to binary fractions, even though you are not necessarily expected to perform such conversions manually.

You will agree that the concept of fixed-point data storage is very simple, and yet it has the serious potential truncation problem mentioned in the discussion of Fig. 3.2. As a further manifestation of the problem, consider a scientist who determines the mass of some substance A to be 0.001111_2 grams. Substance B is found to have a mass of 0.00000000000001111_2 grams, and the mass of substance C turns out to be $0.000000000000000001111_2$ grams. You will notice that each of these three masses has been determined to four significant digits. The scientist now uses a computer to add the three masses by first storing each in a word of memory and then performing the addition. Figure 3.9 shows what happens, on the assumption that 32-bit fixed-point representation is used with an implied binary point between the sixteenth and seventeenth bits.

You can easily see the problem when you look at these internal fixed-point representations, the last two of which suffered truncation because there simply are not enough digit positions available in the 32-bit words. If the scientist understood the reasons behind the resulting inaccurate sum and if the programming language permitted the relocation of the implied binary point, the cure would be to move the binary point to the left by at least five positions. This remedy would require considerable insight, however, and it would be of tremendous advantage if somehow the binary point could be persuaded to float to an optimum position autonomously, far enough to the left to minimize the number of binary digits dropping off into the void, but not far enough to curtail the magnitude of the largest number to be stored. The automatic adjustment would have to be such that the computer, when faced with simultaneous overflow on the left and on the right, would push the binary point far enough to the right to accommodate the full integer component at the expense of the fractional component. The computer, in other words, would have to be willing to sacrifice precision but not magnitude. The choice between preserving magnitude and retaining precision arises only when very small numbers are added to or subtracted from very large numbers. The problem would not be encountered if the interacting quantities were all of similar magnitude. Wishing

	Mass	Internal representation
SUBSTANCE A	0.001111_2	00000000000000000011110000000000
SUBSTANCE B	0.00000000000001111_2	00000000000000000000000000000111
SUBSTANCE C	$0.000000000000000001111_2$	00000000000000000000000000000000

Figure 3.9 The three masses are stored in fixed-point mode.

aside, fixed binary points do not float, but the idea of a floating binary point is rather appealing.

How does all this relate to FORTRAN? The FORTRAN programmer does have access to fixed-point representation, but cannot control the position of the binary point. Instead, the designers of FORTRAN pushed the binary point all the way to the right, and hence out of the way. This permits the representation of large integers in fixed-point mode, but no fractional components, i.e., no real numbers, and we are right back to Chapter 2. We can now summarize Chapter 2 by stating that the type of internal representation discussed there was two's complemented fixed-point, with the implied binary point to the right of the last bit. A datum stored in this mode is said to be of type integer. It turns out that there are many applications that lend themselves to so-called integer arithmetic, and computations using this limited type of fixed-point representation can be very rapid, efficient, and completely accurate. When real numbers are required, FORTRAN provides a different form of internal storage, not surprisingly known as floating-point.

3.7 INTERNAL FLOATING-POINT REPRESENTATION REVISITED

The number of molecules in 1 gram molecule of a substance is very large, approximately 602,204,500,000,000,000,000,000 (about 1 percent more or less, depending on the reference). This number, known as *Avogadro's number,* is extremely large, far in excess of 2,147,483,647, the maximum capacity of 32-bit fixed-point storage with the binary point pushed all the way to the right. Avogadro's number could not, in other words, be stored as a FORTRAN integer.

And then there is a number like pi, the ratio of a circle's circumference to its radius. The value of pi is 3.1415926, a real number in the FORTRAN sense because it has not only an integer, but also a fractional component. A FORTRAN programmer would be unable to store that value in fixed-point mode because the location of the binary point would exclude the fractional part of pi.

The solution to this apparent dilemma is rather straightforward. We simply convert both of these troublesome numbers to normalized floating-point form and develop some scheme for storing floating-point numbers in words of memory. Avogadro's number now becomes 0.6022045×10^{24} and pi becomes 0.31415926×10^{1}. The essence of floating-point storage is to divide a word of memory into approximate quarters. One of these quarters is used to store the exponent, and the mantissa, the fractional component, is assigned to the remaining three quarters. This causes some crowding in the word, and therefore the mantissa is allowed to bring only a limited number of digits aboard, typically around seven or eight. The exponent also has limited elbow room and cannot grow beyond a certain size, usually between about 64 and 256, depending on the machine. In actual fact, the number is first converted either to hex, octal, or to binary, depending on the hardware. It is then expressed in normalized floating-point form in that system before being loaded into the word of memory. For purposes of closer examination, we will assume a hex-based system, but we will also look at a binary-based scheme later. The differences are subtle, but when you think about it, an exponent has considerably more clout in a system based on 16 than in a system based on 2.

Anyway, we will now give some specific examples. They are surprisingly simple and easy to understand, and it is hoped that you will follow along carefully; you will benefit greatly from a modest investment of time. When base conversions are required, you will generally be supplied with the equivalents in the appropriate systems—so don't get hung up worrying about such conversions.

Example 3.1 shows a simplified scheme for representing floating-point numbers internally.

Example 3.1

Deduce the internal 32-bit floating-point representation of 128.452_{10} given that $128.452_{10} = 80.73B645A1CAC0_{16}$.

Solution The first step is to convert the given hex number to normalized floating-point form:

$$80.73B645A1CAC0_{16} = 0.8073B645A1CAC0 \times 10^{2}_{16}$$

We now load the exponent into the first byte (eight bits) of a 32-bit word, and load the mantissa into the remaining three bytes. Only six of the mantissa digits will fit; the remaining ones must be discarded. Recall that one hex digit is equivalent to four bits. The following storage results:

028073B6

It's as simple as that. Take a good look at it: the exponent and the mantissa are clearly identifiable. Based on Fig. 1.4, this is the hex-condensed form of the following bit pattern:

00000010	100000000111001110110110
exponent	mantissa

As you might suspect, the internal floating-point representation of a negative number is simply the two's complement of its positive counterpart. If, as we have just shown, the internal floating-point representation of 128.452 is 028073B6, then the internal floating-point representation of −128.452 must be FD7F8C4A, which is the two's complement of 028073B6. You should verify this by adding the two representations, either on the binary or on the hexadecimal levels.

We now know how to store both positive and negative floating-point numbers in words of memory, but there is one more important issue to be dealt with, namely negative exponents. When a large number is represented in normalized floating-point form, it has a positive exponent. As the number is made smaller, the exponent becomes smaller until it shrinks to zero. If the number is made smaller yet, the exponent becomes negative, although the number is still positive. And so the question arises of how to represent such negative exponents. A possible way might be to two's complement just the exponent, and this is exactly what some manufacturers do. Honeywell's 36-bit hardware is a specific example of this approach. Another way might be to reserve one of the exponent bits to act as a sign bit. There are obviously other ways to deal with the situation, one of which is the excess-40 approach. This scheme is used by much of the IBM mainframe hardware and by other machines of similar architecture. We will study this representation in some detail because of its elegant simplicity.

In the excess-40 scheme, the raw exponent, still expressed as a hexadecimal number, is added to 40_{16}. An exponent of 2, for example, is stored as 42_{16}, whereas an exponent of -2 ends up as $3E_{16}$. Yes, $40_{16} - 2 = 3E_{16}$ and not 38_{16}.

The clever trick of a 40_{16} offset allows positive and negative exponents to be stored as positive quantities. Anything above 40_{16} implies a positive exponent and anything below 40_{16} is clearly a negative exponent. Exponents more negative than -40_{16} can obviously not be accommodated. Figure 3.10 shows several positive and negative exponents offset by 40_{16}.

We are now able to return to Ex. 3.1 and state that the internal excess-40 32-bit floating-point representation of 128.452 is $428073B6_{16}$.

We must deal with one more issue that might have been nagging you. In Ex. 3.1, we were given the mantissa 0.8073B645A1CAC0 and discovered that only six of the 14 significant digits would fit the 32-bit word. The remaining eight digits had to be discarded, leaving a number slightly smaller than 128.452_{10}. When the machine discards digits in this manner, it looks at the first digit discarded. If this digit is equal to or greater than 8_{16}, then the preceding digit is rounded up, causing the internal storage to be slightly larger than might be expected. In our particular case, the first of the discarded digits was 4 and therefore no rounding occurred. The point is that floating-point storage is not necessarily 100 percent accurate. Some numbers fit precisely, some get inflated due to rounding, and others are slightly under. The culprit, of course, is the small capacity of a memory word. Single-

Exponent	Excess-40_{16} equivalent	First byte of word
−40	00	00000000
−3F	01	00000001
...	...	...
−9	37	00110111
−8	38	00111000
−7	39	00111001
−6	3A	00111010
−5	3B	00111011
−4	3C	00111100
−3	3D	00111101
−2	3E	00111110
−1	3F	00111111
0	40	01000000
1	41	01000001
2	42	01000010
3	43	01000011
4	44	01000100
5	45	01000101
6	46	01000110
7	47	01000111
8	48	01001000
9	49	01001001
A	4A	01001010
...	...	...
3F	7F	01111111

Figure 3.10 The exponent expressed in excess-40 form.

word floating-point storage is frequently called *short floating-point*. You will be pleased to hear that it is possible to store floating-point numbers in double words of memory. The first word still contains the exponent in the first byte, stored in some manner such as excess-40. The remaining three bytes of the first word hold the first six digits of the mantissa, and the second word holds another eight digits of the mantissa. This permits a total of 14 significant digits to be stored in such a double word, greatly increasing the precision of the stored datum. Many machines do not round the last digit when storing a datum in a double word of memory. Double-word floating-point storage is known as *long floating-point*. The FORTRAN programmer has access to long floating-point storage, and refers to a datum stored in a double word as being of type *double precision*. Some systems even offer extended double precision storage, involving four or more words of memory.

3.8 EXAMPLES OF 32-BIT EXCESS-40 FLOATING-POINT REPRESENTATIONS

Example 3.2

$504.21_{10} = 1F8.35C28F5C28F_{16}$. Show the internal 32-bit excess-40 floating-point representation of 504.21_{10}.

Solution The normalized floating-point form of the number is $0.1F835C28F5C28F \times 10^3_{16}$. The exponent is 3, which is added to 40_{16}. The resulting internal representation is 431F835C. The actual 32 bits are 01000011000111111000001101011100.

Example 3.3

$504.21_{10} = 1F8.35C28F5C28F5C2_{16}$. Show the internal 32-bit excess-40 floating-point representation of -504.21_{10}.

Solution The given number is negative. We simply determine the internal representation of its positive counterpart and two's complement that bit pattern—all 32 bits. In the previous example, we found the internal representation of +504.21 to be 431F835C. The two's complement is BCE07CA4, or 10111100111000000111110010100100, which is the internal representation of -504.21_{10}.

(Please note that you can perform the two's complementing on the binary level, or you can take a shortcut and do it directly on the hex level. If you do it on the binary level, write all 32 bits, invert each to find the one's complement, and add 1. If you wish to do it on the hex level, simply look at each hex digit and deduce, using your fingers, or the sequence of the first 16 hex digits written on a piece of paper, what you would have to add to each digit to make the sum equal to F_{16}. Don't be embarrassed to use a slip of paper with the hex column; it makes things very graphic and you are not likely to make too many mistakes. To complement the digit F, for example, you realize that $F + 0 = F_{16}$. Therefore, the desired complement is 0. Because $A + 5 = F_{16}$, 5 is the complement of A. The complement of 8 is 7 because $8 + 7 = F_{16}$. After complementing each hex digit, add 1 to the resulting number and you have the desired two's complement in hex-condensed form. Complementing each digit of 431F835C, we get BCE07CA3. This is the one's complement in hex-condensed form. Now, add 1 to that, giving us BCE07CA4, which is the desired two's complement.)

Example 3.4

Deduce the internal 32-bit excess-40 floating-point representation of $0.213_{10} = 0.36872B020C49BA_{16}$.

Solution The normalized floating-point form is $0.36872B020C49BA \times 10^{0}_{16}$. The internal representation is, therefore, 4036872B, i.e., 01000000001101101000011100101011.

Example 3.5

Deduce the internal 32-bit excess-40 floating-point representation of $0.003412_{10} = 0.00DF9BDC69F8C21E_{16}$.

Solution The normalized floating-point form is $0.DF9BDC69F8C21E \times 10^{-2}_{16}$. The resulting internal storage is, therefore, 3EDF9BDC. (Careful when you subtract 2 from 40_{16}. It is always safest to write the appropriate range of hex numbers on a piece of paper to allow you to count as you add and subtract, unless, of course, you perform hex arithmetic frequently enough to be good at it.)

Example 3.6

Show the internal 32-bit excess-40 floating-point representation of $-0.003412_{10} = -0.00DF9BDC69F8C21E_{16}$.

Solution The internal storage of +0.003412 was found to be 3EDF9BDC. Therefore, −0.003412 is represented as C1206424, or 11000001001000000110010000100100.

Example 3.7

Show the internal 32-bit excess-40 floating-point storage of $928481002312324392_{10} = CE2A08D63865528_{16}$.

Solution The normalized floating-point form of the number is $0.CE2A08D63865528 \times 10^{F}_{16}$. The internal representation is 4FCE2A09. Notice that the last digit was rounded up because the first digit of the discarded portion of the mantissa is D, which is greater than 7. Also notice that we had to move the hexadecimal point F_{16} positions when we normalized, not 15_{16}.

Example 3.8

Deduce the internal 32-bit excess-40 representation of $0.000000000000000000000000004_{16}$.

Solution $0.000000000000000000000000004_{16} = 0.4 \times 10^{-18}_{16}$. The internal representation is 28400000. ($40_{16} - 18_{16} = 28_{16}$.)

Example 3.9

Show the internal 32-bit excess-40 representation of $-0.000000000000000000000000004_{16}$. Note that the number is negative.

Solution $-0.000000000000000000000000004_{16} = -0.4 \times 10^{-18}_{16}$. The internal representation is the two's complement of 28400000, which is D7C00000.

Example 3.10

Deduce the internal 64-bit excess-40 long floating-point representation of $0.1_{10} = 0.19999999999999999_{16}$.

Solution Long floating-point storage (64 bits) allows the storage of an additional eight mantissa digits. The resulting internal storage is 4019999999999999. Note that the last digit in the double word might or might not be rounded, depending on the hardware. We did not round up in this case. Short floating-point storage always performs rounding, however.

Example 3.11

What is the largest positive floating-point number that can be represented in 32-bit excess-40 floating-point form?

Solution Because two's complementing is used, the positive numbers can use all the bits except the very first one, which is reserved for the negative numbers. The largest positive number is, therefore, 01111111111111111111111111111111 = 7FFFFFFF, which is the representation of 0.FFFFFF × 10_{16}^{3F}. The decimal equivalent is approximately 10^{76}.

3.9 DEC VAX-11 INTERNAL FLOATING-POINT REPRESENTATIONS

This section is of considerable general interest, but will be of particular interest to those using VAX-11 computers, manufactured by the Digital Equipment Corporation.

The DEC VAX-11 family has a 32-bit architecture, but for historical reasons calls a 16-bit grouping a *word*. A 32-bit grouping is called a *longword*, 64 bits are called a *quadword*, and 128-bit groupings are known as *octawords*. FORTRAN integers are stored in 32-bit *longwords* in two's complement form, as discussed in Chapter 1.

The floating-point representation, however, is quite different from the excess-40 normalized hex-based scheme examined in the previous section.

The DEC VAX-11 family provides four different types of floating-point storage, namely *F-floating*, *D-floating*, *G-floating*, and *H-floating*. DEC does not use two's complementing for floating-point storage. Instead, the first bit is a true sign bit, set to 0 for positive numbers and to 1 for negative data. The remaining bits of the word are the same for both negative and positive data.

Unlike excess-40 storage, where floating-point data are stored in normalized hexadecimal form, the VAX-11 represents a floating-point number in normalized binary form. To emphasize this difference, we look at several decimal numbers and their normalized hexadecimal and binary equivalents:

Decimal	Hex equivalent	Normalized hex	Binary equivalent	Normalized binary
0.5	0.8	0.8×10^0	0.1	0.1×10^0
1.5	1.8	0.18×10^0	1.1	0.11×10^1
2.5	2.8	0.28×10^1	10.1	0.101×10^{10}
4.5	4.8	0.48×10^1	100.1	0.1001×10^{11}
31.75	1F.C	$0.1FC \times 10^2$	11111.11	$0.1111111 \times 10^{101}$
33.25	21.4	0.214×10^2	100001.01	$0.10000101 \times 10^{110}$

The first thing to notice is that normalization on the binary level always results in a mantissa in which the first bit is 1. Because the first mantissa bit is always 1, it is predictable and need therefore not be stored. The VAX-11 does not store this first mantissa bit.

The exponent, which is a binary number, is stored in excess form. It is, in other words, added to some offset value for positive exponents and subtracted from the offset value for negative exponents. This idea is familiar from the excess-40 storage method, where the offset value is 40_{16}.

The VAX provides three different offsets, depending on which of the four floating-point storage methods is used. The three offsets are 10000000_2, 10000000000_2, and 100000000000000_2.

We can now be a little more specific and summarize the four storage methods, as shown in the following table. Subsequent examples will clarify things even further. The VAX's FORTRAN defaults to F-floating for single precision and to D-floating for double precision.

Storage type	No. of bits	No. of exp bits	Excess	No. of mantissa bits
F-Floating	32 (longword)	8	10000000	23
D-Floating	64 (quadword)	8	10000000	55
G-Floating	64 (quadword)	11	10000000000	52
H-Floating	128 (octaword)	15	100000000000000	112

Example 3.12

Show $8.5_{10} = 1000.1_2$ in VAX-11 F-Floating form.

Solution The normalized binary number is $0.10001 \times 10_2^{100}$. The first bit of the resulting internal storage is 0 because the number is positive. The next eight bits are the exponent, expressed in excess-10000000_2 form, i.e., $10000000_2 + 100_2 = 10000100_2$. The remaining 23 bits are reserved for the mantissa, which is 10001. As mentioned before, however, the first bit is not stored because it is always 1. This results in 0 10000100 00010000000000000000000. The gaps indicate the boundaries between the sign bit and the exponent and between the exponent and the mantissa, deprived of the leading 1. Without the gaps, the storage is 01000010000010000000000000000000 = 42080000 in hex-condensed form.

Example 3.13

Show $-8.5_{10} = -1000.1_2$ in VAX-11 F-floating form.

Solution We derived the internal VAX-11 F-floating representation of $+8.5_{10}$ in the previous example. The internal representation of -8.5_{10} differs only in the first bit, which is now 1. The internal representation is, therefore, 11000010000010000000000000000000, or C2080000 in hex-condensed form.

Example 3.14

Show $8.5_{10} = 1000.1_2$ in VAX-11 D-floating form.

Solution D-floating is the quadword (64-bit) version of 32-bit F-floating storage. The internal D-floating storage of 8.5_{10} is, therefore, 4208000000000000 in hex-condensed form.

Example 3.15

Show $8.5_{10} = 1000.1_2$ in VAX-11 G-floating form.

Solution G-floating stores the exponent in excess-10000000000_2 form and uses quadword (64-bit) storage. The exponent is 100_2 and becomes 10000000100 in excess-10000000000_2 form. 0 10000000100 0001000000000000000000000000000000000000000000000000 is the internal storage, or 4041000000000000 in hex-condensed form.

Example 3.16

Show $8.5_{10} = 1000.1_2$ in VAX-11 H-floating form.

Solution H-floating storage reserves 15 of the 128 bits for the exponent. The exponent, in this particular case, is 100000000000100. The corresponding internal H-floating storage is, therefore, 0 100000000000100 0001000000000000 . . . , or 40041000000000000000000000000000 in hex-abbreviated form.

Example 3.17

Show the internal F-, D-, G-, and H-floating DEC VAX-11 representations of $0.1_{10} = 0.00011001100110011001100110011001100\ldots_2$ and of -0.1_{10}.

Solution The normalized number is 0.11001100110011001100110011001100 . . . $\times\ 10_2^{-11}$. The F and D exponents are $(10000000 - 11)_2 = 01111101_2$. The G exponent is $(10000000000 - 11)_2 = 01111111101_2$, and the H exponent is 011111111111101.

0.1 in F floating = 0 01111101 10011001100110011001101 = 3ECCCCCD (rounded up)
0.1 in D floating = 3ECCCCCCCCCCCCCD (rounded up)
0.1 in G floating = 3FD999999999999A (rounded up)
0.1 in H floating = 3FFD999999999999999999999999999A (rounded up)

−0.1 in F floating = 1 01111101 10011001100110011001101 = BECCCCCD (rounded up)
−0.1 in D floating = BECCCCCCCCCCCCCD (rounded up)
−0.1 in G floating = BFD999999999999A (rounded up)
−0.1 in H floating = BFFD999999999999999999999999999A (rounded up)

Example 3.18

Approximately what is the largest number in F- and D-floating formats?

Solution The largest exponent in excess = 10000000_2 form is $1111111_2 = 127_{10}$. The largest number is, therefore, approximately 2^{127}, which is about $(1.7 \times 10^{38})_{10}$. This is considerably smaller than the approximate capacity of 10^{76} of 32-bit excess-40 storage.

Example 3.19

Approximately what is the largest number in DEC's G-floating format?

Solution The largest exponent in excess-10000000000_2 form is $1111111111_2 = 1023_{10}$. The largest number is, therefore, approximately 2^{1023} , which is about 10^{307}. This is much larger, in other words, than the 10^{76} offered by 32-bit excess-40 floating-point storage. (H-floating can accommodate numbers as large as approximately 10^{4931}.)

3.10 INTERNAL BINARY-CODED DECIMAL (BCD) REPRESENTATION REVISITED

A group of four bits, sometimes called a nibble, can store 16 different bit patterns. It is possible to let each of the 10 decimal digits be represented by a nibble, giving us the ability to store decimal digits directly. As an example, consider the decimal number 45210321, the eight decimal digits of which have the following nibble equivalents:

4 – 0100
5 – 0101
2 – 0010
1 – 0001
0 – 0000
3 – 0011
2 – 0010
1 – 0001

These eight nibbles just fit one 32-bit word of memory, where they appear as shown in Fig. 3.11.

We happen to know that the word in Fig. 3.11 does not contain a binary number, but instead holds eight decimal digits encoded into eight nibble patterns. We say that the word contains eight digits encoded in binary-coded decimal (BCD) form. Now, if a FORTRAN programmer were handed the same word of memory and asked to deduce the decimal equivalent of the stored number, additional information about the data type would need to be supplied. If the word were assumed to contain a datum of type integer, the programmer would conclude that it held 1,159,-791,393. This would be arrived at by a brute-force conversion from binary to decimal. If, however, the word were assumed to contain a floating-point datum, stored in excess-40 form, the programmer would interpret the 32 bits as $0.210321 \times 10^5_{16} = 21032.1_{16} = 135{,}218.0625_{10}$. If, on the other hand, the programmer were told that the word contained a datum of type decimal, the interpretation would require that the word be divided into eight nibbles, each holding a BCD digit, which would then be translated to their decimal equivalents, as shown in Fig. 3.12.

All this emphasizes once again how important it is for the programmer to be aware of data types and how and when to use them.

You can see that there are great differences between integer (fixed-point), real (floating-point), and binary-coded decimal storage. A 32-bit word of memory allows you to store a number as large as 2,147,483,647 using integer storage, 10^{76} using excess-40 floating-point storage, whereas 32-bit BCD storage would limit the maximum to 99,999,999. We have also seen that integer and floating-point storage are able to accommodate both positive and negative numbers through the mechanism of two's complementing, whereas it is not clear how negative numbers

01000101001000010000001100100001.

Figure 3.11 Each of the eight digits of the decimal number 45210321 is encoded as a group of four bits and stored in a word of memory.

0100	0101	0010	0001	0000	0011	0010	0001
4	5	2	1	0	3	2	1

Figure 3.12 Decoding numeric information stored in BCD form.

would be represented when stored in BCD mode. There are various schemes, but they all cost some of the storage capacity of the word, often a full decimal digit position.

Data storage of type decimal is not accessible under FORTRAN, but is available in languages such as COBOL, PL/1, and RPG. It should also be pointed out that the implementation of BCD representation makes it possible for the computer to emulate a mechanical calculator, performing decimal arithmetic with great precision. While there are no simple circuits or devices with 10 stable states, a group of four flip-flops, constituting a nibble, does exhibit 16 distinct states. This permits the implementation of decimal arithmetic, or even hexadecimal arithmetic for that matter. It should be obvious to you that in decimal storage, the nibbles act like the gears of a mechanical calculator.

DECIMAL arithmetic exacts a high cost because it takes more bits to store a given number than similar integer or floating-point storage. The arithmetic unit also finds it much more difficult to deal with decimal data, and computations with data of type decimal typically run significantly more slowly, so much so that machines running a lot of decimal computations must be equipped with special decimal arithmetic circuits to speed up the process. Unlike floating-point arithmetic, decimal arithmetic is 100 percent accurate and also permits the representation of decimal fractions. The decimal point is not actually stored with its datum, but the computer keeps track of it in a special table, again adding to the overhead.

Most fixed-point and floating-point implementations are word-oriented in the sense of using one or more words of storage per datum. BCD implementations, on the other hand, are generally byte-oriented, crossing word boundaries freely; many machines accommodate decimal data with 31 or more digits. This crossing of word boundaries does, however, require extensive bookkeeping on the part of the machine because it must keep track of where one decimal number ends and the next one begins. This is another reason why decimal computations generally consume far more CPU time than fixed- or floating-point calculations.

3.11 CHARACTER DATA

Most of us still think of computers as large automatic calculating machines, dealing mainly with arithmetic problems. Arithmetic requirements were indeed the driving force behind much of the initial research and development, a fact reflected in the names given to some of the early machines. There was, for example, the 1944 Automatic Sequence Controlled Calculator, or ASCC. And then there was the 1945 Electronic Numeric Integrator And Calculator or ENIAC, the forerunner of the UNIVAC family. There was also an SSEC (Selective Sequence Electronic Calculator) and an EDVAC (Electronic Discrete Variable Calculator), to mention only a few.

The early machines were programmed entirely in numeric codes called *machine language*, and it was soon realized that this constituted a very real barrier between the computer and potential users. This barrier stimulated early attempts to develop machines with which a programmer could communicate in written form, through a teleprinter and a keyboard, employing the Latin alphabet and other special characters. The idea was certainly not new, but an extension of existing teleprinter technology dating back to 1874. In that year, Emil Baudot invented the first teleprinter to use a fixed number of bits to represent each character. Morse code, by contrast, used variable combinations of long and short signaling elements per character. Early teleprinters used the so-called *Baudot* code in which each character is represented by a unique five-bit code, also known as a five-level code.

It should be clear to you that a five-bit code permits the representation of only 32 different characters, and therefore proves to be highly restrictive. The Latin uppercase alphabet alone requires 26 unique codes, not to mention the 10 Arabic numerals, the various special symbols, and the punctuation marks. In order to make the 32-character, five-level code usable, special shift modes were introduced. One of the 32 characters, for example, was called the Figures Shift, and all characters following receipt of the Figures Shift character were interpreted as numerics. Another of the 32 characters functioned as the Letters Shift, and five-bit groups arriving after the receipt of the Letters Shift would be interpreted as alphabetic characters. The awkwardness of the situation is brought home when you imagine having to transmit postal codes of the type used by several countries, containing both numeric and alphabetic characters.

The original reason for choosing a five-level code was the feeling that a transmitter and its distant receiver would probably not remain synchronized for longer than it took to transmit five bits, a problem long since overcome. You will be surprised to hear that the five-level code is still alive and well and heavily used by international Telex networks.

In order to permit a user to type instructions into the computer in a high-level language, it becomes necessary to use codes similar to the previously mentioned Baudot code to represent character information inside the machine. It would have been shortsighted to implement a five-bit code because of its limited representation repertoire, and so some designers introduced six-bit codes, permitting the representation of 64 unique characters. They assumed that a 64-character set would satisfy all the requirements of a typical business environment, for example. Others began to sense that the computer could do far more than perform mathematical or business applications. They saw great potential for uses such as typesetting, word processing, text analyses, and information retrieval. They also recognized the fact that many written languages extended the Latin alphabet by introducing various diacritical marks such as accents, and that, therefore, even a six-bit code would be inadequate.

IBM took the previously discussed BCD code and extended the concept to arrive at an eight-bit code called, not surprisingly, Extended Binary-Coded Decimal Interchange Code, or EBCDIC (pronounced EB-see-dic). EBCDIC permits the representation of 256 unique characters and because each character is represented by a pattern of eight bits, one byte is required to store one character. This means that a 32-bit word can accommodate a maximum of four characters. A portion of the EBCDIC code table is shown later, but at this point concepts should be made somewhat more tangible by presenting a concrete example.

11000001110000101100001111000100

Figure 3.13 The character string ABCD stored as C1C2C3C4 in EBCDIC code in a 32-bit memory word.

In the EBCDIC code, the Latin character A is assigned the bit pattern 11000001, or hex C1. B is represented by hex C2, C by hex C3, and D by hex C4. The character string ABCD, when expressed in EBCDIC, will fit one 32-bit word, encoded as C1C2C3C4. This is shown in Fig. 3.13.

Now if someone went to the computer, pulled out that particular word of memory, and asked you what it contained, you would have no idea whether it were an integer (fixed-point), a real (floating-point), or character. If it were an integer, you would conclude that it must be negative because the first bit is on. To find the number, you would take the two's complement of C1C2C3C4, which is 3E3D3C3C, and conclude that the word contains -1044200508. If you assumed the word to contain an excess-40 real number, you would again look at the first bit and conclude that the number is negative. After examining the two's complement, you would deduce that the number must be $(-0.3D3C3C \times 10^{-2})_{16} = -0.003D3C3C_{16}$, which is approximately -0.0009343_{10}, certainly vastly different from the integer interpretation.

If, however, you assumed the word to contain character information, you would divide it into the four bytes 11000001 11000010 11000011 11000100 = C1 C2 C3 C4, consult an EBCDIC table, and conclude that the word contains the character string ABCD.

Figure 3.14 shows an interesting subset of the EBCDIC table, arranged such that the EBCDIC codes appear in numerically ascending order. This order is important because it determines the order in which character items appear after a sort operation. When sorting character items, the computer compares the internal codes and arranges these in numeric order. The numerically increasing order in which the characters are assigned EBCDIC codes is known as the EBCDIC collating sequence. The gaps in the sample are indicated by lines. The complete EBCDIC table is presented in Appendix A.

As you can see from Fig. 3.14, the EBCDIC collating sequence is such that in a sort operation, the space floats to the top, followed by the special characters such as accents, punctuation, etc., followed by the lowercase alphabet, followed by the uppercase alphabet. The Arabic numeral characters sink to the bottom.

If, therefore, you were to compile a list of items and subject that list to an EBCDIC sort, the item names beginning with a blank would appear at the very top. These would be followed by items beginning with special characters. The names of items beginning with a lowercase letter would be next, followed by those beginning with the uppercase letters. Items beginning with a number would appear at the end of the list.

Although EBCDIC is widely used, especially in IBM-like mainframe environments, a different code has emerged as the standard. This code is known as the American Standard Code for Information Interchange, usually referred to as ASCII and pronounced AS-key. ASCII is generally implemented as a seven-bit code, permitting the representation of 128 unique characters. Virtually all microcomputers, includ-

Graphic character	Hex code	Octal code	Binary code
Space	40	100	01000000
Ampersand	50	120	01010000
Exclamation point	5A	132	01011010
Dollar sign	5B	133	01011011
Asterisk	5C	134	01011100
)	5D	135	01011101
Semicolon	5E	136	01011110
Comma	6B	153	01101011
Percent sign	6C	154	01101100
Underscore	6D	155	01101101
>	6E	156	01101110
Question mark	6F	157	01101111
a	81	201	10000001
b	82	202	10000010
c	83	203	10000011
d	84	204	10000100
A	C1	301	11000001
B	C2	302	11000010
C	C3	303	11000011
D	C4	304	11000100
0	F0	360	11110000
1	F1	361	11110001
2	F2	362	11110010
3	F3	363	11110011
4	F4	364	11110010
5	F5	365	11110101
6	F6	366	11110110
7	F7	367	11110111
8	F8	370	11111000
9	F9	371	11111001

Figure 3.14 A portion of the EBCDIC table.

ing those sold by IBM, use ASCII internally. The ASCII and EBCDIC collating sequences are quite different, as can be seen from the portion of the ASCII code chart in Fig. 3.15. Appendix B presents the complete seven-bit ASCII table.

You will notice that in both EBCDIC and ASCII code assignments, the space (blank) sits at the top. In the EBCDIC table, the special characters, such as punctuation marks, lie between the blank and the lowercase alphabet. In the ASCII table, the special characters are distributed, some follow the Arabic numerals, others follow the uppercase alphabet, and still others come after the lowercase alphabet. In the ASCII collating sequence, the numerals come before uppercase characters, and these precede the lowercase characters: the order is NUL (i.e., Numerals–Upper–Lower). The EBCDIC collating sequence is LUN. You should devise some scheme for remembering NUL and associating it with ASCII, and for associating LUN with EBCDIC.

Graphic character	Hex code	Octal code	Binary code
Space	20	040	00100000
Exclamation point	21	041	00100001
Double quote	22	042	00100010
Number (pound) sign	23	043	00100011
Dollar sign	24	044	00100100
Percent sign	25	045	00100101
0	30	060	00110000
1	31	061	00110001
2	32	062	00110010
3	33	063	00110011
4	34	064	00110100
5	35	065	00110101
6	36	066	00110110
7	37	067	00110111
8	38	070	00111000
9	39	071	00111001
colon	3A	072	00111010
semicolon	3B	073	00111011
<	3C	074	00111100
=	3D	075	00111101
>	3E	076	00111110
Question mark	3F	077	00111111
@	40	100	01000000
A	41	101	01000001
B	42	102	01000010
C	43	103	01000011
W	57	127	01010111
X	58	130	01011000
Y	59	131	01011001
Z	5A	132	01011010
[	5B	133	01011011
Backlash	5C	134	01011100
]	5D	135	01011101
Circumflex	5E	136	01011110
Underscore	5F	137	01011111
Grave accent	60	140	01100000
a	61	141	01100001
b	62	142	01100010
c	63	143	01100011
x	78	170	01111000
y	79	171	01111001
z	7A	172	01111010
Left brace	7B	173	01111011
Or bar	7C	174	01111100
Right brace	7D	175	01111101
Tilde	7E	176	01111110
Delete	7F	177	01111111

Fig. 3.15 A partial list of seven-bit ASCII code assignments.

Because the two collating sequences are so different, a sorting operation performed on one machine can disagree with a sort performed on a different machine. For this reason, most machines allow the user to specify whether a particular sort is to be performed as an ASCII sort or as an EBCDIC sort.

You will be interested to learn about a new eight-bit code approved in 1985 as part of the National Information Standards Organization (NISO) Z39.47–1985 standard. The standard defines an Extended Latin Alphabet Coded Character Set for Bibliographic Use, and constitutes a superset of the previously mentioned seven-bit ASCII codes. The most interesting feature of Z39.47–1985 is the addition of 32 so-called *diacritics*, which are special symbols used to modify the basic Latin character set. Examples of diacritics are accents, umlauts, tilde, breve, dot above, dot below, macron, circle above, double acute accent, etc. On a terminal equipped to handle the new eight-bit ASCII codes, there would be a special set of keys for these diacritics, probably in the location of the current numeric keypad. When the user hits one of these diacritics, it appears on the screen, but the cursor does not advance to the next cell. The user then strikes the Latin character to be modified, and the two appear superimposed on the screen. To generate an A-umlaut, for example, the user would first hit the special umlaut key, causing the two dots to appear on the screen. The cursor would not advance until the user has typed the character A, after which the cursor advances to the next cell. Because diacritics are defined as nonspacing, several diacritics could be used to modify a basic character. You could, for example, generate a W with two dots above, a circle above and a half circle below, all superimposed. The NISO standard addresses very directly and effectively a long-standing problem in international communications. It is intended to handle all languages based on the Latin alphabet, including Romanized Chinese, Vietnamese, Navaho, Romanized Japanese, Tibetan, French, Spanish, Italian, German, Lao, Telugu, and many others. The importance of Z39.47–1985 will be appreciated by individuals who have tried to write properly accented French on computer terminals, not to mention Spanish or German. The Z39.47–1985 standard makes specific reference to 35 languages that can be dealt with directly. It mentions another 52 languages that can be handled in transliterated (Romanized) forms.

3.12 LOGICAL DATA

There are only two possible logic states, namely true and false. FORTRAN provides the ability to compute the truth values of complex logical expressions very easily and rapidly. You will see details when we get to the appropriate section, but at this stage we are interested only in the internal representations of these two truth values. Some manufacturers set all the bits of a word to 1 to indicate true and they set all the bits to 0 to indicate false. Other manufacturers use a half word to store truth values, and still others do it on a byte level. On Honeywell's 36-bit hardware, for example, a word is assumed to contain the truth value true when the first 18 bits are set to 1. When the same bits contain 0, the word is assumed to store false. Figure 3.16 illustrates Honeywell's approach, and Fig. 3.17 shows the representation of the two truth values on DEC's VAX-11 hardware.

111111111111111111XXXXXXXXXXXXXXXXXX TRUE
000000000000000000XXXXXXXXXXXXXXXXXX FALSE

Figure 3.16 True and False on Honeywell's 36-bit hardware.

11111111111111111111111111111111 TRUE
00000000000000000000000000000000 FALSE

Figure 3.17 True and False on DEC's VAX-11 32-bit hardware.

A manufacturer will always choose a representation compatible with optimum performance of the arithmetic unit.

3.13 PROBLEMS

3.1. Two's complement the following binary numbers. Check with the answers provided. If you study the two's complement columns carefully, you will notice some interesting patterns.

Binary number	Two's complement	Binary number	Two's complement
1	1	1110	0010
10	10	1111	0001
11	01	10000	10000
100	100	100000	100000
101	011	110110	001010
110	010	1000000	1000000
111	001	1011011	0100101
1000	1000	100111000	011001000
1001	0111	1110011000101011	0001100111010111
1010	0110	1011010111111011	0100101000000101
1011	0101	1110101110000101	0001010001111011
1100	0100	1100101111111110	0011010000000010
1101	0011	1100101111100000	0011010000100000

3.2. Given the hex-condensed binary patterns, deduce the appropriate two's complements. Perform the complementing operation directly on the hex level, as discussed in Ex. 3.3.

Hex-condensed binary number	Two's complement hex-condensed	Hex-condensed binary number	Two's complement hex-condensed
1	F	FFFFFE	000002
2	E	FFFFF	00001
4	C	7BCDEF00	84321100
6	A	12345678	EDCBA988
8	8	77654321	889ABCDF
A	6	70F0F0F0	8F0F0F10
C	4	70E0E0E0	8F1F1F20
E	2	5BBBFFFF	A4440001
F	1	49999999	B6666667
10	F0	10000001	EFFFFFFF
100	F00	7000000F	8FFFFFF1
1000	F000	700F00F0	8FF0FF10
10000	F0000	70000000	90000000

3.3 Deduce the 32-bit fixed-point (integer) storage of each of the given decimal numbers. The hexadecimal equivalents are supplied. Check your answers against the answers provided.

Decimal number	Hex equivalent	Answer
1_{10}	1_{16}	00000001
-1_{10}	-1_{16}	FFFFFFFF
$4\ 096_{10}$	$1\ 000_{16}$	00001000
$-4\ 096_{10}$	$-1\ 000_{16}$	FFFFF000
$1\ 048\ 576_{10}$	$100\ 000_{16}$	00100000
$-1\ 048\ 576_{10}$	$-100\ 000_{16}$	FFF00000
$1\ 234\ 567\ 890_{10}$	$49\ 960\ 2D2_{16}$	499602D2
$-1\ 234\ 567\ 890_{10}$	$-49\ 960\ 2D2_{16}$	B669FD2E
$2\ 147\ 000\ 000_{10}$	$7F\ F89\ EC0_{16}$	7FF89EC0
$-2\ 147\ 000\ 000_{10}$	$-7F\ F89\ EC0_{16}$	80076140
$2\ 147\ 483\ 647_{10}$	$7F\ FFF\ FFF_{16}$	7FFFFFFF
$-2\ 147\ 483\ 647_{10}$	$-7F\ FFF\ FFF_{16}$	80000001
$-2\ 147\ 483\ 648_{10}$	$-80\ 000\ 000_{16}$	80000000

3.4. Decimal numbers and their hex equivalents are given. Deduce the 32-bit single-precision (short floating-point), and the 64-bit double-precision (long floating-point) excess-40 internal representations. Assume rounding for short floating-point only.

Decimal number	Hex equivalent of number	Short floating-point	Long floating-point
1.23	1.3AE147AE147AE148	4113AE14	4113AE147AE147AE
45.231	2D.3B22D0E560418938	422D3B23	422D3B22D0E56041
98788.1	181E4.199999999999A	45181E42	45181E4199999999
0.00000001	0.0000002AF31DC4611873C	3A2AF31E	3A2AF31DC4611873
990179845234.05	E68B516472.0CCCCCCCC	4AE68B51	4AE68B5164720CCC
−18.7	−12.B333333333333333	BDED4CCD	BDED4CCCCCCCCCCD
−0.125	−0.2	BFE00000	BFE0000000000000
−0.08	−0.147AE147AE147AE2	BFEB851F	BFEB851EB851EB86
−0.000001	−0.000010C6F7A0B5ED8D36	C3EF3908	C3EF39085F4A1273
−0.3	−0.4CCCCCCCCCCCCCCCCC	BFB33333	BFB3333333333334

3.5. Decimal numbers and their binary equivalents are given. Deduce the DEC VAX-11 F-floating internal representation. You will recall that D-floating differs from F-floating only in precision. D-floating will accommodate an additional 32 mantissa bits.

Decimal number	Binary equivalent	DEC VAX-11 F-floating
3.8	11.1100110011001100110011001100 1	41733333
−3.8	−11.11001100110011001100110011001	C1733333
159.7	10011111.1011001100110011001 1001	441FB333
−159.7	−10011111.10110011001100110011001	C41FB333
4986.74	1001101111010.1011110101110000 10	469BD5EC
−4986.74	−1001101111010.101111010111000010	C69BD5EC
50984103.91	11000010011111010010100111.11101	4D427D2A
−50984103.91	−11000010011111010010100111.11101	CD427D2A

3.6. Decimal numbers and their hexadecimal equivalents are given. Deduce the DEC VAX-11 G-floating internal representation. The decimal numbers' hex equivalents are provided to save space; you will have to convert these to binary, of course, because DEC normalizes on the binary level.

Decimal number	Hex equivalent	DEC VAX-11 G-floating
421083.92	66CDB.EB851EB851EB8	4139B36FAE147AE1
−421083.92	−66CDB.EB851EB851EB8	C139B36FAE147AE1
0.0000000059213	0.000000196E89C793A808	3E596E89C793A808
−0.0000000059213	−0.000000196E89C793A808	BE596E89C793A808
7.31243	7.4FFB69984A0E410C0	403D3FEDA6612839
−7.31243	−7.4FFB69984A0E410C0	C03D3FEDA6612839
493.18214837	1ED.2EA1468C2B71F3B	409ED2EA1468C2B7
−493.18214837	−1ED.2EA1468C2B71F3B	C09ED2EA1468C2B7

3.7. Perform an ASCII sort on the following list of 10 items, i.e., sort the items in ascending ASCII order.

Word
Byte
word
BYTE
!WORD
!word
4-byte
4-o'clock
??WHY
$money

3.8. Perform an ascending EBCDIC sort on the 10 items in the list of the previous problem.

3.9. The contents of 21 words of memory were dumped (printed) below in hexcondensed form. It is known that the dumped section of memory contains character data, stored in ASCII form. Using Appendix B, decode the character information. To help you get going, you are told that the first three words contain the character string "she was so h." Please take the trouble to decode the rest. The ability to analyze the contents of blocks of memory is an invaluable asset.

73686520 77617320 736F2068 756E6772 79207468 61742073 6865204E

4942424C 45442061 74207468 6520636F 6D707574 65722C20 74616B69

6E672073 65766572 616C2042 59544553 206F7574 206F6620 69742E20

3.10. The 21 words of memory given contain a continuation of the account begun in the previous problem. This time, however, the information is encoded in EBCDIC. Using the EBCDIC table in Appendix A, decode the 21 words.

C69699A3 A49581A3 8593A840 A3888540 A3858388 95898389 81954099

A4A28885 84408995 40819584 40A39696 9240A388 8540E6D6 D9C4E240

99898788 A34096A4 A3409686 40888599 409496A4 A3885C40 40404040

3.14 SUGGESTED RESEARCH

What type of floating-point storage is used on your machine? Does the machine use ASCII or EBCDIC internally? Is there decimal hardware, or is decimal arithmetic simulated in software?

4

Assignment Statements and FORTRAN Functions

FORTRAN statements can be divided into *imperatives* and *specification statements*, the latter also called *declaratives*. Specification statements declare or specify a particular computing environment, whereas imperatives give direct orders to the computer at program execution time. The word "imperative" is derived from the Latin *imperare*, to command.

We will not be looking at specification statements at this stage (they appear later in a very natural way), but Fig. 4.1 shows a list of seven FORTRAN imperatives, the first six of which are obviously commands. The seventh is also an imperative, a very special one, called an *assignment statement*, and we will now take a close look at such assignment statements.

4.1 ASSIGNMENT STATEMENTS

The function of the assignment statement is probably most readily understood through a specific example, and we will illustrate it by showing a simple but complete FORTRAN program in Fig. 4.2. The subsequent explanation may seem somewhat lengthy, but the intent is to make some highly specific and important points to make things easier later. In the discussion, we will appear to wander away from the assignment statement, the central issue, but we will come full circle in the end, so please follow along patiently but carefully. And now for the program of Fig. 4.2.

```
GO TO
PAUSE
STOP
WRITE
READ
DO
SUM = 3.4
```

Figure 4.1 Seven FORTRAN imperatives.

```
SUM = 3.4
PRINT *, SUM
END
```

Figure 4.2 A complete FORTRAN program.

This is a complete program, written in FORTRAN, a language referred to as a high-level language, because it is easily written and read by humans.

4.2 DIGRESSION: THE FORTRAN COMPILER AND MACHINE LANGUAGE

The computer can only operate on bit patterns, and, therefore, some bridge must be established to convert a high-level language program to machine language. This conversion is accomplished by another program, resident in the machine, and called a FORTRAN *compiler*. The compiler translates FORTRAN statements into the native language of the particular hardware for which it was designed. The input to the compiler is standard FORTRAN, understood by all standard FORTRAN compilers. The machine language produced by the compiler, however, is highly hardware-dependent and will only execute on machines for which a particular compiler is designed. The user is not at all concerned about this machine dependence because most computers are highly compatible on the FORTRAN level.

4.3 DIGRESSION: SOURCE PROGRAMS, OBJECT PROGRAMS, AND LOAD MODULES

A program written in a high-level language, as was our previous three-liner, is known as a *source program*. Some refer to it as a *subject program*. The compiler translates this source program into an equivalent machine language version called the *object program*.

In our example, we have only three source lines. The END statement, in reality, is not part of the program, instead it is a so-called sentry statement to mark the end of the program to halt the compiler. It may sound like a tall tale when you hear that on some older computers an omitted END statement would cause the compiler to run out of control, compiling whatever it encountered in the file system, until something yielded, but this situation did occur on some systems.

The point is that the END statement is not really a FORTRAN statement at all, but a system watchdog. This leaves us with a complete FORTRAN program containing only two lines.

The object version of this two-liner might contain several dozen machine language instructions, especially if the source program contains a statement like the PRINT statement. Instead of generating a lengthy block of object code whenever a complicated source statement is encountered, the compiler simply inserts a pointer in the object program, identifying a particular block of code (machine language instructions) to be borrowed from the FORTRAN library.

Because the object program usually depends so heavily on code borrowed from the library, the object program cannot run until it has access to the library. It is the function of another program to link the object program with the library, and this special program is called a *linker*.

The linking process can be slow and hard on resources, but the final product will run. This final version is known as an *executable load module* or simply as a *load module*, but some call it a *run unit* or an *executable*.

It is obvious that we are dealing with three separate entities. We start with the source program, which was written by us. This source program is then translated into machine code by the compiler. This translation is known as the object program. This object program is then linked to the library by a program called a linker. The library contains hundreds of blocks of useful code that can be borrowed by a program. Code that is borrowed need not be generated by the compiler, thus making the compile process significantly more efficient. The linked product is called a load module or a run unit. The steps are summarized in Fig. 4.3.

```
SOURCE PROGRAM  -->  OBJECT PROGRAM + LIBRARY  -->   LOAD MODULE
```

Figure 4.3 Compiling and linking a program.

You can see that it takes considerable effort to get a program to run. If the same program is to be run repeatedly, it seems wasteful to go through the compile and link phases each time. Fortunately, it is possible to capture a load module in a file, complete with all library linkages. When the program is required, it can be invoked in a fraction of a second rather than consuming considerable computer time just getting it to the executable stage. It is interesting to note that in a student environment, a program is discarded once it works. In a production environment, the final product, the load module, or run unit, is saved on disk and used over and over again.

4.4 RETURNING TO THE ASSIGNMENT STATEMENT

We have covered a lot of important ground in circumambulating our little program, but we will have to walk around it a few more times, in tighter circles.

Take another look at the imperative statement, the first statement in the program in Fig. 4.2. The equal sign is misleading; it should really be an arrow pointing to the left because the computer is asked to take the real number 3.4 and transfer it

```
SUM <-- 3.4
```

Figure 4.4 The left arrow would have been a better choice.

to the memory location with the symbolic name SUM. See Fig. 4.4. Old keypunches had no left arrow and so the equal sign was chosen as a poor substitute.

The computer has millions of words of memory and FORTRAN mercifully spares us the responsibility of having to pinpoint a specific physical location. Through the medium of FORTRAN, we are really telling the computer that it can store the 3.4 in any memory location it chooses, provided it can keep track of it. As far as we are concerned, the memory location is called SUM and we are putting the onus on the machine to associate an actual physical location with this symbolic address.

In the second line of the program, we ask the machine to print the content of the word with the name SUM. It should be pointed out that the PRINT statement is a simplified output imperative. It will make life very easy until we are ready to deal with the more formal WRITE statement.

The END statement was dealt with earlier and doesn't even appear in the object program nor in the final load module; its sole purpose was to stop the compiler. The absence of the END statement in the object program and in the load module has interesting implications later.

Another walk around the program in an even tighter circle is now possible. When the compiler translates the assignment statement into object code, it stores the constant 3.4 in a special area of the memory called the *literal pool*. When the program is actually executed, the 3.4 is pulled from this literal pool and assigned to the memory word SUM, hence, the name assignment statement.

4.5 DIGRESSION: CHOICE OF VARIABLE NAME

In our two-line program, SUM is not only the name of a word of memory, but also the name of the contents of that word. Because the contents of a word of memory are variable, SUM can also be called a *variable name*. The structure of variable names follows some strict rules. Specifically, a variable name can be from one to six letters or digits long, the first of which must be a letter. The initial letter determines whether the datum is stored as an integer or as a real number. If the initial letter is one of I, J, K, L, M, or N, then integer (fixed-point) storage results. If the variable name begins with any other letter, then real (floating-point) storage is chosen. This is a very important rule, and a FORTRAN programmer is very much aware of it. Figure 4.5 shows two small programs. The only difference between the two is the choice of variable name, but what an important difference. In the left program, the variable SUM is of type real and will end up with 3.4, stored in short floating-point mode. In the right program, the variable ISUM is of type integer. It receives 3, stored in fixed-point mode. The fraction is lost.

```
SUM = 3.4                ISUM = 3.4
PRINT *, SUM             PRINT *, ISUM
END                      END
```

Figure 4.5 What a difference a variable name makes!

4.6 RETURNING TO THE ASSIGNMENT STATEMENT

FORTRAN assignment statements can be far more complex than we have seen thus far. The following two assignment statements contain not a simple constant, but a more complex arithmetic expression:

```
XXX = 3.4 * 12.8 - 3.2
LLL = 3.4 * 12.8 - 3.2
```

When compiling these two assignment statements, the machine reserves two words of memory, XXX to store a datum of type real and LLL to store a datum of type integer. The constants 3.4, 12.8, and 3.2 are all stored in the literal pool in floating-point form because each appears in the expressions with a decimal point. At execution time, the computer evaluates the expressions in the floating-point arithmetic unit, and then assigns the results to XXX and to LLL. XXX will end up with real 40.32 whereas the word LLL receives the integer 40.

And now for a more general look at possible arithmetic expressions. The treatment is rather formal and employs the technical terms of the ANSI X3.9–1978 FORTRAN standard, usually referred to as the FORTRAN 77 standard. (X3.9–1978 is a revision of X3.9–1966, the FORTRAN IV standard, sometimes referred to as FORTRAN 66.)

The material is rather obvious and the accompanying illustrations and digressions will clarify it. Just keep in mind that we are still discussing arithmetic assignment statements and that these have the general form:

```
VARIABLE_NAME = ARITHMETIC EXPRESSION
```

where the VARIABLE_NAME refers to some memory location to which the value of the ARITHMETIC EXPRESSION on the right is assigned and stored, either as an integer or as a real, depending on the choice of variable name.

The ANSI X3.9–1978 document states that "An arithmetic expression is used to express a numeric computation. Evaluation of an arithmetic expression produces a numeric value."

4.7 DIGRESSION: ARITHMETIC EXPRESSIONS IN ASSIGNMENT STATEMENTS

The simplest arithmetic expression is an unsigned arithmetic constant, and we already saw an arithmetic assignment statement involving such a constant:

```
SUM = 3.4
```

Another simple form of arithmetic expression is a variable reference. An example is found in the following assignment statement:

```
SUM = W
```

In that example, the memory location W was probably assigned some value earlier in the program, and the contents of W are now assigned to SUM. This assignment does not alter the value stored in W.

A third simple form of arithmetic expression involves an arithmetic function reference. In the following example, the square root of W is computed and assigned to SUM:

```
SUM = SQRT(W)
```

This last example, of course, raises questions about the sort of functions provided by FORTRAN, but these will be deferred for a while. Suffice it to say, at this time, that FORTRAN provides a very rich set of functions.

X3.9–1978 then states that "More complicated arithmetic expressions may be formed by using one or more arithmetic operands together with arithmetic operators and parentheses." An example illustrating this slight escalation in complexity would be the following arithmetic assignment statement. Again, it is implicit that W contains an assigned value before this statement is executed:

```
SUM = (2.8-W) * SQRT(W)
```

4.8 DIGRESSION: THE FIVE ARITHMETIC OPERATORS

We have now opened the issue of arithmetic operators, of which there are five, shown in Fig. 4.6. Figure 4.7 illustrates the action of the operators.

4.9 DIGRESSION: PRECEDENCE AMONG ARITHMETIC OPERATORS

When the computer evaluates an arithmetic expression, it scans that expression from left to right. Should two or more operators appear in that expression, a well-defined hierarchy determines the order in which the operands are combined, unless

Operator	Representing
**	Exponentiation
/	Division
*	Multiplication
−	Subtraction or negation
+	Addition or identity

Figure 4.6 The five arithmetic operators.

Application	Meaning	Example
M ** N	Exponentiate M to power N	4 ** 2 = 16
M / N	Divide M by N	10/5 = 2
M * N	Multiply M and N	4 * 2 = 8
M − N	Subtract N from M	10 − 4 = 6
− M	Negate M (acts like 0 − M)	−(5) = −5
M + N	Add M and N	3 + 4 = 7
+ N	Same as N (acts like 0 + N)	+(9) = 9

Figure 4.7 The five arithmetic operators in action.

Operator	Precedence
**	Highest
* and /	Intermediate
+ and −	Lowest

Figure 4.8 The precedence among the arithmetic operators.

the order is changed by the presence of parentheses. X3.9–1978 calls the hierarchy among the arithmetic operators a *precedence*, as shown in Fig. 4.8.

This precedence means that when the computer encounters an arithmetic expression, it will make several passes through it. On the first pass, it will perform all exponentiations. On the second pass, it performs all multiplications and divisions in the order in which these are encountered. On the third pass, it performs additions, subtractions, and negations in the order of occurrence. Expressions in parentheses and functions are evaluated first. Keep these simple rules in mind as you work through the examples presented in Fig. 4.9.

```
                   3*10**2*3 - 5 =     895
                 (3*10)**2*3 - 5 =    2695
                 3*10**(2*3) - 5 = 2999995
                 3*10**(2*3 - 5) =      30
             -12/4-4*3**2 + 100 =      61
                     (2**3)**2 =      64
3.2 + 2.0*SQRT(2.0*3.0 + 10.0) =    11.2
                       2**3**2 =     512
                         -4**2 =     -16
```

Figure 4.9 Evaluating arithmetic expressions.

When the computer evaluates an expression containing two successive exponentiation operations without parentheses, it performs the exponentiations from right to left. That is, it interprets 2**3**2 as 2**(3**2), and 1.1**1.2**1.3**1.4 as 1.1**(1.2**(1.3**1.4)). This is quite a departure from the normal left-to-right evaluation, and must be remembered.

The expression −4**2 might also give you pause, but it yields to a brute-force application of the precedence rules. The rules state that the exponentiation must be performed first, followed by the negation: −(4**2), in other words.

4.10 DIGRESSION: ARITHMETIC TERMS AND EXPRESSIONS DEFINED

If you were able to follow the previous examples without difficulty, you understand how expressions are evaluated. You might be interested to know that X3.9–1978 goes to considerable length to define the various types of arithmetic operands and ultimately arrives at the definition of an arithmetic *term* and an arithmetic *expression*. Instead of presenting the details, it is easier to show a particular example. The following is an arithmetic assignment statement of the form VARIABLE = EXPRESSION:

```
X = 3.1*4.2-SQRT(16.)*12.+12./3.**2.
```

Because of the precedence among the arithmetic operators, the expression is evaluated in the order indicated by the parentheses:

```
X = (3.1*4.2) - (SQRT(16.)*12) + (12./(3.**2))
```

which, in effect, reduces it to three items separated by the subtraction and addition operators. These items are called terms. An arithmetic expression, therefore, ultimately consists of one or more terms that are separated by the addition operator or the subtraction operator, or both. A term can be as simple as a single constant. In our earliest example, we encountered the following arithmetic assignment statement:

```
SUM = 3.4
```

The arithmetic expression on the right consists of a single term that happens to be a constant.

You may sense that the concept of a term is rather artificial, but it is the direct consequence of the order or precedence among the arithmetic operators.

4.11 MIXING OF DATA TYPES IN ASSIGNMENT STATEMENTS

So far, we have delicately skirted the issue of mixing data types in assignment statements, although we did hint earlier that a real value can be assigned to an integer variable. It is also true that an integer value can be assigned to a real variable. We can, in other words, mix data types across the equal sign, but we must understand the implications clearly; they are illustrated in the following two examples:

```
SAMPLE = 128 + 12
```

The arithmetic expression in this assignment statement contains two integer terms. The value of the expression is 140, of type integer, which is then assigned to SAMPLE in floating-point form. Another example follows:

```
ISAMP = Ø.33 + Ø.66
```

In this case, the expression contains two real terms, and the sum is therefore performed in floating-point arithmetic. The value of the expression is 0.99, which is then assigned to the integer variable ISAMP. Integer storage, as you well know, cannot accommodate a fraction—and there is no rounding. ISAMP ends up with the integer 0. There is no warning issued.

It should be mentioned that the mixing of data types was traditionally referred to as the mixing of *modes*. The X3.9–1978 document no longer uses the term mode, preferring instead the term *type*. Many older versions of FORTRAN did not permit data-type mixing in expressions, but FORTRAN 77 permits this according to the following rules: When the two operands of an arithmetic operator are both of type real, the arithmetic is performed in the floating-point arithmetic unit and the result is real. When the two operands of an arithmetic operator are of type integer, the arithmetic operation is performed in the integer arithmetic hardware unit and the result is of type integer. When one operand of an arithmetic operator is of type real and the other is of type interger, the integer value is converted to type real and the arithmetic operation is performed by the floating-point hardware, yielding a real result. A few illustrations are presented and explained:

```
X = 1ØØ./3.
```

In this example, the operands of the division operator are both of type real, as indicated by the presence of the decimal points. X is assigned the approximate value 33.33333.

```
X = 1ØØ./3
```

The above is a case of data type mixing in an expression—a real is divided by an integer. The system treats the 3 as a real because the dividend is real. The division is therefore performed in the floating-point hardware, yielding a real result. X is assigned the approximate value 33.33333.

```
X = 1ØØ/3
```

This time both operands of the division operator are of type integer. The division is therefore performed in the integer arithmetic hardware, which cannot handle fractions nor rounding. The result is the integer 33, which is then converted to floating point for storage in the real variable X. X ends up with the value 33.00000.

```
MAL = 1ØØ./3.
```

Again, both operands of the division operator are real, causing the division to be performed by the floating-point hardware, which produces the result 33.33333. When this real result is transferred to the integer word MAL, the fraction is truncated. MAL ends up with the integer value 33.

```
MAL = 1ØØ/3.
```

The operands are of mixed data type, causing the division to be performed in the floating-point hardware. The resulting real result is then assigned to the integer variable MAL, which ends up with 33.

```
MAL = 1ØØ/3
```

The above division is performed by the integer hardware, yielding the integer result 33, which is then assigned to an integer variable. MAL again ends up with 33.

```
SUM = 2Ø./6. + 2.
```

The above expression contains two terms. The division is performed in the floating-point arithmetic unit, as is the subsequent addition. The variable SUM ends up with the approximate value 5.33333.

```
SUM = 2Ø./6. + 2
```

The above assignment statement contains an expression with mixed data types. The division is performed first, yielding the real result 3.33333. The subsequent addition is also performed in the floating-point arithmetic unit even though one of the operands is of type integer. SUM ends up with the approximate value 5.33333.

```
SUM = 2Ø/6. + 2
```

The division in the above expression yields a real result because the divisor is of type real. This causes the addition to be performed by the floating-point hardware as well. SUM again receives the approximate value 5.33333.

```
SUM = 2Ø/6 + 2.
```

The division in this assignment statement is performed by the integer hardware, yielding an integer value of 3. The subsequent addition is performed in the floating-point hardware. This particular example illustrates an important difference between FORTRAN 77 and older implementations. Many FORTRAN 66 implementations would perform the entire expression in the floating-point arithmetic unit if the expression contained just a single floating-point constant or variable. FORTRAN 77 makes data-type decisions on the level of a term rather than the entire expression. Some FORTRAN 66 compilers behaved like FORTRAN 77 in this respect, but others did not, leading to dangerous inconsistencies as programs were taken to different machines. The general rule in FORTRAN 66 was *not* to mix data types if at all possible. This rule can now be relaxed somewhat to the exhortation that you *ought* not mix data types unless you know exactly what you are doing. A caveat might also be added: you should not mix data types in an expression unless you are willing to keep your program away from older FORTRAN compilers. More examples follow:

```
SUM = 2Ø/6 + Ø.888
```

It is obvious that the value of the above expression is 3.888, which is successfully stored in the variable SUM.

```
ISUM = 2Ø./6. + Ø.888
```

It should be obvious to you that ISUM above will be assigned the integer 4.

```
ISUM = 2Ø/6 + Ø.888
```

In this last example, the variable ISUM receives the integer value 3, even though the expression on the right yields a real result.

So much for data-type mixing in expressions and across the equal sign. The principles are easily grasped and do not present an obstacle. On the contrary, if you understand all the hows and whys, you can use them to considerable advantage. If you don't understand the principles, you will be confronted by all sorts of subtle programming errors that take much longer to diagnose and straighten out than the time required to learn it properly in the first place.

4.12 INTRINSIC FUNCTIONS

A FORTRAN programmer has access to various predefined functions such as SQRT, SIN, COS, etc. The ANSI X3.9–1978 document specifies the functions that must be available if the FORTRAN implementation is to conform to the standard. The functions required by the standard are known as the *intrinsic* functions. A particular installation can provide additional functions, but must support all the intrinsic functions. Some of the more important intrinsic functions will now be discussed and illustrated. They are not presented in alphabetic order, but in the order in which they appear in the X3.9–1978 standard.

The best way to get a feeling for the functions about to be illustrated is to have a good look at the programs demonstrating their use. Whenever possible, follow through the programs with a calculator to see whether you agree with the output. The output is shown below each sample program.

INT

The INT function is used for data-type conversion. It accepts a single real argument, removes the fractional component, and presents the value in integer mode. A trivial example could be the following:

```
X = 128.34
PRINT *, INT(X)
END
```

```
INT(X) = 128
```

In older versions of FORTRAN, there were two functions with the same behavior. These were the INT and IFIX functions. Both insisted on a real argument and produced an integer result. If you fed them an integer argument, which is nonsense, of course, there would be loud complaints from the compiler. FORTRAN 77 has combined these two under a so-called generic name, namely INT. The generic version of INT will even accept an integer argument without complaining. If you choose to use the older name IFIX, FORTRAN 77 will still recognize it to be compatible.

REAL

The function REAL is the complement of the INT function. It is designed to take an integer argument and make it look like a real number. This function had two names in older versions of FORTRAN, namely REAL and FLOAT. Its new generic name is simply REAL, and the argument should be integer but can be real. Again, a real argument isn't all that sensible, but it is accepted without run-time errors. The following program illustrates its use:

```
I = 1ØØ
J = 21
PRINT *, REAL(I/J)
END
```

```
REAL(I/J) = 4.ØØØØØØ
```

AINT

The AINT function is known as the *truncation function*. Its argument is real and it produces a real result. It removes the fractional part from its argument and reports the integral portion as a real number. The following program illustrates the function:

```
PRINT *, AINT(33.46789)
END
```

```
AINT(33.46789) = 33.ØØØØØ
```

It is obvious that if the AINT function did not exist, the INT and REAL functions could be used as substitutes. The INT function would perform the necessary truncation, while the REAL function would carry out the required type conversion from integer to real, as the following program shows:

```
PRINT *, INT(33.46789)
PRINT *, REAL(INT(33.467))
END
```

```
INT(33.46789) = 33
REAL(INT(33.46789)) = 33.ØØØØØ
```

ANINT

The ANINT function is used with a real argument. It produces a real result that is the nearest whole number to its argument. The ANINT function, in other words, produces a result that is the rounded equivalent of its argument. This is illustrated by the next example:

```
      PRINT *, ANINT(3.4), ANINT(3.49), ANINT(3.5), ANINT(3.51)
      PRINT *, ANINT(-3.4), ANINT(-3.49), ANINT(-3.5), ANINT(-3.51)
      END
```

```
ANINT(3.4) = 3.000000
ANINT(3.49) = 3.000000
ANINT(3.5) = 4.000000
ANINT(3.51) = 4.000000
ANINT(-3.4) = -3.000000
ANINT(-3.49) = -3.000000
ANINT(-3.5) = -4.000000
ANINT(-3.51) = -4.000000
```

NINT

The NINT function is similar to the ANINT function, except that an integer result is produced. The next program illustrates the function:

```
      PRINT *, NINT(3.4), NINT(3.49), NINT(3.5), NINT(3.51)
      PRINT *, NINT(-3.4), NINT(-3.49), NINT(-3.5), NINT(-3.51)
      END
```

```
NINT(3.4) = 3
NINT(3.49) = 3
NINT(3.5) = 4
NINT(3.51) = 4
NINT(-3.4) = -3
NINT(-3.49) = -3
NINT(-3.5) = -4
NINT(-3.51) = -4
```

ABS

In older FORTRANS, there was an IABS and an ABS function. The IABS function required an integer argument and produced the absolute value of that argument as an integer. The ABS function expected a real argument and produced a real result. These functions are still available under these specific names, but FORTRAN 77 also makes them available under the generic name ABS. The data type of the result is the same as the data type of the argument, as illustrated by the following program:

```
      PRINT *, ABS(-3), ABS(3), ABS(-3.Ø), ABS(3.Ø)
      PRINT *, ABS(-3.87), ABS(3.87)
      END
```

```
ABS(-3) = 3
ABS(3) = 3
ABS(-3.Ø) = 3.ØØØØØØ
ABS(3.Ø) = 3.ØØØØØØ
ABS(-3.87) = 3.87ØØØØ
ABS(3.87) = 3.87ØØØØ
```

MOD

The MOD function is known as the *remaindering function*. It has two arguments. The first argument is divided by the second argument, and the function produces the remainder of the division. The function traditionally had two names, MOD and AMOD. MOD expected an integer argument and produced an integer result, whereas AMOD expected a real argument and produced a real result. These specific versions are still accessible, but FORTRAN 77 makes them available under the generic name MOD, in which the data type of the result is determined by the data type of the arguments. The function is illustrated:

```
      I=1ØØ
      J=15
      A=23.Ø
      B=4.Ø
      PRINT *, MOD(1Ø,3), MOD(1Ø.,3.), MOD(I,J), MOD(A,B)
      END
```

```
MOD(1Ø,3) = 1
MOD(1Ø.,3.) = 1.ØØØØØØ
MOD(I,J) = 1Ø
MOD(A,B) = 3.ØØØØØØ
```

SIGN

The SIGN function is known as the *transfer of sign function*. It has two arguments, transfers the sign of the second argument to the first argument, and reports the first argument with its new sign. SIGN is the generic name, and the function accepts both real and integer arguments, the mode of its result being determined by the mode of the arguments. The older specific names of the function were ISIGN and SIGN. ISIGN expected integer arguments and produced an integer result, whereas SIGN expected real arguments, producing a real result. These specific versions of the function are still available. The SIGN function is illustrated by the following program:

```
      I=34
      J=-2
      X=123.456
      Y=17.3
      Z=-84.32
      PRINT *, SIGN(I,J), SIGN(J,I), SIGN(X,Y), SIGN(Z,Y)
      PRINT *, SIGN(Y,Z), SIGN(3,-4), SIGN(-3,4)
      END
```

```
SIGN(I,J) = -34
SIGN(J,I) = 2
SIGN(X,Y) = 123.456Ø
SIGN(Z,Y) = 84.32ØØØ
SIGN(Y,Z) = -17.3ØØØØ
SIGN(3,-4) = -3
SIGN(-3,4) = 3
```

DIM

The DIM function is called the *positive difference function*. Its two arguments are either real or integer. The data type of the result is that of the arguments. The function subtracts the second argument from the first, and reports the difference if it is positive. If the difference is negative, the function reports 0.

The function's older specific names were IDIM and DIM. The former required integer arguments and produced an integer result. The latter required real arguments and produced a real result. FORTRAN 77 still accepts these specific versions. The following program shows the use of the new generic version of the DIM function:

```
      I=1Ø
      J=7
      X=1Ø.5
      Y=5.1
      PRINT *, DIM(I,J), DIM(J,I), DIM(X,Y), DIM(Y,X)
      PRINT *, DIM(-5,-3), DIM(5,-1Ø), DIM (-5,-1Ø)
      END
```

```
DIM(I,J) = 3
DIM(J,I) = Ø
DIM(X,Y) = 5.4ØØØØØ
DIM(Y,X) = Ø.ØØØØØØ
DIM(-5,-3) = Ø
DIM(5,-1Ø) = 15
DIM (-5,-1Ø) = 5
```

MAX

The MAX function has two or more arguments, either integer or real, but not mixed. It reports the largest argument with a data type determined by the data type of the arguments. The name MAX is generic, covering the specific names MAXØ, MAX1, AMAXØ, AMAX1. MAXØ and AMAXØ expect integer arguments, and produce integer and real results, respectively. MAX1 and AMAX1 expect real arguments, producing integer and real results, respectively. These four specific functions are still available, but you will prefer to use the generic version illustrated here:

```
          PRINT *, MAX(4, 1ØØ, 54, 65, 123, 812)
          PRINT *, MAX(-54.3, -23.2, Ø., 3.4, 5.8)
          END

     MAX(4, 1ØØ, 54, 65, 123, 812) = 812
     MAX(-54.3, -23.2, Ø., 3.4, 5.8) = 5.8ØØØØØ
```

MIN

The MIN function is similar to the MAX function, except that it reports the smallest of the arguments. MIN is a generic name, covering the specific functions MINØ, MIN1, AMINØ, and AMIN1, all of which are still accepted by FORTRAN 77. Again, you will prefer to invoke the function by its new generic name. MIN is illustrated as follows:

```
          PRINT *, MIN(4, 1ØØ, 54, 65, 123, 812)
          PRINT *, MIN(-54.3, -23.2, Ø., 3.4, 5.8)
          END

     MIN(4, 1ØØ, 54, 65, 123, 812) = 4
     MIN(-54.3, -23.2, Ø., 3.4, 5.8) = -54.3ØØØØ
```

SQRT

The SQRT function has a single real argument. It reports the square root of its argument as a real number:

```
          X=54.34
          Z=9.43
          PRINT *, SQRT(X**2 + 2*X*Z)
          PRINT *, SQRT (32.12)
          END

     SQRT(X**2 + 2*X*Z) = 63.Ø6891
     SQRT (32.12) = 5.667451
```

EXP

The EXP is known as the *exponential function*. Its argument must be real and it produces a real result. It raises *e*, the base of the natural log system, to the power of the argument. (The value of *e* is approximately 2.718282.) The function is illustrated:

```
PRINT *, EXP(Ø.), EXP(1.), EXP(2.)
END
```

```
EXP(Ø.) = 1.ØØØØØØ
EXP(1.) = 2.718282
EXP(2.) = 7.389Ø56
```

LOG

The older, specific name of this function is ALOG. It requires a real argument and produces a real result. The same function can now be called by its new generic name LOG. The LOG function produces the log to the natural base *e* of its argument. The function is illustrated:

```
PRINT *, LOG(1.), LOG(2.718282), LOG(7.389Ø56)
END
```

```
LOG(1.) = Ø.ØØØØØØ
LOG(2.718282) = 1.ØØØØØØ
LOG(7.389Ø56) = 2.ØØØØØØ
```

LOG10

Same as LOG, but a base of 10 is assumed. Its older, but still recognized name is ALOG10. It is illustrated:

```
PRINT *, LOG1Ø(1.), LOG1Ø(1Ø.), LOG1Ø(1ØØ.), LOG1Ø(1ØØØ.)
PRINT *, LOG1Ø(1ØØØØ.), LOG1Ø(1ØØØØØ.)
END
```

```
LOG1Ø(1.) = Ø.ØØØØØØ
LOG1Ø(1Ø.) = 1.ØØØØØØ
LOG1Ø(1ØØ.) = 2.ØØØØØØ
LOG1Ø(1ØØØ.) = 3.ØØØØØØ
LOG1Ø(1ØØØØ.) = 4.ØØØØØØ
LOG1Ø(1ØØØØØ.) = 5.ØØØØØØ
```

SIN, COS, TAN

These three trigonometric functions compute the sine, cosine, and tangent of the argument. The argument must be real and the functions return a real result. The argument must be expressed in radians rather than degrees. The functions are illustrated by the following program:

```
PI=3.1415926
PRINT *, SIN(PI/4.), COS(PI/4.), TAN(PI/4.)
END
```

```
SIN(PI/4) = .7Ø71Ø68
COS(PI/4) = .7Ø71Ø68
TAN(PI/4) = 1.ØØØØØØ
```

This summarizes the most frequently used FORTRAN 77 intrinsic functions. You will encounter these again, and some additional functions, when we get into double-precision, complex, and character data applications. Appendix C provides a list of all the intrinsic functions.

4.13 PLACEMENT OF FORTRAN SOURCE STATEMENTS

You are now in a position to write and run your own small FORTRAN programs. Such experimentation will be an invaluable asset at this stage. By now, you should know how to access the computing facilities, and hopefully you will have become an edit expert. Your instructor has probably explained the procedures for invoking the FORTRAN compiler, and for bringing FORTRAN programs to execution.

And now you are confronted by the question of how to present your FORTRAN statements to the computer. Part of the answer is that you create a file containing the source statements, but to do this properly, the FORTRAN compiler will expect you to observe some well-defined etiquette.

Keep in mind that each new FORTRAN source statement is placed on a new line in the source file, where it begins in column 7. For historical reasons, a source statement may not extend beyond column 72, even though most video screens can display 80 columns. The FORTRAN compiler simply will not read beyond column 72, and, in most cases, will not even generate error messages when you trespass into the forbidden zone.

The historical reasons take us back to the days of the Hollerith cards onto which FORTRAN source statements were punched. The standard Hollerith card has 80 columns, but columns 73 to 80 are reserved for card sequence numbers, just in case you dropped a large deck of cards. After a major card spill, the sequence numbers made it possible to reconstruct the original deck. An even nastier reason manifested itself in the form of card readers that occasionally performed a bit of card shuffling in the output hopper. This unsolicited interference gave rise to unpredictable computational results the next time the same deck was run, creating considerable dismay and despondency among programmers and operators alike. The sequence numbers made it possible, however, to monitor such card readers more closely. Although cards are no longer used, columns 72 to 80 are still ignored by most FORTRAN compilers.

When a FORTRAN source statement is too long to fit between columns 7 to 72, that statement can be continued on the next line. The programmer simply places any arbitrary nonzero character in column 6 of the following line, indicating to the compiler that the line is a continuation of the previous line.

X3.9–1978 states that ". . . a statement must not have more than 19 continuation lines." While it may be convenient to continue the occasional FORTRAN statement over four or five lines, few good programmers would ever approach the limit of 19.

In the next chapter, you will meet numeric statement labels. Such labels are placed between columns 1 to 5, inclusively. This implies that numeric labels can range from 1 to 99999 in magnitude.

If you place an asterisk (*) in column 1 of a FORTRAN source line, then that line is not processed by the compiler, but does appear in program listings. This feature provides an ideal medium for program documentation because it allows the programmer to spice a program liberally with comments to explain the flow of the logic. Such comment statements are invaluable when it becomes necessary to return to an earlier program for debugging or modifications. Traditionally a C was placed in column 1 to flag the line as a comment line, but the C makes the reading of the comments more difficult, especially when these begin in columns 2 or 3. FORTRAN 77 still accepts the C as a comment flag, but the asterisk creates a more pleasing appearance.

If the word *column* fails to communicate clearly, substitute *space* and reread the entire section. The word column has been in use since the early Hollerith card days. On a punched card, each character is represented by a column of holes. It is easy to picture a column on a card, but less so when thinking in terms of lines. A card, incidentally, despite its size, accommodates only a single line of source code. In that sense, a deck of cards, with a single FORTRAN source statement per card, is functionally identical to a file containing FORTRAN source lines.

It must be mentioned that there is a tendency for manufacturers to offer a free-form compiler option. When this option is exercised, the compiler will no longer enforce the statement placement etiquette. This relaxation appears to be a desirable feature at first, but it is soon realized that programs become virtually unreadable unless the source statements are presented in some sort of organized fashion.

At the risk of wearying you, it is emphasized that the above FORTRAN source etiquette does not apply to the output generated by a program. That output can appear anywhere on the output line. The programmer is in charge of the appearance of the output. At execution time, programs can also read data from files or from the terminal keyboard. Some people feel, erroneously, that they should also observe the column rules there. The column rules apply only to FORTRAN source statements. They do not apply to program output, nor do they apply to data entered at execution time.

4.14 PROBLEMS

Note: If you do not already know how to create and edit files on your system, you must learn how to do so now. You must also be able to bring small FORTRAN programs to execution. The study of FORTRAN is meaningful only if you can experiment with newly learned concepts. Your learning process will accelerate beyond your greatest expectations when you see new concepts in action, and when you observe these with an open, questioning, and intelligent curiosity.

4.1. Run the two programs in Fig. 4.5. Examine the output to be sure it agrees with the discussion.

4.2. If you wanted to compute the value of an arithmetic expression such as 3.4 * 12.8 − 3.2, you could use either of the following two FORTRAN programs.

```
XXX = 3.4 * 12.8 - 3.2
PRINT *, XXX
END
```

```
PRINT *, 3.4 * 12.8 - 3.2
END
```

Run these two programs to convince yourself. At first glance, you might also expect the following two programs to produce the same answer, but not so.

```
M = 3.4 * 12.8 - 3.2
PRINT *, M
END
```

```
PRINT *, 3.4 * 12.8 - 3.2
END
```

The output of the left program is 40, whereas the right program produces 40.32. The reasons for this difference should be obvious. In the left program, we are dealing with an assignment statement in which a real value is assigned to an integer variable. The fraction is lost. On the right, we are simply printing the value of an expression. The value happens to be real because the terms in the expression are real. Choosing a suitable approach from among these three approaches, write one or more FORTRAN programs to test the nine arithmetic expression examples in Fig. 4.9. If you wish to test all nine expressions in a single program using the second of the three options, it would look something like the following:

```
PRINT *, 3*1Ø**2*3-5
PRINT *, (3*1Ø)**2*3-5
PRINT *, 3*1Ø**(2*3)-5
.......................
.....................  .
END
```

4.3. Test all 15 assignment statements in Section 4.11 using the first and third approaches suggested in problem 4.2. You can test all fifteen assignment statements in a single program by simply extending the sample shown.

```
SAMPLE = 128 + 12
PRINT *, SAMPLE
ISAMP = Ø.33 + Ø.66
PRINT *, ISAMP
...................
...................
END
```

It is easiest if you do it all in a single program, but if you prefer 15 smaller programs, the choice is yours.

4.4. Review Section 4.12 carefully and run all the illustrations on the machine. This may seem tedious, but it will be a highly rewarding exercise. Before running each example, review the output shown in Section 4.12. Make sure you agree with this output by computing the particular function in your head or on a calculator.

4.5. In each of the following assignment statements, a value is assigned to the variable on the left. Deduce the value ending up in that variable, and use the computer to verify your conclusions. Some nonsense assignment statements are included. Identify these, pointing out the problem(s), and discard them. If you feel confident, handle all these assignment statements in a single program by simply alternating the statements with PRINT statements.

```
3.14 * 2. + 1. = PARA
PARA - 1. = 3.14 * 2.
3.14 = (PARA-1.)/2.
PARA = 3.14 * 2. + 1.
PARA = 3.14 * 2 + 1
PARA = 3.14 * 2. + 1
NEXT = 3.14 * 2. + 1
NEXT = 3.14 * 2 + 1
TERM = 3Ø./7. + 15./4.
MILL = 3Ø./7. + 15./4.
TERM = 3Ø./7 + 15./4
MILL = 3Ø./7 + 15./4
TERM = 3Ø/7. + 15/4.
MILL = 3Ø/7. + 15/4.
TERM = 3Ø/7 + 15/4.
MILL = 3Ø/7 + 15/4.
TERM = 3Ø/7 + 15/4
MILL = 3Ø/7 + 15/4
TERM = REAL(3Ø/7 + 15/4)
MILL = REAL(3Ø/7+15/4)
MILL = REAL(3Ø/7) + REAL(15/4)
MILL = REAL(3Ø)/7 + REAL(15)/7
MILL = REAL(3Ø)/7. + 15/REAL(7)
TERM = REAL(3Ø)/7. + 15/REAL(7)
TERM = INT(REAL(3Ø)/7.+15/REAL(7))
```

```
MILL = AINT(3Ø./7.+15/7.)
PARA = 2**3+1Ø/9
PARA = 2**3+REAL(1Ø/9)
PARA = REAL(2**3)+1Ø./9
NEXT = REAL(2**3)+1Ø./9.
TERM = MAX(3.2,5.1,-128.,45.)*2. * MIN(2.1,2.Ø,1.9,1.8)
MILL = MAX(3.2,5.1,-128.,45.)*2. * MIN(2.1,2.Ø,1.9,1.8)
TERM + MILL = MIN(SQRT(6.4))
TERM = MIN(SQRT(16.),SQRT(17.),SQRT(18.))
MILL = MIN(SQRT(16.),SQRT(17.),SQRT(18.))
MILL = MAX(SQRT(16.),SQRT(17.),SQRT(18.))
TERM = MIN(SQRT(REAL(16)),SQRT(27.3),SQRT(REAL(3Ø)))
MILL = MAX(ABS(-28),25,INT(34.54))
TERM = NINT(3.3) + NINT(3.8)
MILL = ANINT(3.3)+ANINT(3.8)
MILL = ANINT(3.3)+NINT(3.8)
NAND = MOD(1Ø,3) + MOD(3Ø,2) + ABS(MIN(-126,-23,56))
OTRO = SIGN(ABS(SQRT(16.)),-1.)
JUMP = DIM(ABS(SQRT(16.)),1.)
```

4.6. Predict the output from each of the following programs. Use the computer to verify your predictions:

```
X = 12.
Y = 2. * X + 12
Z = X + Y
PRINT *, Z
END
```

```
X = 12.
X = X + 1.
X = X + 1.
PRINT *,X
END
```

```
M1 = 2
M2 = 3
M3 = 4
M4 = MIN(M1,M2,M3)
M5 = MAX(M1,M2,M3,M4)
M6 = MIN(M4,M5)
M7 = MAX(M4,M5,M6)
M8 = M1+M2+M3+M4+M5+M6+M7
M8 = M8+1
PRINT *, M8
END
```

```
L1 = 3Ø
L2 = 21
L3 = DIM(L1,L2) + DIM(L2,L1)
PRINT *, L1,L2,L3
L3 = MOD(L1,L2)
L4 = MOD(L2,L1)
PRINT *, L1,L2,L3,L4
L3 = SIGN(L1,L2-L1)
PRINT *, L3
```

```
L1 = -17
L2 = 15
L1 = SIGN(L2,L1)**2 - INT(SQRT(REAL(ABS(L1))))
PRINT *, L1,L2
PRINT *, 'NOW I KNOW IT ALL - IT FEELS GREAT'
END
```

4.7. Predict the output from the following program after thinking about it carefully. Then run the program to see how well the computer agrees with you.

```
PRINT*,3-2+10/4*2**3*2
PRINT*,3.-2+10/4*2**3*2
PRINT*,3-2.+10/4*2**3*2
PRINT*,3-2+10./4*2**3*2
PRINT*,3-2+10/4.*2**3*2
PRINT*,3-2+10/4*2.**3*2
PRINT*,3-2+10/4*2**3.*2
PRINT*,3-2+10/4*2**3*2.
PRINT*,2**2
PRINT*,2**2.
PRINT*,2**(-2)
END
```

4.8. X3.9–1978 states in Section 6.1.2.4 that ". . . an arithmetic expression is formed from a sequence of one or more terms separated by either the addition operator or the subtraction operator. The first term in an expression may be preceded by the identity or the negation operator. . . . Note that these formation rules do not permit expressions containing two consecutive arithmetic operators, such as A**−B or A+−B. However, expressions such as A**(−B) and A+(−B) are permitted."

With this in mind, try to run the following program on your machine. Many systems will not accept any of the three statements, but some will. The program will run, for example, under DEC's VMS FORTRAN. It is best, with program portability in mind, to avoid this type of statement.

```
PRINT*,2**-2.9
PRINT*,2*-2.9
PRINT*,2+-2.9
END
```

Now replace all occurrences of −2.9 with (−2.9) and run the program again. Study the output and be sure that you agree.

4.9. The following program demonstrates a most important assignment statement concept. Step through the program mentally and deduce the output. Then run it to confirm your deduction.

```
SUM=Ø.
PRINT*,SUM
SUM=SUM+12.
PRINT*,SUM
SUM=SUM+SUM+12
PRINT*,SUM
SUM=1Ø*SUM
PRINT*,SUM
SUM=SUM+1
PRINT*,SUM
SUM=(SUM+SUM+SUM+SUM+SUM)/1ØØ.
PRINT*,SUM
END
```

5

Output

When contemplating the immense popularity of FORTRAN, much credit must be given to that language's output flexibility. The programmer is given complete control over the output format and can exercise that control readily, simply, and concisely. FORTRAN is more than 30 years old now, and over those years many languages have come and gone, their early demise, in many cases, hastened by the authors' lack of recognition of the importance of simple and effective output format control.

A very simple but formal FORTRAN program is shown in Fig. 5.1. It contains a WRITE statement and a FORMAT statement in place of the PRINT statement encountered in the previous chapter. The program will be used to define basic terms and concepts. You will do well to dwell on this simple example until you understand every detail; it will make the subsequent output features easy to grasp.

The first statement in Fig. 5.1 is the familiar assignment statement in which we assign the constant 719 to the integer variable NANCY. The second statement is a WRITE statement in which we instruct the machine to write the value stored in the variable NANCY. The WRITE statement includes the so-called *control information list* in which the destination of the output is specified and where a specific output format reference occurs. You will notice this control information list enclosed by brackets in the WRITE statement. In our particular example, the control information list specifies that the output is to be sent to *unit* 6 under control of FORMAT statement 12. It is understood that somewhere in the program there is a FORMAT

```
      NANCY = 719
      WRITE(UNIT=6,FMT=12)NANCY
   12 FORMAT(1X,I5)
      END

  719
```

Figure 5.1 A formal FORTRAN program using the WRITE and FORMAT statements.

statement with the *label* 12 in which the computer receives specific information about the desired appearance of the output. In our example, the FORMAT statement happens to follow the WRITE statement, although it could appear anywhere in the program. The choice of 12 as a label reference is completely arbitrary, the only requirement being that the FORMAT reference in the control information list of the WRITE statement point to an existing FORMAT statement somewhere within the program body. This is a good place to emphasize that the 12 associated with the FORMAT statement is not referred to as a line number. In FORTRAN, there are *no* line numbers, only *labels*.

Output from a program can be channeled to the screen of a terminal or microcomputer, or it might be sent to a high-speed printer near a larger, centralized machine. It could also be sent to a file on disk or tape, or it might be transmitted to a remote printer, or to a plotter, or perhaps a laser printer. The programmer selects the desired output device by specifying a so-called *unit number* in the control information list of the WRITE statement. Traditionally, unit 6 was the high-speed line printer near the main computer, but for on-line work, unit 6 now usually defaults to the screen. Unit 7 might be a plotter, whereas unit 8 could be a tape drive. While unit numbers were usually associated with highly specific output devices in the past, FORTRAN 77 allows the user considerable freedom in this area, as you will soon discover. Before continuing, take another look at the control information list, UNIT=6, FMT=12 in Fig. 5.1.

And now for a closer look at the FORMAT statement which, in our case, contains the explicit format specification (1X, I5). 1X simply asks the machine to skip over the first space in the output medium, whereas I5 tells it that the integer NANCY is to be printed into the next five spaces. Please note that the "I" in I5 is the letter I, and not the number 1. The I is a mnemonic for integer. The resulting output is shown below the program. The pattern beneath the output is not generated by the computer, but was added to make it easy for you to verify the spacing. Check the output carefully. It occupies six spaces, one for the 1X and five for the integer output field I5. Note that the integer is pushed against the right side of the output field; we say that it is *right-justified*.

Take a parting look at the example in Fig. 5.1; it is simple, and yet it contains all the essential concepts. Several technical terms were introduced, but these will be used frequently enough in the subsequent treatment to make them second nature.

5.1 DIGRESSION: THE PLACEMENT OF FORTRAN STATEMENT LABELS

The FORMAT statement marks your first encounter with a labeled statement; there will be others. The labels are numeric, and can be placed anywhere within columns 1 to 5, inclusively, and they must not intrude on column 6. This implies that the largest possible label is 99999. The actual FORTRAN source statements, excluding labels, begin in column 7, as you will recall from the previous chapter. To dress up a program, source statements can actually be indented to begin beyond column 7, but they must keep clear of columns 1 to 6. Many programmers right-justify their labels in columns 4 or 5 to give the programs a neat appearance.

Before we continue, you must be absolutely sure that you understand everything that was said in connection with the program in Fig. 5.1. You will be short-changing yourself sadly if you do not make a point of running it on the machine. Seeing the program in action will add an invaluable component of reality to your understanding of the subsequent material.

The control information list shown in the WRITE statement in Fig. 5.1 can be abbreviated, as shown in Fig. 5.2. In this condensed form, it is always assumed that the first item in the control information list refers to the unit number and that the second item is the FORMAT reference:

```
      NANCY = 719
      WRITE(6,12)NANCY
   12 FORMAT(1X,I5)
      END

  719
----+----+----+----+----+----+----+----+----+----+----+
```

Figure 5.2 The control information list is usually abbreviated.

While running the programs of Figs. 5.1 and 5.2, you may have noticed that your output appeared shifted to the left by one character position. You may also find this in all subsequent examples. Don't worry about this for now, a logical explanation will be offered in due course. If your output wasn't displaced, don't worry either. Everything will be explained.

5.2 FORMAT EDIT DESCRIPTORS

The (1X,I5) in Fig. 5.1 and 5.2 is known as the *format specification*. Stripped of the parentheses, we are left with 1X,I5, which is called the *format list*. 1X and I5 are called *edit descriptors*. A format list, in other words, consists of one or more edit descriptors, and we will now focus on such edit descriptors, mainly through numerous examples. The terms *format specification* and *format list* can be used interchangeably much of the time, but you should be aware of the subtle difference in meaning.

Iw.m Output Editing

Iw.m is the general edit descriptor used in conjunction with the output of integer data. The I tells the machine that an integer output field is to be prepared and that the total field width is to be w spaces. The integer written into the w spaces is to be right-justified, and it is to be presented with a minimum of m digits, even if it means that the integer must be preceded by zeros to fulfill this minimum width requirement. We already saw a special case of Iw.m output editing in our previous example in the form of I5, which specified a total field width of five character spaces, but imposed no minimum width requirements on the output.

The program of Fig. 5.3 will illustrate all aspects of the Iw.m edit descriptor. Study the width and the position of each output item to convince yourself that the output editing in the format list of the program was adhered to. You should also run the program, but be reminded that your output will probably appear shifted to the left by a single character position. The reason won't remain a mystery much longer.

And now for a careful analysis of the program: The WRITE statement specifies unit 6 as the output device, causing the output to appear at the terminal. The output list in the WRITE statement is NANCY, NANCY, NANCY, NANCY, NANCY, NANCY. This output list consists of six integer items, and you will notice that the format list provides six I fields with specific editing instructions for the printing of each of these six integer data. Let's go through the format list, item by item, and check the corresponding output. Use the convenient ruler below the output to count the spaces.

The computer wishes to print the first item in its output list and scans the format list for specific instructions. The first edit descriptor to be encountered is 1X, which simply instructs the output pen to skip one space. The machine then finds the first I edit descriptor, I1Ø.6, specifying an output field width of 10 spaces and a minimum width of 6 character positions for the actual output. The machine prints the output as requested. Count off the spaces. You will notice that the 1X consumed 1 space, and that the first integer appears right-justified within the next 10 spaces. In order to fulfill the minimum width requirement of six spaces, the machine introduced three leading zeros.

```
      NANCY = 719
      WRITE(6,218)NANCY,NANCY,NANCY,NANCY,NANCY,NANCY
  218 FORMAT(1X, I1Ø.6, I1Ø.5, I1Ø.4, I1Ø, I5, 5X, I3)
      END
```

```
     ØØØ719    ØØ719     Ø719       719  719      719
----+----+----+----+----+----+----+----+----+----+----+----+
```

Figure 5.3 Integer output editing.

The machine has five more items to print, and so it continues to scan the format list for suitable edit descriptors, finding I1Ø.5 next. As expected, it takes the next 10 spaces in the output medium and right-justifies the integer output item within that field, presenting it with a total width of 5 characters. Check the output to make sure things worked as expected. The third item is then printed according to I1Ø.4, the fourth according to I1Ø, which imposes no minimum width requirements on the output. The fifth item is printed according to I5, after which the machine encounters 5X in the format list, causing it to leave five blank spaces. The final datum is then printed according to I3. It is hoped that you followed the output, counting the spaces carefully as we went along.

Fw.d Output Editing

The Fw.d edit descriptor is used for real output. The w again specifies the total output field width, while the d requests *d* decimal places in the output. The program in Fig. 5.4 illustrates its use.

Note the assignment statement in which a real number with 10 significant decimal digits is assigned to a real word AMP. Short floating-point can only accommodate a limited number of significant digits, however, six hex digits in 32-bit excess-40 representation and seven hex digits in a 36-bit word. You will notice the resulting inaccuracy clearly when you examine the output produced by the program. The output list contains five items, and the format list provides five F edit descriptors.

Again, the first edit descriptor in the format list is 1X, causing the first space to be left blank. The first numeric edit descriptor is F15.8, specifying an output field with a total width of 15 spaces, into which the first item in the output list is to be printed right-justified with eight decimal places. Take a good look at the output and note that the decimal point takes up a space. Allowances must be made for this when estimating the width of output. If you haven't done so already, compare the magnitude of the output with the magnitude of the constant in the assignment statement. You will be startled to realize just how real internal truncation is.

The next item in the output list is edited according to F15.6. Again, the total field width is 15 spaces, but this time only six decimal places were requested. Note that the output appears right-justified in the specified field. The third item is to be edited according to F1Ø.4. Count the output spacing to confirm that the machine obeyed. This time only four decimal places are requested.

The fourth output item is to be edited according to F1Ø.2. Note that the output appears with the second decimal place appropriately rounded. Such rounding on

```
      AMP = 876.9876543
      WRITE(6,1)AMP,AMP,AMP,AMP,AMP
    1 FORMAT(1X, F15.8, F15.6, F1Ø.4, F1Ø.2, F5.Ø)
      END
```

```
   876.98764ØØØ     876.98764Ø  876.9876     876.99 877.
----+----+----+----+----+----+----+----+----+----+----+----
```

Figure 5.4 Fw.d output editing for real data.

output is an important FORTRAN feature. The fifth item is subjected to F5.Ø editing. The decimal point appears, but there are no decimal places as none had been requested. Again, notice that automatic rounding occurred.

Ew.d and Ew.dEe Output Editing

If you prefer your output in normalized floating-point form, the Ew.d edit descriptor is available. The E suggests exponential and is therefore easily remembered. Again, the w is the total width of the output field, and d specifies the number of decimal places. Figure 5.5 presents an example of Ew.d output editing.

A number such as .8769876E+03 is to be interpreted as $0.8769876 \times 10^{+03}$. Ew.d output editing is usually preferred when very large, or very small, numbers are expected, or when the programmer cannot predict the magnitude of a certain computational result. You should study the output carefully, dutifully counting the spaces. Notice that the machine again performs appropriate rounding on output. It should be mentioned that some machines precede the decimal points with a zero. This does not affect the magnitude of the output, of course, but some people feel that it makes the output more readable, especially since naked decimal points and flyspecks are easily confused. X3.9–1978 suggests the leading zero as an option.

If you like to see your exponents with more than the default two digits, you can request more or fewer by specifying Ew.dEe editing. The final "e" will determine the number of digits in the exponent. Study the program in Fig. 5.6 and you will see how simple this option is.

For standard two-digit exponent E-type editing, the output field width should be at least seven spaces greater than the number of decimal places requested because of the overhead inherent in the structure of the edited output. The E+XX alone requires four spaces, and because some machines also like to present the output

```
      AMP = 876.9876543
      WRITE(6,1)AMP,AMP,AMP,AMP
    1 FORMAT(1X, E15.7, E15.5, E15.3, E15.1)
      END

   .8769876E+Ø3      .87699E+Ø3          .877E+Ø3            .9E+Ø3
----+----+----+----+----+----+----+----+----+----+----+----+-
```

Figure 5.5 Ew.d output editing produces scientific notation.

```
      AMP = 876.9876543
      WRITE(6,1)AMP,AMP,AMP,AMP
    1 FORMAT(1X,E15.7E5, E15.5E3, E15.3E2, E15.1E1)
      END

 .8769876E+ØØØØ3    .87699E+ØØ3         .877E+Ø3            .9E+3
----+----+----+----+----+----+----+----+----+----+----+----+
```

Figure 5.6 The number of exponent digits can be controlled.

with a leading zero, a space must be provided for it. The decimal point and a potential sign require another two spaces, for a total overhead of seven spaces. If you now request that the exponent be presented with more than the standard two digits, the minimal field width has to grow correspondingly.

Gw.d and Gw.dEe Output Editing

The Gw.d edit descriptor acts much like Fw.d or like Ew.d, depending on the occasion. For this reason, G is known as the *general* edit descriptor. As before, the w specifies the total output field width, but this time the d refers to the number of significant digits rather than to the number of decimal places. G editing is only used for real data, and it will present these data in F-edited form whenever possible. It automatically switches to E-edited form whenever the magnitude of the output datum and the requested number of significant digits conspire to make F editing impossible. A number like 12345.67, for example, cannot be F edited unless at least five significant digits are requested. If you ask for four significant digits, the system is forced to resort to E editing, or else it would be unable to report the correct magnitude of the datum.

Whenever the system resorts to E-type editing, the output is presented right-justified within the output field. When it chooses F-type editing, four spaces are left between the output and the right boundary of the output field. These four spaces are reserved in case the system finds it necessary to change to E-type editing. The example of Fig. 5.7 will make it all very clear, but only if you take the time to look at it carefully, counting out the spaces and noting the output field boundaries. As you might have anticipated, Gw.dEe editing is used whenever you wish to overrule the default two-digit exponent for E-type output.

When you study the output, you will notice that G12.5 did indeed produce five significant digits, and that there are four spaces between the output and the right field boundary. G1Ø.4 produced the expected four significant digits, and again there are four blanks between the output and the field boundary. G1Ø.3 produced three significant digits and the four blanks. Notice that rounding occurred as required.

When the system is asked to edit the output according to G1Ø.2, we are permitting only two significant digits to appear and the system is forced to resort to normalized floating-point output that appears right-justified within the specified output field. For the final output item, we allow only a single significant digit, and we also insist on a four-digit exponent. The output confirms that our request was honored.

```
      X = 456.789
      WRITE(6,33) X, X, X, X, X, X
   33 FORMAT(1X, G12.5, G1Ø.4, G1Ø.3, G1Ø.2, G1Ø.1, G1Ø.1E4)
      END
```

```
   456.79     456.8      457.       .46E+Ø3    .5E+Ø3  .5E+ØØØ3
----+----+----+----+----+----+----+----+----+----+----+----+----+----+
```

Figure 5.7 Gw.d and Gw.dEe output editing.

H Output Editing

The H output field is named in honor of Herman Hollerith, who developed punched-card tabulating equipment about 100 years ago. Computer cards are still properly referred to as Hollerith cards. Hollerith output editing is used to produce character strings, such as headings. Figure 5.8 illustrates it well.

In Fig. 5.8, we find a write statement without an output list. The format statement contains the usual 1X to skip over output column 1. This is followed by 51H, which tells the computer that a character string containing 51 characters follows, and that this string is to be reproduced faithfully in the output. The string is usually called a *Hollerith string* and the 51 is called the *Hollerith count.*

One of the more frustrating problems is to have a program rejected because of a wrong Hollerith count, a very common occurrence. To alleviate this frustration, FORTRAN permits the Hollerith string to be enclosed by single quotes, forcing the computer to perform the necessary counting. This valuable simplification is demonstrated in Fig. 5.9. Note that the single quote is used, rather than the double quotation mark. While it is true that many compilers accept either, X3.9–1978 specifies the single quote, which it calls an apostrophe.

The program in Fig. 5.10 is simple and highly instructive. It combines many of the format features discussed to this point, and it deserves very careful study, line by line. Notice how text and numeric output are combined, and also notice that a particular FORMAT statement can be referenced by several WRITE statements. The illustration combines many of the features of a useful program because it computes and reports. The program can serve as a template for more ambitious efforts, in other words, and it is hoped that you are truly impressed by how far you have already come.

```
      WRITE(6,1)
    1 FORMAT(1X, 51HTHIS IS A LONG CHARACTER STRING, A HOLLERITH STRING)
      END

 THIS IS A LONG CHARACTER STRING, A HOLLERITH STRING
----+----+----+----+----+----+----+----+----+----+----+----+----+----+
```

Figure 5.8 H editing of character strings.

```
      WRITE(6,1)
    1 FORMAT(1X, 'THIS IS A LONG CHARACTER STRING, A HOLLERITH STRING')
      END

 THIS IS A LONG CHARACTER STRING, A HOLLERITH STRING
----+----+----+----+----+----+----+----+----+----+----+----+----+----+
```

Figure 5.9 Single quotes are used to delimit a character string.

```
      WRITE(6,1)
    1 FORMAT(1X,'                 +')
      WRITE(6,2)
    2 FORMAT(1X,'                +++')
      WRITE(6,3)
    3 FORMAT(1X,'           +++++++++++++')
      WRITE(6,4)
    4 FORMAT(1X,'     +++++++++++++++++++++++++')
      ITEM1 = 492
      ITEM2 = 6Ø1
      COST1 = 3.43
      COST2 = 7.91
      TOTCOST = ITEM1*COST1 + ITEM2*COST2
      WRITE(6,5)ITEM1,COST1
    5 FORMAT(1X,I5,' ITEMS WERE BOUGHT AT $',F5.2)
      WRITE(6,5)ITEM2,COST2
      WRITE(6,6)TOTCOST
    6 FORMAT(1X,'  FOR A TOTAL COST OF $',F1Ø.2)
      WRITE(6,7)TOTCOST
    7 FORMAT(1X,'  OR, EXPRESSED DIFFERENTLY, $',E12.5)
      WRITE(6,4)
      WRITE(6,3)
      WRITE(6,2)
      WRITE(6,1)
      END
```

```
                +
               +++
          +++++++++++++
    +++++++++++++++++++++++++
492 ITEMS WERE BOUGHT AT $ 3.43
6Ø1 ITEMS WERE BOUGHT AT $ 7.91
FOR A TOTAL COST OF $    6441.47
OR, EXPRESSED DIFFERENTLY, $  .64415E+Ø4
    +++++++++++++++++++++++++
          +++++++++++++
               +++
                +
```

Figure 5.10 A milestone program.

5.3 HORIZONTAL FORMAT CONTROL

nX Editing

We have already encountered the X edit descriptor as a means of generating blank horizontal fields in the output medium. The X field is an empty field, and provides the programmer with considerable horizontal format control. The example in Fig. 5.11 is worth 2000 words.

```
      WRITE(6,1)
    1 FORMAT(25X,'HI YOU ALL')
      Y = 184534.12
      ROOT = SQRT(Y)
      WRITE(6,2)Y,ROOT
    2 FORMAT(5X,'FEW KNOW THAT THE ROOT OF',F10.2,2X,'IS',F8.2,5X,'!')
      WRITE(6,3)
    3 FORMAT(17X,'NOT THAT IT REALLY MATTERS')
      END
```

```
.........................HI YOU ALL
.....FEW KNOW THAT THE ROOT OF 184534.12..IS  429.57.....!
.................NOT THAT IT REALLY MATTERS
----+----+----+----+----+----+----+----+----+----+----+----+
```

Figure 5.11 X-editing is used to generate horizontal spaces.

As you can see, whenever nX appears in a format statement, n spaces are skipped. Study the program carefully. The blank spaces caused by the X edit descriptor are emphasized by dots (.) to help you as you count.

Tp Editing

When the computer encounters Tp in a format statement, it moves the pen to the absolute TAB position p in the output medium. You will recall that the X edit descriptor causes the pen to move to the right relative to its current position, but the T descriptor permits absolute pen positioning, as the program in Fig. 5.12 shows clearly. Study the output and relate it to the format list. You may be a bit

```
      WRITE(6,1)5,6,7,8
    1 FORMAT(T60,I3,T50,I3,T40,I3,T30,I3)
      END
```

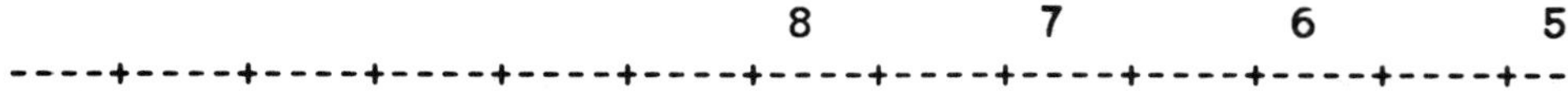

Figure 5.12 T-editing permits absolute pen positioning.

surprised that constants rather than variables appear in the output list, but this is quite legal. It makes this type of demonstration program delightfully simple.

In the program, the output list contains four items and the format statement contains four I-fields for them. The first format instruction T60 causes the pen to tab to column 60, after which the first item 5 is printed into I3. The pen then tabs to column 50, where it starts the I3 field for the 6, etc. And, so you see that absolute tabbing is possible in both directions.

The T descriptor also has a modified form, but in this form it overlaps with the function of X-editing. To be specific, if the computer encounters TRn in a FORMAT statement, it means tab n spaces to the right. Most FORTRAN programmers would probably prefer the nX directive in this case. Similarly, TLn means tab left n spaces. TR and TL are demonstrated in Fig. 5.13. Dots are used to mark the blank spaces in the output to facilitate counting as you check out the behavior of these edit descriptors.

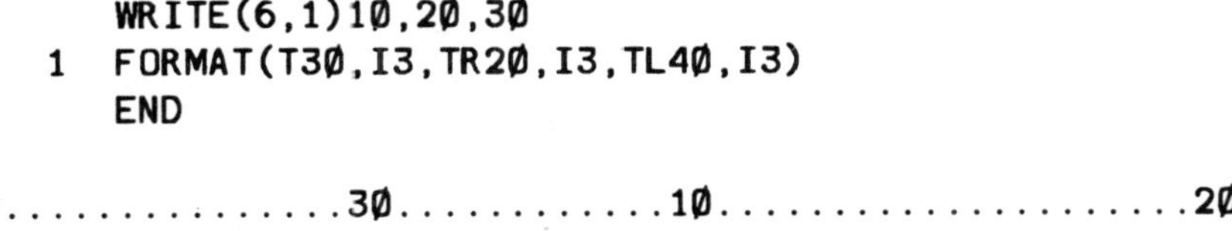

```
      WRITE(6,1)1Ø,2Ø,3Ø
    1 FORMAT(T3Ø,I3,TR2Ø,I3,TL4Ø,I3)
      END

.................3Ø.............1Ø......................2Ø
```

Figure 5.13 TL and TR permit relative pen motion in both directions.

The first edit descriptor in Fig. 5.13 is T3Ø, which means tab to position 30. An I3 field starts at this tab position, ending at column 32 (i.e., it occupies columns 30, 31, and 32). The pen now sits in 33. The next edit descriptor is TR2Ø, which acts exactly like 2ØX and the pen is moved 20 spaces to the right, landing in column 53, which marks the beginning of another I3 field occupying 53, 54, and 55. The pen comes to rest in 56 when TL4Ø is encountered. The pen now ends up in column 16, which marks the beginning of the last I3 field, which occupies columns 16, 17, and 18.

5.4 VERTICAL FORMAT CONTROL

You now know a great deal about formatting FORTRAN output horizontally, and the picture will be complete once you realize how easily and cleverly FORTRAN controls vertical paper motion. If you were observant, then you probably noticed that in all the examples presented above we always left the first space blank—and with good reason. In older versions of FORTRAN, as implemented on many machines, you would probably get away with attempting to print into column 1, but certain characters would never reach this first column. The printer hardware was designed such that if you tried to get a 1 into the first column of a line, the printer would intercept it and give you a page eject instead. A Ø sent to column 1 of an output line would also disappear into the void, but the printer would issue a double line feed. A blank sent to column 1 would be intercepted to trigger a single line feed, and if you sent a + to column 1, the printer would not issue a line feed at all and the + would never be seen nor heard from again. Should other characters be sent to column 1, the behavior of the printer would be unpredictable, but, in most cases, they would probably get through, so you can imagine that the first output column could look rather messy.

ANSI 77 FORTRAN does not even show you the first column of any line, but everything you send to it is inspected carefully. If you transmit a blank, a zero, a 1, or a +, carriage control (vertical format control, VFC) results and all other characters arriving in column 1 are channeled into the proverbial bit bucket behind the machine.

Figure 5.14 presents a summary of vertical format control (VFC) character action, but it must be understood that VFC results only when a VFC character is sent to the very first print position of a particular line.

Please note that in all the examples to date the first ouput print position, although left blank, was always shown; it would have been difficult to explain otherwise. From now on, however, column 1 will not be shown again. This is consistent with ANSI 77 FORTRAN.

Figure 5.15 presents a specific example of VFC in action. Before you look at it, though, it should be pointed out that top of form (TOF) could be difficult to perform on a video terminal; it's easier on a special paper printer. Terminals usually respond to the TOF command by issuing one or two line feeds, or they might even clear the screen. The DO statement near the end of the program is new to you. It is introduced deliberately as a sneak preview.

This example is well worth studying in detail. You will find it instructive, especially if you run it. It contains a little surprise that can only be observed during a live run, either on a screen or on a paper terminal.

Before we continue with VFC, a point must be clarified: You will recall that the format list consists of a series of edit descriptors enclosed by parentheses. These edit descriptors should all be separated by commas to make the program as readable as possible. The comma is optional in special cases where its absence would not lead to confusion. Two such special situations will soon be encountered.

/ Editing

We are now ready to look at the last VFC edit descriptor, the slash (/), which can appear before, after, or between other legal format directives, or even alone in a format statement. To use it properly, keep in mind the following rules:

1. If N slashes appear as the first format edit descriptors, N blank lines precede the output.
2. If N slashes appear as the last format edit descriptors, N blank lines follow the output.
3. If N slashes appear between two other format edit descriptors, N − 1 blank lines appear in the output.
4. If N slashes appear in a format statement without any other edit descriptors, N + 1 blank lines result.

+	no line feed
blank	1 line feed
Ø	2 line feeds
1	Top of new form (TOF)

Figure 5.14 These four characters effect vertical format control (VFC) when sent to column 1 of a terminal or printer.

```
      WRITE(6,1)
    1 FORMAT('1','A DUMB SAYING HAS IT THAT:')
      WRITE(6,2)
    2 FORMAT('Ø','  ONE HAIR ON THE HEAD')
      WRITE(6,3)
    3 FORMAT(' ','IS WORTH TWO IN THE BRUSH.')
      WRITE(6,4)
    4 FORMAT(' ')
      WRITE(6,5)
    5 FORMAT('ØWHILE ANOTHER MAINTAINS THAT IF YOU FALL INTO')
      WRITE(6,6)
    6 FORMAT(' A VAT OF MOLTEN OPTICAL GLASS, YOU WILL MAKE ')
      WRITE(6,7)
    7 FORMAT(12X,'A SPECTACLE OF SELF.')
      WRITE(6,4)
      DO 9 I = 1,5Ø
    9 WRITE(6,8)
    8 FORMAT('+HA HA HA HA HA HA HA HA HA HA HA HA HA HA HA HA')
      END
```

```
A DUMB SAYING HAS IT THAT:

  ONE HAIR ON THE HEAD
IS WORTH TWO IN THE BRUSH.


WHILE ANOTHER MAINTAINS THAT IF YOU FALL INTO
A VAT OF MOLTEN OPTICAL GLASS, YOU WILL MAKE
           A SPECTACLE OF SELF.
HA HA HA HA HA HA HA HA HA HA HA HA HA HA HA HA
```

Figure 5.15 Vertical format control in action.

The example in Fig. 5.16 will make it all perfectly clear. You will be rewarded handsomely if you take the time to study all the little wrinkles carefully; there's a lot more to this than just the slash. You will be doubly rewarded if you run this program on the machine to see it in action. The program output is printed as if on lined paper to make it easier to count the blank lines (shown as dotted lines).

Figure 5.16 contains three different FORMAT statements, and you will notice that all four slash rules are tested successfully. The third FORMAT statement is so

```
*-----THE FOLLOWING PROGRAM ILLUSTRATES SLASH EDITING.
*-----IT WILL TEST ALL 4 SLASH RULES.
*-----
      WRITE(6,2)
    2 FORMAT(///, ' FORMATS AND THINGS', /, ' +++++++++++++++++')
      A = 74.12
      B = 119.21
      M = 91
      N = 298
      INTPROD = M*N
      REALPROD = A*B
      WRITE(6,3)
    3 FORMAT(//)
      WRITE(6,1)A, B, REALPROD, M, N, INTPROD
*-----
*-----THE FOLLOWING FORMAT STATEMENT IS MESSY BECAUSE IT IS
*-----TOO LONG.  IT SHOULD HAVE BEEN BROKEN UP INTO SMALLER
*-----CHUNKS - BUT IT WILL ILLUSTRATE CONTINUATION OF
*-----LONG FORTRAN STATEMENTS.
*-----
    1 FORMAT(' THE TWO REALS', F6.2, ' AND', F7.2 , ' WERE',/,
     +' MULTIPLIED TOGETHER FORMING THE PRODUCT', F8.2, //, ' AFTER',
     +' WHICH THE TWO INTEGERS', I3, ' AND', I4, ' WERE',
     +' MULTIPLIED', /, ' TO YIELD A PRODUCT OF', I6, /)
      END
```

```
.................................................................
.................................................................
.................................................................
FORMATS AND THINGS...............................................
+++++++++++++++++................................................
.................................................................
.................................................................
.................................................................
THE TWO REALS 74.12 AND 119.21 WERE..............................
MULTIPLIED TOGETHER FORMING THE PRODUCT 8835.85..................
.................................................................
AFTER WHICH THE TWO INTEGERS 91 AND 298 WERE MULTIPLIED..........
TO YIELD A PRODUCT OF 27118......................................
.................................................................
```

Figure 5.16 Slash editing.

long that it has to be continued over several lines. A good programmer avoids such FORMAT statements, breaking the output into several smaller WRITE and FORMAT combinations. But suffer through this one; it will show you how to continue FORTRAN statements, how to break in the middle of a Hollerith string, and how not to write FORMAT statements. That particular FORMAT statement tests two of the slash rules.

The slash edit descriptor need not be separated from other edit descriptors by commas because the omission of the comma does not cause confusion. These commas were not omitted in Fig. 5.16, although no commas were placed between adjacent slashes in that example. Commas could, of course, separate slashes from neighboring slashes.

There are only two other special cases where commas can be omitted between edit descriptors, one of which you will encounter in the section after next. We won't meet the third special case because it appears in a more obscure context.

S, SP, and SS Output Editing

When the computer prints a negative number, it must precede that number with a minus sign; it has no choice in the matter. Most computers do not precede positive numeric output with plus signs, although some do. Whether or not a computer does, depends on the default designed into it. A default action is an action taken in the absence of specific instructions. And so we can say that some computers print a + before a positive numeric quantity by default whereas others omit the + by default.

FORTRAN provides the programmer with the ability to set switches in the FORMAT statement to turn on + printing, to turn if off, or to return to the default mode. The three switches are summarized in Fig. 5.17. Any of these sign-printing directives can be issued at any point in the FORMAT statement and it will then be in effect for the remainder of that FORMAT statement, unless one of the other two directives is encountered, which then takes over. Sign-printing directives do not spill over into the next FORMAT statement. All this will seem very simple after you examine the program of Fig. 5.18, along with its output.

1. SP: to turn on + sign printing
2. SS: to suppress + sign printing
3. S: to return to the machine's default

Figure 5.17 The three sign printing switches.

nP Editing

nP is another format switch. When it appears in a format list, all subsequent numeric items written into F- and E-fields have the decimal point shifted to the right *n* positions. −nP would cause all subsequent decimal points to be shifted *n* positions to the left of the normal position. The effect does not spill over into the next FORMAT statement. Shifting the decimal point has some interesting implications because it inflates or deflates F-type output. In E-type output, the exponent is adjusted to keep things even, and I-type output is immune because it has no decimal point to be moved about. It is important to realize that G-type output escapes with its magnitude unscathed, even when it resorts to F-type editing, and so the potential damage hits only F-type output.

The nP format switch is an edit descriptor, and as such should be separated

```
      M = 11
      N = -12
      X = 13.21
      Y = -14.87
*-----WE'LL LET THE SYSTEM DEFAULTS ACT IN THE FOLLOWING FORMAT:
*-----
      WRITE(6,1)M,N,X,Y
    1 FORMAT(I5,I5,F9.2,F9.2,1ØX,'SYSTEM DEFAULT')
*-----
*-----AND NOW WE'LL FORCE '+' PRINTING WITH THE 'SP' DIRECTIVE:
*-----
      WRITE(6,2)M,N,X,Y
    2 FORMAT(SP,I5,I5,F9.2,F9.2,1ØX,'FORCED "+"')
*-----
*-----DOES 'SP' CARRY OVER TO THE NEXT FORMAT STATEMENT ????
*-----THE FOLLOWING WILL TELL -  IT SHOULD NOT CARRY OVER !
*-----
      WRITE(6,3)M,N,X,Y
    3 FORMAT(I5,I5,F9.2,F9.2,1ØX,'NO, DOES NOT CARRY OVER !')
*-----
*-----THIS TIME WE'LL TURN ON 'SS' (SIGN SUPPRESSION) IN THE MIDDLE !
*-----
      WRITE(6,4)M,N,X,Y
    4 FORMAT(SP,I5,I5,SS,F9.2,F9.2,1ØX,'FIRST ON - THEN OFF !')
*-----
*-----NOW WE START WITH SP ON, AND CHANGE TO DEFAULT MODE MIDWAY.
      WRITE(6,5)M,N,X,Y
    5 FORMAT(SP,I5,I5,S,F9.2,F9.2,1ØX,'BACK TO DEFAULT IN MIDDLE')
      END
```

```
   11  -12    13.21   -14.87          SYSTEM DEFAULT
  +11  -12   +13.21   -14.87          FORCED "+"
   11  -12    13.21   -14.87          NO, DOES NOT CARRY OVER !
  +11  -12    13.21   -14.87          FIRST ON - THEN OFF !
  +11  -12    13.21   -14.87          BACK TO DEFAULT IN MIDDLE
```

Figure 5.18 The sign-printing directives in action.

from other edit descriptors by commas. The comma, however, is optional between the nP edit descriptor and an immediately following F, E, or G edit descriptor—and many programmers omit it under these conditions. Its use is still recommended, however, because it highlights the fact that the nP edit descriptor acts like a switch, affecting the remaining edit descriptors, instead of acting like some sort of local modifier of the F or E edit descriptor to which it appears attached in the absence of a comma. Study the program in Fig. 5.19 carefully and you will understand the action of nP editing.

```
*-----THE FOLLOWING PROGRAM INVESTIGATES THE ACTION OF THE
*-----nP EDIT DESCRIPTOR.  nP ACTS LIKE A SWITCH.
*-----
      I = 329
      X = 145.43
      WRITE(6,1)I,X,X,X,X
    1 FORMAT(1X, I6, F14.4, E16.5, G15.4, G1Ø.2)
*-----
      WRITE(6,2)I,X,X,X,X
    2 FORMAT(1X, 2P, I6, F14.4, E16.5, G15.4, G1Ø.2)
*-----
      WRITE(6,3)I,X,X,X,X
    3 FORMAT(1X, -2P, I6, F14.4, ØP, E16.5, G15.4, G1Ø.2)
      END

   329      145.43ØØ      .14543E+Ø3       145.4        .15E+Ø3
   329   14543.ØØØØ     14.543ØE+Ø1       145.4       14.5E+Ø1
   329        1.4543      .14543E+Ø3       145.4        .15E+Ø3
```

Figure 5.19 nP editing.

The n in nP is known as the scale factor. Note the ØP in the last FORMAT statement; it returns things to normal for the last three output items. As you studied the program of Fig. 5.19, you probably noticed a seeming inconsistency. The third datum in the second line of output appears with only four decimal places, even though we specified E16.5 output editing. The explanation is that when P-editing is used with a positive scale factor, to shift the decimal point to the right in E-type output, the computer is forced to produce significant digits on the right in order to print the requested number of decimal places. The computer will produce only a single additional significant digit, however, and hence the apparent discrepancy.

5.5 FORTRAN 77 LIST-DIRECTED OUTPUT: WRITE(UNIT,*) AND PRINT*,

The FORTRAN output editing facilities are simple to use and they are very powerful. Few other computer languages provide similar elegance and flexibility; the few that do borrowed freely from FORTRAN. Despite this simplicity, there are those who want it even easier and thus FORTRAN 77 makes it possible to omit the format reference in the WRITE statement simply by blotting it out with an asterisk in the control information list and by omitting the format statement entirely. This shortcut is illustrated in Fig. 5.20.

The program produces so-called *list-directed* output rather than formatted output, and many aspiring FORTRAN programmers are introduced to the FORTRAN WRITE statement in this manner. Through our opposite approach, however, you are in a position to recognize that there really is a FORMAT statement behind the scenes

```
M = 33
X = 987.543
Y = 4543221234.432
WRITE(6,*)M,X,Y
END

33   987.543Ø   .4543221E+1Ø
```

Figure 5.20 The asterisk replaces the format reference.

and you even recognize its structure. The exact default output editing can vary somewhat from machine to machine.

The term *list-directed* was chosen because the programmer need specify only the output list without concern about formatting. The term isn't necessarily a good one, but we don't have too much control over it. List-driven or free-field might have been better choices.

A statement like WRITE(6,3) requires the programmer to understand the purpose of the unit number 6 and the format reference 3. The list-directed WRITE deals with one of these two obstacles by eliminating the format reference, invoking default output editing. It may be difficult to believe, but there are people who feel that having to specify the unit number of the output device is too demanding. For such FORTRAN 77 provides the list-directed PRINT statement, already encountered in the previous chapter. The PRINT statement is shown in Fig. 5.21. The output unit number and the format reference are both gone now.

```
M = 33
X = 987.543
Y = 4543221234.432
PRINT *, M,X,Y
END

33   987.543Ø   .4543221E+1Ø
```

Figure 5.21 PRINT * and list-directed output.

Figure 5.21 is another example of list-directed output, and it obviously defaults to the same type of editing as did Fig. 5.20. And so, the question is, what additional price are we paying? We are obviously sacrificing control over the output channel, which is potentially a serious matter, because now we can no longer direct output to devices other than the screen.

There is a little kink to all this, hinted at by the presence of the asterisk in the PRINT statement. As you might have guessed, the asterisk does hide a potential format reference; just look at the next example in Fig. 5.22.

And so, we are on the way back to our starting point, although we haven't regained control over the output channel.

Things can get a little more perverse yet, as you will see in Fig. 5.23, where the asterisk is not replaced with a format reference as in Fig. 5.22, but by an actual format specification, complete with parentheses, and surrounded by quotes. When this approach is used, the format specification may *not* contain Hollerith strings delimited by quotes. Instead, H-editing must be used. (See Fig. 5.8.)

Formal FORTRAN programming should use the proper standard form of the

```
      M = 33
      X = 987.543
      Y = 4543221234.432
      PRINT 3, M,X,Y
    3 FORMAT(' I HAVE RETURNED!  M =',I3,'  X =',F7.2,'  Y =',E12.5)
      END

I HAVE RETURNED!  M = 33  X = 987.54  Y =  .45432E+10
```

Figure 5.22 The FORMAT statement can be used with the PRINT statement.

```
      M = 33
      X = 987.543
      Y = 4543221234.432
      PRINT '(1X, I3, F7.2, E12.5)', M, X, Y
      END

 33 987.54  .45432E+10
```

Figure 5.23 The format specification precedes the output list of the PRINT statement.

WRITE statement, although list-directed output can be quite convenient at times, especially when testing and debugging program segments.

5.6 VALUABLE ODDS AND ENDS

Quotes Within Hollerith Strings

Hollerith strings within FORMAT statements are delimited by single quotes ('). Although many compilers will accept the double quote (''), it should not be used. The question is, what happens when a single quote is to appear in a Hollerith string? An example might be found in the following incorrect format statement:

```
3  FORMAT (' DON'T GO')
```

The compiler would count the number of quotes, find an odd number and conclude that something is wrong. It would then issue a suitable error message. To get around it, you simply use two single quotes for every single quote inside the Hollerith string. Only one of these will appear on the output. The above FORMAT statement is thus corrected as shown:

```
3  FORMAT (' DON''T GO')
```

```
  2  FORMAT(///////,1X,F5.1,F5.1,F5.1,F5.1,I1Ø,I1Ø,I1Ø,///////)
 36  FORMAT(1X,'--------------------',I5,I5,I5,I5,I5,I5,I5,I5,I5)
129  FORMAT(1X,F5.2,I5,I1Ø,F5.2,I5,I1Ø,F5.2,I5,I1Ø,F5.2,I5,I1Ø)
```

are equivalent to

```
  2  FORMAT(7(/),1X,4F5.1,3I1Ø,7(/))
 36  FORMAT(1X,2Ø'-',9I5)
129  FORMAT(1X,4(F5.2,I5,I1Ø))
```

Figure 5.24 Repeat specifications condense format lists.

Repeat Specifications

When the same edit descriptor appears several times in succession, a repeat specification can be used to condense the format list. Figure 5.24 shows three FORMAT statements in which the format lists contain repreated descriptors. The same three FORMAT statements are then shown condensed through the use of repeat specifications.

Partially Used Format Lists and the : Edit Descriptor

Should a FORMAT statement provide more numeric output edit descriptors than required by the output list, only the required number of numeric edit descriptors will be used. Any Hollerith editing immediately following the last used numeric editing will also be performed. Figure 5.25 shows a program with a single output item. The FORMAT statement provides two numeric edit descriptors, with Hollerith editing between them. How the program functions is evident from the output, but you might be justified in wondering why a FORMAT statement would ever be more generous than required. Just remember that several WRITE statements are allowed to refer to a single FORMAT statement, and that this might involve output lists of various lengths.

If you place the colon edit descriptor (:) after a numeric output edit descriptor, processing of the format list will cease if that numeric output edit descriptor satisfies

```
      WRITE(6,1)1Ø
    1 FORMAT(/,' THE OUTPUT LIST CONTAINS',I3,' AND ',I8)
      END

 THE OUTPUT LIST CONTAINS 1Ø AND
```

Figure 5.25 An incompletely used format list and a trailing Hollerith string.

```
      WRITE(6,1)10
    1 FORMAT(/,' THE OUTPUT LIST CONTAINS',I3,:,' AND ',I8)
      END

 THE OUTPUT LIST CONTAINS 10
```

Figure 5.26 An incompletely used format list and : editing

the last item in the output list. This is demonstrated in Fig. 5.26 where the Hollerith string AND is now no longer produced.

Rescanning and Partial Rescanning of FORMAT Lists

Should a format list contain fewer edit descriptors than required by the output list, the format list is rescanned until all of the output list items have been printed. An example of such rescanning is shown in Fig. 5.27, where the output list contains three items, whereas the format specification provides for the editing of only a single numeric item. Note that the entire format list, including the initial slash, is rescanned three times until the output list is exhausted.

In Fig. 5.27, the entire format list is rescanned, but it is possible to confine rescanning to a subset by using parentheses. To be more specific, if you approach the format specification from the right, you will, of course, encounter the closing parenthesis. If you then continue scanning to the left, you might encounter a second right parenthesis. That parenthesis will have a matching left parenthesis further on, and it is this matching left parenthesis that determines the point at which rescanning of the format list occurs. A repeat specification just outside this left parenthesis is included when rescanning occurs. Such rescanning continues to the end of the entire format specification. It does not, in other words, stop when the matching right parenthesis is encountered. All this sounds complicated, but you will see from the following examples how simple the concept really is. Figure 5.28 shows a program with a three-item output list. The format specification again contains a single numeric edit descriptor, but this time there are nested parentheses, and, according to the above rule, 1X,I2 will be rescanned. The output confirms that this is exactly what happens.

Figure 5.29 presents another illustration of partial rescanning. This time the

```
      WRITE(6,1)8,7,6
    1 FORMAT(/,' ITEM =',1X,I2)
      END

 ITEM =  8

 ITEM =  7

 ITEM =  6
```

Figure 5.27 The rescanning of a format specification.

```
      WRITE(6,1)8,7,6
    1 FORMAT(/,' ITEM =',(1X,I2))
      END
```

```
 ITEM =  8
  7
  6
```

Figure 5.28 Partial rescanning of a format list.

```
      WRITE(6,1)8,7,6
    1 FORMAT(/,(' ITEM =',1X,I2))
      END
```

```
 ITEM =  8
 ITEM =  7
 ITEM =  6
```

Figure 5.29 Another rescanning example.

parentheses include the Hollerith string. The slash is excluded and will therefore only act during the first scan.

Figure 5.30 emphasizes that rescanning proceeds to the end of the format list, rather than halting at the first matching parenthesis.

```
      WRITE(6,1)8,7,6
    1 FORMAT(/,(' ITEM ='),1X,I2)
      END
```

```
 ITEM =  8
 ITEM =  7
 ITEM =  6
```

Figure 5.30 Rescanning proceeds to the end of the format list.

The last example, shown in Fig. 5.31, illustrates that a repeat specification, parked outside the left parenthesis that defines the rescan entry point, is included in the rescan. The colon edit descriptor in the format specification prevents a dangling AND in the output.

```
      WRITE(6,1)8,7,6,5,4
    1 FORMAT(/,2(' ITEM =',1X,I2:,' AND'))
      END
```

```
 ITEM =  8 AND ITEM =  7 AND
 ITEM =  6 AND ITEM =  5 AND
 ITEM =  4
```

Figure 5.31 The repeat specification is incorporated.

5.7 PROBLEMS

5.1. Predict the output produced by the following four-line program. Run the program on the computer to verify your prediction.

```
      ITEM = 155
      WRITE(6,1)ITEM,ITEM,ITEM,ITEM,ITEM,ITEM,ITEM
    1 FORMAT(1X,7I5)
      END
```

5.2. Substitute each of the following FORMAT statements in the program of Prob. 5.1. Predict the output in each case and test your predictions with actual runs on the computer.

```
1 FORMAT(1X,6I5)
1 FORMAT(1X,5I5)
1 FORMAT(1X,4I5)
1 FORMAT(1X,3I5)
1 FORMAT(1X,2I5)
1 FORMAT(1X, I5)
1 FORMAT(SP,1X,7I5)
1 FORMAT(SP,1X,4I5,SS,3I5)
1 FORMAT(1X,7I5.4)
1 FORMAT(SP,1X,7I5.4)
1 FORMAT(1X,7I5.5)
1 FORMAT(SP,1X,7I5.5)
1 FORMAT(2(1X,I5,' AND'))
1 FORMAT(2(1X,I5:,' AND'))
1 FORMAT(2(1X,I5,' AND'),' NEXT LINE')
1 FORMAT(2(1X,I5:,' AND'),' NEXT LINE')
1 FORMAT(1X,I5,' AND',' ALSO SEE',' NEXT LINE')
1 FORMAT(1X,I5:,' AND',' ALSO SEE',' NEXT LINE')
1 FORMAT(1X,I5,' AND',' ALSO SEE',:,' NEXT LINE')
1 FORMAT(1X,'VALUE =',I5)
1 FORMAT(//,' VALUE =',I5)
1 FORMAT(//,(' VALUE =',I5))
1 FORMAT(2(/),(' VALUE =',I5))
1 FORMAT(2(/),('+VALUE =',I5))
1 FORMAT(2(/),(TR5,'VALUE =',I5))
1 FORMAT(5(TR5,'VALUE =',I5))
1 FORMAT(5(T5,'VALUE =',I5))
1 FORMAT(2(T5,'VALUE =',I5))
1 FORMAT(T5,'VALUE =',I5)
1 FORMAT(1X,(I5),I5,I5,I5)
1 FORMAT(1X,(I5,I5),I5,I5)
1 FORMAT(1X,(I5,I5,I5),I5)
1 FORMAT(1X,(I5,I5,I5,I5))
1 FORMAT('+VALUE =',I5)
1 FORMAT('+VALUE =',2I5)
1 FORMAT('+VALUE =',3I5)
1 FORMAT('1VALUE =',3I5)
1 FORMAT('ØVALUE =',I5)
1 FORMAT(' VALUE =',I5)
```

5.3. Predict the output produced by the following four-line program. Run the program on the computer to verify your prediction.

```
      CON=45.679231
      WRITE(6,1)CON,CON,CON,CON,CON,CON,CON
    1 FORMAT(1X,7F1Ø.6)
      END
```

5.4. Substitute each of the following FORMAT statements in the program in Prob. 5.3. Predict the output in each case and test your predictions with actual runs on the computer.

```
1  FORMAT(1X,F1Ø.6,F1Ø.5,F1Ø.4,F1Ø.3,F1Ø.2,2F1Ø.Ø)
1  FORMAT(1X,F1Ø.6,F1Ø.5,F1Ø.4,F1Ø.3,SP,F1Ø.2,2F1Ø.Ø)
1  FORMAT(1X,SP,F1Ø.6,F1Ø.5,F1Ø.4,F1Ø.3,SS,F1Ø.2,2F1Ø.Ø)
1  FORMAT(1X,SP,F1Ø.6)
1  FORMAT(1X,2P,SP,F1Ø.6)
1  FORMAT(1X,2P,SP,(F12.6))
1  FORMAT(1X,-3P,SP,5(F12.6))
1  FORMAT(1X,2P,SP,5(F12.6))
1  FORMAT(1X,-3P,SP,T15,5(F12.6))
1  FORMAT(1X,E2Ø.4)
1  FORMAT(1X,3E2Ø.4)
1  FORMAT(1X,SP,3E2Ø.4)
1  FORMAT(1X,SP,T5,3E2Ø.4)
1  FORMAT(1X,SP,T5,3E2Ø.4)
1  FORMAT(1X,SP,T5,1P,3E2Ø.4)
1  FORMAT(1X,T5,G2Ø.4,(G2Ø.3,G2Ø.2))
1  FORMAT('Ø',2G2Ø.1)
```

5.5. A program and its output are shown. Supply the missing format lists and run your version of the program on the computer. Your output must agree with that shown here.

```
      A1=4.29
      A2=5.Ø4
      SUM=A1+A2
      WRITE(6,1)A1,A2,SUM
    1 FORMAT(     )
      SMALL=MIN(A1,A2)
      WRITE(6,2)SMALL
    2 FORMAT(     )
      BIG=MAX(A1,A2)
      WRITE(6,3)BIG
    3 FORMAT(     )
      DIFF=BIG-SMALL
      WRITE(6,4)DIFF
    4 FORMAT(     )
```

```
      WRITE(6,5)
    5 FORMAT(    )
      END
```

```
A1 IS 4.29, AND A2 IS 5.Ø4.  THEIR SUM IS  9.33
THE SMALLER OF A1 AND A2 IS 4.29
THE BIGGER OF A1 AND A2 IS 5.Ø4
THE DIFFERENCE BETWEEN A1 AND A2 IS  .75
THIS IS THE END.
```

5.6. Write a program to compute the value of X, where X is defined by the following equation:

$$X = \frac{1.489 \sin (4.3) - 0.3}{\cos (4.3) - 99.42}$$

The program and its output follow. Your output should look identical. This may seem like an unnecessarily tedious exercise, but don't underestimate how much you will learn by doing it.

```
      WRITE(6,1)
    1 FORMAT(   )
      WRITE(6,2)
    2 FORMAT(   )
      X = you supply the appropriate expression here
      WRITE(6,3)X
    3 FORMAT(   )
      WRITE(6,2)
      WRITE(6,4)
    4 FORMAT(   )
      END
```

```
------------EVALUATING AN EXPRESSION------------
I                                              I
I    THE VALUE OF THE EXPRESSION IS  .Ø1667    I
I                                              I
------------------------------------------------
```

Example 5.1

Compute the value of RT in the following equation, where $P = 3.2$, $A = 195.32$, $V = 571.2$, and $B = 69.13$.

$$RT = \left(P + \frac{A}{V^2}\right)(V - B)$$

Solution There are several ways of approaching this problem. The simplest, but not necessarily the most desirable, is shown:

```
      PRINT *, (3.2+195.32/571.2**2)*(571.2-69.13)
      END

 16Ø6.925
```

This approach is one-shot in the sense that it is meaningless to run this program more than once. The same evaluation could be performed less painfully using languages like BASIC or APL, both of which provide convenient desk-calculator modes. A simple pocket calculator would also produce the answer with modest effort.

A second approach involves assignment statements to get the constants into the formula. If the formula is to be evaluated with different constants, it is simply a matter of editing the appropriate assignment statements. It could be argued that this is not much better than the first approach, but you will notice that it allows us to attack much more complicated formulas in a more structured fashion. It also prepares us for the next chapter in which we learn how to parachute constants into a program at run-time, providing us with the ultimate flexibility. The second approach follows:

```
*-----GIVEN THE FOLLOWING FOUR VALUES
      P=3.2
      A=195.32
      V=571.2
      B=69.13
*-----RT IS COMPUTED
*------------------------------------
      RT=(P + A/V**2) * (V - B)
*------------------------------------
*-----THE RESULT IS REPORTED
      WRITE(6,1)RT
    1 FORMAT(/,' THE COMPUTED VALUE OF RT IS:',F9.2)
      END


 THE COMPUTED VALUE OF RT IS:  16Ø6.92
```

5.7. If $R_1 = 31.9$, $R_2 = 61.2$, and $R_3 = 92.74$, write a program to evaluate R_{eq}, where R_{eq} is defined in the equation that follows. Use the more formal approach illustrated in the previous example. The output should be the same as shown. Call R_{eq} REQ in the program.

$$R_{eq} = \frac{R_1R_2R_3}{R_1R_2 + R_2R_3 + R_3R_1}$$

```
EQUIVALENT RESISTANCE
=====================
THE RESISTANCE OF R1 IS 31.9ØØ OHMS
THE RESISTANCE OF R2 IS 61.2ØØ OHMS
THE RESISTANCE OF R3 IS 92.74Ø OHMS
REQ, THE EQUIVALENT RESISTANCE OF THE NETWORK IS 17.1Ø3 OHMS
```

5.8. Evaluate P_{av} using the equation that follows. The various symbols, the suggested equivalent FORTRAN variable names, and the corresponding values are supplied.

$$P_{av} = \frac{\epsilon_{rms}^2 R\omega^2}{L^2(\omega^2 - \omega_0^2)^2 + \omega^2 R^2}$$

ϵ_{rms}	= EPSRMS	= 118
R	= R	= 1000
L	= EL	= 17.3
ω	= OMEGA	= 387
ω_0	= OMEGAØ	= 500
P_{av}	= POWAV	= ?

The computed output should appear exactly as shown.

```
-----------------------------------------
THE COMPUTED AVERAGE POWER IS  .661 WATTS.
-----------------------------------------

WHERE:

THE RMS VOLTAGE (EPSRMS) IS  118.
THE RESISTANCE (R) IN THE CIRCUIT IS 1ØØØ.Ø OHMS
THE INDUCTANCE (EL) IS 17.3 HENRYS
THE FREQUENCY OF THE SIGNAL (OMEGA) IS 387.
THE RESONANT FREQUENCY (OMEGAØ) OF THE CIRCUIT IS 5ØØ.
```

5.9. Evaluate E, defined by the formula that follows. All variables must be real. Recall that e^x becomes EXP(X) in FORTRAN. The symbols, the suggested variable names, and the values are supplied. The computed output must have the form shown.

$$E = \frac{hc/\lambda}{e^{hc/\lambda kT} - 1}$$

h	= H	$= 4.136 \times 10^{-15}$	(4.136E−15)
c	= C	$= 2.998 \times 10^{8}$	(2.998E8)
λ	= XLAM	$= 4.02 \times 10^{-20}$	(4.02E−20)
k	= XK	$= 8.988 \times 10^{9}$	(8.988E9)
T	= T	= 40000	(40000)
E	= E	= ?	

```
              EXPERIMENTAL DETERMINATION OF E
.............................................................
THE EMPIRICALLY DETERMINED VALUE OF H IS:        4.136E-15
THE EMPIRICALLY DETERMINED VALUE OF C IS:        2.998E+Ø8
THE EMPIRICALLY DETERMINED VALUE OF XLAM IS:     4.Ø2ØE-2Ø
THE EMPIRICALLY DETERMINED VALUE OF XK IS:       8.988E+Ø9
THE TEMPERATURE OF THE APPARATUS WAS KEPT AT:    4.ØØØE+Ø4
.............................................................
           THE COMPUTED VALUE OF E IS  34.43E+13
```

6

Data Type-Statements

This chapter shows how the FORTRAN programmer can override default data types, should this be desirable or necessary. The issue, although very simple and brief, is important enough to warrant a chapter.

6.1 REAL AND INTEGER SPECIFICATIONS

As you are aware, when a variable name begins with I, J, K, L, M, or N, integer (fixed-point) storage is assumed by default. When it begins with any one of the remaining 20 letters, real (floating-point) storage is invoked. This default data typing is tremendously convenient, and greatly appreciated by experienced FORTRAN programmers. Occasionally, however, the convention restricts our ability to use a certain highly mnemonic variable name. The word *mnemonic*, incidentally, is pronounced "knee-monnic," and means *designed to assist the memory*.

MILAMP is a good example of a highly mnemonic variable name when computing electric currents measured in milliamperes. Because the initial letter is M, however, it cannot store fractional values, and so we are caught between a highly desirable variable name and an unsuitable data type. FORTRAN provides a ready resolution to the problem by giving the programmer the ability to specify, at the beginning of the program, that MILAMP is to be treated as real. It is possible, in other words, to overrule the data-type defaults. The appropriate FORTRAN statement has the form:

```
REAL MILAMP
```

This is our first encounter with a so-called *specification statement,* a concept introduced at the beginning of Chapter 4. Specification statements, unlike imperatives, declare a specific computing environment. They set the stage before the action begins, and must therefore precede all imperative statements. You should review the opening paragraph of Chapter 4 if you are uncertain about the concept of an imperative statement. Figure 6.1 shows two programs, the one on the left depends on the FORTRAN data-type defaults, whereas the program on the right specifically declares the data type of the variable MILAMP. Compare the outputs produced by the two programs.

Figure 6.2 demonstrates both INTEGER and REAL type-statements. Notice that a single type-statement can be used to declare the data type of several variables. The program is trivial; follow it through to the output.

There are those who feel that a FORTRAN programmer should not depend on the built-in real/integer defaults at all, but should declare every single variable name in appropriate data type-statements at the beginning of each program. Without such declarations, they would consider a program to be incomplete, sloppy, and unstructured. Others feel that having to declare every single variable complicates a program needlessly because you must continually refer back to the type-statements in order to read a program properly. They point out that it might make program

```
VOLTS=11Ø.
OHMS=27.3
MILAMP=VOLTS/OHMS * 1ØØØ.
PRINT *,'CURRENT =',MILAMP
END
```

```
CURRENT = 4Ø29
```

```
REAL MILAMP
VOLTS=11Ø.
OHMS=27.3
MILAMP=VOLT/OHMS * 1ØØØ.
PRINT *,'CURRENT =',MILAMP
END
```

```
CURRENT = 4Ø29.3Ø4
```

Figure 6.1 The data type-statement provides additional flexibility.

```
INTEGER X,Y,Z
REAL I,J,K
X = 5
Y = 9
Z = X + Y
I = Ø.854
J = 23.991
K = I + J
PRINT *, 'Z =', Z, 'AND K =', K
END
```

```
Z = 14 AND K = 24.845ØØ
```

Figure 6.2 A type-statement can declare the data type of several variables.

```
CHARACTER TOM,JANE,LINE,PAGE
COMPLEX Z,Z3,M4,L1
DOUBLE PRECISION L,SPEED,DIST
INTEGER XRAY,ZETA,ALBERT,MICRO,TERM
LOGICAL REL1,L5,MM
REAL NANO,ABLE,MEGA,JOULE
```

Figure 6.3 The six data type-statements.

updates and maintenance more difficult, especially where long programs are involved. They also argue that when it becomes necessary to add code to a program, you are forever going back to the type-statements to add variable names, and when you remove code from a program, you should also go back to remove certain variable names from the type-statements, lest you allow the ghosts of excised code to linger and to haunt the person who might inherit your program.

You can see that there are valid arguments on both sides. A possible compromise position holds that you should overrule the default real/integer data typing whenever this permits the greater use of mnemonic variable names because good mnemonics are one essential key to program clarity.

Overriding the implicit real/integer storage defaults is only a relatively minor part of the story. You will recall that FORTRAN also provides double-precision (long floating-point), character, and logical data storage. In addition, there is a data type, to be discussed later, known as *complex*, where one complex datum consists of a pair of real numbers. FORTRAN provides no defaults for these data types, and if such data are to be used in a program, they must be explicitly specified. Representative type-statements are shown in Fig. 6.3 but not discussed further because they will all be encountered again in their home environments. Just keep in mind that type-statements are specification statements, and as such are nonexecutable. Instead, they define a specific environment in which the subsequent imperatives act.

6.2 THE IMPLICIT SPECIFICATION

The data type-statements discussed in the previous section all have one characteristic in common in that they assign a specific data type to explicitly mentioned variables.

```
      IMPLICIT CHARACTER (A-F)
      IMPLICIT DOUBLE PRECISION (G-K)
      IMPLICIT LOGICAL (L-M)
      IMPLICIT COMPLEX (N)
      IMPLICIT REAL (O-Y)
      IMPLICIT INTEGER (Z)
      WRITE(6,2)
2     FORMAT(' THE STAGE IS SET - LET THE ACTION UNFOLD')
      ETC
```

Figure 6.4 The IMPLICIT specification creates a custom default environment.

Data typing can also be accomplished on a more global basis through the use of the IMPLICIT specification. The IMPLICIT specification allows a programmer to define a unique default environment, in which, for example, all variable names beginning with the letters A through F are associated with character data, whereas variable names with the initial letters G through K might involve double-precision data, initial letters L to M logical, N complex, and O to Y real, and Z integer.

The opening program segment in Fig. 6.4 specifies precisely this environment. The old I, J, K, L, M, N default environment no longer exists within the framework of this particular program. Such flexibility is quite impressive.

6.3 PROBLEMS

6.1. The following program defines a default environment for variable names beginning with all the letters of the alphabet with the exception of L and X. The question is whether or not the old defaults show through these two holes. Run the program, study the output, and draw your conclusions.

```
IMPLICIT REAL (A-K, M-P)
IMPLICIT INTEGER (Q-W, Z)
L=Ø.543
X=Ø.543
PRINT *, 'L=', L, ' X=', X
END
```

7

Input

To this point, we used only assignment statements to load data into words of memory, but we now learn how this can also be done at execution time by means of the FORTRAN READ statement. As always, an example is the best teacher.

Figure 7.1 shows a program containing a READ statement along with its format specification, reminding us strongly of the WRITE statement. In fact, much of what we already learned about the FORMAT statement in connection with output applies here as well, making things very easy. The 5, as you might expect, is the address, or *unit* number, of the device through which the program receives data, and the 8 is the familiar format reference. The choice of 5 as the input unit number is quite arbitrary, but 5 and 6 are the traditional input and output unit numbers at many sites.

Upon encountering the READ statement, most computers issue some sort of prompt character, such as a question mark(?), to alert the user that data are to be entered. Other computers just wait for you to make the next move. When the computer encounters the READ statement in Fig. 7.1, it opens the keyboard to memory word M and lets you type a datum straight into it. The FORMAT statement informs the machine to expect an integer entry within the first five spaces on the input line. Because of this format specification, the computer looks only in the first five spaces; and if it finds the field blank, assumes it to contain 0. If the integer entry is not right-justified, it will add zeros to it, up to and including the fifth space.

Let's actually run the program in Fig. 7.1 to see just how it behaves. A little ruler is included below the prompt line to show the spaces in the input medium. Because the prompt character "?" is issued by the machine, the space consumed

```
      READ(5,8)M
    8 FORMAT(I5)
      WRITE(6,9)M
    9 FORMAT(' JUST READ',I5,' INTO M')
      END
```

Figure 7.1 Reading data at run time.

by it is not included in the count. If you are content to only study the program without running it on your computer, the reality and simplicity of FORTRAN input will elude you. Anyway, here is the run, but beware that your particular machine might not prompt you for input.

```
?  192
----+----+----+----+----+-
JUST READ  192 INTO M
```

The prompt "?" was issued when the computer reached the READ statement. The 192 was preceded by two blanks to right-justify it within the first five spaces specified by the FORMAT statement. Use the ruler to verify this, and check the output.

To illustrate the importance of observing the field width specified in the FORMAT statement and the importance of right-justification, various possible inputs and resulting outputs are shown. The ruler is included for your convenience; don't expect it on the screen. The program is run five more times. Check the input and the output in each case. (Please be aware that on some operating systems, including DEC's VMS, you must actually type the trailing blanks to fill an input field in cases where the input is not right-justified. If you fail to do so, some of the subsequent runs will yield different results. An example is the very next run. If you enter 192, followed by a carriage return, such systems read 192. If you entered 192␣␣, however, 19200 would be read, as shown. Several other systems ignore the trailing blanks entirely, but some simple experimentation will give you insight into the behavior of your machine.)

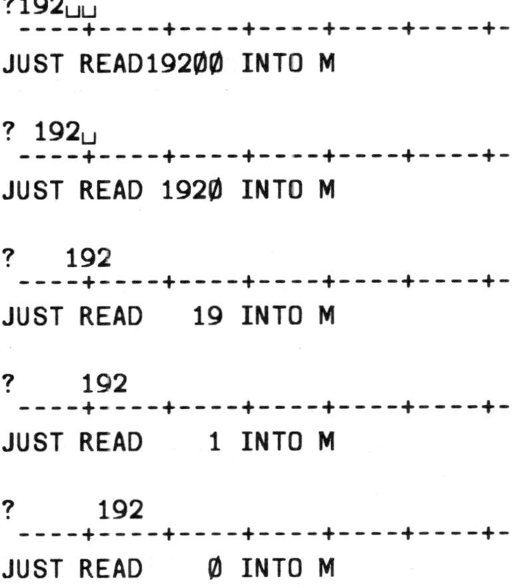

```
?192␣␣
----+----+----+----+----+-
JUST READ19200 INTO M

? 192␣
----+----+----+----+----+-
JUST READ 1920 INTO M

?   192
----+----+----+----+----+-
JUST READ   19 INTO M

?    192
----+----+----+----+----+-
JUST READ    1 INTO M

?     192
----+----+----+----+----+-
JUST READ    0 INTO M
```

7.1 READING UNDER F-EDITING

In the next example, we read into the real word X, instructing the computer to look for our input within the first 10 spaces of the input medium. The program is also run several times to let you study the output. Appropriate comments are made along the way. Take the trouble to study the input and output in each case.

```
      READ(5,8)X
    8 FORMAT(F1Ø.3)
      WRITE(6,9)X
    9 FORMAT(' JUST READ',F1Ø.4,' INTO X')
      END
```

```
?   3.14323
 ----+----+----+----+----+----+-
JUST READ    3.1432 INTO X
```

```
? 3.14323␣␣
 ----+----+----+----+----+----+-
JUST READ    3.1432 INTO X
```

```
?3.14323␣␣␣
 ----+----+----+----+----+----+-
JUST READ    3.1432 INTO X
```

Notice that only the first entry was right-justified in the F1Ø field. The computer padded the other entries with zeros, but because of the decimal point, this padding has no effect on the magnitude of the value read. A few more examples will be helpful:

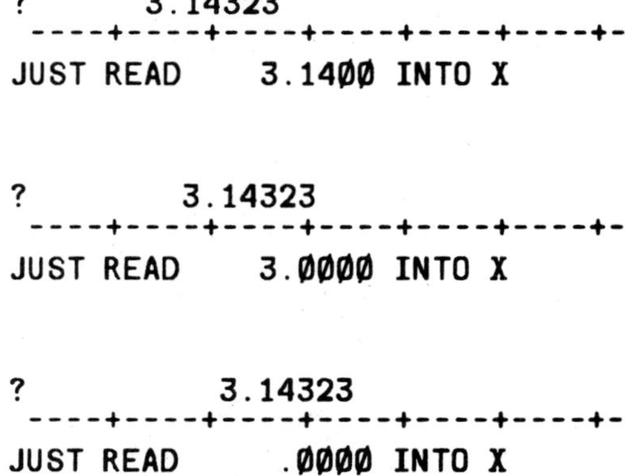

```
?      3.14323
 ----+----+----+----+----+----+-
JUST READ    3.14ØØ INTO X
```

```
?        3.14323
 ----+----+----+----+----+----+-
JUST READ    3.ØØØØ INTO X
```

```
?          3.14323
 ----+----+----+----+----+----+-
JUST READ     .ØØØØ INTO X
```

By now you are probably wondering why we specified F1Ø.3 in the input FORMAT statement and then entered a number with five decimal places. The fact is that if the input datum carries a decimal point, the number of decimal places suggested by an input format edit descriptor such as F10.3 is simply ignored. Had F10.0 been specified, the program would have run the same.

To probe this mystery, we will run our test program again, but this time no decimal point is provided in the input datum:

```
?     31415
 ----+----+----+----+----+----+-
JUST READ   31.4150 INTO X
```

Because the input has no decimal point, the computer consults the format edit descriptor F10.3 and decides to assume a decimal point in the input, three positions from the right end of the field, and this is obvious from the output. Two more examples follow:

```
?       123
 ----+----+----+----+----+----+-
JUST READ    0.1230 INTO X
```

```
?    123␣␣␣␣
 ----+----+----+----+----+----+-
JUST READ 1230.0000 INTO X
```

7.2 READING UNDER E-EDITING

When reading under E-editing, everything is as you might expect, provided that the input datum has a decimal point and is right-justified in the input field. The input datum can even appear without an exponent, in which case E+00 is assumed.

If the number entered has no decimal point, the d in Ew.d will act just as it did when reading under F-editing, assuming a decimal point d digits from the end. The examples that follow will make it clear.

If the input datum is not right-justified within the specified input field, padding with zeros results; and when you add zeros to exponents, numbers become large fairly fast. This is all illustrated in the following 10 live runs. Think about each one carefully and all will become very clear, especially after a few good sessions at the computer.

```
      READ(5,2)X
    2 FORMAT(E10.2)
      WRITE(6,3)X
    3 FORMAT(' JUST READ',E15.5,' INTO X')
      END
```

```
?  123.E+01
 ----+----+----+----+----+----+----+----
JUST READ      .12300E+04 INTO X
```

```
? 123.E+Ø1␣
 ----+----+----+----+----+----+----+----
JUST READ     .123ØØE+13 INTO X


? 123.E+Ø3␣
 ----+----+----+----+----+----+----+----
JUST READ     .123ØØE+33 INTO X


?   123E+Ø1
 ----+----+----+----+----+----+----+----
JUST READ     .123ØØE+Ø2 INTO X


?      123.
 ----+----+----+----+----+----+----+----
JUST READ     .123ØØE+Ø3 INTO X


?   123.␣␣␣
 ----+----+----+----+----+----+----+----
JUST READ     .123ØØE+Ø3 INTO X


?123.␣␣␣␣␣␣
 ----+----+----+----+----+----+----+----
JUST READ     .123ØØE+Ø3 INTO X


?       123
 ----+----+----+----+----+----+----+----
JUST READ     .123ØØE+Ø1 INTO X


?   123␣␣␣␣
 ----+----+----+----+----+----+----+----
JUST READ     .123ØØE+Ø5 INTO X


?123␣␣␣␣␣␣␣
 ----+----+----+----+----+----+----+----
JUST READ     .123ØØE+Ø8 INTO X
```

7.3 READING REAL DATA UNDER G-EDITING

The next example shows that reading under G-editing is the same as reading under F and E-editing. Again, you will profit if you take the time to analyze each input and the resulting output.

```
      READ(5,1)X
    1 FORMAT(G1Ø.2)
      WRITE(6,2)X
    2 FORMAT(' JUST READ',E14.5,' INTO X')
      END
```

```
?      123.
 ----+----+----+----+----+----+----+----
JUST READ    .123ØØE+Ø3 INTO X

?123.␣␣␣␣␣␣
 ----+----+----+----+----+----+----+----
JUST READ    .123ØØE+Ø3 INTO X

?       123
 ----+----+----+----+----+----+----+----
JUST READ    .123ØØE+Ø1 INTO X

?123␣␣␣␣␣␣␣
 ----+----+----+----+----+----+----+----
JUST READ    .123ØØE+Ø8 INTO X

?  123.E+Ø1
 ----+----+----+----+----+----+----+----
JUST READ    .123ØØE+Ø4 INTO X

? 123.E+Ø3␣
 ----+----+----+----+----+----+----+----
JUST READ    .123ØØE+33 INTO X

?   123E+Ø1
 ----+----+----+----+----+----+----+----
JUST READ    .123ØØE+Ø2 INTO X

?  123E+Ø3␣
 ----+----+----+----+----+----+----+----
JUST READ    .123ØØE+31 INTO X

?␣␣␣␣␣␣␣␣␣␣
 ----+----+----+----+----+----+----+----
JUST READ    .ØØØØØE+ØØ INTO X
```

You can see from all this that it makes no difference whether you read real data under similar F, E, or G-fields. The one thing we did not illustrate is the reading of data in exponential form under F-editing, but it works, as you can easily verify.

7.4 AN ILLUSTRATION

A tape arrives containing thousands of records (lines) of census data. A typical record looks as shown:

```
3998576453421234 3EØ166565645342424 2ØØØ95Ø5949281747465643524133445 4656633
----+----+----+----+----+----+----+----+----+----+----+----+----+---
```

Suppose that you are interested in only four different data items on each record, specifically:

1. A four-digit integer between columns 10 to 13
2. A number in exponential form with an implied decimal point zero positions from the end, in columns 16 to 20
3. A real number with an implied decimal point four spaces from the end, between columns 33 to 38 inclusively
4. An integer between columns 63 and 67

The program in Fig. 7.2 extracts the required data. Step through it to see whether you agree with the output. You will find this example highly instructive.

```
     READ(5,1)I,X,Y,L
   1 FORMAT(9X, I4, 2X, E5.Ø, 12X, F6.4, 24X, I5)
     WRITE(6,2)I,X,Y,L
   2 FORMAT(' THE VALUES ARE:', I6, E12.3, F9.4, I8)
     END

?39985764534212343EØ1665656453424242ØØØ95Ø59492817474656435241334454656633
 ----+----+----+----+----+----+----+----+----+----+----+----+----+----+----

 THE VALUES ARE:  3421    .43ØE+Ø3  24.2ØØØ   34454
```

Figure 7.2 Selecting specific data from an input record.

7.5 / EDITING ON INPUT

The action of the slash (/) in an input FORMAT statement is very simple. Whenever a slash is encountered, the computer moves to the next input record. The program in Fig. 7.3, for example, prompts for seven input records, and you should run it

```
      READ(5,1)X,Y
    1 FORMAT(//,F1Ø.Ø,////,F1Ø.Ø)
      WRITE(6,2) X,Y
    2 FORMAT(1X,2F2Ø.5)
      END
```

Figure 7.3 / editing on input.

to confirm this. Before we even enter the format list, the first record is in position to be read. The first slash then causes the second record to be called, and the second slash makes the machine move to the third input record, where F1Ø.Ø permits the computer to read X. The third slash then causes the system to move to the fourth record, and the fourth, fifth, and sixth slashes space the machine to the seventh input record. On the seventh record, it finds an open F1Ø.Ø field, allowing it to read Y.

7.6 FORMAT RESCANNING AND PARTIAL FORMAT RESCANNING

Should the input list contain more items than the number of format fields specified, the FORMAT statement will be rescanned. Whenever the FORMAT specification is rescanned, the computer automatically moves to the next record in the input medium. This is very similar to format rescanning on output, where every rescan generates a new output record. Based on your knowledge of output formatting, you will expect that partial rescanning is forced by enclosing a subset of the format specification within parentheses.

The next example, a highly instructive program, is shown in Fig. 7.4. Although the input list consists of only eight items, the program will read sixteen input records, a fact you should confirm on the computer. When the machine enters the format list, it sits at the first input record on which it is allowed to read A under F5.Ø. It then encounters the slash and immediately moves to the second input record. Upon looking for further input format instructions, it reaches the end of the format list and is forced to rescan. This rescan causes the machine to move to the third input record, on which it reads B under F5.Ø. The slash moves the attention to the fourth record, and the subsequent rescan focuses on the fifth record, where C is read. It is obvious that 16 input records are required to satisfy the input list.

```
      READ(5,1)A,B,C,D,E,F,G,H
    1 FORMAT(F5.Ø,/)
      WRITE(6,2)A,B,C,D,E,F,G,H
    2 FORMAT(1X,4F15.5)
      END
```

Figure 7.4 Format rescanning on input.

Analyze the following program and deduce how many input records it requires and run it on the machine to confirm your findings. You should conclude that three records are read and you should be able to explain why.

```
      READ(5,1)A,B,C,D,E,F,G,H
    1 FORMAT(2F5.Ø,(2F5.Ø))
      WRITE(6,2)A,B,C,D,E,F,G,H
    2 FORMAT(1X,4F15.5)
      END
```

If the format specification were changed to (2F5.Ø,2(F5.Ø)), the program would still require only three input records because the repeat factor 2 outside the inner set of parentheses acts as though it were inside.

7.7 LIST-DIRECTED INPUT

You recall list-directed output from the previous chapter. Not surprisingly, list-directed input is also available, as the program in Fig. 7.5 shows. Note that the input FORMAT statement is gone. At run time, the computer does not care how many input records are entered so long as it gets the eight data items it wants. If you simply hit the carriage return, it will not pick up zeros as would be the case with the formatted read. If you put all eight items on a single record, separated by blanks or commas, the computer will not prompt for more. If you place one datum on every third record, it will prompt 24 times. List-directed input has some highly desirable features—even more so than list-directed output, and you will probably become rather fond of it—but keep in mind that a problem such as the earlier census example could not be handled in this manner because it requires the masking out of specific data and the special interpretation of other data. In general, however, list-directed input is ideal for interactive computing, where data are supplied through the keyboard.

```
      READ(5,*)A,B,C,D,E,F,G,H
      WRITE(6,2) A,B,C,D,E,F,G,H
    2 FORMAT(1X,4F15.5)
      END
```

Figure 7.5 List-directed input.

If you were willing to lose control over the input channel, a sacrifice you cannot make when reading from files, an even simpler form is available, as illustrated in Fig. 7.6. This form is still suitable for keyboard input, however.

```
      READ *,A,B,C,D,E,F,G,H
      WRITE(6,2)A,B,C,D,E,F,G,H
    2 FORMAT(1X,4F15.5)
      END
```

Figure 7.6 The simplest form of list-directed input.

7.8 THE FULLY DRESSED READ STATEMENT

The format-directed and list-directed READ statements have some attractive additional features that take the form shown in Fig. 7.7. The END=LABEL1 option causes the logic of the FORTRAN program to branch to the statement with label LABEL1 as soon as the read operation encounters an end-of-file condition (EOF).

```
READ(5,2,END=LABEL1,ERR=LABEL2,IOSTAT=MESSAGE)input list
                          or
READ(5,*,END=LABEL1,ERR=LABEL2,IOSTAT=MESSAGE)input list
```

Figure 7.7 End-of-file and error branching on input.

Should some error condition occur during a read operation, the logic will branch to the statement with label LABEL2. In the process, the variable MESSAGE receives a special numeric code detailing the error condition. Such numeric error codes are designed for systems people, and you need not worry too much about them. The system usually also produces a parellel English explanation of the error condition. IOSTAT, incidentally, is a mnemonic for I/O status, where I/O is the customary short form for input/output. Specific forms of these READ statements might have the following appearance:

```
READ(5,2,END=99,ERR=98,IOSTAT=MESS)A,B,C,D,E
                    or
READ(5,*,END=99,ERR=98,IOSTAT=MESS)A,B,C,D,E
```

Have a thorough look at these two READ statements. They inform the computer to read on input unit 5. Should an end-of-file (EOF) condition be encountered during the read operation, the system will automatically branch to a statement with label 99. Should some other error condition arise during the read operation, the logic will branch to the statement bearing label 98, at the same time assigning a numeric explanatory error code to the variable MESS. The programmer may or may not decide to make use of this error code.

The error condition you are most likely to encounter occurs when you enter an alpha character when the machine expects a numeric datum. Without the ERR and IOSTAT options in the READ statement, the program would trip, and not very gracefully. With these options (and they must be used together), you can intercept the error condition and branch to some other part of your program from where you might issue some suitable warning.

7.9 ILLUSTRATIONS

The first illustration, presented in Fig. 7.8, is rather primitive. It contains a READ statement, list-directed for simplicity, and a WRITE statement to echo the input. This is followed by an unconditional GO TO, sending control back to the READ. This is your first informal, but easily understood encounter with the GO TO statement. It will be met again later. The program keeps reading until it runs out of data. If the program were reading from a file, it would ultimately encounter the end-of-file (EOF) marker and abort. When the program reads from a keyboard, you will need to know how to simulate the EOF conditions. On many systems, control-Z or

```
*-----READ EXPERIMENTS:
    1  READ(5,*)M
       WRITE(6,2)M
    2  FORMAT(' M =',I2)
       GO TO 1
       END

?1
M = 1

?  2
M = 2

?  3
M = 3

?          4
M = 4

? (The user simulates EOF from keyboard here.)

FORTRAN run-time error
I/O error on Unit +5 (SEQUENTIAL, LIST DIRECTED, READ)
End-of-File in input.
Step aborted.
```

Figure 7.8 The program aborts upon encountering an unexpected EOF condition.

escape-F is the required signal, but you may have to ask about your particular machine.

The program will now be run and the simplicity of list-directed input is emphasized by disregarding any sort of input field width. When we tire of playing the infinite loop game, the appropriate keystrokes are issued to simulate the EOF condition, and the job aborts. Study the program and the interaction carefully. The error message shown is peculiar to the Honeywell CP6 system and may look quite different on your machine. The essential content of the error message produced by any system will probably be similar.

You will benefit from a careful look at the error message that tells us that a FORTRAN run-time error has occurred. Run-time error implies that the problem did not occur until the program was actually in execution mode. The machine then gets rather specific, telling us that it was an I/O error on Unit 5, which is the read channel used in this program.

Please note that many systems produce rather specific error messages that can be remarkably helpful, but only if we can overcome our natural reluctance to read what we perceive as being obscure or even incomprehensible.

7.10 THE READ OPERATION WITH EOF PROTECTION

The next example is found in Fig. 7.9. Here we use the END= option in the READ statement to instruct the machine to branch to the statement with label 57 should it encounter the EOF condition. The statement with label 57 is the STOP imperative, followed by an optional Hollerith string. The program is self-explanatory. It is important to realize that the programmer takes control of the EOF error condition in the example. Note that there is no error message from the system, and that the program exit is rather graceful.

```
*-----READ EXPERIMENTS - INTERCEPTING EOF CONDITION
*-----
    1  READ(5,*,END=57)M
       WRITE(6,2)M
    2  FORMAT(' M =',I3)
       GO TO 1
   57  STOP '  NATURAL EXIT - TRIGGERED BY EOF CONDITION'
       END


? 45
M = 45

? 3
M =  3

? 129
M =129

? (The user simulates EOF from keyboard here.)
 *STOP*   NATURAL EXIT - TRIGGERED BY EOF CONDITION
```

Figure 7.9 A program protected against EOF aborts.

7.11 OTHER ERROR CONDITIONS DURING READ OPERATIONS

Another common READ problem occurs when the user enters invalid data. An example would be nonnumeric data when the computer expects numeric data. In Fig. 7.10, the same program is run again, but this time ABCDEF is entered in response to the input prompt. The resulting error message is representative of what you might expect.

Again, the error message is highly specific on many systems, to the point of showing us the record that caused the problem. On some systems, this is not a

```
*-----READ EXPERIMENTS - ENTERING INVALID DATA:
*-----
    1 READ(5,*,END=57)M
      WRITE(6,2)M
    2 FORMAT(' M =',I6)
      GO TO 1
   57 STOP '  NATURAL EXIT - TRIGGERED BY EOF CONDITION'
      END


?5432
M =  5432

?ABCDEF


FORTRAN run-time error
I/O error on Unit +5 (SEQUENTIAL, LIST DIRECTED, READ)
An expected character not found.
Input found was: ABCDEF
Skipping to next input record.

? (The user simulates EOF from keyboard here.)
 *STOP*   NATURAL EXIT - TRIGGERED BY EOF CONDITION
```

Figure 7.10 Invalid data types will create run-time error conditions.

fatal error, and program execution might resume. The EOF condition is then deliberately triggered by the user to cause a natural program exit. On other systems, such an error might be fatal, causing the job to abort.

7.12 INTERCEPTING READ ERROR CONDITIONS

In Fig. 7.11, the program is modified once more, this time to include the ERR= and IOSTAT= options. It is then executed, and bad data are supplied at run time. Be sure to work through the program; it is easy to follow.

You can see that this is a sophisticated program because it can handle EOF and bad input data internally. Don't worry about the error code produced by the IOSTAT option. It's designed for systems people and is shown here only for the sake of interest. It is stressed, however, that on some systems the ERR= branch will not be taken if you fail to include the IOSTAT indicator in the control information list of the READ statement.

```
*-----READ EXPERIMENTS - ENTERING INVALID DATA AND CATCHING IT !
*-----
    1  READ(5,*, END=57, ERR=92, IOSTAT=ICODE)M
       WRITE(6,2)M
    2  FORMAT(' M =',I6)
       GO TO 1
*-----
*-----EOF BRANCH
   57  STOP '  NATURAL EXIT - TRIGGERED BY EOF CONDITION'
*-----
*-----ERROR BRANCH
   92  WRITE(6,3)ICODE
    3  FORMAT(/,' YOU ENTERED GARBAGE, ERROR CODE = ',I1Ø,
      +'  PLEASE RETRY',/)
       GO TO 1
       END


?12345
M = 12345

?ABCDEF

YOU ENTERED GARBAGE, ERROR CODE = 1Ø365319   PLEASE RETRY

?76543
M = 76543

? (The user simulates EOF from keyboard here.)

 *STOP*   NATURAL EXIT - TRIGGERED BY EOF CONDITION
```

Figure 7.11 The program now also deals with bad input data.

7.13 BN AND BZ EDITING

FORTRAN provides two interesting format switches, namely BZ and BN. They have no effect when found in an output format specification, but on input, they determine how blanks that are found in numeric input fields are treated. If you specify BZ, the blanks are interpreted as zeros, but if you specify BN, the blanks are squeezed out, in other words, treated like nulls. BZ is usually the default, but BN can also be made the default when the READ statement is associated with an input file in the OPEN statement, the subject of the next chapter. The exact action

```
   1  READ(5,8,END=99)M
   8  FORMAT(BZ,I5)
      WRITE(6,9)M
   9  FORMAT(' JUST READ',I6,' INTO M')
      GO TO 1
  99  STOP
      END

?␣␣␣␣␣
JUST READ     Ø INTO M

?␣␣1␣␣
JUST READ   1ØØ INTO M

?␣␣␣1␣
JUST READ    1Ø INTO M

?␣␣1␣1
JUST READ   1Ø1 INTO M

?1␣1␣1
JUST READ 1Ø1Ø1 INTO M

? (EOF simulated here)
 *STOP*
```

Figure 7.12 The BZ format switch causes blanks to be treated as zeros.

of these two switches will be demonstrated in the examples that follow. It is first pointed out, however, that if a numeric input field is completely filled with blanks, the computer will always read Ø, even if the BN switch is set. The examples clarify the actions of BN and BZ very effectively.

Figure 7.12 is a modified version of our opening program of Fig. 7.1. Read this simple program to understand it, and then follow the various inputs and the corresponding outputs. The blanks under consideration are indicated. Note the placement of BZ in the format specification.

The last two inputs and the resulting outputs may surprise you somewhat. The same inputs would have produced the same outputs when we examined the program in Fig. 7.1. There, however, we avoided this type of fragmented input because it would have been somewhat unsettling. Just be aware that BZ already acted in Fig. 7.1 by default.

Figure 7.13 shows the same program again, but the BZ switch has been set to BN, causing the blanks to be squeezed out.

7.14 AFTERMATH

This chapter is easily summarized by stating that for interactive, that is, keyboard-based computing, you will find list-directed input to be the best possible way to feed data to your program. When data are read from tape, or from disk files, you

```
    1  READ(5,8,END=99)M
    8  FORMAT(BN,I5)
       WRITE(6,9)M
    9  FORMAT(' JUST READ',I6,' INTO M')
       GO TO 1
   99  STOP
       END

?␣␣␣␣␣
JUST READ     Ø INTO M

?␣␣1␣␣
JUST READ     1 INTO M

?␣␣␣1␣
JUST READ     1 INTO M

?␣␣1␣1
JUST READ    11 INTO M

?1␣1␣1
JUST READ   111 INTO M

? (EOF simulated here)
 *STOP*
```

Figure 7.13 The BN format switch causes blanks to be ignored.

will find input editing indispensable when certain data fields need to be blocked out, or when the data appear without space or comma separation. If you understand both edited and list-directed input, you command impressive flexibility, and you will be able to tackle any input situation.

This chapter was very important. If you got bogged down, you probably did not sufficiently appreciate the importance of going to your computer to check all the programs thoughtfully. You must be cautioned that if you failed to master the concepts presented in this chapter, your progress will be fraught with difficulties from this point on.

7.15 PROBLEMS

7.1. In Section 7.4, an illustration was presented in which only certain data were read from an input record. Undesired data were skipped over using nX-editing. Careful counting had to be performed to make sure that the format specification masked out the proper fields. It is obvious that if a mistake were made in the number of spaces to be skipped early in the format list, all subsequent data on the record would be read in error. You recall Tp output editing, which allowed us to tab to an absolute output position. With this in mind, you might try substituting the input format specification in Fig. 7.2 with (T10, I4, T16, E5.0, T33, F6.4, T63, I5). Try this format specification. If it works, it will make this type of input much more palatable.

7.2. The following 12 programs read and write data. The input is shown on the few lines of screen below each program. Show the resulting output on the same screen, then verify your predictions on the computer. Please note that each "␣" represents one space on the screen, and that each "␣" represents a space to be typed by you. Also note that if your system does *not* prompt for input, all input shown should be moved to the left by one position. You are reminded that FORTRAN 77 does *not* show the first output print position on the screen.

The output generated by the first of these 12 programs is shown to clear up any potential misunderstanding. The first line below the program shows the input record. The resulting output record is shown on the second line below the input record. The line before the output is left blank for aesthetic reasons.

```
      READ(5,2)I,J,K,L
    2 FORMAT(4I6)
      WRITE(6,3)I,J,K,L
    3 FORMAT(1X,4I9)
      END
```

```
? ␣ ␣ 1 8 ␣ ␣ ␣ 3 4 2 ␣ ␣ ␣ ␣ ␣ ␣ ␣ 5 5 ␣ ␣ 7 3 1 _ _ _ _ _ _ _ _ _ _ _ _ _ _
_ _ _ _ _ _ _ _ _ _ _ _ _ _ _ _ _ _ _ _ _ _ _ _ _ _ _ _ _ _ _ _ _ _ _ _ _ _ _ _
_ _ _ _ _ 1 8 Ø Ø _ _ _ _ 3 4 2 Ø Ø _ _ _ _ _ _ _ _ _ 5 _ _ _ 5 Ø Ø 7 3 1 _ _
_ _ _ _ _ _ _ _ _ _ _ _ _ _ _ _ _ _ _ _ _ _ _ _ _ _ _ _ _ _ _ _ _ _ _ _ _ _ _ _
```

```
      READ(5,2)I,J,K,L
    2 FORMAT(4I5)
      WRITE(6,3)I,J,K,L
    3 FORMAT(1X,4I9)
      END
```

```
? 1 ␣ ␣ ␣ ␣ 2 ␣ ␣ ␣ ␣ ␣ 3 ␣ ␣ ␣ ␣ ␣ ␣ ␣ 4 _ _ _ _ _ _ _ _ _ _ _ _ _ _ _ _ _
_ _ _ _ _ _ _ _ _ _ _ _ _ _ _ _ _ _ _ _ _ _ _ _ _ _ _ _ _ _ _ _ _ _ _ _ _ _ _ _
_ _ _ _ _ _ _ _ _ _ _ _ _ _ _ _ _ _ _ _ _ _ _ _ _ _ _ _ _ _ _ _ _ _ _ _ _ _ _ _
_ _ _ _ _ _ _ _ _ _ _ _ _ _ _ _ _ _ _ _ _ _ _ _ _ _ _ _ _ _ _ _ _ _ _ _ _ _ _ _
```

```
      READ(5,2)X,Y,Z
    2 FORMAT(F1Ø.Ø,E1Ø.Ø,G1Ø.Ø)
      WRITE(6,3)X,Y,Z
    3 FORMAT(1X,F1Ø.2,E1Ø.2,F1Ø.Ø)
      END
```

```
? 1 . 2 3 ␣ ␣ ␣ ␣ ␣ ␣ ␣ ␣ 3 . 4 E + Ø 2 ␣ ␣ ␣ ␣ ␣ ␣ ␣ ␣ ␣ ␣ 5 _ _ _ _ _ _ _
_ _ _ _ _ _ _ _ _ _ _ _ _ _ _ _ _ _ _ _ _ _ _ _ _ _ _ _ _ _ _ _ _ _ _ _ _ _ _ _
_ _ _ _ _ _ _ _ _ _ _ _ _ _ _ _ _ _ _ _ _ _ _ _ _ _ _ _ _ _ _ _ _ _ _ _ _ _ _ _
_ _ _ _ _ _ _ _ _ _ _ _ _ _ _ _ _ _ _ _ _ _ _ _ _ _ _ _ _ _ _ _ _ _ _ _ _ _ _ _
```

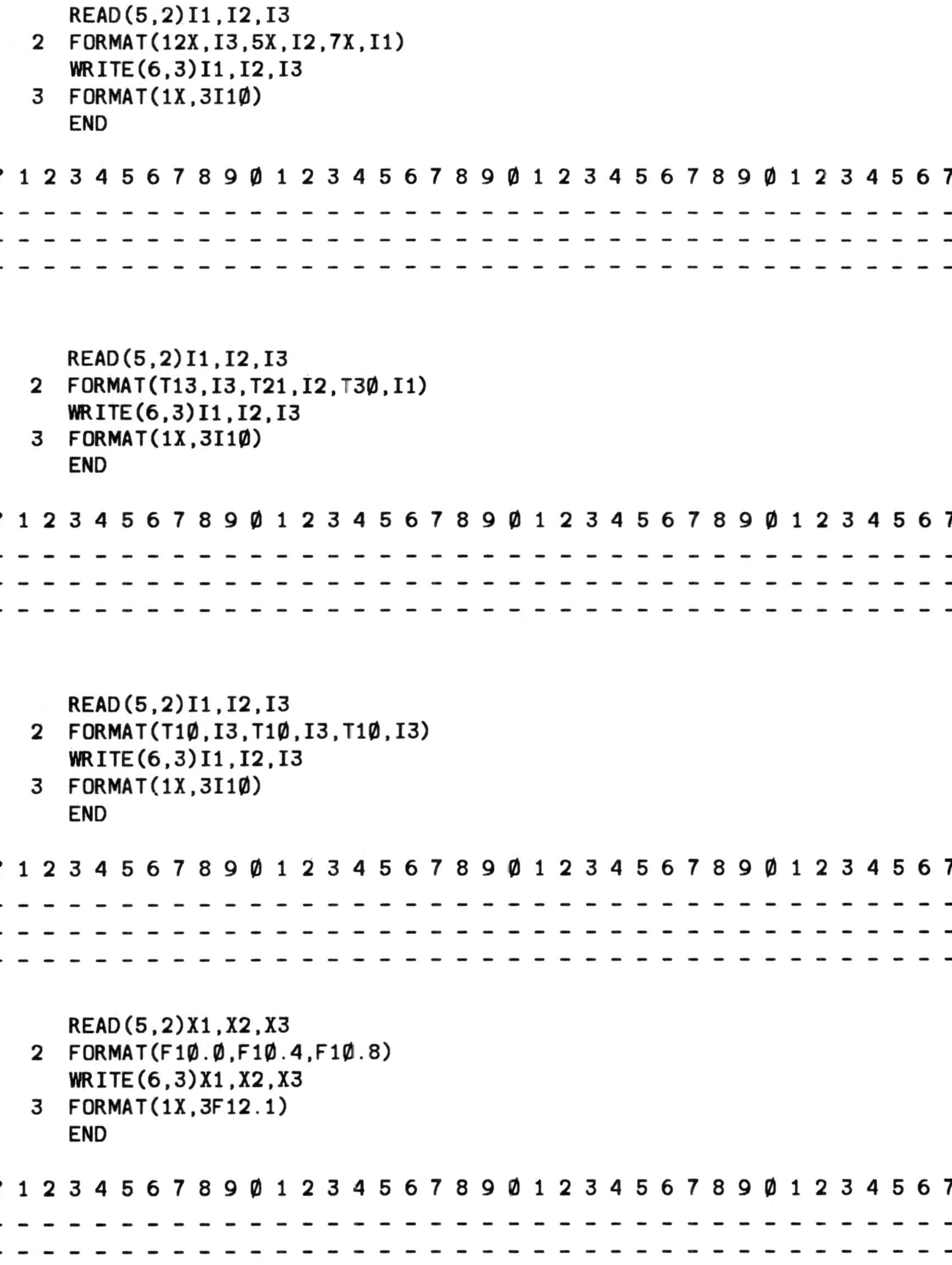

```
      READ(5,2)I1,I2,I3
    2 FORMAT(12X,I3,5X,I2,7X,I1)
      WRITE(6,3)I1,I2,I3
    3 FORMAT(1X,3I1Ø)
      END
```

```
? 1 2 3 4 5 6 7 8 9 Ø 1 2 3 4 5 6 7 8 9 Ø 1 2 3 4 5 6 7 8 9 Ø 1 2 3 4 5 6 7
- - - - - - - - - - - - - - - - - - - - - - - - - - - - - - - - - - - - - -
- - - - - - - - - - - - - - - - - - - - - - - - - - - - - - - - - - - - - -
- - - - - - - - - - - - - - - - - - - - - - - - - - - - - - - - - - - - - -
```

```
      READ(5,2)I1,I2,I3
    2 FORMAT(T13,I3,T21,I2,T3Ø,I1)
      WRITE(6,3)I1,I2,I3
    3 FORMAT(1X,3I1Ø)
      END
```

```
? 1 2 3 4 5 6 7 8 9 Ø 1 2 3 4 5 6 7 8 9 Ø 1 2 3 4 5 6 7 8 9 Ø 1 2 3 4 5 6 7
- - - - - - - - - - - - - - - - - - - - - - - - - - - - - - - - - - - - - -
- - - - - - - - - - - - - - - - - - - - - - - - - - - - - - - - - - - - - -
- - - - - - - - - - - - - - - - - - - - - - - - - - - - - - - - - - - - - -
```

```
      READ(5,2)I1,I2,I3
    2 FORMAT(T1Ø,I3,T1Ø,I3,T1Ø,I3)
      WRITE(6,3)I1,I2,I3
    3 FORMAT(1X,3I1Ø)
      END
```

```
? 1 2 3 4 5 6 7 8 9 Ø 1 2 3 4 5 6 7 8 9 Ø 1 2 3 4 5 6 7 8 9 Ø 1 2 3 4 5 6 7
- - - - - - - - - - - - - - - - - - - - - - - - - - - - - - - - - - - - - -
- - - - - - - - - - - - - - - - - - - - - - - - - - - - - - - - - - - - - -
- - - - - - - - - - - - - - - - - - - - - - - - - - - - - - - - - - - - - -
```

```
      READ(5,2)X1,X2,X3
    2 FORMAT(F1Ø.Ø,F1Ø.4,F1Ø.8)
      WRITE(6,3)X1,X2,X3
    3 FORMAT(1X,3F12.1)
      END
```

```
? 1 2 3 4 5 6 7 8 9 Ø 1 2 3 4 5 6 7 8 9 Ø 1 2 3 4 5 6 7 8 9 Ø 1 2 3 4 5 6 7
- - - - - - - - - - - - - - - - - - - - - - - - - - - - - - - - - - - - - -
- - - - - - - - - - - - - - - - - - - - - - - - - - - - - - - - - - - - - -
- - - - - - - - - - - - - - - - - - - - - - - - - - - - - - - - - - - - - -
```

```
      READ(5,2)X1,X2,X3
    2 FORMAT(3E12.4)
      WRITE(6,3)X1,X2,X3
    3 FORMAT(1X,3E12.4)
      END
```

```
?␣␣␣␣1234E+Ø5␣␣␣1234.E+Ø5␣␣␣1.234E+Ø5_
-------------------------------------
-------------------------------------
-------------------------------------
```

```
      READ(5,2)X1,X2,X3
    2 FORMAT(3F12.4)
      WRITE(6,3)X1,X2,X3
    3 FORMAT(1X,3E12.4)
      END
```

```
?␣␣␣␣1234E+Ø5␣␣␣1234.E+Ø5␣␣␣1.234E+Ø5_
-------------------------------------
-------------------------------------
-------------------------------------
```

```
      READ(5,2)X1,X2,X3
    2 FORMAT(3G12.4)
      WRITE(6,3)X1,X2,X3
    3 FORMAT(1X,3E12.4)
      END
```

```
?␣␣␣␣1234E+Ø5␣␣␣1234.E+Ø5␣␣␣1.234E+Ø5_
-------------------------------------
-------------------------------------
-------------------------------------
```

```
      READ(5,*)X1,X2,X3
      WRITE(6,3)X1,X2,X3
    3 FORMAT(1X,3E12.4)
      END
```

```
? 1 2 3 4 E + Ø 5 ␣ 1 2 3 4 . E + Ø 5 ␣ 1 . 2 3 4 E + Ø 5 _ _ _ _ _ _ _ _ _ _
_ _ _ _ _ _ _ _ _ _ _ _ _ _ _ _ _ _ _ _ _ _ _ _ _ _ _ _ _ _ _ _ _ _ _ _ _ _
_ _ _ _ _ _ _ _ _ _ _ _ _ _ _ _ _ _ _ _ _ _ _ _ _ _ _ _ _ _ _ _ _ _ _ _ _ _
_ _ _ _ _ _ _ _ _ _ _ _ _ _ _ _ _ _ _ _ _ _ _ _ _ _ _ _ _ _ _ _ _ _ _ _ _ _
```

```
      READ(5,*)X1,X2,X3
      WRITE(6,3)X1,X2,X3
    3 FORMAT(1X,3E12.4)
      END
```

```
? 1 2 3 4 E + Ø 5 , 1 2 3 4 . E + Ø 5 , 1 . 2 3 4 E + Ø 5 _ _ _ _ _ _ _ _ _ _
_ _ _ _ _ _ _ _ _ _ _ _ _ _ _ _ _ _ _ _ _ _ _ _ _ _ _ _ _ _ _ _ _ _ _ _ _ _
_ _ _ _ _ _ _ _ _ _ _ _ _ _ _ _ _ _ _ _ _ _ _ _ _ _ _ _ _ _ _ _ _ _ _ _ _ _
_ _ _ _ _ _ _ _ _ _ _ _ _ _ _ _ _ _ _ _ _ _ _ _ _ _ _ _ _ _ _ _ _ _ _ _ _ _
```

7.3. Deduce how many input records each of the following programs reads, keeping in mind that the computer always moves to the next input record when either one of the following two conditions occurs: (1) an input format list is reentered for rescanning, and (2) a slash is encountered in the format list. Verify your conclusions on the computer.

```
    READ(5,2)X,Y,Z
  2 FORMAT(3F5.Ø)
    WRITE(6,3)X,Y,Z
  3 FORMAT(1X,3F1Ø.3)
    END
          (=1)
```

```
    READ(5,2)X,Y,Z
  2 FORMAT(2F5.Ø)
    WRITE(6,3)X,Y,Z
  3 FORMAT(1X,3F1Ø.3)
    END
          (=2)
```

```
    READ(5,2)X,Y,Z
  2 FORMAT(F5.Ø)
    WRITE(6,3)X,Y,Z
  3 FORMAT(1X,3F1Ø.3)
    END
          (=3)
```

```
    READ(5,2)X,Y,Z
  2 FORMAT(6(/),F5.Ø)
    WRITE(6,3)X,Y,Z
  3 FORMAT(1X,3F1Ø.3)
    END
          (=21)
```

```
    READ(5,2)X,Y,Z
  2 FORMAT(6(/),3F5.Ø)
    WRITE(6,3)X,Y,Z
  3 FORMAT(1X,3F1Ø.3)
    END
          (=7)
```

```
    READ(5,2)X,Y,Z
  2 FORMAT(6(/),(F5.Ø))
    WRITE(6,3)X,Y,Z
  3 FORMAT(1X,3F1Ø.3)
    END
          (=9)
```

```
    READ(5,2)X,Y,Z
  2 FORMAT(F5.Ø,/)
    WRITE(6,3)X,Y,Z
  3 FORMAT(1X,3F1Ø.3)
    END
          (=6)
```

```
    READ(5,2)X,Y,Z
  2 FORMAT(2F5.Ø,/)
    WRITE(6,3)X,Y,Z
  3 FORMAT(1X,3F1Ø.3)
    END
          (=3)
```

```
    READ(5,2)X,Y,Z
  2 FORMAT(3F5.Ø,/)
    WRITE(6,3)X,Y,Z
  3 FORMAT(1X,3F1Ø.3)
    END
          (=2)
```

```
      READ(5,2)X,Y,Z
 2    FORMAT(4F5.Ø,/)
      WRITE(6,3)X,Y,Z
 3    FORMAT(1X,3F1Ø.3)
      END
            (=1)
```

```
      READ(5,2)X,Y,Z
 2    FORMAT(F5.Ø,//)
      WRITE(6,3)X,Y,Z
 3    FORMAT(1X,3F1Ø.3)
      END
            (=9)
```

```
      READ(5,2)X,Y,Z
 2    FORMAT(2F5.Ø,//)
      WRITE(6,3)X,Y,Z
 3    FORMAT(1X,3F1Ø.3)
      END
            (=4)
```

```
      READ(5,2)X,Y,Z
 2    FORMAT(3F5.Ø,//)
      WRITE(6,3)X,Y,Z
 3    FORMAT(1X,3F1Ø.3)
      END
            (=3)
```

```
      READ(5,2)X,Y,Z
 2    FORMAT(4F5.Ø,//)
      WRITE(6,3)X,Y,Z
 3    FORMAT(1X,3F1Ø.3)
      END
            (=1)
```

```
      READ(5,2)X,Y,Z
 2    FORMAT(F5.Ø,/,2F5.Ø)
      WRITE(6,3)X,Y,Z
 3    FORMAT(1X,3F1Ø.3)
      END
            (=2)
```

```
      READ(5,2)X,Y,Z
 2    FORMAT(2F5.Ø,/,F5.Ø)
      WRITE(6,3)X,Y,Z
 3    FORMAT(1X,3F1Ø.3)
      END
            (=2)
```

```
      READ(5,2)X,Y,Z
 2    FORMAT(3F5.Ø,/,F5.Ø)
      WRITE(6,3)X,Y,Z
 3    FORMAT(1X,3F1Ø.3)
      END
            (=2)
```

```
      READ(5,2)X,Y,Z
 2    FORMAT(4F5.Ø,/,F5.Ø)
      WRITE(6,3)X,Y,Z
 3    FORMAT(1X,3F1Ø.3)
      END
            (=1)
```

Example 7.1

The following is an example of an interactive program. The program asks you to enter some number, computes and reports the square root of that number, and then prompts for more data. If you generate the end-of-file (EOF) condition, the program halts. If you enter invalid data, such as alpha characters, there is a suitable error message and the program also halts. Again, you will see an obvious use of the GO TO statement, although it has not yet been discussed formally. You will notice that the program uses both formatted and list-directed input/output (I/O) to provide a good mixture of convenience and appearance. Study the program and then run it on your system to get a feel for this type of interaction.

```
*-----THE USER IS PROMPTED FOR DATA
   1  WRITE(6,2)
   2  FORMAT(//,' PLEASE ENTER SOME NUMBER')
*-----LIST-DIRECTED INPUT IS USED SO THAT THE
*-----USER NEED NOT WORRY INPUT FIELD WIDTHS.
*-----THE READ IS PROVIDED WITH EOF AND ERROR BRANCHES.
      READ(5,*,END=5,ERR=6,IOSTAT=M)X
*-----THE COMPUTATION IS PERFORMED IN THE FOLLOWING STATEMENT:
      TIMES5 = X*5.
*-----THE INPUT AND THE COMPUTED RESULTS ARE REPORTED
      PRINT*,'YOU ENTERED',X,'WHICH, WHEN MULTIPLIED BY 5 YIELDS',TIMES5
*-----GOING BACK FOR MORE
      GO TO 1
   5  STOP 'EOF REACHED'
   6  STOP 'YOU ENTERED BAD DATA'
      END
```

7.4. The electric potential V along the axis of a ring charged with q coulombs is given by the formula:

$$V = \frac{q}{4\pi\epsilon\sqrt{z^2 + a^2}}$$

where a is the radius of the ring and z is the distance along the axis, measured from the center of the charged ring. If physics isn't your field, don't worry about the meaning of the formula. The object of the exercise is to write an interactive FORTRAN program that prompts for z and a and computes V. The various symbols, suggested program equivalents, and values are shown.

q = Q = 0.375E-03
π = PI = 3.1415926
ϵ = EPS = 8.8542E-12
z = Z = Entered at run time
a = A = Entered at run time
V = POT = To be computed

The program has the ability to handle bad data and EOF. It generates the following interaction:

```
------ PLEASE ENTER Z AND A, SEPARATED BY A BLANK OR COMMA:
?18, 23
WHEN Z = 18.ØØØØØ
AND A =  23.ØØØØØ
THE COMPUTED VALUE OF THE POTENTIAL IS 115397.8
-----------------------------------------------------------
------ PLEASE ENTER Z AND A, SEPARATED BY A BLANK OR COMMA:
?18, 5ØØ
WHEN Z = 18.ØØØØØ
AND A =  5ØØ.ØØØØ
THE COMPUTED VALUE OF THE POTENTIAL IS 6736.291
-----------------------------------------------------------
------ PLEASE ENTER Z AND A, SEPARATED BY A BLANK OR COMMA:
?1ØØ, 1
WHEN Z = 1ØØ.ØØØØ
AND A =  1.ØØØØØØ
THE COMPUTED VALUE OF THE POTENTIAL IS 337Ø1.59
-----------------------------------------------------------
------ PLEASE ENTER Z AND A, SEPARATED BY A BLANK OR COMMA:
?FIVE, TWELVE
- ERROR - YOU ENTERED NON-NUMERIC CHARACTERS - PLS RETRY
------ PLEASE ENTER Z AND A, SEPARATED BY A BLANK OR COMMA:
?5, 12
WHEN Z = 5.ØØØØØØ
AND A =  12.ØØØØØ
THE COMPUTED VALUE OF THE POTENTIAL IS 259255.9
-----------------------------------------------------------
------ PLEASE ENTER Z AND A, SEPARATED BY A BLANK OR COMMA:
?   (EOF supplied here)
 *STOP* EOF ENCOUNTERED
```

8

File Input/Output

There are two basic file structures. One is called *sequential* and the other is known as a *random-access*. The best example of a sequential file might be a collection of records on a magnetic tape. In order to get to a particular record, the user must get to it sequentially, reading all preceding records until the desired one is encountered.

In a random-access file, each record has an identifying key of some sort, making it possible to hop through the file randomly, picking the last record, then the first, then one in the middle, and so on. Your best example of a random-access file is the type of file associated with a disk-based editor, where each record has a numeric key. The editor has the ability to access the file randomly, presenting a particular record with a single disk access, rather than combing through the entire file to search for it. The keys of the records of random-access files need not necessarily be numeric; they could also be character strings, such as a person's last name, or an address.

Early versions of FORTRAN provided access only to sequential file structures, allowing a user to write a series of records to a magnetic tape, and to read from such tapes. This magnetic tape history survives in modern versions of FORTRAN in imperative statements such as REWIND and BACKSPACE.

When disks appeared in computing systems, many manufacturers were not quick to implement more flexible file structures in their versions of FORTRAN, although languages like COBOL soon provided random-access files, taking advantage of a disk's ability to access any point on its surface randomly. There were several notable early implementations of FORTRAN, however, that provided good random-access features, even though the FORTRAN standards of the day did not require this.

It could be said that by the late sixties some FORTRAN programmers already had access to exceptionally well-implemented random-access file structures, while others were still using tapes or sequential disk files that emulated tape behavior. This uneven distribution of FORTRAN file-handling abilities probably explains why some maintain that FORTRAN is not a suitable language for business applications, while others are adamant that the language has a definite place there.

X3.9–1978 does define random-access structures, but these are rather modest by COBOL standards. Many manufacturers have gone far beyond these minimal requirements, and many current versions of FORTRAN provide all conceivable random-access features. Such enriched versions of the language make excellent programming vehicles in a business environment. X3.9–1978, incidentally, refers to random-access files as direct-access files. The term *random* is somewhat richer, but in keeping with the standard, we refer to such files as *direct* from here on.

We begin by looking at FORTRAN sequential file handling, and it will be easy to extend the concepts to direct files.

As mentioned previously, the FORTRAN READ and WRITE statements were traditionally routed to devices such as the card reader or the line printer near the central computer. On modern time-sharing systems and microcomputers, they default to the user's keyboard, printer, or screen. In addition, FORTRAN 77 makes it very easy to associate the READ and WRITE statements with files, allowing a programmer to read from files and to write to other files. On some systems, a single program could have 20 or more files open at any one time, reading from some and writing to others, while at the same time interacting through the screen and the keyboard.

FORTRAN 77 connects read and write units with files through the OPEN statement, and terminates the connection with the CLOSE. Some unit number appears in the open, along with the name of a file. The same unit number then appears in the appropriate READ and WRITE statements, and finally in the CLOSE statement. While the file is open, any I/O directed to that unit number will automatically travel to or from the file with which that unit number is associated in the OPEN.

8.1 THE FORTRAN OPEN AND CLOSE STATEMENTS

Figure 8.1 presents a specific example of a program that writes to a file, which is probably the best way to introduce the OPEN and CLOSE imperatives. The program first opens a file, writes to it, closes the file, and then terminates. In this example, the first statement is the OPEN statement, requesting that a file called TESTFILE be associated with I/O unit 7. The 7 is quite arbitrary; 17 would serve just as well. You should be warned, however, that some systems impose restrictions on the choice of unit number, and it might be best to ask if you collide with such restrictions. You will notice that the WRITE statement also specifies unit 7, and it is this unit number that links the OPEN statement, and hence the file, with the WRITE.

```
*-----THIS PROGRAM WRITES THREE RECORDS TO A FILE CALLED 'TESTFILE'
*-----THROUGH UNIT # 7, AN ARBITRARY NUMBER.  FIRST THE FILE IS OPENED:
      OPEN(UNIT=7,FILE='TESTFILE',STATUS='NEW',IOSTAT=M1,ERR=88,
     +ACCESS='SEQUENTIAL',FORM='FORMATTED')
      A=12.1
      B=13.2
      C=14.3
*-----NOW THE ACTUAL WRITE OPERATION:
      WRITE(7,1)A,B,C
    1 FORMAT(1X,F5.1)
*-----AND NOW THE FILE IS CLOSED:
      CLOSE(UNIT=7,IOSTAT=M2,ERR=99,STATUS='KEEP')
      WRITE(6,2)
    2 FORMAT(//,' FILE WRITTEN SUCCESSFULLY')
      STOP
*-----IF 'OPEN' ATTEMPT ENCOUNTERS PROBLEMS, LOGIC WILL BRANCH HERE:
   88 WRITE(6,3)M1
    3 FORMAT(' HAD TROUBLE OPENING FILE.  ERROR CODE:',I12)
      STOP
*-----IF 'CLOSE' ATTEMPT ENCOUNTERS PROBLEMS, LOGIC WILL BRANCH HERE:
   99 WRITE(6,4)M2
    4 FORMAT(' HAD TROUBLE CLOSING FILE.  ERROR CODE:',I12)
      END

FILE WRITTEN SUCCESSFULLY
```

Figure 8.1 The OPEN statement connects the WRITE statement with a file.

The OPEN statement in Fig. 8.1 looks formidable with all its options. These options are easily remembered, however, because they are sensible, and each is now discussed.

UNIT=u

u is the unit number subsequently used in READ and WRITE statements. It also appears in the CLOSE statement. It is an integer, and many systems place no restriction on its size. Most programmers choose single- or double-digit unit numbers. You should be aware that several systems reserve some unit numbers, but you are not likely to run into difficulties. If some number fails to work, you can always try another.

FILE='fname'

'fname' is the name of the file to which the I/O unit u is to be connected. The file name is a character string, and must therefore be enclosed by quotes. (On many systems, the name of a file must include a so-called extension, and possibly an

explicit version number. On a DEC VMS system, for example, you might use a name like TEST.DAT;1. The file-naming convention of your system, in other words, should be followed when you specify the name of a file in the OPEN statement.)

STATUS='NEW' or 'OLD' or 'SCRATCH' or 'UNKNOWN'

A program can either read data from an existing file or it can create a file and write to it. If we specify STATUS='OLD', we are telling the program to open an existing file. Should the file not exist, this option will trigger an error message. If, on the other hand, we specify STATUS='NEW', we are informing the system that the program is to create the file. Should the file already exist, the program will abort with an error message, and the existing file is not overwritten.

Sometimes it is convenient to use a file like a scratchpad to which we write information, only to read it back into the same program a little later. Such scratchpad files have no name and the STATUS='SCRATCH' option makes this facility available. An example is presented later. Just remember that when you specify 'SCRATCH', the file is not given a name.

If you declare STATUS='UNKNOWN', the system determines the status of the file and assigns certain defaults. If you omit the status option from the OPEN statement, the system inserts 'UNKNOWN'. You are not likely to use this specification often.

ACCESS='SEQUENTIAL' or 'DIRECT'

This one is obvious. If you omit the option, ACCESS='SEQUENTIAL' is assumed.

IOSTAT=IVAR, ERR=LABEL

These two options look very familiar because we already met them in connection with the READ statement. It was stressed that the two should always be used together, and the same applies here as well. Should a problem occur during the execution of the OPEN, the system will assign a machine-dependent numeric error code to the integer variable IVAR. The logic then branches to the statement bearing the label LABEL. That statement could be a WRITE statement to warn the user that the open failed, reporting the error code contained in IVAR. After a successful OPEN, incidentally, IVAR contains Ø.

FORM='FORMATTED' or 'UNFORMATTED'

We will see later that data can be written to files in binary form, bypassing format conversions. Such files are not intended for human consumption; instead, they usually become input to some other program. When dealing with such binary files, you would specify FORM='UNFORMATTED', otherwise FORM='FORMATTED'. Don't worry about this yet as a specific example will be shown before long. If you omit the FORM- option, the machine defaults to FORMATTED for sequential files and to UNFORMATTED for direct-access files.

RECL=N

This option is not invoked in Fig. 8.1. It is used only when direct-access files are opened, and it specifies the length of the records. The record length is specified in bytes for formatted files and, depending on the system, in words or bytes for unformatted files.

BLANK='NULL' or 'ZERO'

This option is also not used in Fig. 8.1, but is included here for completeness. You recall that near the conclusion of the chapter on input, the BN and BZ format switches were illustrated. These two determine whether, on input, blanks shall be treated like nulls, or like zeros, respectively. It was mentioned that the zero treatment is usually the default, but that this default can be altered at the time the file is opened, in cases where the input comes from a file rather than the keyboard. To make a long story short, if you specify BLANK='NULL' in the OPEN statement, blanks are treated as nulls, and if you specify BLANK='ZERO', blanks are treated as zeros. You can, in other words, establish a default environment when you open the file, but that default can still be overruled through the use of the BN or BZ switches in input FORMAT statements. In cases where a program reads from several files, the 'NULL' default could be assigned to some of the files, and the 'ZERO' default could be invoked for the rest.

You will see the CLOSE statement near the middle of the program in Fig. 8.1. Again, you will notice the specific reference to the unit number to which the file is attached. Should any problems be encountered during the close operation, the IOSTAT and ERR options fulfill their usual roles. The STATUS='KEEP' option instructs the machine to retain the file rather than delete it after the program quits. STATUS='DELETE' causes the file to be deleted after the program terminates.

8.2 RUNNING THE PROGRAM

It is strongly urged that you run the program exactly as it appears in Fig. 8.1, carefully observing the file-naming conventions of your particular system. After the run, list your file directory. The file TESTFILE (or whatever you called it) should be represented. Now copy the file to your screen; it should contain three records because the FORMAT statement was rescanned three times. The records should contain the numbers shown:

```
12.1
13.2
14.3
```

If you now attempt to run the program again, it will trigger error branch 88 because the file TESTFILE now exists. (DEC VMS users should be aware that if they do not specify an explicit version number of the file in the OPEN statement, the system will assign such a version number. A subsequent run will succeed because the system simply generates a new version of the file.)

To become more familiar with the various options, you should delete the file TESTFILE and change the STATUS='KEEP' to STATUS='DELETE' in the CLOSE statement of Fig. 8.1. Recompile and execute the program again. It will still tell you that the file was written successfully, but if you list your file directory after the run, the file will not be there, having been deleted right after the CLOSE statement was executed.

You will be pleased to learn that the OPEN and CLOSE are usually used in a much less rigorous form, allowing the system's defaults to act. The program in Fig. 8.2 is the program with which we started, but the comment lines have been removed and the OPEN and CLOSE statements have been simplified to allow the defaults to act.

The first thing to notice in Fig. 8.2 is that we removed error handling from both the OPEN and CLOSE, allowing the system error messages to be invoked automatically in case of difficulties. You will also notice that the word *unit* was omitted. That should not really surprise you; just take a look at the WRITE statement in Fig. 5.1. Also note that there is no longer any reference to the file disposition in the CLOSE statement—the default is STATUS='KEEP'. You recall that if the access mode is not specified, ACCESS='SEQUENTIAL' is assumed, and that for sequential files, the default is FORM='FORMATTED'. Things couldn't really get much simpler.

```
      OPEN(7,FILE='TESTFILE',STATUS='NEW')
*-----
      A=12.1
      B=13.2
      C=14.3
*-----
      WRITE(7,1)A,B,C
    1 FORMAT(1X,F5.1)
*-----
      CLOSE(7)
*-----
      WRITE(6,2)
    2 FORMAT(//,' FILE WRITTEN SUCCESSFULLY')
      END

FILE WRITTEN SUCCESSFULLY
```

Figure 8.2 Simplified OPEN and CLOSE statements.

8.3 BACKSPACE AND REWIND

BACKSPACE and *REWIND* are FORTRAN imperatives dating back to when tapes were the only medium on which to write files under program control. These two commands are still important because they can also be used with sequential disk files, as shown by Fig. 8.3. The program reads the file TESTFILE created by the program in Fig. 8.1. If you no longer have that file, recreate it before running Fig. 8.3. You will find it rewarding and stimulating to work through, Fig. 8.3 thoughtfully.

```
      OPEN(7,FILE='TESTFILE',STATUS='OLD')
*
    3 READ(7,1,END=99)X
    1 FORMAT(1X,F5.Ø)
      WRITE(6,2)X
    2 FORMAT(' JUST READ',F5.1)
      GO TO 3
*
   99 REWIND(7)
    4 READ(7,1,END=77)X
      WRITE(6,2)X
      GO TO 4
*
   77 BACKSPACE(7)
      BACKSPACE(7)
      READ(7,1)X
      WRITE(6,2)X
      CLOSE(7)
      END

JUST READ 12.1
JUST READ 13.2
JUST READ 14.3
JUST READ 12.1
JUST READ 13.2
JUST READ 14.3
JUST READ 13.2
```

Figure 8.3 BACKSPACE and REWIND in action.

The program opens the 'OLD' file TESTFILE, reads the datum on the first record into the variable X, and reports X to the screen. Notice that the program has units 6 and 7 open, 7 connected to the file TESTFILE, and 6 to the screen. After reporting the value of X, the logic branches back to read and report the datum in the second record of the file. When the machine ultimately attempts to read a fourth record, it encounters the EOF marker. This directs the logic to the REWIND statement labeled 99. REWIND is an imperative, causing the file to be positioned at the first record. Again, we read the data on the records and report these to the screen. Upon hitting the EOF for the second time, the logic branches to the BACKSPACE statement labeled 77. Each BACKSPACE causes the file to be backspaced a single record. The EOF marker is, in effect, record 4. The first BACKSPACE positions the file at record 3, and the second BACKSPACE at record 2, containing the value 13.2. The record is read, and the value is printed. The file is then closed. The program and the resulting output deserve careful thought.

8.4 UNFORMATTED DATA TRANSFER (I/O)

Chapters 5 and 7 dealt with input and output, with very specific emphasis on I/O editing. The term *editing* came into common usage with FORTRAN 77, and was formerly known as *format conversion*. The word *conversion* is quite appropriate because data are stored internally in binary form, but are used in decimal or character form in the external world. Format conversions allow the external world to communicate with the computer and vice versa. It has to be recognized that the purpose of the FORMAT statement is twofold: it not only permits us to match our decimal and character notations to the computer's binary system, but it also allows us to impose desired spacing and appearance on the output, and hence the newer term *editing*.

When you see the term *unformatted I/O*, you might be tempted to think of statements like WRITE(6,*), READ(5,*), READ *, or PRINT * because all of these so-called list-directed I/O statements do not require you to specify a format. In actual fact, however, there certainly is a format conversion process behind the scenes because all four of these statements deal with decimal or character data in the outside world and with binary inside the computer. Although there is definite format conversion involved here, the format directives themselves cannot be accessed by the programmer, who has to make do with the appearance and spacing of the output offered by the machine. List-directed I/O is certainly *not* unformatted, but it might more appropriately be called format-statementless I/O, or free-field I/O.

When we refer to unformatted I/O, we have something much more radical in mind, namely the transfer of data between the machine and the outside world in binary form. On the surface, it doesn't appear to be all that useful to be able to send binary data to the outside, until we understand that the format conversion process is very expensive, sometimes consuming more CPU time than the rest of the program.

In order to understand the situation in perspective, consider a case involving programs A and B. Program A generates massive amounts of data, let's say several hundred thousand records. The output from program A is written to tape, and flown to some other site to be used as input to program B. If we approached the situation thoughtlessly, we would force program A to convert its output to decimal form before writing it to tape. Program B would then be compelled to convert this decimal input back to binary form, the conversions at both ends costing dearly. Would it not be more rational to permit program A to write the tape in binary form because this is how it ultimately ends up in program B anyway? FORTRAN does provide this facility, as the program in Fig. 8.4 shows. That program looks normal enough with the exception of the missing format reference in the WRITE statement. There is not even an asterisk to imply unseen format instructions.

```
M1=1
M3=3
M5=5
M7=7
M9=9
WRITE(6)M1,M3,M5,M7,M9
END
```

Figure 8.4 Unformatted data transfers.

The absence of any sort of format reference is a clear signal to the machine that the output is *not* to undergo format conversion, but is to be transferred to the exteranl world in binary form. Try to run Fig. 8.4 on your system. Some machines will transmit the binary output to the screen, where it manifests itself as random characters, but other machines block the data transfer, issuing suitable error messages to the effect that such binary data transfers are illegal.

If we cannot see the output on the screen, we might attempt to capture it in a file. This is done in Fig. 8.5, where the file receiving the binary data is called BINFILE. Be sure to observe the file-naming conventions of your system when experimenting. You will recall that FORM='FORMATTED' is the default for sequential files. In this case, we overrule the default with the FORM='UNFORMATTED' specification.

After you run Fig. 8.5, a file called BINFILE will appear in your directory. Attempt to copy that file to your screen. Again, you might get random characters on some systems, and others will inform you that binary writes to the screen are illegal, and so we seem to be back where we started. Fortunately, many machines permit you to request that the file be copied to your screen either in hex or in octal. You may have to ask about the appropriate command, but you will consider it worth the effort once you see the five data sitting there in fixed-point form. Some chaff will accompany the data to the screen, but it should be quite easy to pick out the wheat.

Figure 8.6 shows a companion program to read the binary data from the file BINFILE created by the previous program. Again, you will notice the missing

```
OPEN(6,FILE='BINFILE',STATUS='NEW',FORM='UNFORMATTED')
M1=1
M3=3
M5=5
M7=7
M9=9
WRITE(6)M1,M3,M5,M7,M9
CLOSE(6)
END
```

Figure 8.5 Transferring unformatted data to an external file.

```
      OPEN(5,FILE='BINFILE',STATUS='OLD',FORM='UNFORMATTED')
      READ(5)M1,M3,M5,M7,M9
      WRITE(6,2)M1,M3,M5,M7,M9
    2 FORMAT(1X,5I5)
      CLOSE(5)
      END

    1    3    5    7    9
```

Figure 8.6 Reading unformatted data from a file.

format reference in the READ statement and the FORM='UNFORMATTED' specification in the OPEN statement.

The program of Fig. 8.6 opens the file BINFILE and perform a single unformatted read on it. It then converts these data to decimal and displays them, confirming that the unformatted data transfer was successful.

Before leaving unformatted data tranfers, several points should be noted:

1. Each unformatted write operation generates a single record. The length of that record is determined by the number of items in the output list. A long output list generates a long record, and a short output list generates a short record. Many systems impose no restriction on the length of such records, but some impose a ceiling.
2. Each unformatted read operation involves a single record. In order to interpret the contents of that record properly, it must be known exactly how it was generated. The input list of the program reading the record must be matched, item for item, with the output list of the program that generated the record. Compare the output list in Fig. 8.5 with the input list in Fig. 8.6, for example.
3. Most systems permit the records to be of variable length. The first record, for example, might be longer than the remaining records.

8.5 SCRATCH FILES

The concept of a *scratch* file was introduced earlier. A scratch file is sometimes a convenient medium for storing intermediate data. A potential application might involve a program that writes several million random numbers to a file. The program then combs through the file to perform some statistical analyses on these random numbers. Such work could be done directly in memory if there were enough of it, but there are still modest memories around. Figure 8.7 illustrates the use of a scratch file. The file is connected to unit 3, but it is *not* given a name. We choose unformatted reading and writing because of the greater efficiency. The program assigns 12.456 to X and writes it to the file. The file is then rewound and read into Y. Y is then printed to confirm that everything worked.

```
      OPEN(3,STATUS='SCRATCH',FORM='UNFORMATTED')
      X=12.456
      WRITE(3)X
      REWIND(3)
*-----------------------------------------------------
      READ(3)Y
      PRINT *,Y
      CLOSE(3)
      END

12.456
```

Figure 8.7 Using a scratch file.

8.6 DIRECT-ACCESS FILES

A direct-access file, as mentioned near the beginning of this chapter, permits direct access to any record in the file without the need to wade through all the preceding records. Such files are essential if applications such as payroll programs are to be flexible. It would be unacceptable if someone whose last name begins with Z were to call the payroll department to notify them of an address change, and if the payroll people had to read all the way to Z to make the change. Actually, the situation is much worse than implied. To update a sequential file, it is necessary to copy the file to be updated to a new file, record by record. When the record to be updated is encountered, the change is made and this updated record is copied to the new file. All the records following the updated record must also be copied. Needless to say, file updates were major adventures in the days of sequential-only files.

A direct-access file is vastly more flexible. The record to be updated is brought into memory with as few as one or two disk accesses. The change is made, and the record is written back to the file, the whole procedure taking very little time.

In Fig. 8.8 a direct-access file is created. Notice the OPEN statement in which

```
OPEN(4,FILE='RANDFILE',ACCESS='DIRECT',RECL=1Ø,STATUS='NEW')
M=1Ø99
WRITE(4,REC=99)M
M=1Ø87
WRITE(4,REC=87)M
M=1119
WRITE(4,REC=119)M
M=1847
WRITE(4,REC=847)M
CLOSE(4)
END
```

Figure 8.8 Writing the records in random order while creating a direct-access file.

```
      OPEN(3,FILE='RANDFILE',STATUS='OLD',ACCESS='DIRECT',RECL=1Ø)
      READ(3,REC=119)M
      PRINT*,'JUST READ',M
      M=-1119
      WRITE(3,REC=119)M
      READ(3,REC=119)L
      PRINT*,'JUST READ',L
      READ(3,REC=99)L
      PRINT*,'JUST READ',L
      CLOSE(3)
      END

JUST READ 1119
JUST READ -1119
JUST READ 1Ø99
```

Figure 8.9 Reading and updating a direct-access file.

ACCESS='DIRECT' is specified. Each record in this particular program will be only a single word long, and RECL=1 would probably work quite well on systems that measure the record length in words. But this program has to work on all systems, so we specify RECL=10, just in case your system measures the record length in bytes. You can scale the RECL specification down to make such programs run economically on your system. Because the file will have very few records in it anyway, you need not feel too guilty about records that are longer than needed.

You recall that FORM='UNFORMATTED' is the default for direct-access files, and because we wish to write to the file in unformatted form, this default suits us.

Note the WRITE statements. The control information list contains the unit number and the key (record number) of the record. If we were writing formatted records, the format reference would appear there as well.

The program writes four records in random order. After the program terminates, a file called RANDFILE will appear in your directory. That file is then used by the program shown in Fig. 8.9, which displays and updates certain records.

Take the time to look over the program, making sure you agree with the output. The logic is very simple, but the output won't make sense if you fail to relate this program back to Fig. 8.8 in which the file RANDFILE was created.

There is one final point: What happens when you try to access a record with a record number that does not exist? Needless to say, the program would cause the computer problems and this would result in some appropriate error message. Fortunately, however, such conditions can be intercepted by the programmer, who would include the familiar ERR and IOSTAT options in the READ statement. A typical READ statement would now have the following form:

```
READ(3,REC=34,ERR=55,IOSTAT=M)L
```

8.7 PROBLEMS

8.1. Write a program similar to the one shown in Fig. 8.2. to create a sequential formatted file called DATAFILE, containing the following five records:

```
1.11
2.22
3.33
4.44
5.55
```

Be sure to observe your system's file-naming convention. After the program has been run, copy the file to your screen to satisfy yourself that it exists and that it contains the expected data. The file DATAFILE is used as input in the next two problems.

8.2. Using the file DATAFILE created in Prob. 8.1 as the input file, predict and explain the output generated by the following program:

```
OPEN(3,FILE='DATAFILE',STATUS='OLD')
READ(3,*)
READ(3,*)
READ(3,*)
READ(3,*)X
PRINT*,X
BACKSPACE (3)
READ(3,*)X
PRINT*,X
BACKSPACE(3)
BACKSPACE(3)
BACKSPACE(3)
READ(3,*)X
READ(3,*)X
READ(3,*)X
PRINT*,X
BACKSPACE(3)
BACKSPACE(3)
PRINT*,X
READ(3,*)X
PRINT*,X
REWIND(3)
PRINT*,X
READ(3,*)X
PRINT*,X
CLOSE(3)
END
```

Run the program to see how accurate your analysis was, but only after thinking about it carefully.

8.3. Write a program in which you sequentially access the file DATAFILE created in Prob. 8.1. The program reads the file backwards and generates the following output:

```
RECORD 5 CONTAINS 5.55
RECORD 4 CONTAINS 4.44
RECORD 3 CONTAINS 3.33
RECORD 2 CONTAINS 2.22
RECORD 1 CONTAINS 1.11
```

Hint: Read the file sequentially until you hit the EOF condition. Then use the backspace facility to allow the records to be accessed in the desired sequence.

8.4. Does your system place restrictions on the magnitude of I/O unit numbers? Write a three- or four-line program to investigate. Try unit numbers such as 10, 20, 40, 80, 100, 500, and 1000. (See Section 8.1 under *'UNIT=u'*)

8.5. Run the following program to create a direct-access file called DIRFILE. The next problem requires that file. (Please note: The program writes under F6.2, generating six-byte records, and we therefore declare a record length of six units in the open statement. For formatted I/O, this means six bytes, but it is possible that your system will require more than six bytes per record because of overhead, but this is unlikely. If you have difficulty in getting the program to run, you might declare a more generous record size in the OPEN statement.)

```
      OPEN(7,FILE='DIRFILE',ACCESS='DIRECT',FORM='FORMATTED',
     +RECL=6,STATUS='NEW')
      X=1.11
      KEY=1
      WRITE(7,1,REC=KEY)X
    1 FORMAT(F6.2)
      X=2.22
      KEY=2
      WRITE(7,1,REC=KEY)X
      X=3.33
      KEY=3
      WRITE(7,1,REC=KEY)X
      X=4.44
      KEY=4
      WRITE(7,1,REC=KEY)X
      X=5.55
      KEY=5
      WRITE(7,1,REC=KEY)X
      CLOSE(7)
      END
```

Copy the file DIRFILE to your screen to take a look at it. On the surface, it should look much like the file DATAFILE of Problem 8.1, although its internal organization is probably quite different to enable the system to access the records in random order.

8.6. Write a program that generates the interaction shown. The program accesses the file DIRFILE created in the previous problem. The error messages are triggered by the ERR/IOSTAT options in the READ statement. A more flexible version of this program appears in the problem section of the next chapter, using some of the features of that chapter.

```
WHICH RECORD WOULD YOU LIKE TO READ
?4
FOUND 4.44 ON RECORD 4
WHICH RECORD WOULD YOU LIKE TO READ
?1
FOUND 1.11 ON RECORD 1
WHICH RECORD WOULD YOU LIKE TO READ
?7
ERROR:      7 IS NOT A VALID RECORD NUMBER - PLS RETRY
WHICH RECORD WOULD YOU LIKE TO READ
?6
ERROR:      6 IS NOT A VALID RECORD NUMBER - PLS RETRY
WHICH RECORD WOULD YOU LIKE TO READ
?4
FOUND 4.44 ON RECORD 4
WHICH RECORD WOULD YOU LIKE TO READ
?2
FOUND 2.22 ON RECORD 2
WHICH RECORD WOULD YOU LIKE TO READ
?5
FOUND 5.55 ON RECORD 5
WHICH RECORD WOULD YOU LIKE TO READ
?3
FOUND 3.33 ON RECORD 3
WHICH RECORD WOULD YOU LIKE TO READ
? (simulate the EOF conditions from the keyboard here)
*STOP* USER-SUPPLIED EOF
```

Discussion: In Probs. 8.5 and 8.6, we worked with a direct-access file. Direct-access I/O defaults to UNFORMATTED, i.e., to binary, but we overruled the default by declaring FORM='FORMATTED' with a record length of six bytes. The fact that we did declare FORM='FORMATTED' has some interesting implications. Because RECL=6 refers to bytes for formatted I/O, it means that 999.99 is the largest positive datum we can write to a record, and −99.99 is the most negative.

If, on the other hand, we had declared FORM='UNFORMATTED', one word (four bytes) would have been sufficient to store any number from approximately. -10^{75} to $+10^{75}$, assuming excess-40 32-bit floating-point storage. There is an important lesson in this. This is also a good place to remind you one more time that when you specify RECL=N in the OPEN statement, N refers to bytes when formatted I/O is involved, and to either bytes or words, depending on the system, when unformatted I/O is performed.

9

Transfer of Control and Selection Control Structures

Executable FORTRAN statements, also known as *imperative* statements, are executed in the order in which they appear. Control, in other words, moves through the statements sequentially. There are, however, special executable FORTRAN statements that have the ability to redirect control to different parts of a program. Such redirection is known as *branching*, and the special FORTRAN statements are called *transfer-of-control* statements. We can now modify the opening statement by saying that control moves through a program sequentially unless redirected by transfer-of-control statements.

If sequential processing were the only available mode, computers could only work on problems that require step-by-step brute-force processing. The ability to select branches, however, allows the computer to follow one of several available paths through a program, guided by various conditions, thus creating the impression of intelligence. The technical term for this type of execution sequence is *selection.*

In this chapter various *conditional* and *unconditional* transfer-of-control statements are discussed and illustrated, and there is a special emphasis on selection control structures.

9.1 UNCONDITIONAL TRANSFER OF CONTROL: THE STOP STATEMENT

The *STOP* statement is regarded as a transfer-of-control statement because it provides a path out of the program. In the early days, STOP actually brought the computer to a halt, requiring the operator to restart it. This, however, was undesirable on multiuser systems, and the action of the STOP was soon toned down to effect a simple program exit without shutting the machine down.

The STOP statement is a tremendously convenient facility in programs that have several different potential exit points, depending on the logic path selected. Because it is useful to know which particular STOP is chosen by the program, it is possible to attach a modifier to the STOP statement that is either a character constant or a number with up to five decimal digits. Then, when the program logic leaves through one of these modified STOP statements, the modifier is printed to identify the particular STOP involved. In the chapter on input, you saw several examples of STOP statements modified by character constants, which we called *Hollerith strings*. The two forms of the STOP are:

```
STOP 'THIS IS ONE WAY OF MARKING THE STOP'
STOP 12345
STOP 1
```

9.2 UNCONDITIONAL TRANSFER OF CONTROL: THE PAUSE STATEMENT

The action of the *PAUSE* statement is similar to that of STOP, except that the door is left open to reenter the program after some external action has been taken. In the same manner as the STOP statement, PAUSE can also be modified by an optional numeric constant with a maximum of five digits or by a character constant. When the PAUSE statement is executed in an interactive environment, the logic branches to the printer or screen, where the optional modifier is displayed. Execution then resumes upon receipt of a carriage return or some special command. (In DEC's VMS, for example, the user would be expected to type CONTINUE, EXIT, or DEBUG before control reenters the program.) In a batch environment, the optional modifier is usually displayed on the operator's console, and execution is suspended until the operator takes some predefined action. The PAUSE statement could be used, for example, to request special paper in the printer, or to request that some specific tape or diskette be mounted. The PAUSE statement is illustrated in Fig. 9.1.

```
CURR = 45.32
PAUSE 'PLS MOUNT TAPE ON UNIT 7'
WRITE(7)CURR
REWIND 7
END
```

Figure 9.1 The PAUSE statement temporarily suspends program execution.

The following shows that, at least on the surface, PAUSE acts much like a WRITE and READ sequence, and many programmers usually follow this second approach, especially in an interactive setting.

```
CURR = 45.32
PRINT *,'PLS MOUNT TAPE ON UNIT 7'
READ *
WRITE(7)CURR
REWIND 7
END
```

9.3 UNCONDITIONAL TRANSFER OF CONTROL: THE END STATEMENT

Originally, the *END* statement was a signal to the compiler, informing it that the end of the source statements had been reached. As such, END was considered to be a control statement rather than a FORTRAN source statement and did not survive the compile phase. Because it did not survive, it would have been meaningless to label the END statement. The END statement is now considered to be an executable FORTRAN statement and can be labeled. Although we have not yet encountered subprograms formally, we state that the END statement must be the last statement of a main program or of a subprogram. When END is executed in a main program, it has the action of a STOP statement, and when it is executed in a subprogram, it acts like RETURN.

9.4 UNCONDITIONAL TRANSFER OF CONTROL: THE CONTINUE STATEMENT

The *CONTINUE* statement can also be regarded as a transfer-of-control statement because it always transfers control to the next statement in the execution sequence. CONTINUE does nothing more than that, but it serves a highly useful purpose as a label holder. Whenever it is necessary to send control to a certain block of statements, that block can start with a labeled CONTINUE statement. You will soon see some very obvious applications.

9.5 UNCONDITIONAL TRANSFER OF CONTROL: THE GO TO STATEMENT

The *GO TO* statement is so obvious that we were already able to use it without formal introduction. GO TO 12, for example, forces control to transfer to the statement bearing the label 12; no alternative is possible.

The unconditional GO TO statement should be used as little as possible because its indiscriminate use results in unreadable spaghetti programming. Some people feel that it should be exorcised from the language and some books on programming pretend that it doesn't exist. The GO TO actually does have a valid place in FORTRAN and sometimes its careful use results in more elegant code than its dogmatic avoidance.

9.6 CONDITIONAL TRANSFER OF CONTROL: THE COMPUTED GO TO STATEMENT

The *computed GO TO* statement has the general form:

```
GO TO(L1,L2,L3,L4,L5,.....,LN),I
```

where L1,L2,L3,L4,L5, . . . ,LN are labels within the program body. The I outside the closing parenthesis is either an integer variable or some integer expression. The comma preceding this I is optional, although older versions of FORTRAN insist on it.

Execution of the computed GO TO causes I to be evaluated, followed by a transfer to the statement bearing the Ith label in the label list of the computed GO TO statement. To illustrate, consider the following computed GO TO statement:

```
GO TO(18,32,18,12,1,3,2,9,18,32)K+2
```

Assume that K has a value of 2 when the statement is encountered. Control will then transfer to the statement with label 12 because 12 is the fourth label in the label list, and the integer expression K+2 has the value 4.

If the expression I has a value less than 1 or greater than the number of labels in the label list, the computed GO TO acts like a CONTINUE statement, and control drops through to the next statement. Figure 9.2 shows the action of the computed GO TO statement symbolically. Just keep in mind that I is not necessarily just an integer variable, it could also be an integer expression.

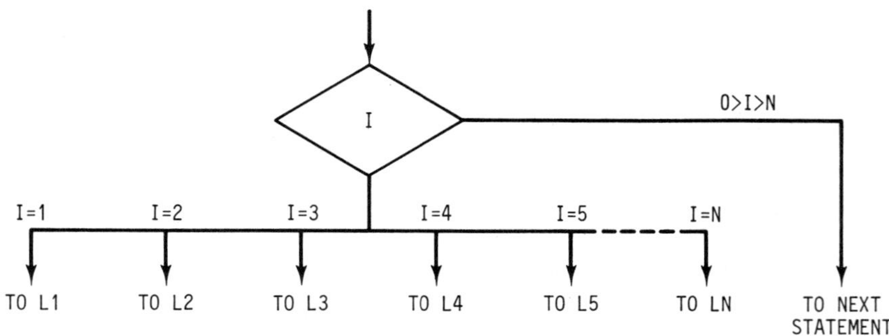

Figure 9.2 The computed GO TO statement evaluates I and selects branch I.

Figure 9.3 illustrates an application of the computed GO TO statement in a simple program. The program's structure is represented by the flowchart in Fig. 9.4. Please take the trouble to understand the flowchart and the program. Follow the logic to see whether you agree with each line of output.

```
*
*
*
    1  PRINT *,'PLEASE ENTER SOME NUMBER'
       READ *,J
*
       GO TO(3,4,5,6,7)J
*
       PRINT *,'YOU FELL RIGHT THROUGH'
       GO TO 1
    3  PRINT *,'YOU HIT THE STATEMENT WITH LABEL 3'
       GO TO 1
    4  PRINT *,'YOU HIT THE STATEMENT WITH LABEL 4'
       GO TO 1
    5  PRINT *,'YOU HIT THE STATEMENT WITH LABEL 5'
       GO TO 1
    6  PRINT *,'YOU HIT THE STATEMENT WITH LABEL 6'
       GO TO 1
    7  STOP 'YOU HIT THE STOP STATEMENT - BYE'
       END
```

```
PLEASE ENTER SOME NUMBER
?-1ØØ
YOU FELL RIGHT THROUGH
PLEASE ENTER SOME NUMBER
?88
YOU FELL RIGHT THROUGH
PLEASE ENTER SOME NUMBER
?4
YOU HIT THE STATEMENT WITH LABEL 6
PLEASE ENTER SOME NUMBER
?3
YOU HIT THE STATEMENT WITH LABEL 5
PLEASE ENTER SOME NUMBER
?2
YOU HIT THE STATEMENT WITH LABEL 4
PLEASE ENTER SOME NUMBER
?1
YOU HIT THE STATEMENT WITH LABEL 3
PLEASE ENTER SOME NUMBER
?5
*STOP* YOU HIT THE STOP STATEMENT - BYE
```

Figure 9.3 The computed GO TO statement in action. (See Fig. 9.4.)

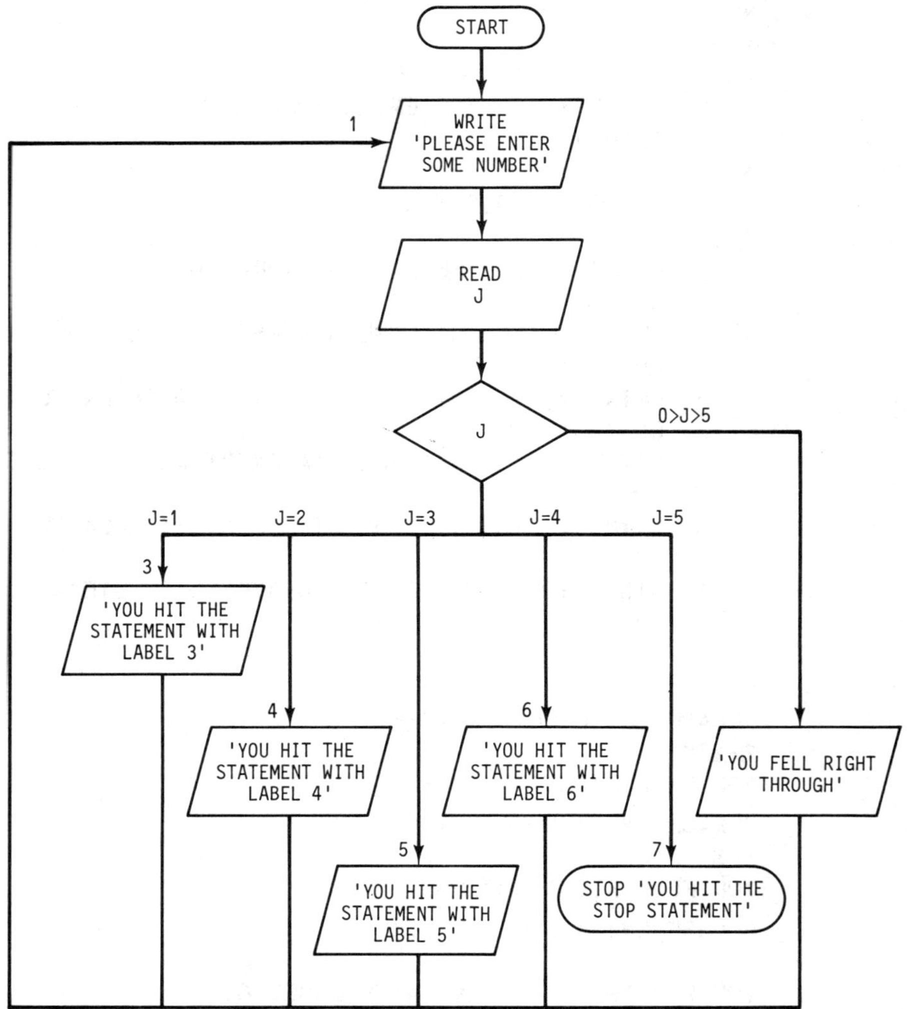

Figure 9.4 The flowchart for Fig. 9.3.

9.7 CONDITIONAL TRANSFER OF CONTROL: THE ARITHMETIC IF STATEMENT

The *arithmetic IF* statement has its roots in the earliest days of FORTRAN. Its structure is such that at execution time very few machine language instructions are involved, making it highly efficient, but its careless application will result in twisted spaghetti logic. The arithmetic IF statement has the following form:

```
IF(expression)N,Z,P
```

where N, Z, and P are three numeric labels, and "expression" is any integer or floating-point arithmetic expression. At execution time, the expression is evaluated, and if the value is negative, control transfers to the statement with label N. If the expression has a value of 0, control transfers to the statement with label Z. If the expression has a positive value, the logic branches to the statement with the label P. Figure 9.5 shows the logic of the arithmetic IF statement symbolically. Figure 9.6 shows a small program using the arithmetic IF statement and Fig. 9.7 shows the flowchart of the program's logic.

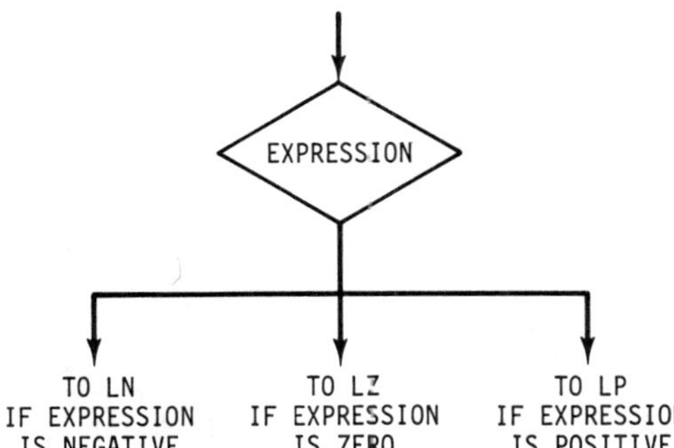

Figure 9.5 The logical representation of the arithmetic IF statement.

```
      9  PRINT *,'PLS ENTER X AND Y'
         READ *, X,Y
*
         IF(X**2 -Y)1,2,3
*
      1  PRINT *,'EXPRESSION IS NEGATIVE'
         GO TO 9
      2  PRINT *,'EXPRESSION IS ZERO'
         GO TO 9
      3  STOP 'EXPRESSION IS POSITIVE - BYE'
         END

PLEASE ENTER X AND Y
?3.Ø, 1Ø.Ø
EXPRESSION IS NEGATIVE

PLEASE ENTER X AND Y
?3.Ø, 9.Ø
EXPRESSION IS ZERO

PLEASE ENTER X AND Y
?3.Ø, 8.Ø
*STOP* EXPRESSION POSITIVE - BYE
```

Figure 9.6 The arithmetic IF statement in action.

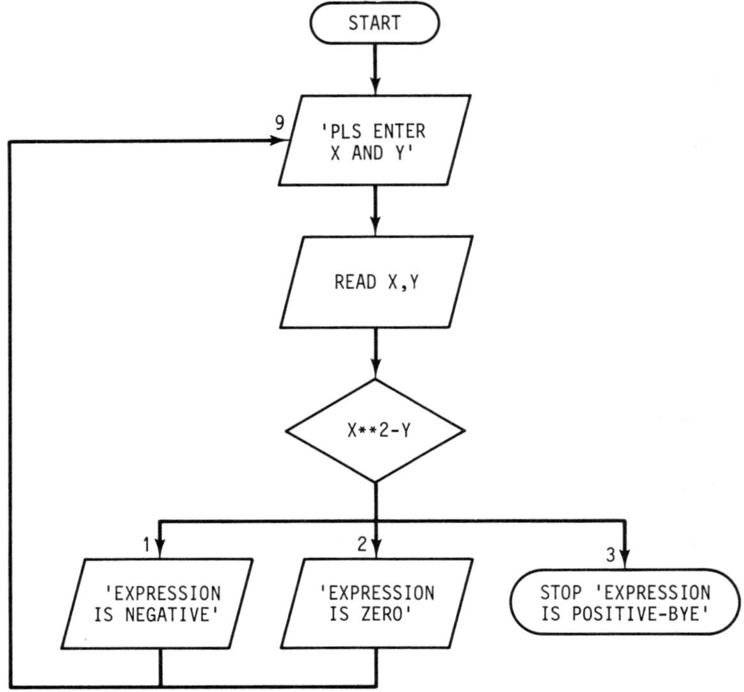

Figure 9.7 The flowchart for Fig. 9.6.

9.8 CONDITIONAL TRANSFER OF CONTROL: THE LOGICAL IF STATEMENT

The *logical IF* and the *block IF* statements are the pride and joy of FORTRAN. Chronologically, the logical IF arrived some years after the arithmetic IF, greatly enhancing the attractiveness of FORTRAN. The block IF statement arrived later yet, appearing as a standard FORTRAN 77 feature. The block IF will be dealt with after we have taken a close look at the logical IF statement, which has the general form:

```
IF (Logical Expression) a single FORTRAN Imperative
```

The single FORTRAN imperative is executed if and only if the logical expression within the parentheses is true. The essence of the logical IF construct is shown symbolically in Fig. 9.8. The logical expression appears in the diamond. If the condition is true, the logic leaves the diamond through the true (T) branch to execute the FORTRAN imperative, but only one such executable statement can appear. If the logical expression is false, the logic leaves the diamond through the false (F) branch, and the FORTRAN statement is bypassed.

To give you a better feeling for the logical IF statement, three typical examples are given before a more rigorous treatment is offered. Remember that the item

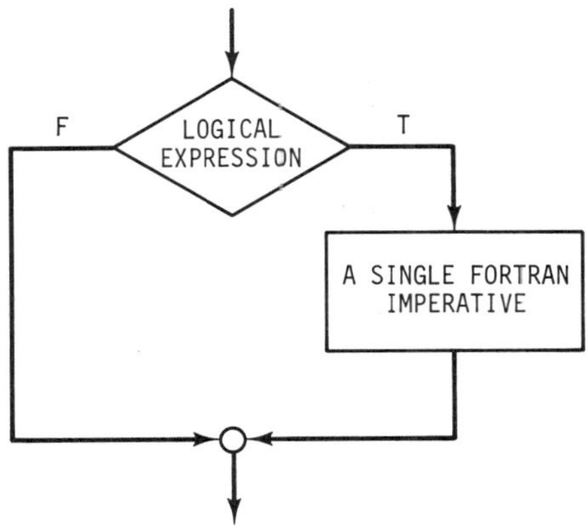

Figure 9.8 The logical representation of the logical IF statement.

within the parentheses is called a *logical expression*. Such logical expressions will receive considerable attention later, but they are almost self-explanatory once you recognize that ".EQ." means *equal to*, ".LE." means *less than or equal to*, and ".LT." simply means *less than*.

```
IF(M .EQ. N)STOP
IF(M+N .LE. 5)WRITE(6,2)X
IF(Y .LT. SIN(12.))GO TO 99
```

The logical expressions are obviously the key to the usefulness of the logical IF statement, and they are treated in greater depth after the example in Figure 9.9, which shows the logical IF statement in the context of a program. The program's logic structure is shown in the flowchart of Fig. 9.10. Make the effort to understand the flowchart clearly, and then relate it to the program.

```
*
*      THIS PROGRAM ILLUSTRATES THE SIMPLE LOGICAL IF STATEMENT.
*      THE LOGIC CASCADES THROUGH THE PROGRAM SEQUENTIALLY.
*      WHENEVER A LOGICAL CONDITION IS TRUE, THE APPROPRIATE
*      'PRINT' STATEMENT IS ACTIVATED.  THE USEFULNESS OF THE
*      SIMPLE LOGICAL IF STATEMENT MUST NOT BE UNDERESTIMATED!
*
   1   PRINT *,'PLEASE ENTER SOME NUMBER'
       READ *,N
*
       IF(N.LT.Ø)PRINT *,'NEGATIVE INPUT'
       IF(N.EQ.Ø)PRINT *,'ZERO INPUT'
       IF(N.GT.Ø)PRINT *,'POSITIVE INPUT'
       IF(N.EQ.99)STOP'YOU ENTERED 99 - BYE'
*
       GO TO 1
       END
```

Figure 9.9 The logical IF statement in action.

```
PLEASE ENTER SOME NUMBER
?7
POSITIVE INPUT
PLEASE ENTER SOME NUMBER
?4
POSITIVE INPUT
PLEASE ENTER SOME NUMBER
?-1ØØ
NEGATIVE INPUT
PLEASE ENTER SOME NUMBER
?Ø
ZERO INPUT
PLEASE ENTER SOME NUMBER
?88
POSITIVE INPUT
PLEASE ENTER SOME NUMBER
?99
POSITIVE INPUT
*STOP* YOU ENTERED 99 - BYE
```

Figure 9.9 (Cont.)

9.9 LOGICAL EXPRESSIONS, RELATIONAL OPERATORS, AND LOGICAL OPERATORS

Now that you have a general feeling for the logical IF statement, it is time to look at possible logical expressions. Whatever you learn here carries over directly to the block IF statement to be discussed in the next section.

Logical expressions can contain arithmetic expressions, so-called *relational operators* and *logical operators*. There are six relational operators, namely:

`.EQ.`	equal to
`.NE.`	not equal to
`.LT.`	less than
`.LE.`	less than or equal to
`.GT.`	greater than
`.GE.`	greater than or equal to

Notice the periods surrounding each of these six relational operators. A simple logical expression using one of these relationals might be

5.LT.10

All logical expressions have a *truth value*, in the sense that they are either true or false. 5.LT.10 is obviously true, whereas 5.GE.10 is false.

The next expression is a little more complex, containing arithmetic expressions

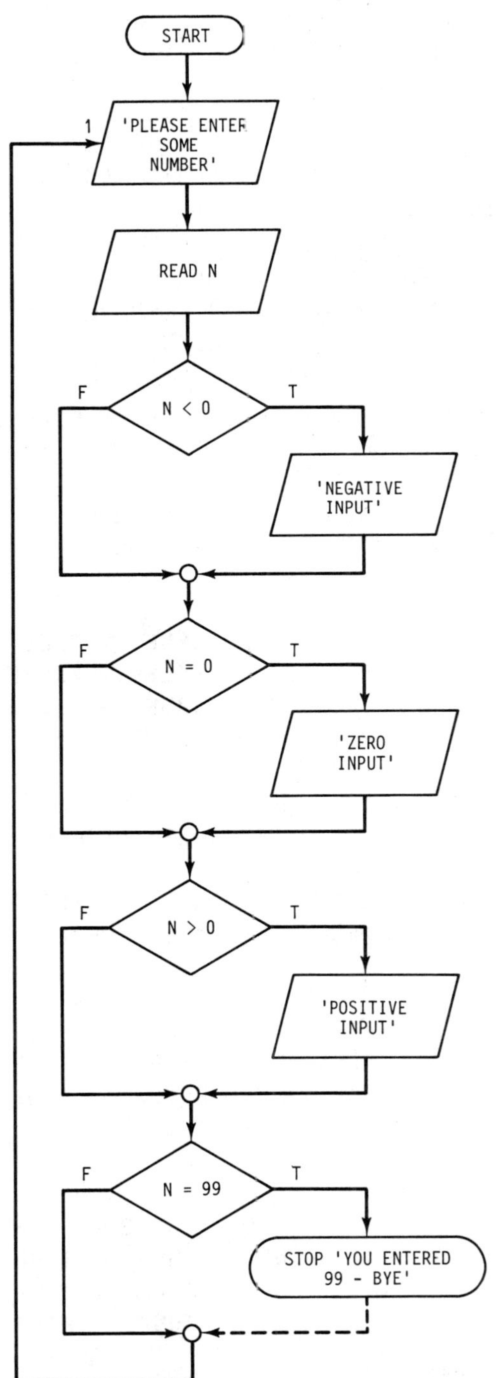

Figure 9.10 The flowchart for Fig. 9.9.

and a relational operator. The arithmetic expressions are always evaluated first, after which the relational operators act. The resulting truth value is obviously false.

5+3.LT.4+3

Logical expressions can also contain LOGICAL OPERATORS in addition to the six relational operators. The five logical operators are

.NOT.	LOGICAL NEGATION
.AND.	LOGICAL CONJUNCTION
.OR.	LOGICAL INCLUSIVE DISJUNCTION
.EQV.	LOGICAL EQUIVALENCE
.NEQV.	LOGICAL NON-EQUIVALENCE

The action of the logical operators is shown in Figure 9.11. The figure may be regarded as the definition of the operators.

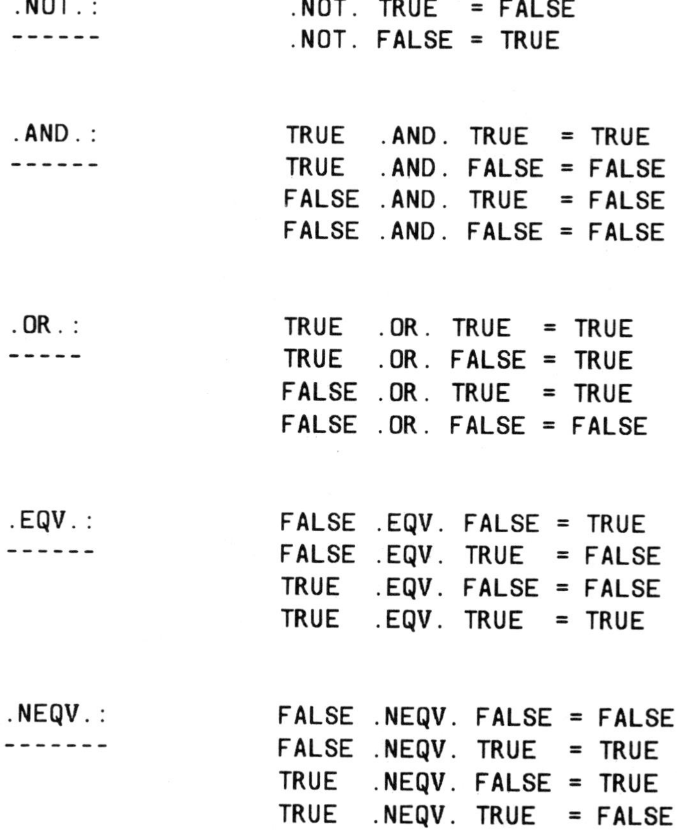

```
.NOT.:          .NOT. TRUE  = FALSE
------          .NOT. FALSE = TRUE


.AND.:          TRUE  .AND. TRUE  = TRUE
------          TRUE  .AND. FALSE = FALSE
                FALSE .AND. TRUE  = FALSE
                FALSE .AND. FALSE = FALSE


.OR.:           TRUE  .OR. TRUE  = TRUE
-----           TRUE  .OR. FALSE = TRUE
                FALSE .OR. TRUE  = TRUE
                FALSE .OR. FALSE = FALSE


.EQV.:          FALSE .EQV. FALSE = TRUE
------          FALSE .EQV. TRUE  = FALSE
                TRUE  .EQV. FALSE = FALSE
                TRUE  .EQV. TRUE  = TRUE


.NEQV.:         FALSE .NEQV. FALSE = FALSE
-------         FALSE .NEQV. TRUE  = TRUE
                TRUE  .NEQV. FALSE = TRUE
                TRUE  .NEQV. TRUE  = FALSE
```

Figure 9.11 The five logical operators.

Several logical expressions are now evaluated to show how the computer deals with them. This is an important area that deserves careful attention. The next logical expression combines an arithmetic expression with relational and logical operators to produce a truth value of false, as explained:

```
3+4.GE.8 .AND. 5.EQ.5
```

The truth value of a logical expression is always evaluated according to a simple hierarchy that has already partially emerged. On the first scan, the computer evaluates all the arithmetic expressions. On the second scan, all the relational operators act in the order of appearance. On the third scan, .NOT. is allowed to act. .AND. and .OR. operate on the fourth and fifth scans, respectively. .EQV. and .NEQV. function on the sixth scan in the order in which they appear. Applying these rules to this particular logical expression yields false. The evaluation hierarchy is summarized in Figure 9.12.

First scan:	Arithmetic expressions
Second scan:	Relational expressions
Third scan:	.NOT.
Fourth scan:	.AND.
Fifth scan:	.OR.
Sixth scan:	.EQV. and .NEQV.

Figure 9.12 The logical expression evaluation hierarchy.

Example 9.1

```
                  2.LT.3.OR.1.GT.2+5

After scan 1:      2.LT.3.OR.1.GT.7
After scan 2:        TRUE.OR.FALSE
After scan 5:            TRUE
```

Example 9.2

```
    .NOT.2.GT.3.AND.2.GT.1
=   .NOT.FALSE .AND.TRUE
=   TRUE       .AND.TRUE
=   TRUE
```

Example 9.3

```
    2+6.LE.1+3**2.AND.2.GT.3.OR.1.EQ.1
=   8  .LE.1Ø     .AND.2.GT.3.OR.1.EQ.1
=   TRUE          .AND.FALSE .OR.TRUE
=   FALSE                    .OR.TRUE
=   TRUE
```

Example 9.4

```
    .NOT.5.LT.4.AND..NOT.6.GT.21.OR.5.LE.1Ø.AND.4.EQ.4
=   .NOT.FALSE .AND..NOT.FALSE  .OR.TRUE   .AND.TRUE
=   TRUE       .AND.TRUE        .OR.TRUE   .AND.TRUE
=   TRUE                        .OR.TRUE
=   TRUE
```

Example 9.5

```
    .NOT.5.GT.3.OR.3.EQ.1.EQV.Ø.LT.5.OR.1.GT.3.OR..NOT.5.EQ.5
 =  .NOT.TRUE  .OR.FALSE .EQV.TRUE  .OR.FALSE .OR..NOT.TRUE
 =  FALSE      .OR.FALSE .EQV.TRUE  .OR.FALSE .OR.FALSE
 =  FALSE                .EQV.TRUE            .OR.FALSE
 =  FALSE                .EQV.TRUE
 =  FALSE
```

Example 9.6

```
    .NOT.(5.GT.3.OR.3.EQ.1).EQV.Ø.LT.5.OR.1.GT.3.OR..NOT.5.EQ.5
 =  .NOT.(TRUE  OR. FALSE.).EQV.TRUE  .OR.FALSE .OR..NOT.TRUE
 =  .NOT.(TRUE)             .EQV.TRUE  .OR.FALSE .OR.FALSE
 =  FALSE                   .EQV.TRUE            .OR.FALSE
 =  FALSE                   .EQV.TRUE
 =  FALSE
```

Example 9.7

```
    .NOT.5.GT.3.OR.3.EQ.1.EQV.Ø.LT.5.OR.(1.GT.3.OR..NOT.5.EQ.5)
 =  .NOT.TRUE  .OR.FALSE .EQV.TRUE  .OR.(FALSE .OR..NOT.TRUE)
 =  .NOT.TRUE            .EQV.TRUE  .OR.(FALSE .OR.FALSE)
 =  FALSE                .EQV.TRUE  .OR.(FALSE)
 =  FALSE                .EQV.TRUE
 =  FALSE
```

Example 9.8

```
    .NOT.5.GT.3.OR.(3.EQ.1.EQV.Ø.LT.5).OR.1.GT.3.OR..NOT.5.EQ.5
 =  .NOT.5.GT.3.OR.(FALSE .EQV.TRUE)  .OR.1.GT.3.OR..NOT.5.EQ.5
 =  .NOT.5.GT.3.OR.(FALSE)            .OR.1.GT.3.OR..NOT.5.EQ.5
 =  .NOT.TRUE  .OR.(FALSE)            .OR.FALSE  .OR..NOT.TRUE
 =  FALSE      .OR.(FALSE)            .OR.FALSE  .OR.FALSE
 =  FALSE                             .OR.FALSE  .OR.FALSE
 =  FALSE                                        .OR.FALSE
 =  FALSE
```

Example 9.9

```
    45+2.NE.7.AND..NOT.TRUE.NEQV.4-2.LT.3.OR..NOT.TRUE.AND.TRUE.OR.FALSE
 =  47  .NE.7.AND..NOT.TRUE.NEQV.2  .LT.3.OR..NOT.TRUE.AND.TRUE.OR.FALSE
 =  TRUE    .AND..NOT.TRUE.NEQV.TRUE     .OR..NOT.TRUE.AND.TRUE.OR.FALSE
 =  TRUE    .AND.FALSE     .NEQV.TRUE    .OR.FALSE     .AND.TRUE.OR.FALSE
 =  FALSE                  .NEQV.TRUE    .OR.FALSE               .OR.FALSE
 =  FALSE                  .NEQV.TRUE                            .OR.FALSE
 =  FALSE                  .NEQV.TRUE
 =  TRUE
```

9.10 THE BLOCK IF STATEMENT

The block IF statement has the general form:

```
IF (LOGICAL EXPRESSION) THEN
```

This block IF statement is the opening statement in the FORTRAN implementation of three fundamental logical constructs, namely:

1. One-way selection
2. Two-way selection
3. Multiway selection

The FORTRAN structural skeletons corresponding to these three logical constructs are:

```
IF( )THEN....END IF
IF( )THEN....ELSE....END IF
IF( )THEN...ELSE IF( )THEN...ELSE IF( )THEN...ELSE...END IF
```

The three logic constructs are now considered in some depth, and you will better sense their true significance once you see them in perspective.

9.11 THE BLOCK IF STATEMENT AND ONE-WAY SELECTION: THE IF ( ) THEN . . . END IF CONSTRUCT

When FORTRAN I was issued early in 1957, the GO TO, the computed GO TO, and the arithmetic IF were contained in the language specification. There was also a so-called *assigned* GO TO, which still exists in FORTRAN 77, but is rarely used today. These four transfer-of-control statements all pointed to labels somewhere in the program, and if a program was not carefully thought out, it easily became a massive tangled web, with logic paths running back and forth in bewildering disarray. Such label-hopping messes were frequently called *spaghetti programs* for obvious reasons, and they were very difficult to maintain.

FORTRAN II was released in June 1958. Its technical highlight was the introduction of subprograms, which made it possible to divide a program into logical units in order to deal with these individually. This provided the basis for a much more rigorous approach to programming, and opened the door to a programming style that might be called *bottom up* in the sense that a programmer could develop all the individual major steps of a program in corresponding subprograms, which could then be combined into a larger, more complex program unit, held together by a so-called *main program*. A large task could thus be constructed from the bottom up by combining several smaller programming steps.

The advent of subprograms had a tremendously beneficial cleanup effect on FORTRAN programming, but within each program unit, you could still find logic tangles, although these were much smaller and therefore somewhat easier to digest.

The fundamental source of spaghetti programming must be understood in order to avoid it. As already stated, all logical branching in early FORTRAN involved labels to which the logic was directed, and label-directed branching automatically, and inexorably, creates tangles. It is true that some programmers create worse tangles than others, but tangle-free programming is impossible when confined to label-directed branching.

Some people soon compared the logic strands in a program to hair, and classified programs into kempt and unkempt. A well-kempt program had most of its logic strands flowing downward in as clean a fashion as possible, with minimal backward looping. This approach imposes definite structure and elegance on programs, but cannot eliminate the strands because these are inherent in the branching statements themselves.

FORTRAN I and II were IBM products that had a profound impact on computing, in effect, making programming widely available. There were similar language developments in progress elsewhere, but none was to have the ultimate impact of FORTRAN. There was even a FORTRAN III, used internally by IBM in the early sixties, by which time other manufacturers offered FORTRAN-like languages, some with features not found in FORTRAN II, but FORTRAN quickly gained astonishing momentum. In May 1962, the American Standards Association established the ASA X3.4.3 Committee to develop a FORTRAN standard. That standard was approved on March 7, 1966 and was called the ASA FORTRAN X3.9–1966 Standard. In August 1966, ASA was reorganized, and its name was change to United States of America Standards Institute, and ASA FORTRAN X3.9–1966 became known as USASI FORTRAN X3.9–1966. USASI, incidentally, ultimately changed its name to ANSI, the American National Standards Institute, and the current standard is ANSI FORTRAN X3.9–1978.

FORTRAN 66 was essentially a consensus on what had become known as FORTRAN IV, which was basically FORTRAN II with numerous extensions. One of these extensions was the *logical IF* statement, which became an important part of the ASA FORTRAN X3.9–1966 standard.

In retrospect, it is easy to see that the logical IF defined a major turning point in programming structure. You will recall that the logical IF has the ability to execute a single FORTRAN imperative statement if a specified logical condition is true, and you saw just how easy it is to formulate highly complex logical conditions. From a structural point of view, the real significance of the logical IF lies in the fact that the statement is not necessarily a source of another strand of hair unless, of course, the conditionally executed statement happens to be a GO TO.

The logical IF statement was received with enthusiasm, but soon fault was found with it. The major criticism focused on the fact that only a single imperative statement is triggered when the logical condition is true. If a whole block of statements is to be executed, it becomes necessary to lay spaghetti ducts to channel the logic appropriately, and this is where the FORTRAN 77 IF() THEN . . . END IF comes in. This construct is nothing more than an extended logical IF statement, allowing the conditional execution of an entire block of statements. The construct has the symbolic representation, shown in Fig. 9.13.

Comparing the structure with the logical IF, you notice that the *only* difference

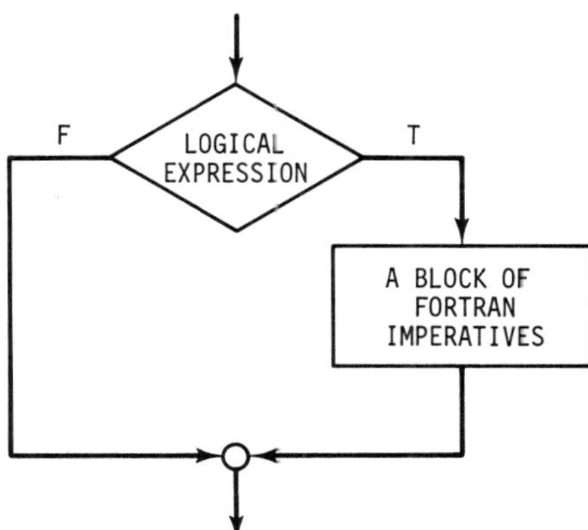

Figure 9.13 The logical representation of the IF()THEN . . . END IF (one-way selection construct).

lies in the ability to execute a block of statements rather than just a single one. The logical IF is, in other words, a subset of the IF()THEN . . . END IF construct.

To highlight some of these points, we design a small program to read a real number X. If X is zero or negative, it is ignored, and another value is read. If X is positive, we define Y as the product of the square root of X and the sine of X. A counter N is then updated by 1, and X is added to the sum accumulating in a variable SUM. Y, N, and the sum are printed each time a positive X is read. No exit path is built into the logic to keep the construct confined to its essence.

In case you are shuddering at the seeming complexity of the problem, you are reacting as intended. This is a golden opportunity to convince you how much more successfully such problems are stated by means of flowcharts. This particular problem is restated by the flowchart in Figure 9.14 from which it is easy to see that we are really dealing with a relatively trivial bit of logic.

If only the arithmetic IF statement were available, the FORTRAN implementation of the program would take the form of the left program in Figure 9.14, whereas access to the logical IF statement would lead the programmer in the direction of the other two programs.

The type of logical construct involved here is known as *one-way selection.* The first two programs are relatively clean because the logic is simple. The third program is considerably less elegant, displaying more spaghetti logic than the other two. The label-driven logic strands are shown beside each program. The author of the third program gave the logic an additional, but unnecessary, strand. It could be argued that good flowcharting would have avoided some of these problems, but ironically, there is nothing wrong with the flowchart, and all three programs follow it more or less faithfully. You will find it profitable to investigate this fact. The secret is to recognize this one-way selection logic, and to know how best to translate it into FORTRAN—and this done in Fig. 9.15 using the IF()THEN . . . END IF construct. Again, the flowchart is the same, and you will notice that the program actually assumes the physical appearance of the flowchart somewhat.

This program is clean, highly readable, and contains only a single label-driven logic strand. The statements between the block IF and the END IF are indented an additional three spaces to highlight the structure of the program, but this additional

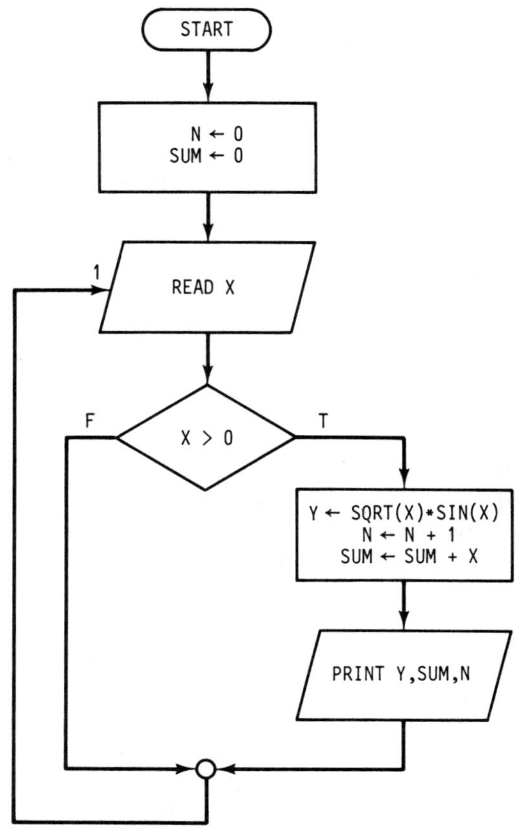


```
  N=Ø
  SUM=Ø.
1 READ(5,*)X
  IF(X)1,1,2
2 Y=SQRT(X)*SIN(X)
  N=N+1
  SUM=SUM+X
  WRITE(6,*)Y,N,SUM
  GO TO 1
  END
```

```
  N=Ø
  SUM=Ø.
1 READ(5,*)X
  IF(X.LE.Ø.)GO TO 1
  Y=SQRT(X)*SIN(X)
  N=N+1
  SUM=SUM+X
  WRITE(6,*)Y,N,SUM
  GO TO 1
  END
```

```
  N=Ø
  SUM=Ø.
1 READ(5,*)X
  IF(X.GT.Ø.)GO TO 2
  GO TO 1
2 Y=SQRT(X)*SIN(X)
  N=N+1
  SUM=SUM+X
  WRITE(6,*)Y,N,SUM
  GO TO 1
  END
```

Figure 9.14 Three programs showing how one-way selection should *not* be implemented.

identation is optional. The indented group of statements is called the *IF-block*, referring to the fact that if the logical condition is true, only then is the block of statements executed.

In summary, it is stated again that the IF()THEN . . . END IF construct is basically an extension of the logical IF construct, which, as you know, permits the

```
      N=Ø
      SUM=Ø.
    1 READ(5,*)X
*
      IF(X.GT.Ø.)THEN
         Y=SQRT(X)*SIN(X)
         N=N+1
         SUM=SUM+X
         WRITE(6,*)Y,N,SUM
      END IF
*
      GO TO 1
      END
```

Figure 9.15 One-way selection and the IF()THEN . . . END IF construct.

conditional execution of only a single FORTRAN statement. The IF()THEN . . . END IF construct, on the other hand, permits the conditional execution of any number of FORTRAN statements sandwiched between THEN and END IF.

9.12 THE BLOCK IF STATEMENT AND TWO-WAY SELECTION: THE IF( )THEN . . . ELSE . . . END IF CONSTRUCT

The benefits of a construct to perform the conditional execution of a block of statements are easily recognized. From this recognition, it is only a small additional step to wish for an extension to the IF()THEN . . . ELSE construct to permit the execution of an alternate block of statements, whenever the logical condition is *not* true. The IF()THEN . . . ELSE . . . END IF construct, shown symbolically in Fig. 9.16, provides precisely this flexibility. The construct is the ideal way to program *two-way selection* without involving a single label-driven logic strand.

To illustrate, we return to the program of the previous section and extend it to process zero and negative values. The desired additions are shown in the flowchart in Fig. 9.17. Whenever X is negative or zero, LOG(ABS(X)+1.) is computed and assigned to Y. A new counter NUMNEG is also introduced, and the former counter

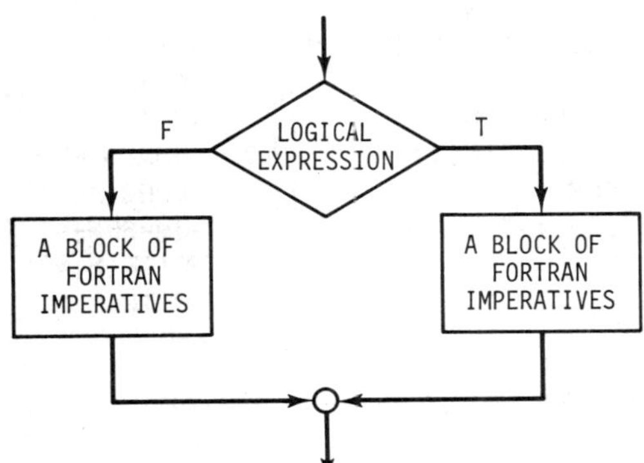

Figure 9.16 The logical representation of the IF()THEN . . . ELSE . . . END IF (two-way selection construct).

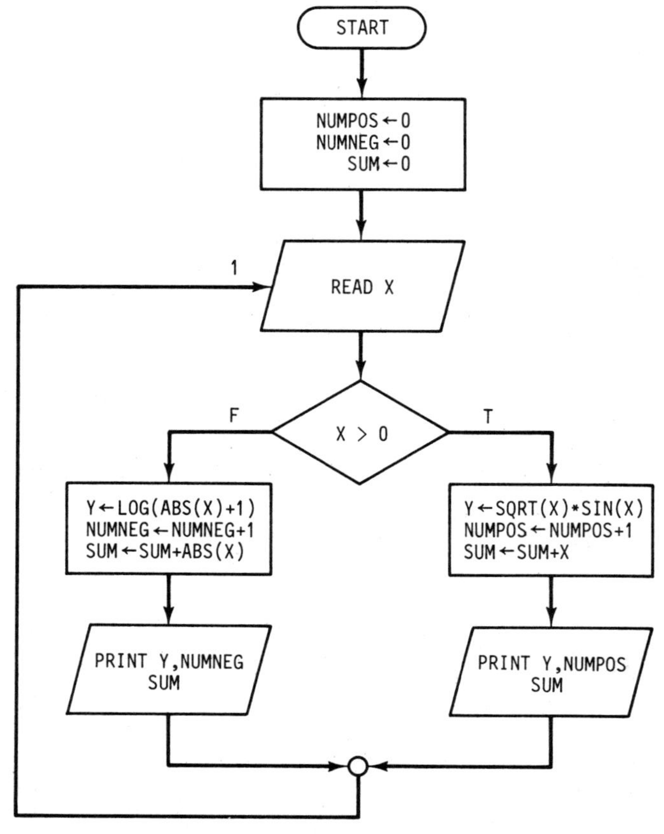

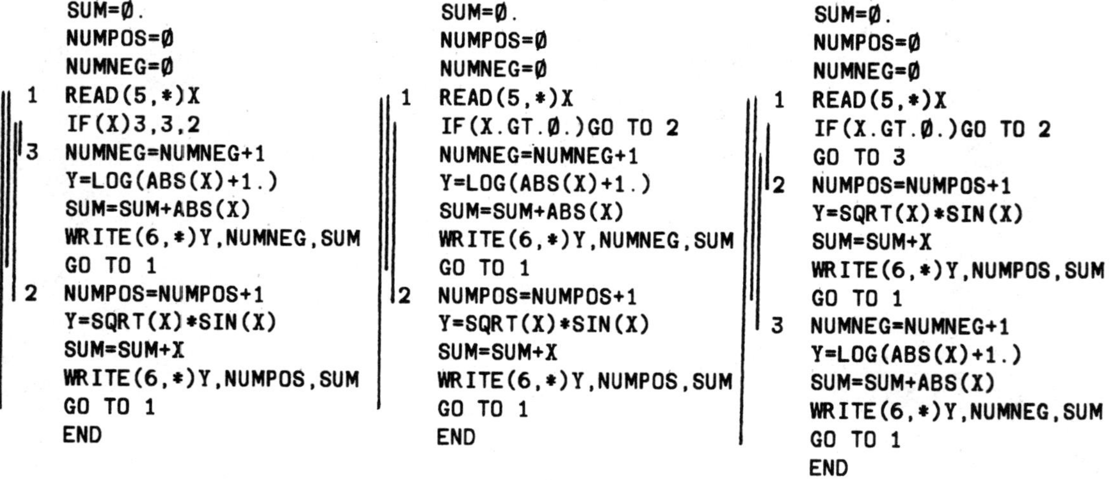

```
      SUM=0.
      NUMPOS=0
      NUMNEG=0
    1 READ(5,*)X
      IF(X)3,3,2
    3 NUMNEG=NUMNEG+1
      Y=LOG(ABS(X)+1.)
      SUM=SUM+ABS(X)
      WRITE(6,*)Y,NUMNEG,SUM
      GO TO 1
    2 NUMPOS=NUMPOS+1
      Y=SQRT(X)*SIN(X)
      SUM=SUM+X
      WRITE(6,*)Y,NUMPOS,SUM
      GO TO 1
      END
```

```
      SUM=0.
      NUMPOS=0
      NUMNEG=0
    1 READ(5,*)X
      IF(X.GT.0.)GO TO 2
      NUMNEG=NUMNEG+1
      Y=LOG(ABS(X)+1.)
      SUM=SUM+ABS(X)
      WRITE(6,*)Y,NUMNEG,SUM
      GO TO 1
    2 NUMPOS=NUMPOS+1
      Y=SQRT(X)*SIN(X)
      SUM=SUM+X
      WRITE(6,*)Y,NUMPOS,SUM
      GO TO 1
      END
```

```
      SUM=0.
      NUMPOS=0
      NUMNEG=0
    1 READ(5,*)X
      IF(X.GT.0.)GO TO 2
      GO TO 3
    2 NUMPOS=NUMPOS+1
      Y=SQRT(X)*SIN(X)
      SUM=SUM+X
      WRITE(6,*)Y,NUMPOS,SUM
      GO TO 1
    3 NUMNEG=NUMNEG+1
      Y=LOG(ABS(X)+1.)
      SUM=SUM+ABS(X)
      WRITE(6,*)Y,NUMNEG,SUM
      GO TO 1
      END
```

Figure 9.17 How *not* to program two-way selection.

N appears as NUMPOS. Again, the verbal description sounds unpalatable, if not confusing, but the flowchart shows the true simplicity of the problem.

The three programs in Fig. 9.17 show how such two-way selection might be programmed in pre-FORTRAN 77 days. Again the label-driven logic strands are shown to the left of each program. By current standards, these programs illustrate bad form, and in order to understand what is meant by bad form in this particular case, you must step through the programs, guided by the flowchart.

The first two programs in Fig. 9.17 are as clean as possible under the circumstances, but the program on the right, although yielding proper results, is unnecessarily tangled. The IF()THEN . . . ELSE . . . END IF structure is now used to produce a clean program, completely faithful to the flowchart, as shown in Fig. 9.18. Again, the program resembles the flowchart in Fig. 9.17 somewhat. The IF and ELSE-blocks are indented to stress this resemblance. It is emphasized once more that this indenting is optional, but very helpful.

```
      NUMPOS=Ø
      NUMNEG=Ø
      SUM=Ø.
    1 READ(5,*)X
*
      IF(X.GT.Ø.)THEN
         Y=SQRT(X)*SIN(X)
         NUMPOS=NUMPOS+1
         SUM=SUM+X
         WRITE(6,*)Y,NUMPOS,SUM
      ELSE
         Y=LOG(ABS(X)+1.)
         NUMNEG=NUMNEG+1
         SUM=SUM+ABS(X)
         WRITE(6,*)Y,NUMNEG,SUM
      END IF
*
      GO TO 1
      END
```

Figure 9.18 The IF()THEN . . . ELSE . . . END IF construct is used to implement two-way selection.

When you compare the symbolic representations of one-way and two-way selection, it will become clear that one-way selection is a special case of two-way selection, with an empty ELSE-block. Figure 9.19 shows our earlier one-way selection program, but this time the empty ELSE-block is included. The program will still compile and execute as before.

The next example involves nested two-way selection. There is an outer two-way selection structure, of which the IF and ELSE-blocks also involve two-way selection. An attempt will be made to explain the problem, but you will find that the flowchart in Fig. 9.20 conveys the logic considerably more effectively. Here is the problem: A number X is read from the keyboard. If that number is zero or positive, it is looked at more closely. If it is greater than or equal to 5, that fact is reported. If it is less than 5 but still positive or zero, that fact is also reported.

```
      N=Ø
      SUM=Ø.
    1 READ(5,*)X
*
      IF(X.GT.Ø.)THEN
         Y=SQRT(X)*SIN(X)
         N=N+1
         SUM=SUM+X
         WRITE(6,*)Y,N,SUM
      ELSE
      END IF
*
      GO TO 1
      END
```

Figure 9.19 Two-way selection with an empty ELSE block reduces to one-way selection.

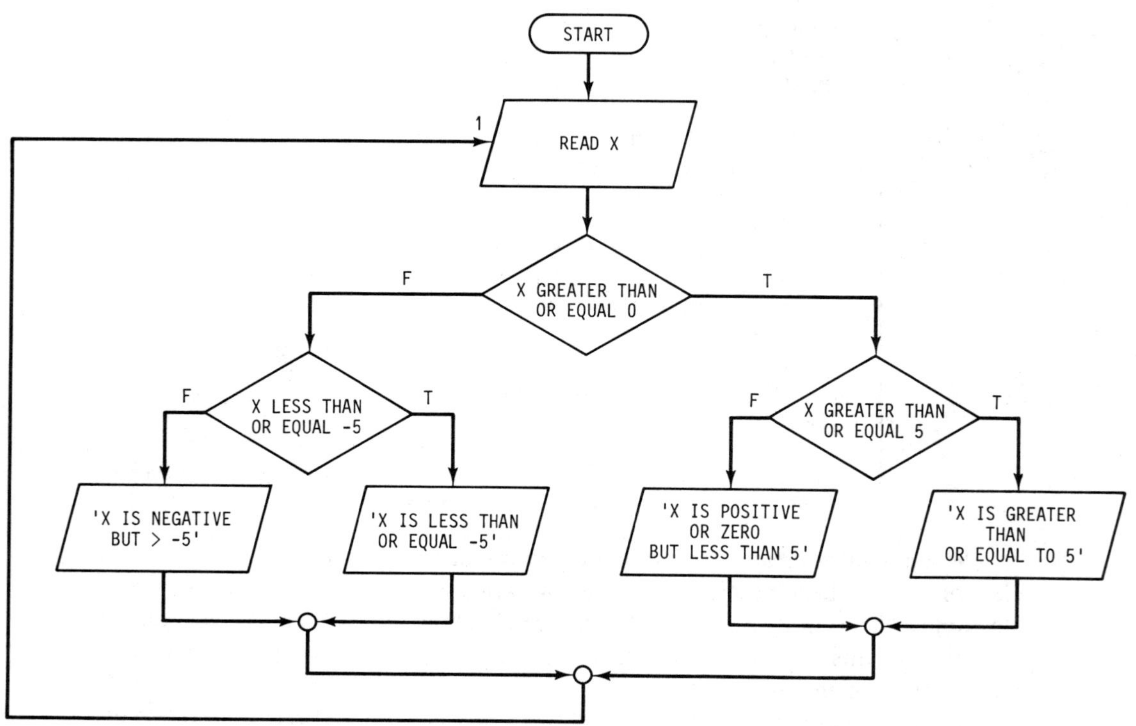

Figure 9.20. Nested two-way selection.

If the input is negative, it is also examined more closely. If it is less than or equal to -5, that fact is reported. If it is greater than -5, but still negative, that fact is reported. The program then prompts for more input. The program as it stands has no exit, but we won't worry about that for now to keep the basic structure as free of clutter as possible.

The flowchart presents the problem so crisply that it becomes easier to state it more effectively. Let's try it again: Read a number. If the number is positive or zero, then if the number is greater than or equal to 5, report that fact. Else report that it is zero or positive, but less than 5.

If, on the other hand, the number is negative, then if the number is less than or equal to −5, report that fact. Else report that it is negative but greater than −5.

Actually, it is debatable whether the second attempt to explain the problem is more successful than the first. The trouble is that human languages lack the necessary constructs to communicate nested logic unambiguously, but the flowchart fills this gap admirably and so do certain computer languages. When scientists wish to convey complex algorithms, they frequently resort to flowcharts or to actual or hypothetical computer languages because these provide them with a medium for expressing certain logical structures without ambiguity. A language such as FORTRAN, therefore, is more than simply a programming language. In a very real way, it must also be regarded as an extension to the human language, supplementing in special areas in which that language has failed to evolve.

We now make a third attempt to state the problem, but this time using FORTRAN. It is done in two steps: first we deal with the outer two-way selection after which we supply the inner two-way constructs.

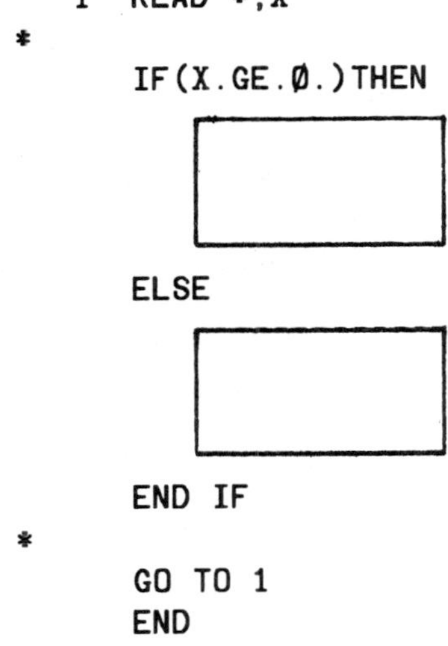

```
    1  READ *,X
*
       IF(X.GE.Ø.)THEN

       ELSE

       END IF
*
       GO TO 1
       END
```

The program is now completed by filling in the two boxes. This is easily accomplished because they contain plain, ordinary two-way selection constructs. The final FORTRAN statement of the algorithm appears in Fig. 9.21. Not only is it a concise statement of the desired procedure, but it is also a working program.

At first glance, the program does not appear to communicate as effectively as the flowchart, but it does come into sharper focus after you become accustomed to it. There is a growing tendency to place less stress on flowcharts, but the various logical constructs under discussion are most readily conveyed through flowcharts.

The reason behind the flowchart's great effectiveness in communicating selection algorithms is that it rests on a more instinctive level of human consciousness than

```
    1 READ *,X
*
      IF(X.GE.Ø.)THEN
         IF(X.GE.5.)THEN
            PRINT *,'X IS GREATER THAN OR EQUAL TO 5'
         ELSE
            PRINT *,'X IS ZERO OR POSITIVE BUT LESS THAN 5'
         END IF
      ELSE
         IF(X.LE.-5.)THEN
            PRINT *,'X IS LESS THAN OR EQUAL TO -5'
         ELSE
            PRINT *,'X IS NEGATIVE BUT GREATER THAN -5'
         END IF
      END IF
*
      GO TO 1
      END
```

Figure 9.21 FORTRAN is more than a language to drive a computation process. It can also be used to communicate algorithms.

the program, which belongs to realm of verbal communication, an acquired skill. You have either been the target or the source of the following statement: ". . . you don't seem to understand what I'm saying. Maybe I should draw a picture." Although intended as a slight, the statement does reflect considerable insight.

The program in Figure 9.21 is certainly not trivial, and yet contains only a single label-driven logic path, allowing us to return to the READ statement for the next datum. To show you just how important the FORTRAN 77 IF()THEN . . . ELSE . . . END IF construct really is, Figure 9.21 is now reprogrammed using the arithmetic IF and shown in Fig. 9.22. The program exhibits the same behavior,

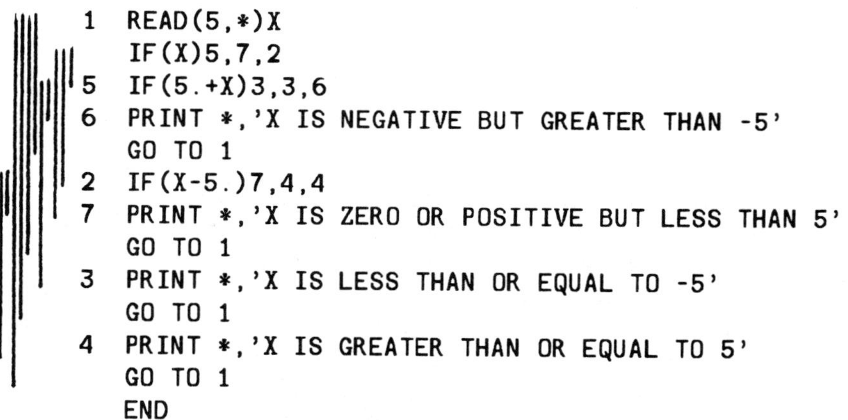

```
    1 READ(5,*)X
      IF(X)5,7,2
    5 IF(5.+X)3,3,6
    6 PRINT *,'X IS NEGATIVE BUT GREATER THAN -5'
      GO TO 1
    2 IF(X-5.)7,4,4
    7 PRINT *,'X IS ZERO OR POSITIVE BUT LESS THAN 5'
      GO TO 1
    3 PRINT *,'X IS LESS THAN OR EQUAL TO -5'
      GO TO 1
    4 PRINT *,'X IS GREATER THAN OR EQUAL TO 5'
      GO TO 1
      END
```

Figure 9.22 Unacceptable tangling results when two-way selection is based on the arithmetic IF statement.

but is difficult to read. Not only is it difficult to read, but it would be difficult to write without the flowchart in Fig. 9.20. The extensive logic strands are indicated to the left of the program.

Notice all the GO TO statements in Fig. 9.22, and all the labels. The logic is so intertwined that any sort of debugging would be difficult. When reading the program, your attention is shifted up and down, and you have to keep various alternative logic paths in mind while pursuing a particular one.

It was this type of program that gave FORTRAN a somewhat negative reputation in its earlier days. Programmers complained about the lack of structure and clarity, and the difficulties associated with program modifications. There was always the fear that any sort of alteration attempt would set into motion a ripple effect in the rest of the program, especially because the programmer could not always grasp the logic flow in its entirety. Various logic streams might pass through blocks of code being considered for modifications, frequently giving rise to the attitude that, although a program might not do all it should or could, it must be left alone because any sort of change might result in unexpected complications.

The program shown in Fig. 9.23 is also based on the flowchart of Fig. 9.20, but it employs the logical IF statement to implement the structure. The resulting program is perhaps somewhat less twisted and correspondingly somewhat more readable, but still far short of the elegance displayed by the earlier, and equivalent, IF()THEN . . . ELSE . . . END IF implementation in Fig. 9.21.

The program forms in Figs. 9.22 and 9.23 are intolerable, of course, and cannot be excused, given the selection constructs offered by FORTRAN 77.

The growing awareness over the years of the necessity of clean and structured programming, and the parallel evolution of the required language constructs, turned out to be a highly significant ingredient in the development of good programming techniques. The magnitude of the advance can best be judged through the benefit of hindsight. It provided new dimensions and vision to an approach to computing that had become stagnant and mired in horrendous tangles. At many major computer

```
    1 READ(5,*)X
*
      IF(X.GE.Ø.)GO TO 2
      IF(X.LE.-5.)GO TO 3
      PRINT *,'X IS NEGATIVE BUT GREATER THAN -5'
      GO TO 1
    2 IF(X.GE.5.)GO TO 4
      PRINT *,'X IS ZERO OR POSITIVE BUT LESS THAN 5'
      GO TO 1
    3 PRINT *,'X IS LESS THAN OR EQUAL TO -5'
      GO TO 1
    4 PRINT *,'X IS GREATER THAN OR EQUAL TO 5'
      GO TO 1
*
      END
```

Figure 9.23 The logical IF is used to implement two-way selection.

sites, the development of new software had virtually ceased, with all available programming resources dedicated to the maintenance of previously developed code. The loss of a particular programmer often meant the death of an undocumented, tangled creation that no other person could understand without a disproportionate investment of time.

To cope with the dilemma, companies hired more programming staff, raiding the data processing operations of other companies, compounding the overall problem. The evolution of structured programming approaches, in retrospect, salvaged a situation that was drifting inexorably along a dead-end path.

For many, structured programming turned into a religion since it offered salvation. By the midseventies it had become surrounded by high priests, elaborate theology, definitions of sin and gatherings for purposes of worship. The inevitable split into various denominations soon followed. The GO TO statement became the antithesis of goodness and the object of choruses of condemnation.

The earlier fervor has yielded to a mature commitment to structured techniques, and today it is relatively safe to admit that the GO TO statement does have a place at times, and that its occasional and thoughtful deployment can simplify certain problems considerably, without fear of excommunication or the auto-da-fe.

9.13 THE BLOCK IF STATEMENT AND MULTIWAY SELECTION: THE IF()THEN . . . ELSE IF()THEN . . . ELSE IF()THEN . . . ELSE . . . END IF CONSTRUCT

To this point, we have encountered simple one-way selection in which a so-called IF-block of code is either executed or not executed, depending on the truth value of some logical expression. When either one block of code or another block is to be executed, again depending on the truth value of some logical expression, we are dealing with two-way selection for which the IF()THEN . . . ELSE . . . END IF construct is used. The two blocks of code, of which either one or the other is selected, are known as the IF and ELSE-blocks.

Sometimes we have more than two blocks of code from which only one is to be selected. This is an example of multiway selection for which FORTRAN 77 provides the IF()THEN . . . ELSE IF()THEN . . . ELSE IF()THEN . . . ELSE . . . END IF construct, shown symbolically in Fig. 9.24. The logic flow enters the construct from the top and cascades through the various logic tests indicated by the diamonds. The very first test to be found true causes the logic to leave the diamond through the true branch to execute the appropriate IF or ELSE IF-block. The last block in the structure is an ELSE block. The logic reaches this ELSE-block only if no single logical condition along the cascade is found to be true.

Figure 9.25 shows a simple application of the construct. A value of M is read. If that value is 0, the first logical test is true, the value of M is reported, and the logic returns to read the next M. If M = 1, the first logical condition is false, and the flow cascades to the next logical test that is true. Again, the true branch is

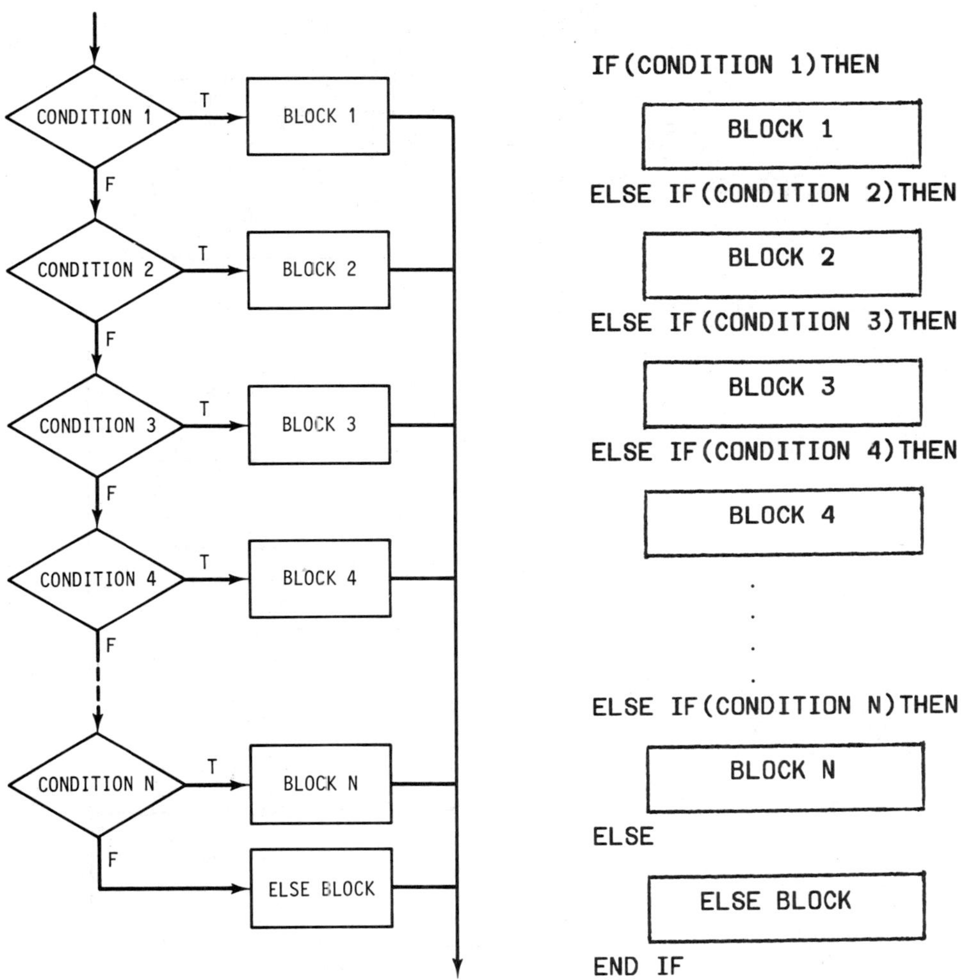

Figure 9.24 Multiway selection.

taken, M is reported, and the logic returns to the READ statement. It is important to realize that the logic flow through this construct cascades from one logical test to the next until a logical condition is true, in which case the true branch is taken and the logic ceases to cascade. This is quite different from the logic flow portrayed by the flowchart in Fig. 9.10 in which cascading continues through the chain even after the first true condition is encountered. The program in Fig. 9.25 contains EOF and ERROR branching in the READ statement. Look at the flowchart to see how these branches are represented. The flowchart also shows connectors, represented by labeled circles. Simply picture connectors with like labels to be joined. This saves running long and awkward lines. After the "finger problems," error message is issued, for example, the logic branches back to the READ statement.

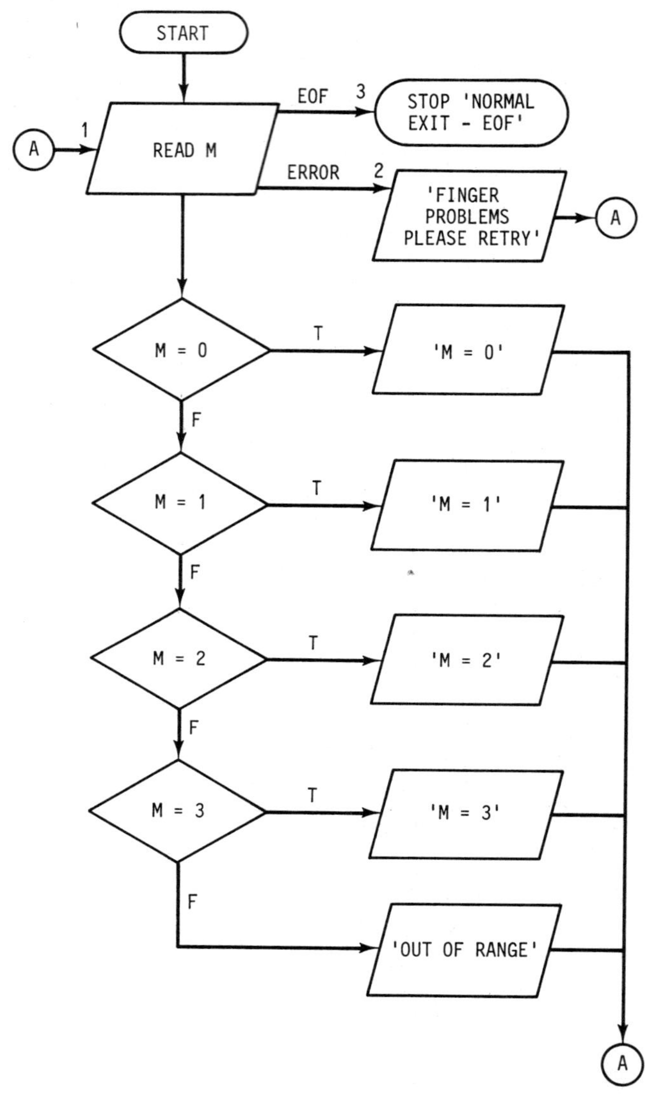


```
    1  READ(5,*,END=3,ERR=2,IOSTAT=L)M
*-----MULTIWAY SELECTION CONSTRUCT
*-----STARTS HERE
       IF(M.EQ.Ø)THEN
          PRINT *,'M = Ø'
       ELSE IF(M.EQ.1)THEN
          PRINT *,'M = 1'
       ELSE IF(M.EQ.2)THEN
          PRINT *,'M = 2'
```

Figure 9.25 Multiway selection applied.

```
      ELSE IF(M.EQ.3)THEN
         PRINT *,'M = 3'
      ELSE
         PRINT *,'OUT OF RANGE'
      END IF
*-----END OF CONSTRUCT
      GO TO 1
*-----ERROR HANDLING
    2 PRINT *,'FINGER PROBLEMS - PLEASE RETRY'
      GO TO 1
*-----EOF BRANCH
    3 STOP 'NORMAL EXIT - EOF'
      END
```

Figure 9.25 (Cont.)

Example 9.10

Translate the flowchart of Fig. 9.26 into a FORTRAN program.

Solution It is possible to come up with many different programs that exhibit the logic flow shown in the flowchart, but some of these require 10 or more GO TO statements. Making use of all the FORTRAN 77 features studied thus far, however, permits it to be done with as few as two GO TO statements. The program on the left employs two GO TO statements. It is a faithful transliteration of the flowchart. The program on the right incorporates a slightly different interpretation of the flowchart and is down to a single GO TO. This right program is somewhat more elegant than the left, but the left program is possibly more faithful to the flowchart. When you compare the two programs, you should be clear on the fact that if something is *not* greater than 99, it must be less than *or equal to* 99. It is tempting to assume that if something is not greater than 99, it must be less than 99. Many programmer stub their toes on that one.

```
    1 READ(5,*,END=99)L
      IF(L.GT.99)GO TO 1
*
      IF(MOD(L,2).EQ.Ø)THEN
        PRINT *,'L IS EVEN'
      ELSE
        IF(L.GT.21)PRINT *,'*'
        IF(L.GT.41)PRINT *,'**'
      END IF
*
      IF(L.EQ.19)THEN
        PRINT *,'***'
      ELSE IF(L.EQ.21)THEN
        PRINT *,'****'
```

```
    1 READ(5,*,END=99)L
*
      IF(L.LE.99)THEN
*
        IF(MOD(L,2).EQ.Ø)THEN
          PRINT *,'L IS EVEN'
        ELSE
          IF(L.GT.21)PRINT *,'*'
          IF(L.GT.41)PRINT *,'**'
        END IF
*
        IF(L.EQ.19)THEN
          PRINT *,'***'
        ELSE IF(L.EQ.21)THEN
          PRINT *,'****'
```

```
      ELSE IF(L.EQ.23)THEN
        PRINT *,'*****'
      ELSE
        PRINT *,'******'
      END IF
*
      GO TO 1
   99 STOP
      END
```

```
        ELSE IF(L.EQ.23)THEN
          PRINT *,'*****'
        ELSE
          PRINT *,'******'
        END IF
*
      END IF
*
      GO TO 1
   99 STOP
```

Conclusion We set out to write a program to go with the flowchart of Fig. 9.26. The program on the left is that program. The program on the right is perhaps somewhat cleaner, but it goes beyond the flowchart. Treat it as an eloquent commentary on the flowchart.

9.14 SUMMARY

Whenever a single FORTRAN imperative is to be executed when a logical test is true, the simple logical IF statement is the best choice.

Whenever a block of statements is to be executed when a logical condition is true, one-way selection is involved, and the IF()THEN . . . END IF structure is to be used.

Whenever a single statement or a block of statements is to be executed when a logical condition is true, and another single statement or block of statements is to be executed if the same logical condition is false, we are dealing with two-way selection for which the FORTRAN IF()THEN . . . ELSE . . . END IF structure is designed.

Whenever we must select one branch from more than two alternatives, the FORTRAN IF()THEN . . . ELSE IF()THEN . . . ELSE IF()THEN . . . ELSE . . . END IF construct is used. This is a case of multiway selection.

Considering the fact that one-way selection is a special case of two-way selection, this leaves really only two constructs to be recognized.

9.15 PROBLEMS

9.1. Determine the truth value of each of the following logical expressions. You can verify your conclusions on the computer. The following program, for example, produces either T or F, and all these statements can be packed into a single program.

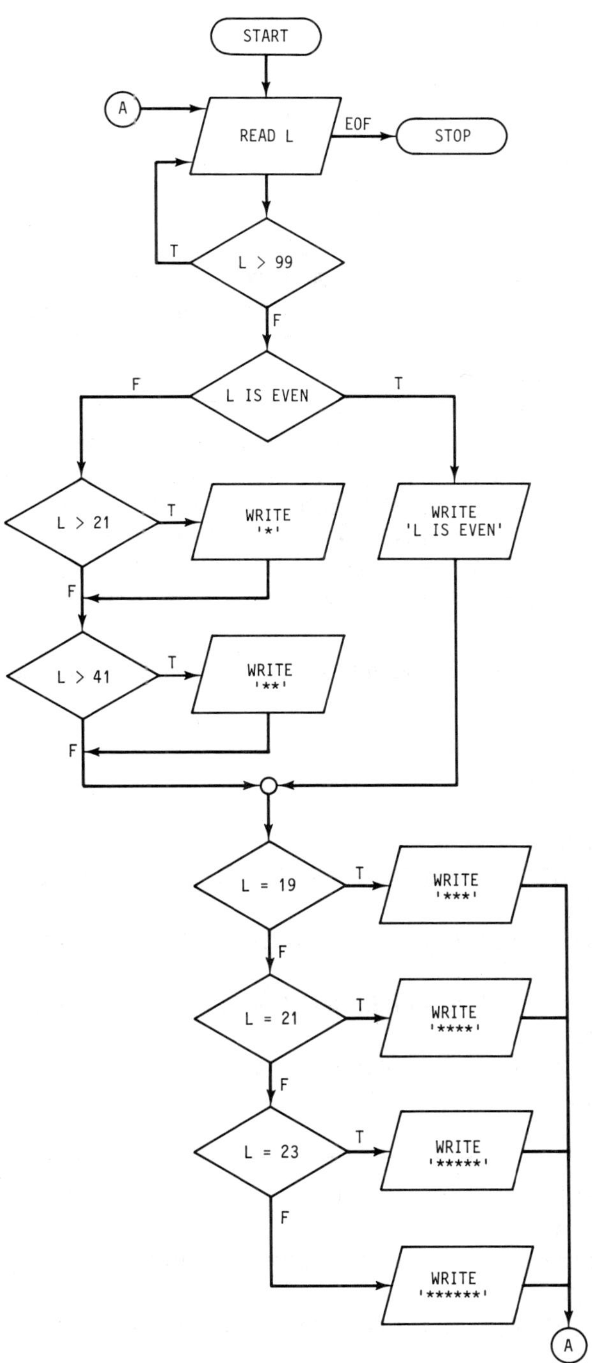

Figure 9.26 Flowchart for Example 9.10.

```
      PRINT *, 5.LT.7.AND.9.GE.8
      END
```

```
5.GE.5
8..LT.8.7
99.LE.21.OR.47.3.NE.21.
1245.NE.9.AND.-45.LT.-25
9.EQ.3+4+2.OR.7.EQ.1+3+3.OR.9.LT.1Ø94
9.EQ.3+4+2.OR.7.EQ.1+3+3.AND..NOT.9.LT.1Ø94
1-9.LT.1+9.EQV.17.GT.-17
.NOT.5.EQ.6
.NOT.1245.NE.9.AND.-45.LT.-25
.NOT.(45+2.LT.45+3.AND..NOT.45+2.GT.45+3).AND.7.LE.7
.NOT.45+2.LT.45+3.AND.(.NOT.45+2.GT.45+3.AND.7.LE.7)
.NOT.(45+2.LT.45+3).AND..NOT.45+2.GT.45+3.AND.7.LE.7
.NOT.(45+2.LT.45+3.OR..NOT.45+2.GT.45+3).AND.7.LE.7
.NOT.45+2.LT.45+3.OR.(.NOT.45+2.GT.45+3.AND.7.LE.7)
.NOT.(45+2.LT.45+3).OR..NOT.(.NOT.45+2.GT.45+3.AND.7.LE.7)
```

9.2. Show the output produced by each of the following programs. Use the computer to verify your conclusion.

```
      M=1Ø/3
      GO TO(1,18,12,3),M
      STOP
 1    PRINT *,' REACHED STATEMENT WITH LABEL 1'
      STOP
 3    PRINT *,' REACHED STATEMENT WITH LABEL 3'
      STOP
12    PRINT *,' REACHED STATEMENT WITH LABEL 12'
      STOP
18    PRINT *,' REACHED STATEMENT WITH LABEL 18'
      END
```

```
      M=1Ø/3
      IF(M)1,18,3
 1    PRINT *,' REACHED STATEMENT WITH LABEL 1'
      STOP
18    PRINT *,' REACHED STATEMENT WITH LABEL 18'
      STOP
 3    PRINT *,' REACHED STATEMENT WITH LABEL 3'
      END
```

```
      M=1Ø/3
      IF(M.LT.3)PRINT *, 'M IS LESS THAN 3'
      IF(M.EQ.3)PRINT *, 'M IS EQUAL TO 3'
      IF(M.GT.3)PRINT *, 'M IS GREATER THAN 3'
      IF(M.GT.Ø)PRINT *, 'M IS A POSITIVE NUMBER'
      IF(M.NE.3.333)PRINT *, 'M IS NOT EQUAL TO 3.333'
      END
```

```
      A=5.2
      B=7.3
      C=1Ø.4
      D=-A
      IF(D.LT.A)PRINT*,'CONDITION 1 TRUE'
      IF(A.GT.B)PRINT*,'CONDITION 2 TRUE'
      IF(A+B.LT.Ø.1)PRINT*,'CONDITION 3 TRUE'
      IF(A+B.GE.Ø.1)PRINT*,'CONDITION 4 TRUE'
      IF(MIN(A,B,C,D).LT.-5.)PRINT*,'CONDITION 5 TRUE'
      IF(MAX(A,B,C,D).GE.5.)PRINT*,'CONDITION 6 TRUE'
      END
```

9.3. Some of the subsequent problems read from two files called DATA1 and DATA2, and those files must exist in your directory. The following program will generate the required files. While you certainly should be interested in the mechanics of this program, you need not worry about it unduly. Simply implement it and run it, making sure to observe *your* system's file-naming convention in the OPEN statement. After the run, copy the files to your screen and study them. There should be exactly 200 records in each of the two files, each record containing a 10-digit integer. The first digit of each number is zero. Be aware, however, that some systems remember that the files were created by a FORTRAN program, and therefore might *not* show you the first digit; it's still there, though. Such systems treat the leading zero as a *vertical format control* (VFC) character and show the records of the file double spaced when you copy them to the screen.

```
*-----THIS PROGRAM CREATES THE TWO FILES 'DATA1' AND 'DATA2'
      OPEN(3,FILE='DATA1',STATUS='NEW')
      OPEN(4,FILE='DATA2',STATUS='NEW')
      N=Ø
      I=1
      J=127
      K=4427
    1 CONTINUE
      I=MOD(I*J+K,K)*491
      N=N+1
      IF(N.GT.2ØØ)THEN
         CLOSE(3)
         CLOSE(4)
         STOP'FILES DATA1 AND DATA2 CREATED'
```

```
      END IF
      M=I+N*2ØØØØØØ
      WRITE(3,2)M
      IF(N.NE.77)M=M+231477
      WRITE(4,2)M
    2 FORMAT(I1Ø.1Ø)
      GO TO 1
      END
```

9.4. The program shown is designed to check the files created in Prob. 9.3. Run this program against your versions of DATA1 and DATA2. The output must be the same as shown here. If it is different, you must find and rectify the cause before proceeding to the remaining problems.

```
*-----CHECKER PROGRAM
      OPEN(3,FILE='DATA1',STATUS='OLD')
      OPEN(4,FILE='DATA2',STATUS='OLD')
      ISUM1=Ø
      ISUM2=Ø
    1 READ(3,2,END=99)I1,I2,I3,I4,I5,I6,I7,I8,I9,I1Ø
      READ(4,2,END=99)M1,M2,M3,M4,M5,M6,M7,M8,M9,M1Ø
    2 FORMAT(1ØI1)
      ISUM1=ISUM1+I1+I3+I5+I7+I9+M1+M3+M5+M7+M9
      ISUM2=ISUM2+I2+I4+I6+I8+I1Ø+M2+M4+M6+M8+M1Ø
      GO TO 1
   99 WRITE(6,3)ISUM2-ISUM1
    3 FORMAT(' THE CHECKSUM IS',I4)
      CLOSE(3)
      CLOSE(4)
      END
 THE CHECKSUM IS 6I5
```

9.5. The file DATA1 created in Prob. 9.3 contains 200 records. Each record contains a single 10-digit integer, or 10 one-digit numbers side by side. Let's pretend that a typical record contains a two-digit integer N1 in columns 1 to 2, another two-digit integer N2 in columns 4 to 5, N3 in column 6, N4 in column 8, and a real datum X5 in columns 9 to 10, with an implied decimal point between columns 9 and 10.

Write a program to read the file DATA1 record by record, summing all 200 N1 values into ISUM1, all 200 N2 values into ISUM2, all 200 N3 values into ISUM3, all 200 N4 values into ISUM4, and all 200 X5 values into SUM5. Report ISUM1, ISUM2, ISUM3, ISUM4, and SUM5. The expected steps are illustrated using the first three records of the file, namely,

```
ØØØ2Ø62357
ØØØ5896733
ØØØ7554997
```

The same three records are shown again, but this time the undesired data are crossed out:

```
ØØx2Ø6x357
ØØx589x733
ØØx755x997
```

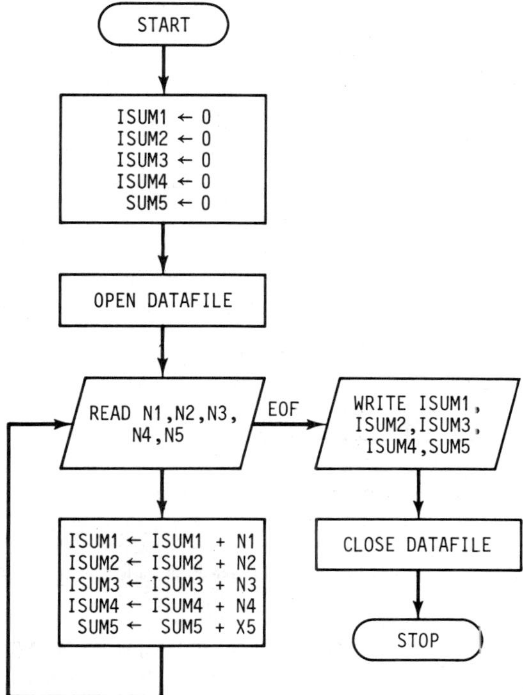

Figure 9.27 Flowchart for Problem 9.5.

For this small sample, ISUM1 = 0, ISUM2 = 153, ISUM3 = 20, ISUM4 = 19, and SUM5 = 18.7

The explanations are lengthy but the problem is simple. The required program can be written with fewer than 20 statements. The flowchart of Fig. 9.27 details the logic. The program has little to do with transfer of control, apart from the EOF branch, but it gives us the basic framework for subsequent programs that do. The correct output is:

```
ISUM1 =    3Ø5
ISUM2 =   9536
ISUM3 =    876
ISUM4 =    896
SUM5  =   1Ø27.1
```

9.6. We have claimed all along that the file DATA1 contains 200 records, and you should now write a program to verify that claim. The program simply performs dummy READs on the file until it hits the end, counting the records along the way. A dummy READ need not specify any variables. The flowchart of Fig. 9.28 displays the logic, and this is a good place to make a few general comments about counting. The flowchart suggests NUMREC as the variable to accumulate the count. Whenever you wish to count, you always start by assigning zero to the accumulating variable to clear it. This is analogous to pushing the clear button on a calculator or to resetting the trip odometer in your car. To add a quantity N to the total already accumulated in NUMREC, you use the following so-called replacement assignment statement:

```
NUMREC = NUMREC + N
```

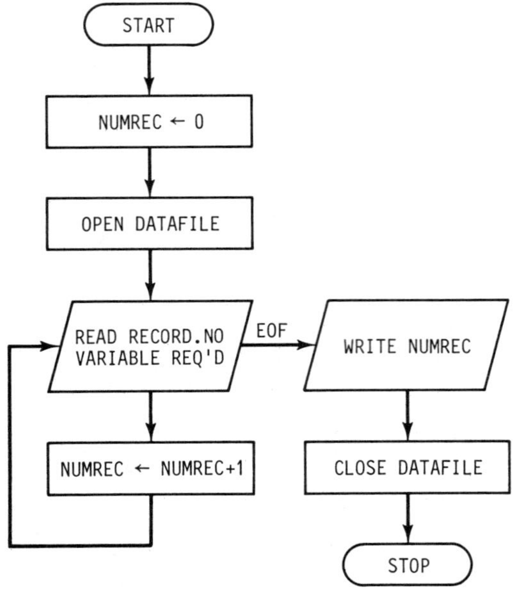

Figure 9.28 Flowchart for Problem 9.6.

IT tells the machine that the new value of NUMREC is the old value of NUMREC with N added to it. We have been using this idea all along, and you probably accepted it intuitively, but this problem presents a golden opportunity to spell it out. Base your counting program on the flowchart.

```
INVESTIGATING 2062357
2062357 IS DIVISIBLE BY 11
----------------------------
INVESTIGATING 5896733
----------------------------
INVESTIGATING 7554997
----------------------------
INVESTIGATING 8282816
8282816 IS DIVISIBLE BY 2
----------------------------
INVESTIGATING 10678071
10678071 IS DIVISIBLE BY 3
----------------------------
INVESTIGATING 12497383
12497383 IS DIVISIBLE BY 19
----------------------------
INVESTIGATING 15573655
15573655 IS DIVISIBLE BY 5
----------------------------
INVESTIGATING 16833227
----------------------------
```

```
INVESTIGATING 18612768
18612768 IS DIVISIBLE BY 3
18612768 IS DIVISIBLE BY 2
---------------------------
INVESTIGATING 21831430
21831430 IS DIVISIBLE BY 5
21831430 IS DIVISIBLE BY 2
---------------------------
INVESTIGATING 22715387
---------------------------
INVESTIGATING 25598205
25598205 IS DIVISIBLE BY 15
25598205 IS DIVISIBLE BY 9
25598205 IS DIVISIBLE BY 5
25598205 IS DIVISIBLE BY 3
---------------------------
INVESTIGATING 27443049
27443049 IS DIVISIBLE BY 19
27443049 IS DIVISIBLE BY 17
27443049 IS DIVISIBLE BY 3
---------------------------
INVESTIGATING 29327664
29327664 IS DIVISIBLE BY 3
29327664 IS DIVISIBLE BY 2
---------------------------
ALL DONE
```

9.7. Assume each record of the file DATA1 to contain a single 10-digit number. Write a program to comb through the file to count the number of even numbers and the number of odd numbers. The logic flow is detailed in the flowchart of Fig. 9.29. You should find 107 odd numbers and 93 even numbers. Hint: If N is even, MOD(N,2) = 0. Conversely, if N is odd, MOD(N,2) = 1 for positive N, and MOD(N,2) = −1 for negative N.

9.8. Assume, as in the previous problem, that the file DATA1 contains a single 10-digit number in each record. Write a program to investigate the first 14 numbers. Report whether each of the numbers is divisible by 19, 17, 13, 11, 9, 7, 5, 3, and 2. The flowchart is Fig. 9.30 and it might intimidate some, but don't let it scare you. The program can be written with as few as 24 statements. It produces the output shown:

9.9 DATA1 and DATA2 are the two files created in Prob. 9.3. Each file has 200 records, each record containing a 10-digit integer. A typical record can therefore be regarded as containing a single 10-digit integer or as containing 10 one-digit integers. Copy portions of each file to your screen to reacquaint yourself with the structure. You are reminded that some systems might not show you the first digit, which happens to be a zero in all 400 records.

Following the flowchart of Fig. 9.31 faithfully, write a program to perform the steps outlined below. Declare IMPLICIT INTEGER(A–Z) at the beginning, because you will be dealing with integers exclusively.

Open the file DATA1. Regard each record as containing 10 one-digit integers. Step through the file, accumulating the ten sums: SUM1, SUM2, . . . , SUM10, where SUM6, for example, is the sum of all the sixth digits of all records. Report the sums.

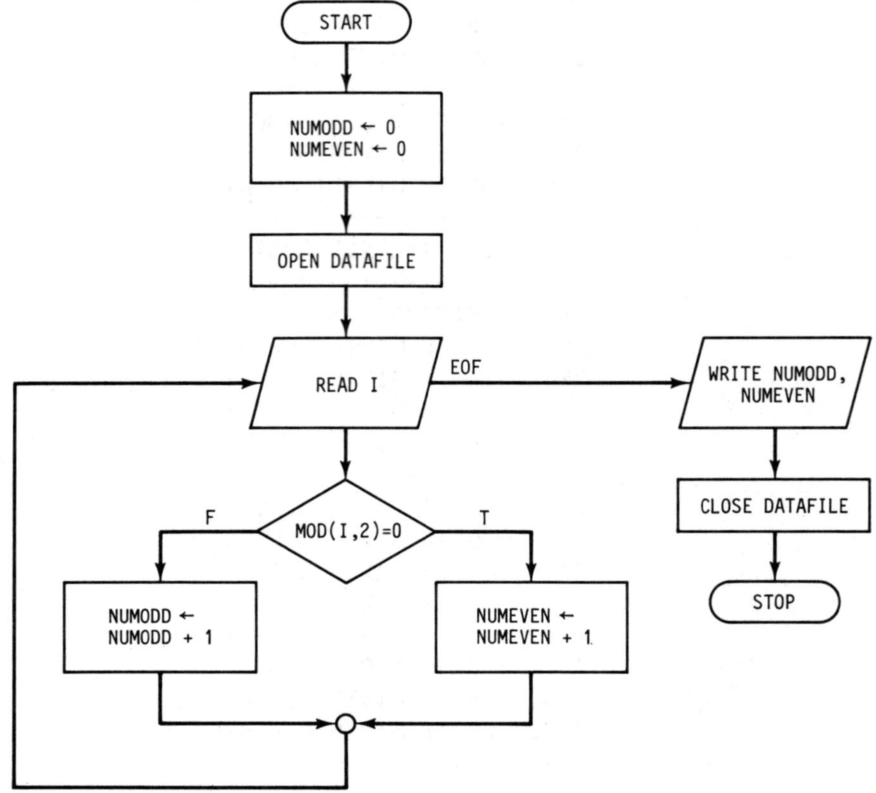

Figure 9.29 Flowchart for Problem 9.7.

Now rewind the file and repeat the above, but this time skip all the even-numbered records, i.e., skip records 2, 4, 6, 8, . . . , 200. This is easily accomplished with / input editing.

Rewind the file again and repeat the above, but this time skip all odd-numbered records, i.e., skip records 1, 3, 5, 7, . . . , 199. This is also easily done through / input editing.

Rewind the file a third time and repeat the above, but this time skip all the records, the last digits of which are not 0 or 5.

Rewind the file again and then space forward until you encounter the first record with a 1 in column 5. Report the position of that record.

Rewind the file DATA1 once again, and also open the file DATA2. These two files have identical records in one location only. Find that location and report it. This step is most readily performed by treating the content of a typical record as a 10-digit integer because only two numbers need be compared for each record rather than ten.

Now close file DATA1 and rewind file DATA2. Regard each record of file DATA2 as containing the 10 one-digit integers K1, K2, K3, . . . , K10. Read a record and form a sum TOTAL depending upon whether K9, K7, and K5 are odd or even. Refer to the flowchart for details.

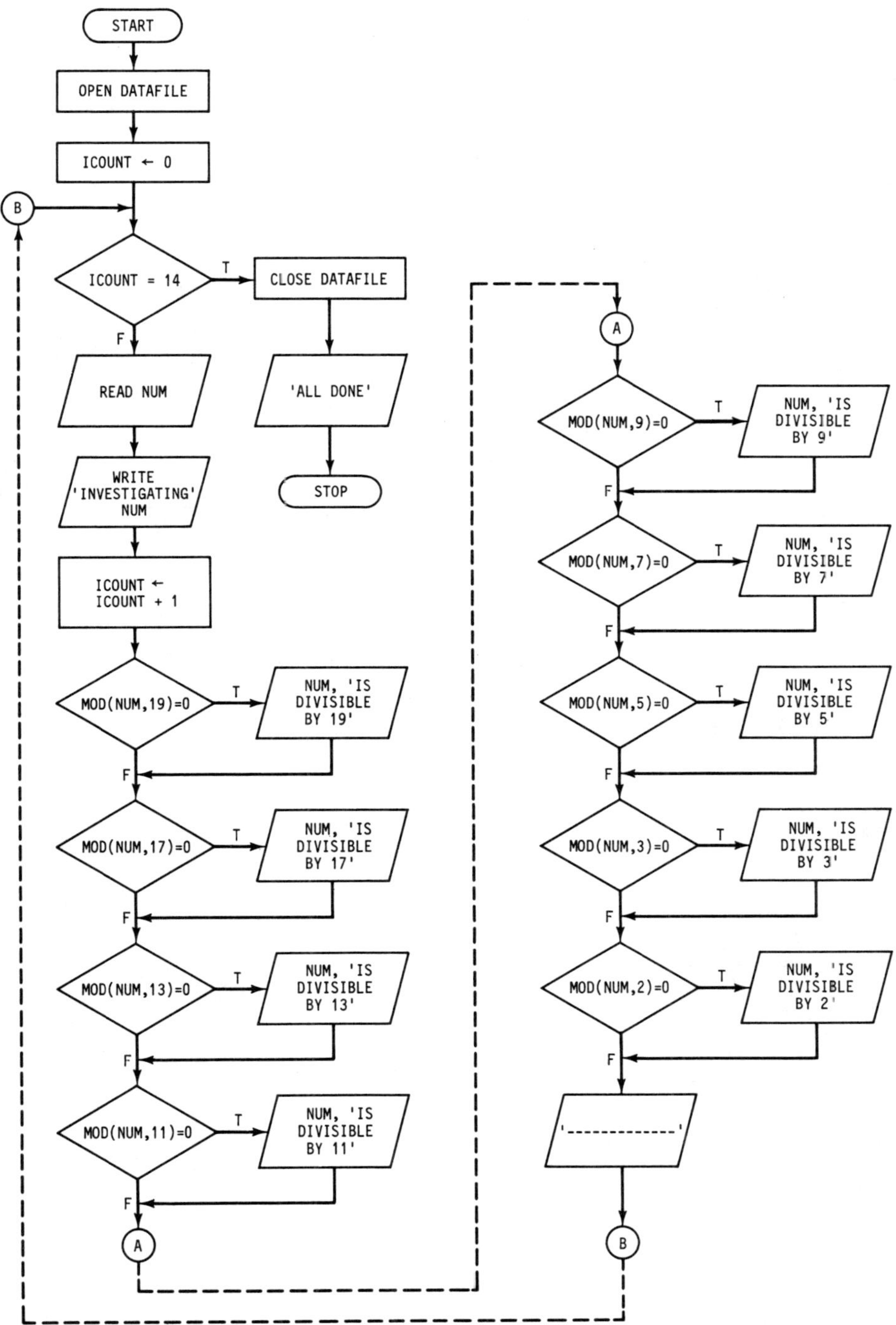

Figure 9.30 Flowchart for Problem 9.8.

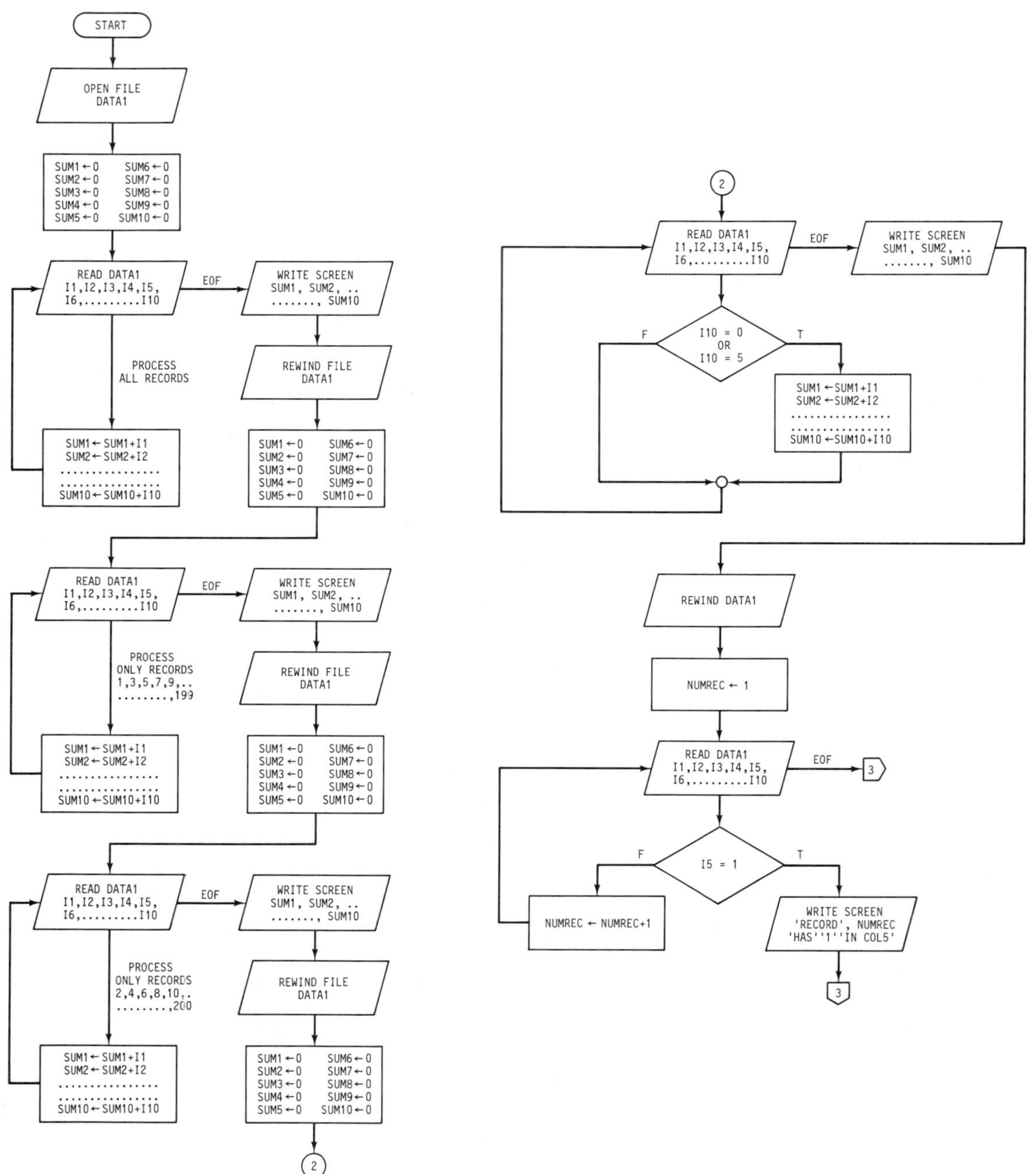

Figure 9.31 Flowchart for Problem 9.9.

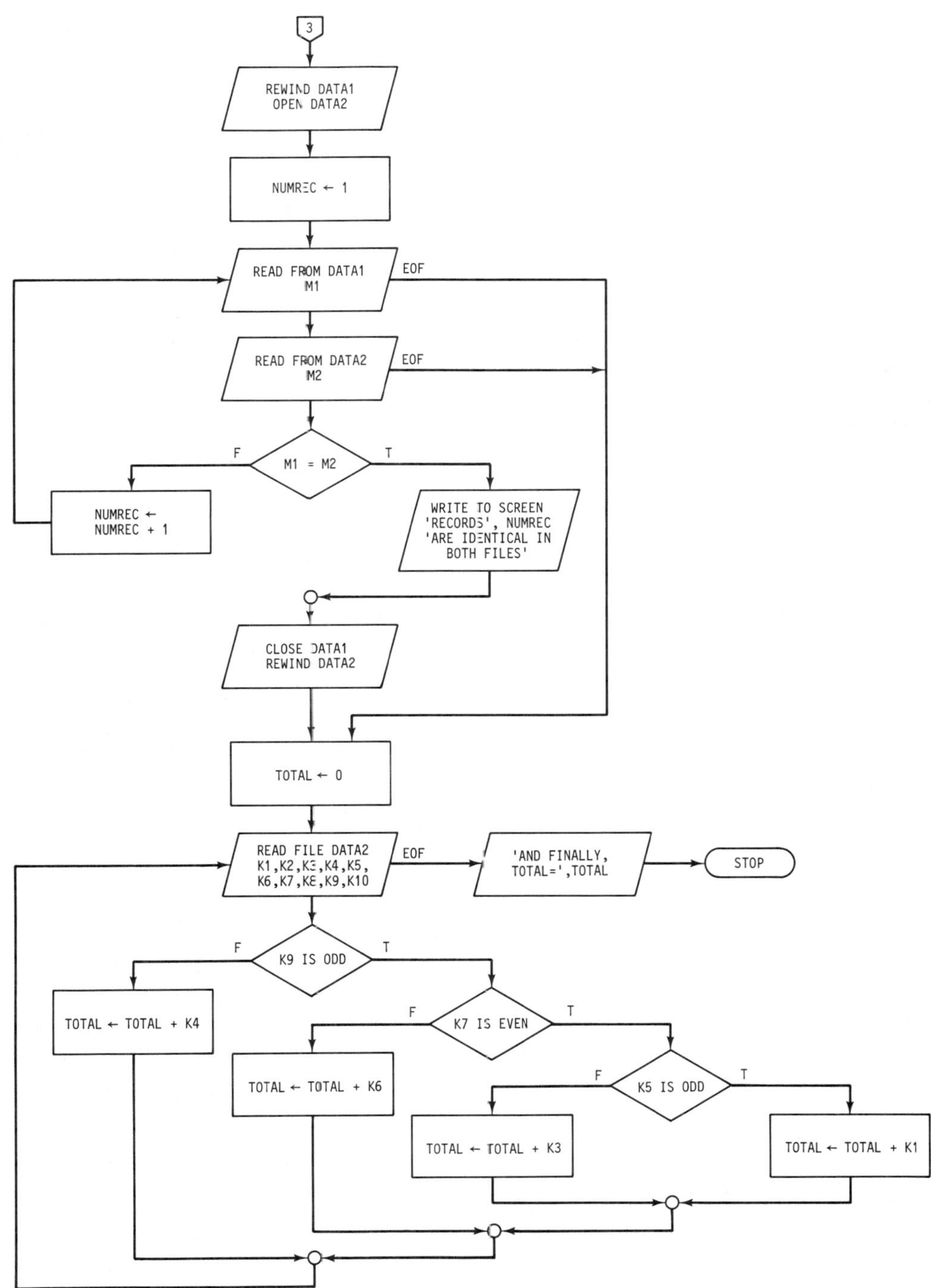

Figure 9.31 (Cont.)

Please note: This problem is not difficult *if* you stick to the flowchart. As you can see, several GO TO statements are required—as many as nine. The entire program can be done in about 120 statements, provided your system allows the following multiple assignment statement:

```
SUM1=SUM2=SUM3=SUM4=SUM5=SUM6=SUM7=SUM8=SUM9=SUM1Ø=Ø.
```

The alternative is to use ten individual assignment statements. Because the sums have to be initialized four times, you save 36 statements. The expected output is

```
                        SUM1 SUM2 SUM3 SUM4 SUM5 SUM6 SUM7 SUM8 SUM9 SUM1Ø
                        ==== ==== ==== ==== ==== ==== ==== ==== ==== =====
ALL RECORDS:               Ø  3Ø5  894  871  826  876  9Ø3  896  934   931
ODD-NUMBERED RECORDS:      Ø  151  454  414  4Ø6  449  452  44Ø  452   483
EVEN-NUMBERED RECORDS:     Ø  154  44Ø  457  42Ø  427  451  456  482   448
LAST DIGIT Ø OR 5:         Ø   57  18Ø  147  155  157  134  168  18Ø   1ØØ
RECORD 16 HAS '1' IN COLUMN 5
RECORDS 77 ARE IDENTICAL IN BOTH FILES
AND FINALLY, TOTAL = 742
```

9.10. This problem is an extension of Prob. 8.6. If you have deleted the file DIRFILE created by the small program in Prob. 8.5, you should recreate it.

In this problem, you are asked to develop a program to maintain the direct-access file DIRFILE. The program has the ability to display the contents of a specific record, it permits you to create new records, and it allows the contents of specified records to be updated. It should be clear that such a program could serve as the skeleton of a payroll program, for example, where files are accessed randomly to display and update employee records, and where it must be possible to create new employee records.

You recall that the file DIRFILE contains formatted six-byte records, the implications of which were discussed in Prob. 8.6. If you don't recall the details, you may wish to refer back to Prob. 8.6. We will carry the six-byte limitations over to this problem for no particularly clever technical reason, other than to illustrate that at times it is possible to live with restrictions.

The program's logic flow is mapped out in the flowchart of Fig. 9.32, and the interaction between you and the final program follows. The flowchart and the sample interaction will give you very clear guidance as you develop the program. The flowchart is designed around the computed GO TO statement, although other approaches are possible and somewhat more elegant. Problem 9.11 examines such an approach. Anyway, follow the flowchart and launch out to write a potent and compact program. You will find that fewer than 60 statements are necessary, but you should be distressed by the relatively large numbers of GO TO statements required—seven, not counting the computed GO TO, which should really be counted as another four, for a total of eleven. After you get over your initial happiness over the impressive abilities of the program, you will realize that the user interface isn't all that clean. The program will be tackled again after the chapter on character data and cleaned up considerably.

The interaction between the user and the computer follows. Study it to understand just how this exceptionally important program behaves.

```
DO YOU WISH TO: (1) READ, (2) CREATE, (3) UPDATE, OR (4) QUIT
SPECIFY 1, 2, 3, OR 4
?1
READ WHICH RECORD
?5
FOUND   5.55 ON RECORD    5
```

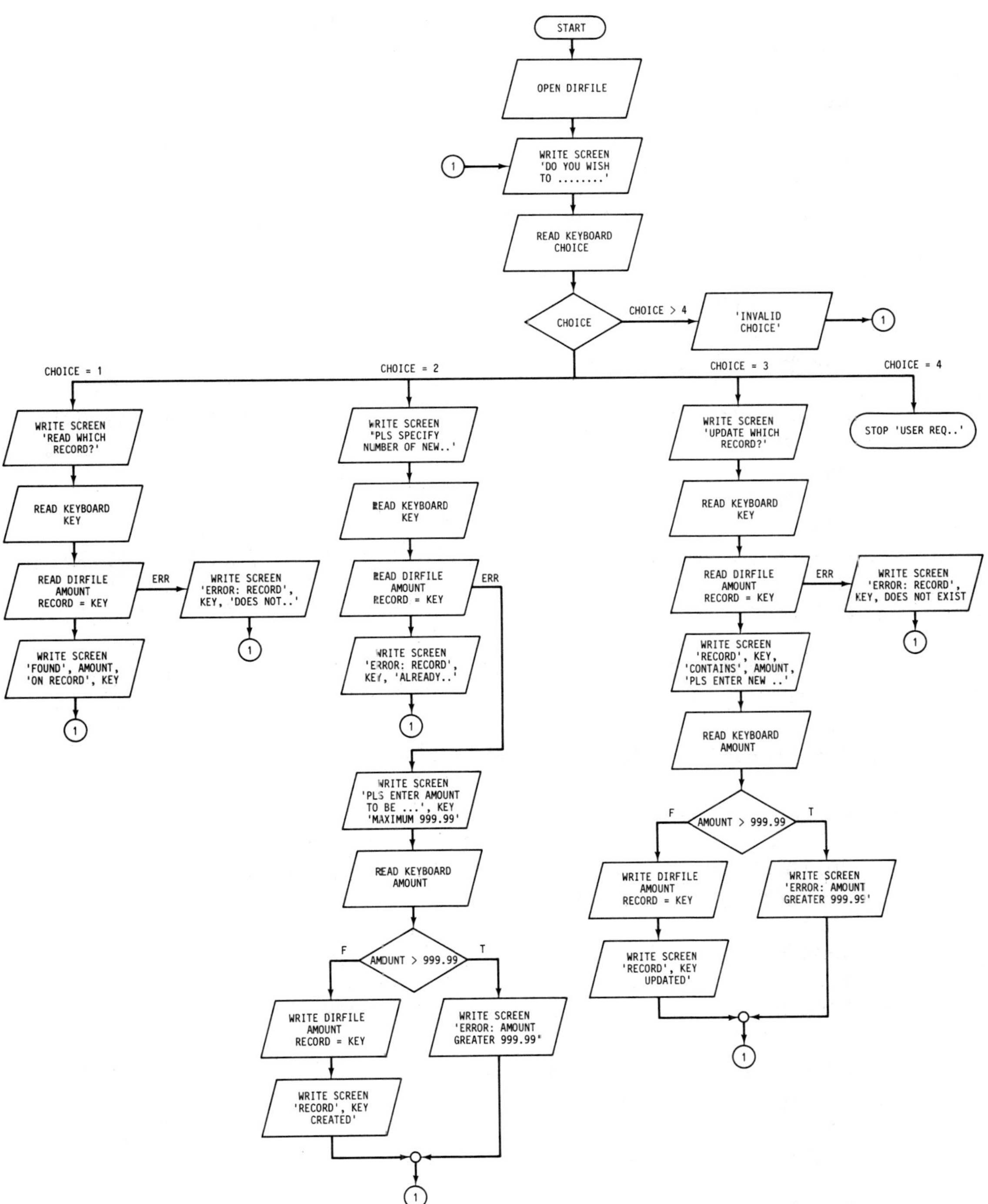

Figure 9.32 Flowchart for Problem 9.10.

```
DO YOU WISH TO: (1) READ, (2) CREATE, (3) UPDATE, OR (4) QUIT
SPECIFY 1, 2, 3, OR 4
?1
READ WHICH RECORD
?2
FOUND   2.22 ON RECORD    2

DO YOU WISH TO: (1) READ, (2) CREATE, (3) UPDATE, OR (4) QUIT
SPECIFY 1, 2, 3, OR 4
?1
READ WHICH RECORD
?14
ERROR: RECORD 14 DOES NOT EXIST

DO YOU WISH TO: (1) READ, (2) CREATE, (3) UPDATE, OR (4) QUIT
SPECIFY 1, 2, 3, OR 4
?2
PLS SPECIFY THE NUMBER OF THE NEW RECORD
?14
PLS ENTER AMOUNT TO BE WRITTEN TO RECORD 14 (MAXIMUM 999.99)
?1Ø3.14
RECORD 14 CREATED

DO YOU WISH TO: (1) READ, (2) CREATE, (3) UPDATE, OR (4) QUIT
SPECIFY 1, 2, 3, OR 4
?2
PLS SPECIFY THE NUMBER OF THE NEW RECORD
?14
ERROR: RECORD 14 ALREADY EXISTS

DO YOU WISH TO: (1) READ, (2) CREATE, (3) UPDATE, OR (4) QUIT
SPECIFY 1, 2, 3, OR 4
?3
UPDATE WHICH RECORD
?12
RECORD 12 DOES NOT EXIST - CANNOT UPDATE

DO YOU WISH TO: (1) READ, (2) CREATE, (3) UPDATE, OR (4) QUIT
SPECIFY 1, 2, 3, OR 4
?3
UPDATE WHICH RECORD
?14
RECORD  14 CONTAINS 1Ø3.14
PLEASE ENTER NEW AMOUNT
?23.99
RECORD 14  UPDATED
```

```
DO YOU WISH TO: (1) READ, (2) CREATE, (3) UPDATE, OR (4) QUIT
SPECIFY 1, 2, 3, OR 4
?1
READ WHICH RECORD
?14
FOUND  23.99 ON RECORD   14

DO YOU WISH TO: (1) READ, (2) CREATE, (3) UPDATE, OR (4) QUIT
SPECIFY 1, 2, 3, OR 4
?8

ERROR:  INVALID CHOICE

DO YOU WISH TO: (1) READ, (2) CREATE, (3) UPDATE, OR (4) QUIT
SPECIFY 1, 2, 3, OR 4
?4
 *STOP* USER-REQUESTED EXIT
```

9.11. The file-maintenance program in Prob. 9.10 was based on the computed GO TO statement. The flowchart of Fig. 9.33 shows how the same program can be based on the IF()THEN . . . ELSE IF()THEN . . . ELSE IF()THEN . . . ELSE . . . END IF construct. Only four GO TO statements are required now. Use the flowchart to write the program. The interaction between the user and the computer must be the same as shown in Prob. 9.10.

9.12. Modify either Prob. 9.10 or 9.11 to remove the six-byte restriction by invoking the unformatted option in the open, and a record length of one word. Keep in mind that some systems expect you to specify the record length in bytes, even when dealing with unformatted records. For more details, refer to the discussion near the end of Prob. 8.6. For this experiment, you will need an unformatted version of DIRFILE. Make the appropriate modification to the program in Prob. 8.5.

9.13. Figure 9.26 presents a flowchart associated with Ex. 9.10. Explain precisely why the program that follows does *not* conform to the flowchart. The difference is subtle, but highly important. The program would appear to behave exactly as required by the flowchart, producing identical output. Can you explain why? Under what conditions would the differences manifest themselves?

9.14. Modify the flowchart of Fig. 9.26 to conform to the right-hand program in Ex. 9.10.

```
    1 READ(5,*,END=99)L
      IF(L.GT.99)GO TO 1
*
      IF(MOD(L,2).EQ.Ø)THEN
        PRINT *,'L IS EVEN'
      ELSE
        IF(L.GT.21)PRINT *,'*'
        IF(L.GT.41)PRINT *,'**'
      END IF
*
        IF(L.EQ.19)PRINT *,'***'
        IF(L.EQ.21)PRINT *,'****'
        IF(L.EQ.23)PRINT *,'*****'
        PRINT *,'******'
*
      GO TO 1
   99 STOP
      END
```

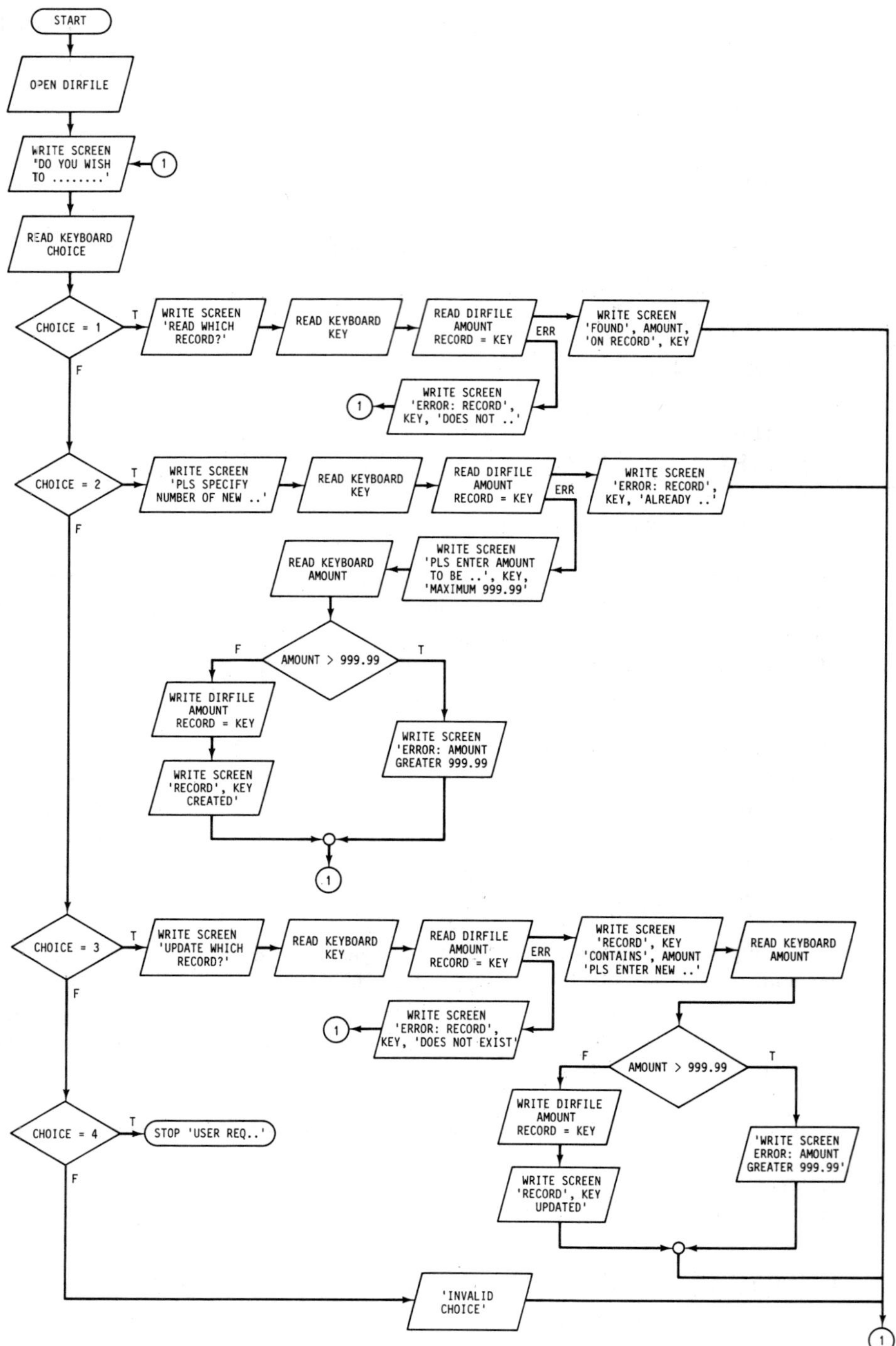

Figure 9.33 Flowchart for Problem 9.11.

10

DO-loops

In programming, it is frequently desired to execute a certain block of code a predetermined number of times. You might wish, for example, to produce a temperature conversion chart from Celsius to Fahrenheit from −200 to +200 degrees Celsius in steps of one degree, requiring similar code to be executed 401 times.

The technical term applied to the repetitive performance of a task is *iteration*, derived from the Latin verb *iterare, to repeat*. Iteration can certainly be built into a FORTRAN program with the aid of a GO TO statement that causes the logic to loop back to some point in the program, in conjunction with some IF statement that terminates the looping after a predetermined number of iterations. Many programmers do precisely that, but FORTRAN provides a simple construct to perform such iterations automatically. This construct is known as the *DO loop*, which has the general form shown in Fig. 10.1.

The first line of this structure is known as the *DO statement*. It is to be read as follows: DO repeatedly all the statements down to and including the statement with the label s, while the DO-variable I moves from LIM1 to the value LIM2 in steps of INCREMENT. The DO-loop behaves in the same manner as the program and flowchart segment shown in Fig. 10.2. If you take several moments to reason through these few lines of code, you will rapidly understand the DO-loop concept.

In Fig. 10.2, I is equivalent to the DO-variable I of Fig. 10.1. LIM1, called the *initial parameter*, can be either a constant or some expression, and its value becomes the initial value of the DO-variable I. The DO-variable is then compared to the *terminal parameter* LIM2, which may also be a constant or some expression.

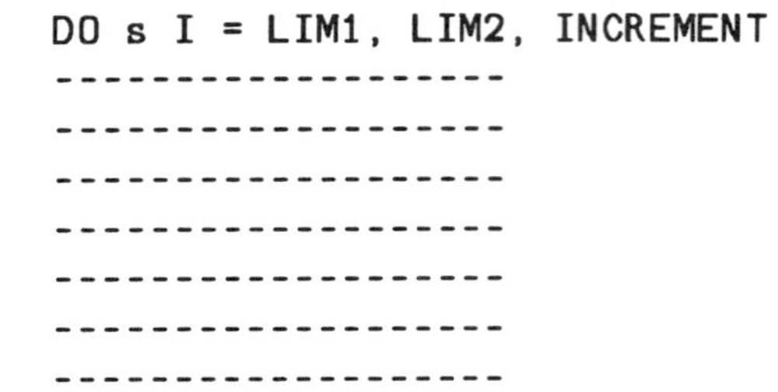

```
      DO s I = LIM1, LIM2, INCREMENT
      --------------------
      --------------------
      --------------------
      --------------------
      --------------------
      --------------------
      --------------------
s     CONTINUE
```

Figure 10.1 FORTRAN's iteration construct, the DO-loop.

If the value of the DO-variable is less than or equal to the terminal parameter, the block of statements is executed. The value of the *incrementation parameter* INCREMENT is then added to the DO-variable before it is again compared against LIM2. When the value of the DO-variable is found to be greater than LIM2, the logic leaves the structure.

It is stressed that the initial parameter LIM1, the terminal parameter LIM2, and the incrementation parameter INCREMENT can be simple integer or real constants or highly complex arithmetic expressions. It is also stressed that if the value of the initial parameter LIM1 is greater than that of the terminal parameter LIM2, the body of the loop is *not* executed, as you can easily deduce from Fig. 10.2.

Take another look at the general structure of the DO-loop in Fig. 10.1. As already mentioned, the opening statement is known as the DO statement. The labeled statement at the end is called the *terminal statement*. The block of statements between the DO statement and the terminal statement, indicated by dashed lines, can be any FORTRAN imperatives or logical constructs. The terminal statement itself need not be the CONTINUE statement, but can be some FORTRAN imperative. It cannot, however, be a branch statement such as GO TO, arithmetic IF, block IF, ELSE IF, END IF, RETURN, STOP, END, or another DO statement. Logical IF statements can appear, but only if they cause no branching. It is *always* safe to use a CONTINUE statement as the terminal statement, which is strongly recommended.

The statements between the DO statement and down to and including the terminal statement constitute the so-called *range* of the DO. As mentioned previously,

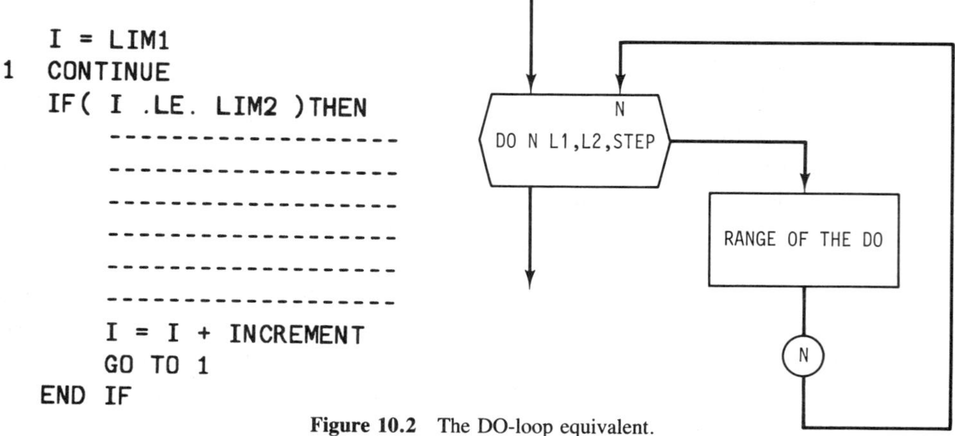

```
      I = LIM1
1     CONTINUE
      IF( I .LE. LIM2 )THEN
         --------------------
         --------------------
         --------------------
         --------------------
         --------------------
         --------------------
         I = I + INCREMENT
         GO TO 1
      END IF
```


Figure 10.2 The DO-loop equivalent.

the DO-variable I can be integer or real, and you can probably sense that the name of this DO-variable is arbitrary, provided it conforms to the standard FORTRAN variable-naming convention. The increment can be positive or negative or even fractional, but no attempt must be made to redefine the DO-variable within the range of the DO although it may be used in computations.

10.1 DO-LOOPS IN ACTION

If all this sounds somewhat obscure, a few examples will make it very tangible. The comments associated with the examples are important and must be considered carefully. The first few examples are small, and are designed to give you a feeling for the behavior of the DO-variable. Although we will stick to the X3.9–1978 convention of calling it the DO-variable, many refer to it as the *counter* or as the *index*.

The DO-variable in the first example is the integer variable I. The initial parameter is set to 1, the terminal parameter to 5, and the incrementation parameter is 1. The range of the DO consists of a PRINT statement and the CONTINUE statement. The output speaks for itself:

```
      DO 1 I = 1,5,1
      PRINT *,' I =',I
    1 CONTINUE
      END

 I = 1
 I = 2
 I = 3
 I = 4
 I = 5
```

You should now go to the computer to try the program. Seeing is more than believing because it adds a note of reality to something otherwise intangible.

In the next example, no incrementation parameter is specified. The machine always defaults to an increment of 1 when none is specified by the programmer.

```
      DO 1 I = 1,5
      PRINT *,' I =',I
    1 CONTINUE
      END

 I = 1
 I = 2
 I = 3
 I = 4
 I = 5
```

In the following example, an increment of 2 is specified. Notice that the DO-variable now has the arbitrary name M.

```
      DO 12 M = 1,5,2
      PRINT *,' M =', M
   12 CONTINUE
      END
```

```
 M = 1
 M = 3
 M = 5
```

The next example illustrates another arbitrary DO-variable name and an increment of 3. Note the last value reported, a case of *undershoot*.

```
      DO 19 MICHEL = 1,5,3
      PRINT *,' MICHEL =', MICHEL
   19 CONTINUE
      END
```

```
 MICHEL = 1
 MICHEL = 4
```

The next example demonstrates that the limits need not be positive. Again an increment of 1 is assumed by default.

```
      DO 3 KNOT = -5,-1
      PRINT *,' KNOT =', KNOT
    3 CONTINUE
      END
```

```
 KNOT = -5
 KNOT = -4
 KNOT = -3
 KNOT = -2
 KNOT = -1
```

The next example shows that the increment can also be negative, provided that the value of the initial parameter is greater than that of the terminal parameter.

```
      DO 17 NEG = 8,1,-1
      PRINT *,' NEG =', NEG
   17 CONTINUE
      END
```

```
 NEG = 8
 NEG = 7
 NEG = 6
 NEG = 5
 NEG = 4
 NEG = 3
 NEG = 2
 NEG = 1
```

A further example of negative incrementing follows. Negative incrementing is also known as *decrementing*.

```
      DO 2 JJJ = 11,1,-3
      PRINT *,' JJJ =', JJJ
    2 CONTINUE
      END
```

```
JJJ = 11
JJJ = 8
JJJ = 5
JJJ = 2
```

This time, the DO-variable is real, and so are the limits and the increment. All three are fractional.

```
      DO 12 X = Ø.Ø1, Ø.25, Ø.Ø4
      PRINT *,' X =', X
   12 CONTINUE
      END
```

```
X = .1ØØØØØØE-Ø1
X = .5ØØØØØØE-Ø1
X = .9ØØØØØØE-Ø1
X = .13ØØØØØ
X = .17ØØØØØ
X = .21ØØØØØ
X = .25ØØØØØ
```

Another real DO-variable is decremented next. The output is highly instructive because it emphasizes once again that internal floating-point representation is not 100 percent accurate. A cursory look at the DO statement would lead you to expect 10 lines of output, but only nine appear. The output, of course, will be highly machine dependent, so don't be surprised if your machine behaves a little differently.

```
      DO 7 ZETA = 1.8,Ø,-Ø.2
      PRINT *,' ZETA =',ZETA
    7 CONTINUE
      END
```

```
ZETA = 1.8ØØØØØ
ZETA = 1.6ØØØØØ
ZETA = 1.4ØØØØØ
ZETA = 1.2ØØØØØ
ZETA = .9999998
ZETA = .7999998
ZETA = .5999998
ZETA = .3999998
ZETA = .1999998
```

The following four examples dispense with the CONTINUE statement to emphasize that the loop can end on FORTRAN imperative statements provided that such statements do not cause unconditional branching. As stressed earlier, however, it is good practice to use CONTINUE as the terminal statement.

This same set of four examples is also designed to illustrate what to expect when LIM1 = LIM2 and what happens when the increment and LIM1 and LIM2 are in conflict. Upon studying the output, you will notice that when the limits are the same, the loop executes one cycle, a fact we already stressed in connection with our discussion of Fig. 10.2. You will recall that if LIM1 is greater than LIM2 and the increment is positive, *no* cycle is executed. Another contradictory situation arises when LIM1 is less than LIM2 and the increment is negative.

In older versions of FORTRAN, the range of the DO was executed before the limits were tested. The range of the DO was, therefore, always executed at least once, even when contradictory limits and increments were specified in the DO statement. In ANSI FORTRAN 77, the limits are tested before the range of the DO is executed, and contradictions are detected. When such contradictions are found, the range of the DO is not executed even once, and this is one of the more important differences between FORTRAN 77 and older implementations.

Study and run the four little tests. Output is produced in only two cases as you can see. The other two tests violate the limits and no ouput results. Because many older implementations of FORTRAN did produce once cycle under contradictory conditions, problems are frequently encountered when programs are taken from one machine to another; the results may differ. The DO limits are one of the first areas to be investigated when searching for the reasons.

```
          DO 122 J = 1Ø,1Ø
    122   PRINT *,' J =',J
          END

  J = 1Ø


          DO 122 J = 1Ø,9
    122   PRINT *,' J =',J
          END


          DO 122 J = 9,9,-1
    122   PRINT *,' J =',J
          END

  J = 9


          DO 122 J = 9,1Ø,-1
    122   PRINT *,' J =',J
          END
```

The next example shows that LIM1, LIM2, and the INCREMENT can be expressions to be computed at run time. This is a very powerful feature. In the example, LIM1 is SQRT(3.2), LIM2 is 3.2**2, and the increment is MOD(3.2,1.)+1.

```
      X=3.2
      DO 1 Y = SQRT(X), X**2, MOD(X,1.)+1.
    1 PRINT *,' Y =',Y
      END
```

```
Y = 1.788854
Y = 2.988854
Y = 4.188854
Y = 5.388855
Y = 6.588855
Y = 7.788855
Y = 8.988855
Y = 10.18885
```

10.2 DO-LOOP FLOWCHART SYMBOL

Several DO-loop flowchart symbols can be found in the literature. The symbol of Fig. 10.3 appears to convey the FORTRAN DO-loop structure and behavior most effectively, but be aware that you will encounter other symbols. If you compare the symbol with Fig. 10.2, you will notice considerable similarity.

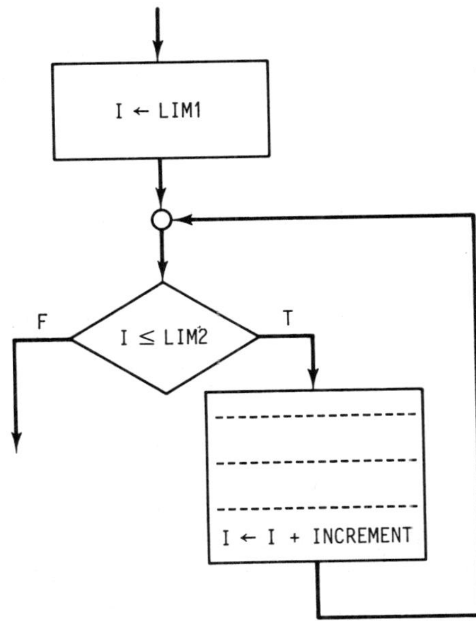

Figure 10.3 DO-loop flowchart symbol.

10.3 NESTED DO-LOOPS

Because the range of a DO-loop can contain executable FORTRAN structures, it should be obvious that it could also contain other DO-loops. A DO-loop within a DO-loop is known as a *nested* DO-loop, and there is no limit to the number of levels of nesting. The only conditions are that the loops cannot intersect, and that an inner loop must not use the same DO-variable as an outer loop, but these conditions are rather self-evident.

An example follows in which I is the DO-variable of the outer loop, and J is the DO-variable of the inner loop. There is a WRITE statement in the inner loop to enable you to watch the process. The flowchart is shown in Fig. 10.4. Study the output with care:

```
      DO 2 I = 1,3
      DO 1 J = 5,15,5
      WRITE(6,3)I,J
    3 FORMAT(' OUTER LOOP I = ',I2,/,' INNER LOOP J = ',I2)
    1 CONTINUE
    2 CONTINUE
      END
```

```
 OUTER LOOP I =  1
 INNER LOOP J =  5
 OUTER LOOP I =  1
 INNER LOOP J = 1Ø
 OUTER LOOP I =  1
 INNER LOOP J = 15
 OUTER LOOP I =  2
 INNER LOOP J =  5
 OUTER LOOP I =  2
 INNER LOOP J = 1Ø
 OUTER LOOP I =  2
 INNER LOOP J = 15
 OUTER LOOP I =  3
 INNER LOOP J =  5
 OUTER LOOP I =  3
 INNER LOOP J = 1Ø
 OUTER LOOP I =  3
 INNER LOOP J = 15
```

Although DO-loops must not intersect, they may share a common terminal statement. The previous program can therefore be abbreviated as shown, although the previous version is preferred.

```
      DO 1 I = 1,3
      DO 1 J = 5,15,5
1     WRITE(6,3)I,J
3     FORMAT(' OUTER LOOP I = ',I,/,' INNER LOOP J = ',I)
      END
```

This is a good point to emphasize that although a DO-variable can be used in calculations, it cannot be redefined within the range of the DO. It must be clearly understood that the DO-variable is under the full control of the DO statement, which determines the lower limit, the upper limit, and the increment. The programmer must not interfere with this autonomy.

It is quite legal to jump out of a DO-loop before the DO-variable has reached its limit. You might include some logical construct, for example, watching for certain conditions to arise, and then transfer control to some labeled statement outside the loop.

While it is legal to jump out of a DO-loop prematurely, it is never legal to jump into the middle of one because such a jump would bypass the DO statement, where the counter is initialized and where the limits and the increment are set.

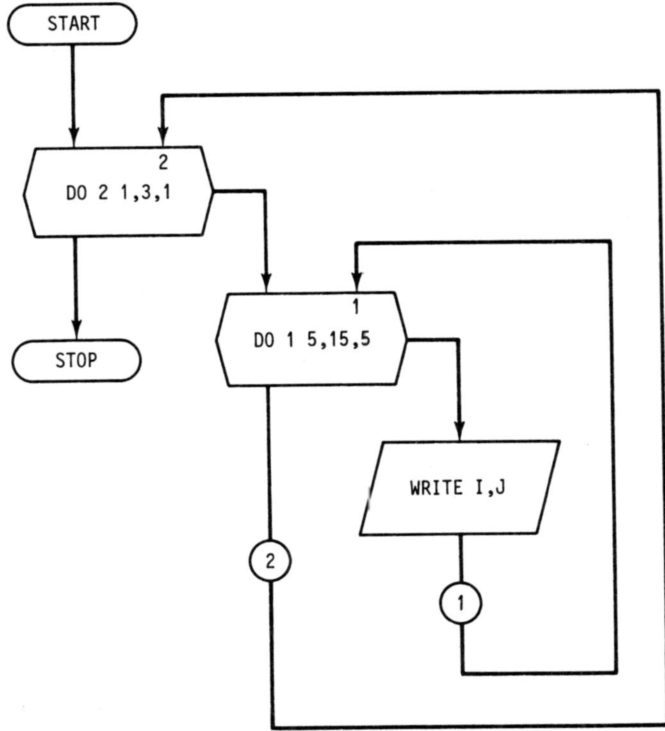

Figure 10.4 Flowchart involving a nested DO-loop.

It must also be realized that the DO-variable is defined only within the range of the DO. Once you get beyond the terminal statement of the DO-loop, the DO-variable can no longer be used in calculations. It is true that the DO-variable still has some value beyond the range of the DO, but that value can vary from machine to machine. On some, it may be the same as the upper limit reached while the DO was in operation, or it might be greater by the increment. It should not be used outside the range of the DO, in other words.

An example follows to illustrate just how the DO-variable can be used in a calculation. It is a delightful application of the FORTRAN DO-loop, one of the most extensively used features of the language. The program is designed to generate a temperature-conversion chart from Celsius to Fahrenheit. The simplicity of the logic is conveyed by the flowchart of Fig. 10.5.

```
      WRITE(6,3)
    3 FORMAT(/,'    CONVERSION CHART   ',/,'    ================',/)
      WRITE(6,4)
    4 FORMAT(' CELSIUS    FAHRENHEIT',/,' -------     ----------')
      DO 1 CELS = -1Ø,11,3
      FAHREN = 32. + 9./5.*CELS
      WRITE(6,2)CELS,FAHREN
    2 FORMAT(1X,F7.2,F13.2)
    1 CONTINUE
      END
```

```
    CONVERSION CHART
    ================

 CELSIUS      FAHRENHEIT
 -------      ----------
  -1Ø.ØØ        14.ØØ
   -7.ØØ        19.4Ø
   -4.ØØ        24.8Ø
   -1.ØØ        3Ø.2Ø
    2.ØØ        35.6Ø
    5.ØØ        41.ØØ
    8.ØØ        46.4Ø
   11.ØØ        51.8Ø
```

The final program generates three copies of the temperature-conversion chart of the previous example by placing the chart-producing code within an outer DO loop executing three cycles. The flowchart is shown in Fig. 10.6.

```
   DO 5 NCOPY = 1,3
   WRITE(6,3)
3  FORMAT(/,'   CONVERSION CHART   ',/,'   ================',/)
   WRITE(6,4)
4  FORMAT(' CELSIUS   FAHRENHEIT',/,' -------     ----------')
   DO 1 CELS = -10,11,3
   FAHREN = 32. + 9./5.*CELS
   WRITE(6,2)CELS,FAHREN
2  FORMAT(1X,F7.2,F13.2)
1  CONTINUE
5  CONTINUE
   END
```

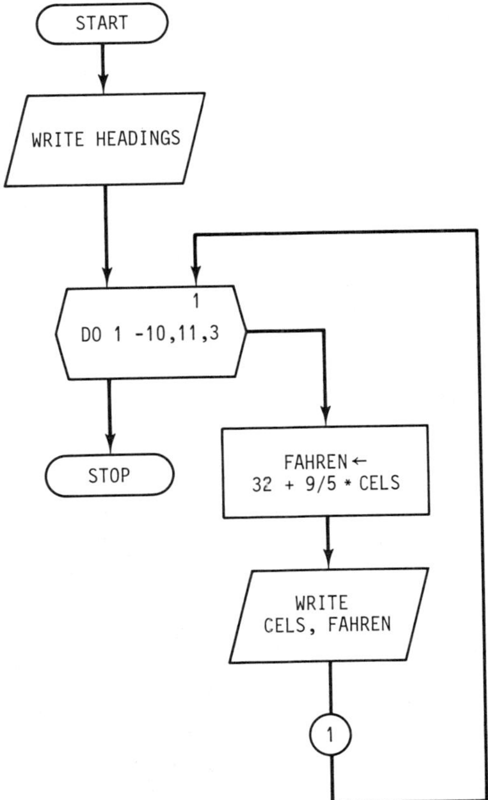

Figure 10.5 Flowchart for the temperature-conversion program.

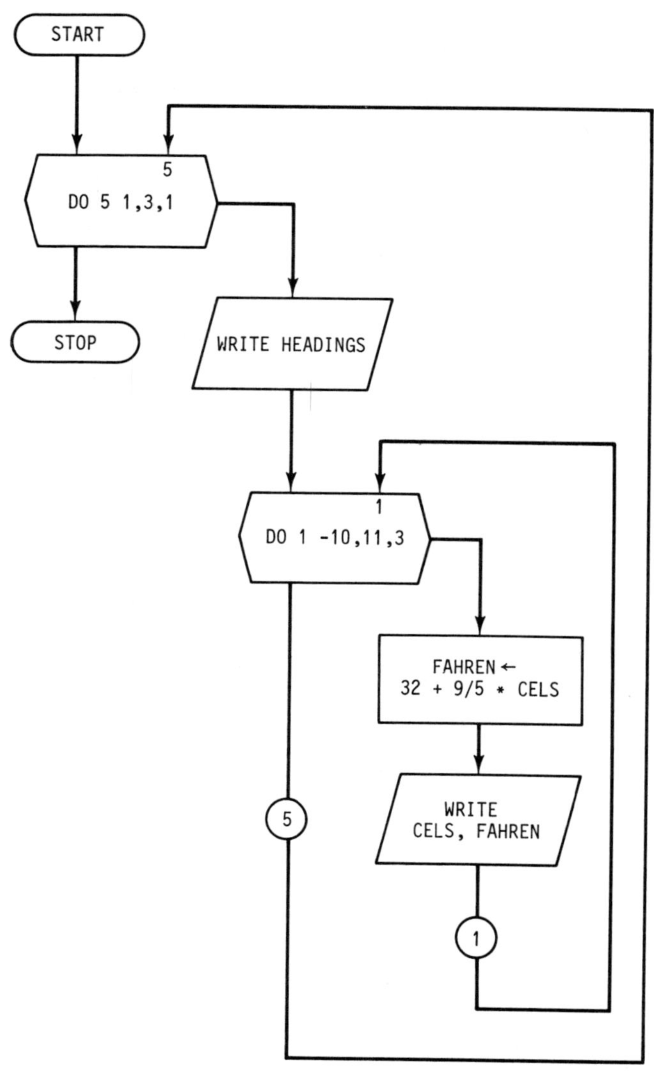

Figure 10.6 Flowchart for generating three copies of the temperature-conversion chart.

10.4 PROBLEMS

10.1. Show the output generated by each of the following programs:

```
      DO 1 MMM=1,6
      PRINT*,MMM
    1 CONTINUE
      END
```

```
      DO 98 K=1,83,20
      PRINT*,K
   98 CONTINUE
      END
```

```
      IMPLICIT INTEGER (A-Z)
      LOW=19
      HIGH=45
      STEP=5
      DO 1 COUNT=LOW,HIGH,STEP
      PRINT*,COUNT
    1 CONTINUE
      END
```

```
      DO 34 L=83,81,-1
      PRINT*,L
   34 CONTINUE
      END
```

```
      DO 12 L=83,81
      PRINT*,L
   12 CONTINUE
      END
```

10.2. Some of the following programs have errors. Describe these clearly. Show the output for programs without errors.

```
      DO 1 X=1.,1Ø.
      PRINT*,X*X*1Ø.
      CONTINUE
      END
```

```
      DO 1 Y=1.,1Ø.,Ø.1
      Y=Y*1ØØ.
      PRINT*,Y
    1 CONTINUE
      END
```

```
      DO 42 W=1.,1Ø.
      Y=W**2
      PRINT*,W,Y
   42 CONTINUE
      END
```

```
      M=19
      GO TO 39
      DO 3 I=1,1ØØ
      PRINT*,I
      CONTINUE
      END
```

```
      DO 3 OUTER=1.,5.
      DO 4 INNER=6,1Ø
      PRINT*,INNER,OUTER
    3 CONTINUE
    4 CONTINUE
      END
```

```
      DO 3 OUTER=1.,5.,1.5
      DO 4 INNER=6,1Ø
      PRINT*,INNER,OUTER
    4 CONTINUE
    3 CONTINUE
      END
```

```
      DO 4 OUTER=1.,5.
      DO 4 INNER=6,1Ø
      PRINT*,INNER,OUTER
      END
```

```
      NUM=6
      DO 19934 K=1,5Ø
19934 WRITE(6,19935)(NUM,L=1,8Ø)
19935 FORMAT(1X,8ØI1)
      END
```

Note that the last program on the right employs a FORTRAN feature that you haven't met before. Try to guess what the program might do, then run it, and study the output. You will meet this feature again soon.

10.3. Explain precisely what each of the following two programs does.

```
      SUM=Ø.
      A=1./3.
      DO 19 I=1,1ØØØØØ
      SUM=SUM+A
   19 CONTINUE
      PRINT*,SUM
      END
```

```
      DO 3 I=1,1Ø
    3 WRITE(6,2)MAX(1,2,3,4,5,I)
    2 FORMAT(1X,I3)
      END
```

10.4. How many multiplications does each of the following programs perform, and how many lines of output does each generate?

<table>
<tr>
<td>

```
      DO 1 I1=1,1ØØ
      X=3.4*12.
    1 CONTINUE
      PRINT*,X
      END
      (1Ø²,1)
```

</td>
<td>

```
      DO 1 I1=1,1ØØ
      DO 2 I2=1,1ØØ
      X=3.4*12.
    2 CONTINUE
    1 CONTINUE
      PRINT*,X
      END
      (1Ø⁴,1)
```

</td>
<td>

```
      DO 1 I1=1,1ØØ
      DO 2 I2=1,1ØØ
      X=3.4*12.
      PRINT*,X
    2 CONTINUE
    1 CONTINUE
      END
      (1Ø⁴,1Ø⁴)
```

</td>
</tr>
<tr>
<td>

```
      DO 1 I1=1,1ØØØ
      DO 2 I2=1,1ØØ
      X=3.4*12.
    2 CONTINUE
    1 CONTINUE
      PRINT*,X
      END
      (1Ø⁵,1)
```

</td>
<td>

```
      DO 1 I1=1,1ØØ
      DO 2 I2=1,1ØØ
      DO 3 I3=1,1ØØ
      DO 4 I4=1,1ØØ
      X=3.4*12.
      PRINT*,X
    4 CONTINUE
    3 CONTINUE
    2 CONTINUE
    1 CONTINUE
      END
      (1Ø⁸,1Ø⁸)
```

</td>
<td>

```
      DO 1 I1=1,1ØØ
      DO 2 I2=1,1ØØ
      DO 3 I3=1,1ØØ
      DO 4 I4=1,1ØØ
      X=3.4*12.
    4 CONTINUE
      PRINT*,X
    3 CONTINUE
    2 CONTINUE
    1 CONTINUE
      END
      (1Ø⁸,1Ø⁶)
```

</td>
</tr>
<tr>
<td>

```
      DO 1 I1=1,1Ø
      DO 2 I2=1,1ØØ
      DO 3 I3=1,1ØØØ
      DO 4 I4=1,1Ø
      X=3.4*12.
    4 CONTINUE
    3 CONTINUE
      PRINT*,X
    2 CONTINUE
    1 CONTINUE
      END
      (1Ø⁷,1Ø³)
```

</td>
<td>

```
      DO 1 I1=1,1ØØ
      DO 2 I2=1,1ØØ
      DO 3 I3=1,1ØØ
      DO 4 I4=1,1ØØ
      X=3.4*12.
    4 CONTINUE
    3 CONTINUE
    2 CONTINUE
      PRINT*,X
    1 CONTINUE
      END
      (1Ø⁸,1Ø²)
```

</td>
<td>

```
      DO 1 I1=1,1ØØ
      DO 2 I2=1,1ØØ
      DO 3 I3=1,1ØØ
      DO 4 I4=1,1ØØ
      DO 5 I5=1,1ØØ
      X=3.4*12.
    5 CONTINUE
    4 CONTINUE
    3 CONTINUE
    2 CONTINUE
      PRINT*,X
    1 CONTINUE
      END
      (1Ø¹Ø,1Ø²)
```

</td>
</tr>
</table>

10.5. Write a program that forms a sum by adding 0.1 100,000 times. Write the sum into F10.3 and study the output to see how far short it falls of the expected 10,000. Pattern your program after the first program in Prob. 10.3 and sketch its flowchart. (If you are using a shared system, other users might object if you repeatedly perform 100,000 additions. In that case, you may wish to scale the problem down to 10,000 additions, rather than lose your computer privileges. The phenomenon being investigated here will still surface sufficiently, but not quite so dramatically.)

10.6. The previous problem clearly demonstrated error accumulation inherent in floating-point calculations. The error has two specific sources, the first resulting from the fact that 0.1_{10} is a nonterminating fraction in the binary and hexadecimal systems (i.e., 0.1_{10} = $0.0001100110011001100110011001100\ldots_2 = 0.1999999999\ldots_{16}$) and therefore cannot be represented completely accurately in the finite number of bits of a word of memory. Most systems, however, round up the internal representation of 0.1_{10}, so that you would really expect the sum in the previous problem to be greater than 10,000 rather than smaller. We must, therefore, take a good look at the other potential source of error, the addition process itself. The next few steps are very easy to follow, and you should make every effort to understand them. To be specific, we try to understand just what happens when the computer is asked to add 0.1_{10} to 9000_{10}. The hex equivalents of these two quantities are shown:

$$0.1_{10} = 0.199999\ldots_{16} = 0.199999\ldots \times 10^0_{16}$$

and

$$9000_{10} = 2328_{16} = 0.2328 \times 10^4_{16}$$

The question is how does the computer go about adding such normalized hexadecimal floating-point representations, that is, how does it add the following two numbers:

$$\begin{array}{r} 0.19999\text{A} \times 10^0_{16} \\ +\ 0.232800 \times 10^4_{16} \end{array}$$

It is obvious that the addition cannot be performed unless the exponents are equal, and so we try again:

$$\begin{array}{r} 0.000019 \times 10^4_{16} \\ +\ 0.232800 \times 10^4_{16} \\ \hline 0.232819 \times 10^4_{16} \end{array}$$

You noticed that as we adjusted the exponent of the first addend, four of the significant digits were lost, and the number became smaller. In fact, the number dropped from very slightly more than 0.1_{10} to approximately 0.0977_{10}.

Let's try another addition. The first addend is still the same, but the second addend is much larger now:

$$\begin{array}{r} 0.19999\text{A} \times 10^0_{16} \\ +\ 0.232800 \times 10^6_{16} \end{array}$$

Again, the exponents must be made the same before the addition can be performed, and we encounter the following situation:

$$\begin{array}{r} 0.000000 \times 10^6_{16} \\ +\ 0.232800 \times 10^6_{16} \\ \hline 0.232800 \times 10^4_{16} \end{array}$$

Notice that the first addend vanished in the process of making the exponents equal. It could be argued, of course, that we did not carry enough mantissa digits, but we did carry six, which is what most computers accommodate in short floating-point mode. Double precision (long floating-point) carries an additional eight digits, greatly improving the situation, but that's for later.

We can summarize by stating that whenever a small floating-point number is added to a much larger floating-point number, the exponents must first be made equal and the small number suffers a loss of significant digits. This loss grows as the difference in the magnitudes of the two addends increases. Ultimately, a situation can be reached in which the small addend vanishes in the process and no longer contributes to the sum.

Now that we understand the source of addition error in detail, we are in a position to attack it. An obvious approach is to break the 100,000 small numbers into several subgroups to produce subtotals. These subtotals are relatively small, the digit sliding is reduced considerably, and these subtotals can then be added to produce the final total. This approach is known as *batch adding* because we add the small numbers in batches.

Write a program that adds 0.1 100,000 times in 100 batches of 1000. The suggested procedure is indicated by the flowchart of Fig. 10.7. The output should have the form:

```
BATCH ADDITION PRODUCES    #####.###
STRAIGHT ADDITION PRODUCES #####.###
```

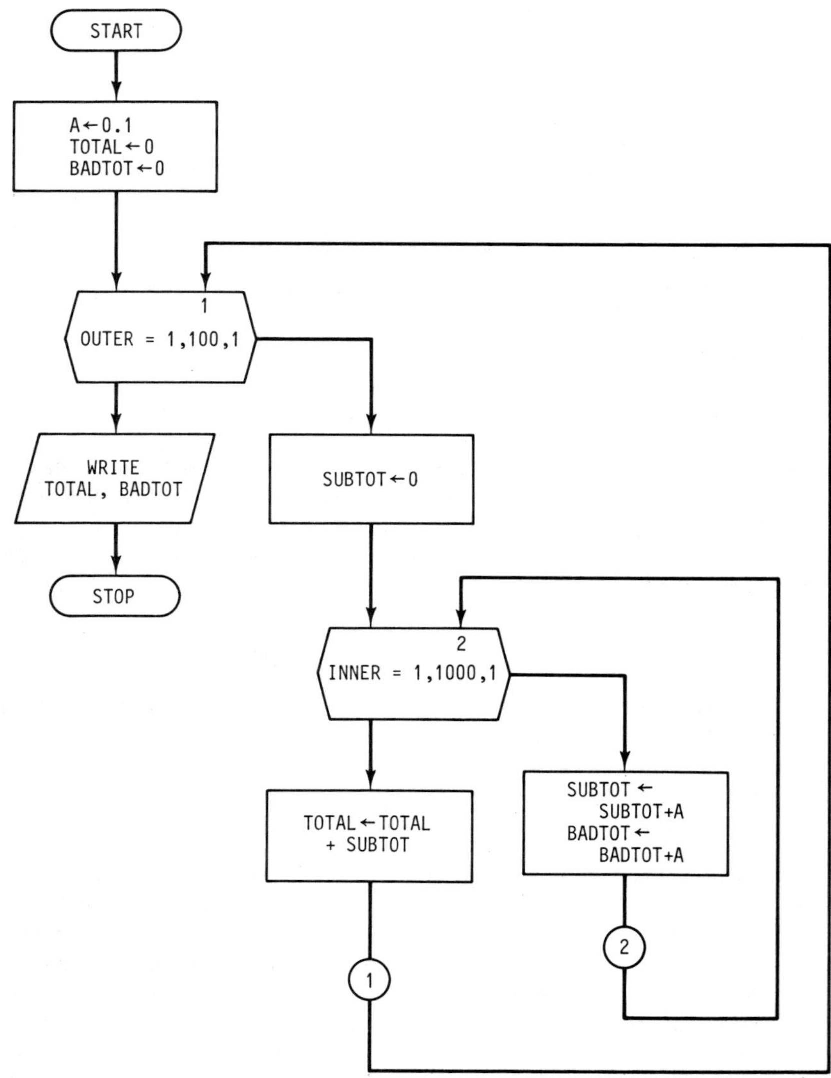

Figure 10.7 Flowchart for Problem 10.6.

10.7. $0.125_{10} = 0.200000_{16}$, suggesting that if 0.125_{10} were to be added 100,000 times, the sum should be very accurate because only the trailing zeros are lost, unless, of course, the difference in the addends becomes too great, and the 2 disappears. Substitute 0.125 for 0.1 in the program in Prob. 10.5 and run it again. All this should be a warning to those who like to compute certain problems in steps of 0.1, when 0.125 would be a far wiser choice.

10.8. Write a program that writes all the octal numbers from 0000 to 7777. A portion of the output follows and the suggested flowchart is shown in Fig. 10.8.

```
ØØØØ
ØØØ1
ØØØ2
ØØØ3
ØØØ4
ØØØ5
ØØØ6
ØØØ7
ØØ1Ø
ØØ11
ØØ12
ØØ13
ØØ14
ØØ15
ØØ16
ØØ17
ØØ2Ø
....
....
7764
7765
7766
7767
667Ø
7771
7772
7773
7774
7775
7776
7777
```

10.9. Modify Prob. 10.8 to count in a system based on 3. The output ranges from 0000 to 2222.

10.10. Modify Prob. 10.8 to count in a system based on 2. The output ranges from 00000000 to 11111111.

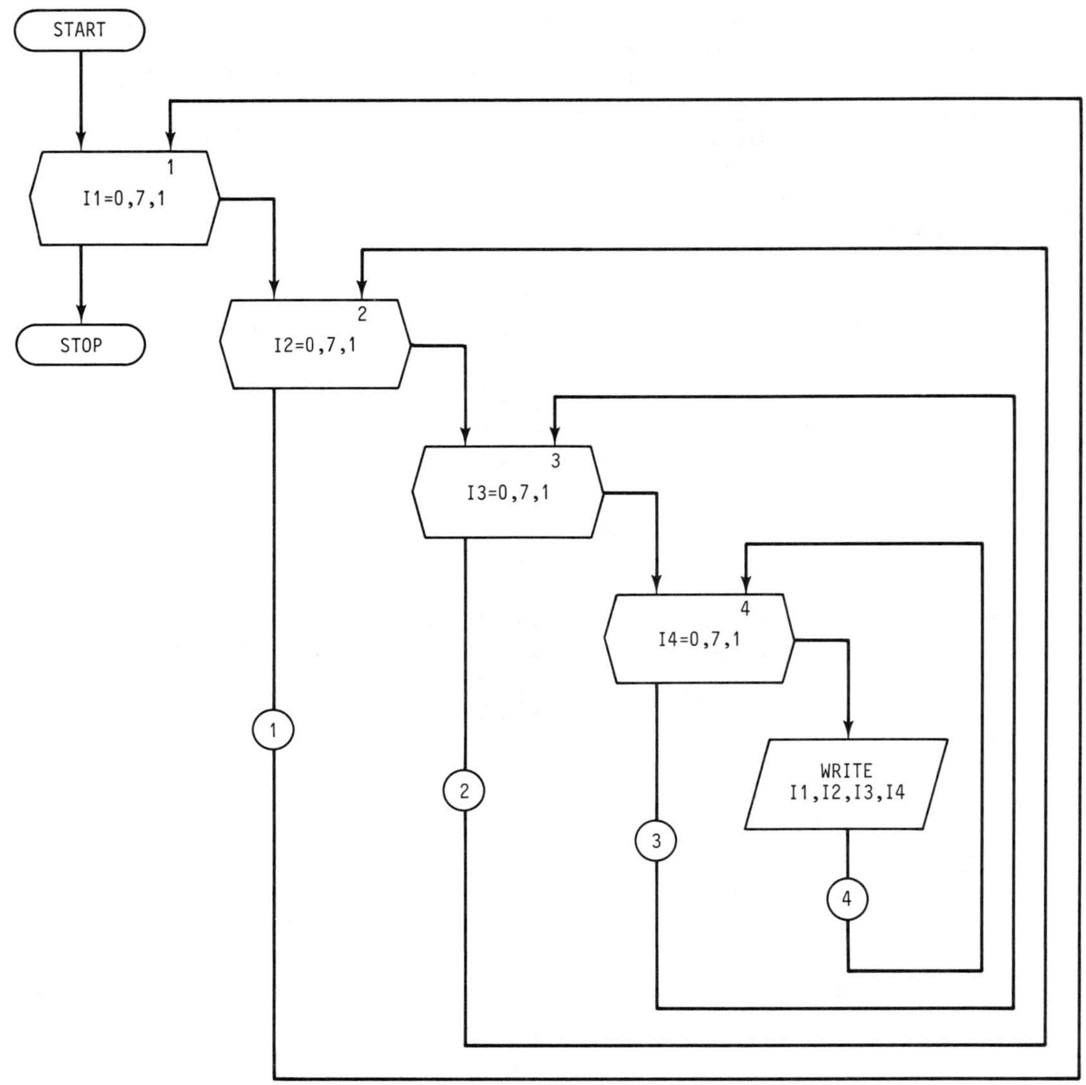

Figure 10.8 Flowchart for Problem 10.8.

10.11. Write a program to produce a time-like display in steps of five minutes from 00:00 to 24:00. The output should looks as shown:

```
ØØ:ØØ
ØØ:Ø5
ØØ:1Ø
ØØ:15
.....
12:55
13:ØØ
13:Ø5
```

```
.....
23:5Ø
23:55
24:ØØ
```

10.12. FORTRAN assumes that the arguments of the sine and cosine functions will be supplied in radians. To convert from degrees to radians, multiply the degrees by 3.1415926/180. Write a program to produce a sine, cosine, and tangent table for the angles from 0 to 90 degrees. Pretend that TAN(X) is not one of the intrinsic functions and resort to the fact that TANGENT(X) = SIN(X)/COS(X). The suggested output should look something like the following. (The last calculation may result in an error condition on some systems because the tangent becomes infinitely large.)

```
                        TRIG TABLE
                        ==========

DEGREES        SINE          COSINE         TANGENT
-------        ----          ------         -------
   Ø        .ØØØØØØ       1.ØØØØØØ        .ØØØØØØ
   1        .Ø17452        .999848        .Ø17455
   2        .Ø34899        .999391        .Ø34921
   .        .......        .......        .......
  ..        .......        .......     ..........
  88        .999391        .Ø349ØØ      28.636156
  89        .999848        .Ø17453      57.289644
  9Ø       1.ØØØØØØ        .ØØØØØØ  **************
```

10.13. Write a program to produce a log and exponential table for numbers ranging from 10 to 0.1 in steps of 0.1. A portion of the suggested output is shown.

```
           LOG AND EXPONENTIAL TABLE
           =========================

     X          LOG(X)           EXP(X)
    ---        --------       ------------
   1Ø.Ø        2.3Ø259        22Ø26.4653Ø
    9.9        2.29253        1993Ø.3696Ø
    ...        .......        ...........
    2.5         .91629           12.18247
    ...         ......           ........
     .3       -1.2Ø398            1.34986
     .2       -1.6Ø945            1.2214Ø
     .1       -2.3Ø261            1.1Ø517
```

10.14. If a DO-loop were introduced by each of the following DO statements, how many iterations would be performed in each case?

```
Ø,1Ø            DO 1 K = 19,27,4         DO 9 X = 6.,5.,-Ø.1
1,1Ø            DO 1 K = 47,25,-2        DO 4 J = 9,2Ø5,5
12,5            DO 1 K = 1ØØ,91,-3       DO 3 J = 952,487,-2Ø
5,1Ø,-2         DO 1 X = 5.,6.,Ø.1       DO 2 Y = 19.7,27.9,Ø.3
```

10.15. The previous problem demonstrates that it would be desirable to have access to a formula to calculate the number of iterations performed by a DO-loop. Try the following formula by substituting values from some of the simpler DO statements in the previous problem. LIM1, LIM2, and INCREMENT were defined near the beginning of the chapter.

$$\text{ITERATIONS} = \text{MAX}\left\{\text{INT}\left(\frac{\text{LIM2} - \text{LIM1} + \text{INCREMENT}}{\text{INCREMENT}}\right),0\right\}$$

10.16. Write a small interactive FORTRAN program, based on the formula in the previous problem, to compute the number of iterations. The program asks you to enter LIM1, LIM2, and INCREMENT, and reports the number of iterations. Use the program to check how well you handled Prob. 10.14.

11

Subscripted Variables and Arrays

11.1 INTRODUCTION

You are reminded that the computer's memory is composed of bits that are grouped into bytes that are grouped into words that are grouped into pages. The words must be thought of as being strung out, one behind the other, much like the cars on a very long train. The memory, in other words, is a one-dimensional structure.

To this point, all our programs make very frugal use of the memory, tying up a few words here and there. As an example, consider the following program:

```
READ*, A,B,C,D,E,F,G,H,P,Q,R,S,T,U,V,W,X,Y,Z
PRINT*, A,B,C,D,E,F,G,H,P,Q,R,S,T,U,V,W,X,Y,Z
END
```

To run this program, the machine takes 19 words of memory that are not necessarily contiguous, i.e., next to each other, and calls them A,B,C,D . . . etc. At execution time, values are read into these 19 words and then printed. We don't really know in which actual words of memory the computer stores the values, nor do we really care. We simply give each word a symbolic address in the form of a variable name, and it is up to the machine to find a location for each.

11.2 THE DIMENSION STATEMENT AND ARRAYS

The program is now modified through the addition of a *DIMENSION statement*, which is then explained in considerable detail. The modified program is shown in Fig. 11.1. The DIMENSION statement is a *specification statement*, and marks our second encounter with such statements. In Chapter 6, we first met specification statements in the form of the two data type-statements: REAL and INTEGER, and the IMPLICIT statement, all used to override, or even to confirm, automatic data typing. It was explained at the time that specification statements, unlike the imperative statements, are not executed. Instead, they specify a certain computing environment to the FORTRAN compiler.

Specification statements are like stage props that are put in place before the play begins. They set the stage, so to speak, for the action to follow, and it is for this reason that FORTRAN insists that all specification statements precede the imperative statements. You should be aware that many programmers still refer to specification statements as *declaratives*, an older term, because they *declare* a specific computing environment.

The opening statement in Fig. 11.1 is DIMENSION X(19). This is a specification statement declaring to the compiler that we wish to reserve 19 *contiguous* words of memory, and that this array of 19 words is to be called by the collective name X. The DIMENSION statement, in other words, specifies the *dimensions* of array X, and, for the remainder of the program, whenever X appears, the machine assumes that you are referring to this *contiguous* group of 19 words. Thus, when you tell the machine to read X, it will expect you to enter 19 values, and when you tell the machine to write X, it will print 19 values. The machine also assumes that you wish to store the data in floating-point form because X was chosen as the collective variable name, and because the choice of the collective variable name conveys the usual real or integer data typing to the compiler. The concept of *contiguity* is very important to programmers. *Contiguous* means to be adjoining without intervening spaces. The American states, for example, are not contiguous, because of Alaska and Hawaii, nor are the Canadian provinces contiguous because of Prince Edward Island and Newfoundland.

The discussion of Fig. 11.1 will be more meaningful if you run this example on your computer. When the machine prompts for input, supply the 19 data and watch as the PRINT statement is executed. After that stimulating experience, your comprehension of the remaining sections of the chapter will be heightened considerably.

In Fig. 11.1, X may be called a *one-dimensional array*, or a *vector*, and as you would expect, the elements of the array are accessible on an individual basis through the use of *subscripts*. Unfortunately, subscripts cannot be printed on standard computer screens and we therefore resort to so-called *linear notation,* which places

```
DIMENSION X(19)
READ*, X
PRINT*, X
END
```

Figure 11.1 The DIMENSION statement.

```
DIMENSION X(19)
READ*, X
PRINT*, X(10), X(5), X(15)
END
```

Figure 11.2 Array elements can be accessed individually and randomly.

the subscript on the same line as the variable, enclosed by brackets. X_4, for example, is represented by X(4), which is the fourth element of the array X, and is read as *X sub four*, whereas X(18) is the second to last element in our particular example.

In Fig. 11.2, we again read all 19 values into the array X, but then print only the tenth, the fifth, and the fifteenth elements. This illustrates that the elements of an array can be addressed individually and randomly.

X is properly called a *one-dimensional array variable*, or a *vector variable*, but some refer to it as a *dimensioned variable* and still others call it a *subscripted variable*. The latter is probably the least precise because X is not really a variable, but a collection of variables. Each of its elements could, however, be called a subscripted variable.

```
DIMENSION X(19)
READ*, X(1),X(3),X(5),X(7),X(9),X(13),X(15),X(17),X(19)
PRINT*, X(1),X(3),X(5),X(7),X(9),X(13),X(15),X(17),X(19)
END
```

Figure 11.3 A program illustrating unwieldy I/O lists.

In Fig. 11.3, we also declare an array X with 19 elements, but this time decide to read and write only the odd-numbered elements. This looks unmanageable and would certainly be if X had 1000 elements. Such lengthy I/O lists can be condensed, however, with the so-called *implied-DO*, but please note that this feature is designed for condensing such lengthy lists only, and cannot be used to perform calculations. The name implied-DO stems from its obvious similarity to the DO statement. The implied-DO is shown in Fig. 11.4, where it is used to condense the unwiedly I/O lists of Fig. 11.3; the two programs are functionally identical. The I/O lists in Fig. 11.4 are to be read as *the Jth element of the array X, where J goes from 1 to 19 in steps of 2*. Please note the brackets around the condensed I/O list. Some extended versions of FORTRAN will accept the implied-DO I/O lists without the parentheses, but these should never be omitted. It is stressed again that the compact program in Fig. 11.4, with its condensed I/O lists, is completely equivalent to the program in Fig. 11.3. Once the compiler reduces these programs to object code, they are indistinguishable. The implied-DO I/O notation must, therefore, be regarded as nothing more than convenient shorthand for the benefit of the programmer.

```
DIMENSION X(19)
READ*, (X(J),J=1,19,2)
PRINT*, (X(J),J=1,19,2)
END
```

Figure 11.4 The implied-DO is used to condense lengthy I/O lists.

11.3 DO-LOOPS AND ARRAYS

DO-loops and arrays seem to be made for each other. Figure 11.5 shows two programs, each declaring a 19-element array X. In the program on the left, X is filled manually with 1, 2, 3, . . . , 19 and then printed.

The program is lengthy, and again it is obvious that this would be intolerable if X had 1000 or more elements; it is bad with 19. The program on the right is functionally identical, but it is much more palatable and concise. You will be rewarded if you take the time to think it through in detail. In the program, we find a DO-loop in which the DO-variable I advances from 1 to 19 in steps of 1. On the first cycle, the terminal statement of the range of the DO moves 1 into X(1). During the second cycle, 2 is moved into X(2), until the last cycle, where 19 is moved into X(19). The program is obviously equivalent to its awkward neighbor on the left, and it is also vastly more convenient from the programmer's point of view. Take the trouble to run these and similar examples on the computer to enhance your general understanding and appreciation.

```
DIMENSION X(19)
X(1)=1.
X(2)=2.
X(3)=3.
X(4)=4.
X(5)=5.
X(6)=6.
X(7)=7.
X(8)=8.
X(9)=9.
X(1Ø)=1Ø.
X(11)=11.
X(12)=12.
X(13)=13.
X(14)=14.
X(15)=15.
X(16)=16.
X(17)=17.
X(18)=18.
X(19)=19.
PRINT*, X
END
```

```
   DIMENSION X(19)
   DO 1 I=1,19
1  X(I)=I
   PRINT*, X
   END
```

Figure 11.5 Two equivalent programs to emphasize the complementary nature of arrays and DO-loops.

11.4 UPPER AND LOWER DIMENSION BOUNDS

Let's take a closer look at the DIMENSION statement we have been using in all the examples to this point, namely

```
DIMENSION X(19)
```

As mentioned earlier, this DIMENSION statement is an example of a nonexecutable specification statement declaring an array. The X(19) is known as an *array declarator* and the 19 as the *dimension declarator*. Because 19 is the largest subscript defined by this DIMENSION statement, it is called the *upper dimension bound*, and when no *lower dimension bound* is specified, it is always assumed to be 1.

Older versions of FORTRAN did not allow the specification of a lower dimension bound, but FORTRAN 77 does permit it. The following DIMENSION statement illustrates this interesting and useful feature:

```
DIMENSION X(-5:13)
```

This modified DIMENSION statement still declares a one-dimensional array with 19 elements, but this time there is a lower dimension bound of −5 and an upper dimension bound of 13, giving us the following 19 elements:

```
X(-5), X(-4), X(-3), X(-2), X(-1), X(Ø), X(1), X(2),...., X(13)
```

The ability to perform this type of *coordinate shifting* could be most helpful at times, as you can deduce from the following scenario: An engineer studies the tension in the cables of a suspension bridge as a function of temperature. The tensions are measured for temperatures in the range from 40 to 110 degrees. The resulting 71 readings are summarized in the following table:

TEMPERATURE	TENSION
40	1212
41	1201
42	1200
43	1192
...	...
...	...
...	...
108	929
109	920
110	873

Assume that for analysis purposes, the engineer needs to store these 71 readings in an array called STRESS. In older versions of FORTRAN, the first part of the program might have looked something like this:

```
DIMENSION STRESS(71)
STRESS(1)=1212.
STRESS(2)=12Ø1.
STRESS(3)=12ØØ.
.............
.............
```

```
STRESS(7Ø)=92Ø.
STRESS(71)=873.
..............
```

With the FORTRAN 77 ability to shift subscripts, however, it becomes much easier to keep things straight because the subscripts can now be brought in line with the temperatures. In real life, needless to say, things don't always start with 1:

```
DIMENSION STRESS(4Ø:11Ø)
STRESS(4Ø)=1212.
STRESS(41)=12Ø1.
STRESS(42)=12ØØ.
..............
..............
STRESS(1Ø9)=92Ø.
STRESS(11Ø)=873.
..............
```

Before moving on to some specific examples, note that the DIMENSION statements and data type-statements can be combined. The following two specification statements

```
REAL M
DIMENSION M(1ØØØ)
```

are equivalent to the following single specification:

```
REAL M(1ØØØ)
```

Similarly, the following two specification statements

```
INTEGER X
DIMENSION X(5ØØ)
```

can be replaced by this single specification statement:

```
INTEGER X(5ØØ)
```

11.5 EXAMPLES INVOLVING ONE-DIMENSIONAL ARRAYS

Example 11.1

The following program generates 20 random numbers and assigns these to the 20-element array M. The array is then written to a file called ARRAYDATA with a single unformatted WRITE. This will make the same data available in subsequent examples. The data are also written to the screen to give you a feeling for the numbers involved. The screen output is shown beside the program. Make the effort to understand this simple program and then run it. After the run, the file ARRAYDATA will appear in your directory, but remember that it is a binary file.

```
      DIMENSION M(20)
*-----                                                                1
*-----THIS 20-ELEMENT ARRAY IS NOW FILLED                            64
*-----WITH 20 'RANDOM' NUMBERS.                                      75
*-----                                                              148
      DO 1 I = 1,20                                                  68
      M(I)=MOD(I**6,2*I+321)                                         36
    1 CONTINUE                                                       64
*-----                                                              295
*-----THE ARRAY IS NOW WRITTEN TO A FILE                            228
*-----'ARRAYDATA' WITH A SINGLE UNFORMATTED WRITE.                  188
*-----                                                              309
      OPEN(7,FILE='ARRAYDATA',STATUS='NEW',FORM='UNFORMATTED')        9
      WRITE(7)M                                                      39
      CLOSE(7)                                                      210
*-----                                                              324
*-----THE ARRAY IS ALSO WRITTEN TO THE SCREEN                       185
*-----TO LET US SEE WHAT WE ARE DEALING WITH                         54
*-----                                                              120
      WRITE(6,2)M                                                     8
    2 FORMAT(1X,I4)                                                 115
      END
```

Example 11.2

The file ARRAYDATA is unformatted and contains a single record with 20 integer data. Read these data into a 20-element integer array M and determine the magnitude of the largest element.

Solution After filling the array from the file, assign M(1) to the variable LARGE. Now compare LARGE to M(2). If M(2) is larger than LARGE, assign M(2) to LARGE, otherwise move on to M(3). Continue this procedure until you reach the end of the array.

```
      DIMENSION M(20)
      OPEN(7,FILE='ARRAYDATA',FORM='UNFORMATTED',STATUS='OLD')
      READ(7)M
      CLOSE(7)
*-----
      LARGE=M(1)
*-----
      DO 1 I=2,20
      IF(M(I).GT.LARGE)LARGE=M(I)
    1 CONTINUE
```

```
*-----
      WRITE(6,2)LARGE
    2 FORMAT(/,' THE VALUE OF THE LARGEST ELEMENT IS',I4)
      END
```

```
THE VALUE OF THE LARGEST ELEMENT IS 324
```

This is another example where the required FORTRAN program communicates more effectively than the parallel verbal description. The heart of the program is obviously the DO-loop. Think about it carefully.

Example 11.3

Modify the program in Example 11.2 to report the magnitude and the location of the largest element, and the magnitude and location of the smallest element.

Solution Assume that the M(1) is the largest and, simultaneously, the smallest element. Modify that assumption by subsequent comparisons with the remaining 19 elements of M. Each time LARGE and SMALL are updated, store the locations in LOCHI and LOCLOW. See the program for details.

```
      INTEGER SMALL
      DIMENSION M(20)
      OPEN(7,FILE='ARRAYDATA',FORM='UNFORMATTED',STATUS='OLD')
      READ(7)M
      CLOSE(7)
*-----
      LARGE=M(1)
      SMALL=M(1)
      LOCHI=1
      LOCLOW=1
*-----
      DO 1 I=2,20
*-----
      IF(M(I).GT.LARGE)THEN
          LARGE=M(I)
          LOCHI=I
      END IF
*-----
      IF(M(I).LT.SMALL)THEN
          SMALL=M(I)
          LOCLOW=I
      END IF
*-----
    1 CONTINUE
```

```
*-----
      WRITE(6,2)LARGE,LOCHI,SMALL,LOCLOW
    2 FORMAT(' THE  LARGEST ELEMENT IS',I4,' LOCATED AT POSITION',I3,/,
     +' THE SMALLEST ELEMENT IS',I4,' LOCATED AT POSITION',I3)
      END
```

```
THE  LARGEST ELEMENT IS 324 LOCATED AT POSITION 15
THE SMALLEST ELEMENT IS   1 LOCATED AT POSITION  1
```

Example 11.4

Read the data from file ARRAYDATA into an integer array M and compute the sum and the average of the elements.

Solution This is a very simple problem, you just have to be careful not to use integer division, even though the answer would turn out the same with our particular data. Study the program.

```
      DIMENSION M(2Ø)
      OPEN(7,FILE='ARRAYDATA',FORM='UNFORMATTED',STATUS='OLD')
      READ(7)M
      CLOSE(7)
      MSUM=Ø
*-----
      DO 1 I=1,2Ø
      MSUM=MSUM+M(I)
    1 CONTINUE
*-----
      AVER=MSUM/2Ø.
      WRITE(6,2)MSUM,AVER
    2 FORMAT(/,' THE      SUM OF THE 2Ø ELEMENTS IS',I7,/,
     +' THE AVERAGE OF THE 2Ø ELEMENTS IS',F7.2)
      END
```

```
THE      SUM OF THE 2Ø ELEMENTS IS   254Ø
THE AVERAGE OF THE 2Ø ELEMENTS IS 127.ØØ
```

Example 11.5

Modify the program in Example 11.4 to compute and report the so-called MEAN DEVIATION for the 20 data. We already computed the global average of the 20 elements in the array. You now calculate the 20 differences between each element and this global average, add together the absolute values of these 20 differences, and divide by 20. That is the definition of the mean deviation. Note that MDEV is real in the program.

```
      REAL MDEV
      DIMENSION M(2Ø)
      OPEN(7,FILE='ARRAYDATA',FORM='UNFORMATTED',STATUS='OLD')
      READ(7)M
      CLOSE(7)
      MSUM=Ø
      DO 1 I=1,2Ø
      MSUM=MSUM+M(I)
    1 CONTINUE
      AVER=MSUM/2Ø.
      DIFSUM=Ø.
*-----
      DO 3 I=1,2Ø
      DIFSUM=DIFSUM+ABS(M(I)-AVER)
    3 CONTINUE
*-----
      MDEV=DIFSUM/2Ø.
      WRITE(6,2)MSUM,AVER,MDEV
    2 FORMAT(/,' THE     SUM OF THE 2Ø ELEMENTS IS',I7,/,
     +' THE AVERAGE OF THE 2Ø ELEMENTS IS',F7.2,/,
     +'             THE MEAN DEVIATION IS',F7.2)
      END
```

```
THE     SUM OF THE 2Ø ELEMENTS IS   254Ø
THE AVERAGE OF THE 2Ø ELEMENTS IS 127.ØØ
            THE MEAN DEVIATION IS  87.1Ø
```

Example 11.6

Write a program to determine how many of our 20 array elements are divisible by the numbers from 1 to 10. Report how many of the elements are divisible by a given number, what the sum of such elements is, and what their average is.

```
      DIMENSION M(2Ø),ICOUNT(1Ø),SUM(1Ø),AVER(1Ø)
      OPEN(7,FILE='ARRAYDATA',FORM='UNFORMATTED',STATUS='OLD')
      READ(7)M
      CLOSE(7)
*-----
      DO 1 I=1,1Ø
      ICOUNT(I)=Ø.
      SUM(I)=Ø.
    1 CONTINUE
*-----
```

```
      DO 2 I=1,2Ø
*-----
      DO 3 J=1,1Ø
      IF(MOD(M(I),J).EQ.Ø)THEN
         ICOUNT(J)=ICOUNT(J)+1
         SUM(J)=SUM(J)+M(I)
      END IF
    3 CONTINUE
*-----
    2 CONTINUE
*-----
      DO 4 I=1,1Ø
      AVER(I)=SUM(I)/ICOUNT(I)
      WRITE(6,5)ICOUNT(I),I,SUM(I),AVER(I)
    5 FORMAT(1X,I2,' ARE DIVISIBLE BY',I3,'. THEIR SUM IS',
     +F7.1,', AND THEIR AVERAGE IS',F7.1)
    4 CONTINUE
      END
```

```
2Ø ARE DIVISIBLE BY  1. THEIR SUM IS 254Ø.Ø, AND THEIR AVERAGE IS  127.Ø
12 ARE DIVISIBLE BY  2. THEIR SUM IS 1512.Ø, AND THEIR AVERAGE IS  126.Ø
1Ø ARE DIVISIBLE BY  3. THEIR SUM IS 14Ø4.Ø, AND THEIR AVERAGE IS  14Ø.4
1Ø ARE DIVISIBLE BY  4. THEIR SUM IS 1248.Ø, AND THEIR AVERAGE IS  124.8
 6 ARE DIVISIBLE BY  5. THEIR SUM IS 1ØØØ.Ø, AND THEIR AVERAGE IS  166.7
 6 ARE DIVISIBLE BY  6. THEIR SUM IS  972.Ø, AND THEIR AVERAGE IS  162.Ø
 1 ARE DIVISIBLE BY  7. THEIR SUM IS  21Ø.Ø, AND THEIR AVERAGE IS  21Ø.Ø
 4 ARE DIVISIBLE BY  8. THEIR SUM IS  256.Ø, AND THEIR AVERAGE IS   64.Ø
 4 ARE DIVISIBLE BY  9. THEIR SUM IS  423.Ø, AND THEIR AVERAGE IS  1Ø5.8
 2 ARE DIVISIBLE BY 1Ø. THEIR SUM IS  33Ø.Ø, AND THEIR AVERAGE IS  165.Ø
```

Discussion This remarkably compact program shows much of the flexibility of FORTRAN. Note that the program declares four arrays. One of these holds the 20 data, of course, and the other three hold the results of the computations. The nth element of the array ICOUNT records how many of the data in M are divisible by n. The nth element of the array SUM records the sum of all the elements divisible by n. The nth element of the array AVER records the average of all the elements divisible by n.

Notice that in the first DO-loop, all the elements of SUM and ICOUNT are set to zero to prepare them for their accumulating roles. You will see the two nested DO-loops next. The outer one steps from 1 to 20 and is obviously used to move through the array M, stopping at each element M(I). The logic now falls into the inner loop, where the element M(I) is tested to see whether it is divisible by any of the numbers from 1 to 10. If it is found to be divisible by n, then the nth element of the array ICOUNT is bumped up by one, and M(I) is added to the nth element of the array SUM. The compactness of these nested loops shows FORTRAN at its best.

We then head for the reporting DO-loop at the end, where a WRITE statement is executed 10 times to generate the impressive report. Note that we included the computation of the average into that loop, rather than providing a separate loop for that purpose. If you really think about it, we didn't actually need the array AVER; a simple variable would have sufficed. But, if we wanted the individual averages later on in the program, the existence of the array AVER could be justified.

If you make the effort to understand the program in detail, you will get a glimpse of the real essence of FORTRAN.

11.6 THE GOLDFISH ALGORITHM

Pretend that you ordered two fish: a baby shark and a goldfish. While waiting for the fish to be delivered, you prepared a large bowl for the shark and a smaller one for the goldfish. Unfortunately, the delivery people erred, and the goldfish wound up in the larger bowl, and the shark in the smaller, and you were faced with the task of switching the fish. It seemed like a simple problem at first. You would simply place the shark in the larger bowl and then remove the goldfish and deposit it in the smaller bowl, but then you sensed that the two would never coexist in the same bowl, not even for that fraction of a second, sharks being what they are. After some thought, you filled a third bowl with water and placed it between the other two bowls. You then took the goldfish out of the larger bowl, placed it into the holding bowl, removed the shark from the smaller bowl and transported it to the larger one, and then you moved the goldfish from the holding bowl to the smaller bowl. The fish were then safely switched, and the holding bowl was no longer needed.

Sometimes it is necessary to interchange the contents of two words of memory without losing either one. The situation is analogous to the goldfish problem because

```
      BOWL1=2.
      BOWL2=1.
      WRITE(6,1)BOWL1,BOWL2
    1 FORMAT(' BOWL1 =',F3.Ø,' AND BOWL2 =',F3.Ø)
*-----
*-----AND NOW THE GOLDFISH ALGORITHM
*-----
      HOLD=BOWL2
      BOWL2=BOWL1
      BOWL1=HOLD
*-----
      WRITE(6,1)BOWL1,BOWL2
      END
```

```
BOWL1 = 2. AND BOWL2 = 1.
BOWL1 = 1. AND BOWL2 = 2.
```

Figure 11.6 The goldfish algorithm is used to interchange the contents of two words of memory.

one word of memory cannot hold two different data simultaneously. The obvious solution is to invoke a third word to permit the switch to be performed. Although the algorithm is simple, and apparently obvious, some don't always think of it under duress, and this is why your attention is drawn to it here. The goldfish algorithm will play a major role when we sort data.

Figure 11.6 illustrates the goldfish algorithm. The variables BOWL1 and BOWL2 are assigned 2 and 1, respectively, and their contents are printed. The goldfish algorithm is then executed, and the two are printed again after the switch. The variable HOLD acts as the intermediate holding tank.

11.7 SORTING

In this section, we consider the sorting of a column of numbers in ascending or descending order. Arranging numbers in ascending or descending order is something most of us have done as far back as we can remember, and it has become an automatic and instinctive process. It is not easy to turn our instincts into programs because programming requires the conscious understanding of all the steps of an algorithm. The purpose of this section is to remind us of the various steps involved in a sort. Consider the following eight numbers:

97
89
19
30
1
0
8
5

A systematic and brute-force approach to arranging these numbers in ascending order involves comparing the first two numbers. If the first number is greater than the second, the pair is interchanged to yield:

89
97
19
30
1
0
8
5

The second and third numbers are now compared, and interchanged if necessary. The third and fourth, the fourth and fifth, the fifth and sixth, the sixth and seventh, and, finally, the seventh and eighth. When you get done, the column looks like this:

89
19
30
1
0
8
5
97

You will notice that the "heaviest" element of this array sank to the bottom. We now make a second pass through the column, interchanging adjacent elements as required. The following results:

19
30
1
0
8
5
89
97

Note that this time the second-heaviest element descended to the bottom, coming to rest on top of the heaviest. A third pass yields:

19
1
0
8
5
30
89
97

You can see that the third-heaviest element now forms part of the sediment at the bottom, with the sediment piling up in ascending order.

It is obvious that after $8 - 1 = 7$ passes, the entire column consists of numbers, sorted in ascending order, and it is possible to generalize that if the column contained n numbers, it would be completely sorted after $n - 1$ passes. Because sorting involves the interchange of data between pairs of memory words, it should be clear to you why we dwelt on the goldfish algorithm in the previous section. In Example 11.7, we read our 20-element array from the file ARRAYDATA and sort it in ascending order.

Example 11.7

Read the 20 data from the file ARRAYDATA into an integer array M. Print the 20 data. Now sort the array in ascending order and print it again.

Solution Because we have 20 data, we need to make 19 passes through our data, and so we simply set up a DO-loop executing 19 cycles. With each cycle, we compare adjacent data, performing a switch if necessary. This is obviously an ideal candidate for another DO-loop. Here is the required program. It will be discussed some more after you look at it.

```
      DIMENSION M(2Ø)
      OPEN(7,FILE='ARRAYDATA',FORM='UNFORMATTED',STATUS='OLD')
      READ(7)M
      CLOSE(7)
*-----WE NOW PRINT THE 2Ø DATA IN THE ORDER IN WHICH THEY APPEAR IN
*-----THE VECTOR (ARRAY) 'M'
      WRITE(6,1)M
    1 FORMAT(/,(1X,1ØI5))
*-----
*-----AND NOW FOR THE SORT:
*-----
      DO 2 J=1,19
*-----
      DO 3 K=1,19
      IF(M(K).GT.M(K+1))THEN
         MHOLD=M(K)
         M(K)=M(K+1)
         M(K+1)=MHOLD
      END IF
    3 CONTINUE
*-----
    2 CONTINUE
*-----
*-----THE SORT IS ALL FINISHED, AND THE VECTOR M IS PRINTED
*-----TO CONFIRM THAT ALL WORKED AS EXPECTED:
      WRITE(6,1)M
      END
```

```
    1   64   75  148   68   36   64  295  228  188
  3Ø9    9   39  21Ø  324  185   54  12Ø    8  115

    1    8    9   36   39   54   64   64   68   75
  115  12Ø  148  185  188  21Ø  228  295  3Ø9  324
```

Discussion The entire sort is performed by the compact nested DO-loops near the middle of the program. You may be wondering why the inner DO-loop had an upper limit of 19 rather than 20, but if you look at the code, you will notice that when the inner DO-loop hits 19, we are comparing elements 19 and 20. Had we allowed the inner loop go to 20, we would have been comparing elements 20 and 21, but there is no element 21, of course.

We only sorted a small number of elements in the preceding example, and not very much CPU time was used. As the arrays get larger, however, more CPU time is expended. Because we are dealing with nested DO-loops, a sort of 20 numbers involves 19 × 19 = 361 comparisons. If we increased the array to 200 elements, 199 × 199 = 39,601 comparisons are performed, while a 20,000 element vector would require almost 400 million comparisons.

You can appreciate that sorting is highly CPU intensive, and it is clear that shortcuts are desirable. An obvious way to save computer time is to take advantage of the phenomenon of sediment buildup. You recall that the heaviest element always sinks to the bottom, followed by the next heaviest element, as the sediment grows from the bottom. Because the sediment is sorted in numeric order, there is no need to compare into it. For this reason, we can make the inner loop more and more shallow with each cycle of the outer loop, and the heart of Example 11.7 is now shown with this dynamic upper limit on the inner loop in Fig. 11.7.

The upper limit on the inner loop is 20 − J. On the first cycle of the outer loop, J = 1 and K − J = 19, causing the vector to be sorted full length. As the outer loop reaches 19, 20 − J = 1, and only the first and the second elements are compared, the rest having already been transformed into sorted sediment. The savings are impressive. Without the dynamic upper limit on the inner loop, a vector with 1000 elements would require 998,001 comparisons. With the dynamic feature, the number of comparisons drops to 499,500.

A second way to save significant CPU time is to quit as soon as you discover that no pair swapping was necessary during a pass. The vector is obviously completely sorted when every element is larger than the preceding one.

This new saving is incorporated in Fig. 11.8. You will notice that just before we drop into the inner loop, we assign 0 to IFLAG. Whenever we interchange two elements, we also assign 1 to IFLAG. It is obvious that when we emerge from the inner loop with a 0 still in IFLAG, then no swapping was necessary, and we are done. In this example, control then transfers to the statement with label 4, outside the outer loop.

It is true that maintaining the flag requires a bit of CPU time, but usually you save vastly more than you spend. An extreme example would involve a vector in which all the elements are already sorted. You would realize that fact right after emerging from the inner loop the very first time, and the sort would be over. The other extreme would involve a vector in which the elements appear sorted in descending order. That situation would involve a maximum of swapping, and maintaining the

```
      DO 2 J=1,19
*-----
      DO 3 K=1,2Ø-J
      IF(M(K).GT.M(K+1))THEN
         MHOLD=M(K)
         M(K)=M(K+1)
         M(K+1)=MHOLD
    3 CONTINUE
*-----
    2 CONTINUE
```

Figure 11.7 The second loop becomes more shallow with each cycle of the outer loop.

```
      DO 2 J=1,19
*-----
      IFLAG=Ø
      DO 3 K=1,19
      IF(M(K).GT.M(K+1))THEN
         MHOLD=M(K)
         M(K)=M(K+1)
         M(K+1)=MHOLD
         IFLAG=1
      END IF
    3 CONTINUE
      IF(IFLAG.EQ.Ø)GO TO 4
*-----
    2 CONTINUE
*-----
    4 CONTINUE
```

Figure 11.8 A flag is used to detect when no more pairs need be interchanged.

flag would introduce a bit of overhead without saving any CPU time, but you are not likely to encounter that situation too often.

There are other ways to save CPU time when performing a sort, but the two methods presented here are probably the most effective and the most fundamental. Other methods frequently involve breaking a large array of numbers into several smaller groups because smaller groups are much more readily sorted. These smaller groups are then recombined in a merging phase.

11.8 TWO-DIMENSIONAL ARRAYS

People often like to arrange numbers in table form, with rows and columns. Such a table is known as a *matrix*, but some call it a two-dimensional matrix, and X3.9–1978 calls it a two-dimensional array, a more general term.

The following two specification statements declare a real array Y with 100 rows and 57 columns:

```
DIMENSION Y(1ØØ,57)
```

or

```
REAL Y(1ØØ,57)
```

The first subscript always specifies the number of rows of the array, and the second subscript declares the number of columns. You won't forget the order if you remember that a matrix is "real cute." In this particular case, the lower dimension bound on both the row and column declarators is 1 by default, although a different lower dimension bound could be chosen as shown:

```
DIMENSION Y(-51:5Ø,11:67)
```

or

```
REAL Y(-51:5Ø, 11:67)
```

Anyway, let's take a closer look at the specification statement DIMENSION Y(100,57). It informs the compiler that space is to be reserved for a two-dimensional array to be called Y, containing 100 rows and 57 columns of real data. It is a very large array, occupying 5700 words of memory.

Each of the 5700 elements has a unique array address, defined by the intersection of the row and the column in which it is located. The element Y(45,29), for example, is located at the intersection of the 45th row and the 29th column of the array Y, the general element being Y(row,column).

A specific example follows, but first a brief digression to point out how such a two-dimensional structure is stored in the computer's memory, given the fact that the memory itself is a long one-dimensional string of words. The answer is that the two-dimensional array is simply dismembered, column by column. These columns are placed into memory, one after the other without intervening spaces, contiguously, in other words. The decision to store the array in column order was an arbitrary one—the creators of FORTRAN could have chosen row order, but they didn't. There is nothing special about column order, so simply accept it without wasting nervous energy on it, and don't look for some cosmic justification. People who read books in row order, that is, a line at a time, feel that this is how the universe should be run, but they forget that there are people who read in column order, and such people would probably consider FORTRAN's matrix storage order to be quite natural. The point must not be beaten to death, but some do get hung up on this issue, sometimes beyond recovery.

In the example, we will step through some of the basic concepts, and you are urged to follow along carefully to spare you considerable discomfort later.

Figure 11.9 shows a two-dimensional matrix with four rows and six columns, usually referred to as a 4 × 6 array or as a 4 × 6 matrix.

3.4	23.1	4.0	11.2	3.4	2.1
10.9	3.1	1.7	1.5	12.1	8.8
7.1	43.2	68.5	11.0	4.7	3.1
0.0	1.2	1.4	1.6	1.8	10.3

Figure 11.9 A 4 × 6 array.

Figure 11.10 shows a very elementary program designed to read data into the 4 × 6 array Y, after which the array is printed. Notice the DIMENSION statement, which instructs the compiler to set aside 24 words of memory to which we give the arbitrary collective name Y. The DIMENSION statement also tells the compiler that Y is to be viewed as a two-dimensional structure with four rows and six columns. The computer responds by selecting a contiguous block of 24 words, reserving the first four words for the first column, the next four words for the second column, and the last four words are reserved for the sixth column of the array.

```
      DIMENSION Y(4,6)
      READ*,Y
      PRINT*,Y
      END


?3.4  1Ø.9  7.1  Ø  23.1  3.1  43.2  1.2  4  1.7  68.5  1.4
?11.2  1.5  11  1.6  3.4  12.1  4.7  1.8  2.1  8.8  3.1  1Ø.3


 3.4ØØ  1Ø.9Ø  7.1ØØ  Ø.ØØØ  23.1Ø  3.1ØØ  43.2Ø  1.2ØØ
 4.ØØØ  1.7ØØ  68.5Ø  1.4ØØ  11.2Ø  1.5ØØ  11.ØØ  1.6ØØ
 3.4ØØ  12.1Ø  4.7ØØ  1.8ØØ  2.1ØØ  8.8ØØ  3.1ØØ  1Ø.3Ø
```

Figure 11.10 A program to read and write a two-dimensional array.

The program in Fig. 11.10 doesn't really prove much, except to confirm that the array Y does indeed have 24 words. It gives no insight into the order in which the elements are stored in memory because it simply writes them in the order in which these were read, which happened to be in column order. Had we entered the elements in row order, the computer would have printed them in row order. The moral is that the programmer has to impose structure on the array; to the computer, it is just a contiguous block of 24 words.

The program in Fig. 11.11 reads the same array. Because you know that the computer stores the data in column order, the data are entered in that order. This

```
      DIMENSION Y(4,6)
*-----THE ARRAY IS READ IN 'NATURAL' FORTRAN ORDER
      READ*,Y
*-----THE ARRAY IS NOW PRINTED IN ROW ORDER
*-----FOR EACH VALUE OF IROW, ICOL STEPS THROUGH 6 VALUES.
      DO 1 IROW = 1,4
      WRITE(6,2)(Y(IROW,ICOL),ICOL=1,6)
    2 FORMAT(1X,6F7.1)
    1 CONTINUE
      END

?3.4  1Ø.9  7.1  Ø  23.1  3.1  43.2  1.2  4  1.7  68.5  1.4
?11.2  1.5  11  1.6  3.4  12.1  4.7  1.8  2.1  8.8  3.1  1Ø.3


    3.4   23.1    4.Ø   11.2    3.4    2.1
   1Ø.9    3.1    1.7    1.5   12.1    8.8
    7.1   43.2   68.5   11.Ø    4.7    3.1
     .Ø    1.2    1.4    1.6    1.8   1Ø.3
```

Figure 11.11 The array is read in FORTRAN's "natural" order, and printed in row order.

time, however, a DO-loop is used to print the array. During the first cycle, all the elements in Row 1 are printed, that is, elements Y(1,1), Y(1,2), Y(1,3), Y(1,4), Y(1,5), and Y(1,6). We then print all the elements in Row 2, Row 3, and Row 4. Notice that as the DO-loop moves through the rows, the implied-DO in the WRITE statement steps through the columns. This example is of pivotal importance; don't underestimate it. Notice the use of highly mnemonic subscript names and DO-variables. You will find these helpful, especially when dealing with three-dimensional arrays.

Figure 11.12 shows the same program again, but this time FORTRAN's "natural" array order is overruled not only on output, but also on input. This is the preferred way of dealing with two-dimensional arrays.

Figure 11.13 shows that a nested implied-DO can also be used to overrule FORTRAN's column order. There is a subtle difference between the programs of Figs. 11.12 and 11.13, however. In Fig. 11.12, the input list contains only six items, but in Fig. 11.13 the list consists of 24 items. The same is true about the output lists in these two illustrations, and the only reason the matrix looks normal in Fig. 11.13 is that the FORMAT statement permits only six elements to be printed on a record. Figure 11.12 definitely requires at least four input records, but Fig. 11.13 would be satisfied with a single input record, provided it contained 24 data.

All this is not difficult to grasp, but it is highly concentrated. The only way to truly grasp it is to try some of these features on your computer. You will be wasting a lot of time otherwise, trying to visualize the unknown when you could be asking the machine to show it to you.

```
      DIMENSION Y(4,6)
*-----THE ARRAY IS READ IN ROW ORDER.
      DO 3 IROW=1,4
      READ *,(Y(IROW,ICOL),ICOL=1,6)
    3 CONTINUE
*-----THE ARRAY IS NOW PRINTED IN ROW ORDER
      DO 1 IROW = 1,4
      WRITE(6,2)(Y(IROW,ICOL),ICOL=1,6)
    2 FORMAT(1X,6F7.1)
    1 CONTINUE
      END

?3.4    23.1    4     11.2    3.4    2.1
?1Ø.9    3.1    1.7    1.5    12.1    8.8
?7.1    43.2    68.5    11    4.7    3.1
?Ø    1.2    1.4    1.6    1.8    1Ø.3

    3.4   23.1    4.Ø   11.2    3.4    2.1
   1Ø.9    3.1    1.7    1.5   12.1    8.8
    7.1   43.2   68.5   11.Ø    4.7    3.1
     .Ø    1.2    1.4    1.6    1.8   1Ø.3
```

Figure 11.12 The array is filled and printed in row order.

```
      DIMENSION Y(4,6)
      READ *,((Y(IROW,ICOL),ICOL=1,6),IROW=1,4)
      WRITE(6,2)((Y(IROW,ICOL),ICOL=1,6),IROW=1,4)
    2 FORMAT(1X,6F7.1)
      END
```

```
?3.4  23.1  4  11.2  3.4  2.1  1Ø.9  3.1  1.7  1.5  12.1  8.8
?7.1  43.2  68.5  11  4.7  3.1  Ø  1.2  1.4  1.6  1.8  1Ø.3

   3.4   23.1    4.Ø   11.2    3.4    2.1
  1Ø.9    3.1    1.7    1.5   12.1    8.8
   7.1   43.2   68.5   11.Ø    4.7    3.1
    .Ø    1.2    1.4    1.6    1.8   1Ø.3
```

Figure 11.13 The nested implied-DO is used to force row order.

Example 11.8

Given the following 5 × 10 integer matrix MAT, write a program to read the array from the keyboard into memory. The matrix is to be read in row order. Write the matrix to a formatted file MATDATA in row order. The file is required by subsequent examples, so you may wish to create it.

3	3	−1	5	10	−33	5	5	1	−1
45	−91	0	9	21	90	12	−73	21	7
10	8	−6	22	1	34	87	34	−51	4
0	5	3	1	3	3	−3	2	87	19
71	20	43	3	0	−7	−32	61	3	3

Solution

```
      DIMENSION MAT(5,1Ø)
*-----READING THE ARRAY INTO MEMORY:
      DO 1 IROW=1,5
      READ*,(MAT(IROW,ICOL),ICOL=1,1Ø)
    1 CONTINUE
*-----THE FILE 'MATDATA' IS OPENED FOR OUTPUT:
      OPEN(7,FILE='MATDATA',FORM='FORMATTED',STATUS='NEW')
*-----THE MATRIX IS WRITTEN TO THE FILE IN ROW ORDER:
      DO 2 IROW=1,5
      WRITE(7,3)(MAT(IROW,ICOL),ICOL=1,1Ø)
    3 FORMAT(1ØI5)
    2 CONTINUE
      CLOSE(7)
      PRINT*,'THE FILE ''MATDATA'' HAS BEEN CREATED'
      WRITE(6,4)((MAT(IROW,ICOL),ICOL=1,1Ø),IROW=1,5)
    4 FORMAT(/,' THIS MATRIX WAS WRITTEN TO THE FILE:',//,(1X,1ØI5))
      END
```

```
?3 3 -1 5 1Ø -33 5 5 1 -1
?45 -91 Ø 9 21 9Ø 12 -73 21 7
?1Ø 8 -6 22 1 34 87 34 -51 4
?Ø 5 3 1 3 3 -3 2 87 19
?71 2Ø 43 3 Ø -7 -32 61 3 3

THE FILE 'MATDATA' HAS BEEN CREATED

THIS MATRIX WAS WRITTEN TO THE FILE:

    3    3   -1    5   1Ø  -33    5    5    1   -1
   45  -91    Ø    9   21   9Ø   12  -73   21    7
   1Ø    8   -6   22    1   34   87   34  -51    4
    Ø    5    3    1    3    3   -3    2   87   19
   71   2Ø   43    3    Ø   -7  -32   61    3    3
```

Example 11.9

Read the 5 × 10 matrix MAT from the file MATDATA of the previous example. Use format-directed input, remembering that the records were written under 10I5, and that the file contains the array in row order. Compute the sum of all the elements of the matrix.

Solution

```
      DIMENSION MAT(5,1Ø)
      OPEN(7,FILE='MATDATA',STATUS='OLD')
      DO 1 IROW=1,5
      READ(7,2)(MAT(IROW,ICOL),ICOL=1,1Ø)
    2 FORMAT(1ØI5)
    1 CONTINUE
      CLOSE(7)
*-----WE NOW SHOW THE MATRIX WE JUST READ
      WRITE(6,3)((MAT(IROW,ICOL),ICOL=1,1Ø),IROW=1,5)
    3 FORMAT(' THE FOLLOWING MATRIX WAS READ:',//,(1X,1ØI5))
*-----AND NOW FOR THE SUM OF THE ELEMENTS:
      ISUM=Ø
      DO 4 IROW=1,5
      DO 4 ICOL=1,1Ø
      ISUM=ISUM+MAT(IROW,ICOL)
    4 CONTINUE
      WRITE(6,5)ISUM
    5 FORMAT(/,' THE SUM OF ALL THE ELEMENTS IS',I4)
      END
```

```
THE FOLLOWING MATRIX WAS READ:

   3    3   -1    5   1Ø  -33    5    5    1   -1
  45  -91    Ø    9   21   9Ø   12  -73   21    7
  1Ø    8   -6   22    1   34   87   34  -51    4
   Ø    5    3    1    3    3   -3    2   87   19
  71   2Ø   43    3    Ø   -7  -32   61    3    3

THE SUM OF ALL THE ELEMENTS IS 466
```

Example 11.10

Compute the sums of all the elements in the individual rows and columns of the matrix MAT of the previous example, and report the 10 column sums and the 5 row sums.

Solution Declare a 10-element integer vector COLSUM, and a 5-element vector ROWSUM to hold the sums. This time, to be different, we use list-directed input when reading the data from the file. Remember that the sum vectors must be initialized to zero.

```
      INTEGER MAT(5,1Ø),ROWSUM(5),COLSUM(1Ø)
      OPEN(7,FILE='MATDATA',STATUS='OLD')
      DO 1 IROW=1,5
      READ(7,*)(MAT(IROW,ICOL),ICOL=1,1Ø)
    1 CONTINUE
      CLOSE(7)
*-----COLSUM AND ROWSUM ARE ZEROED OUT:
      DO 2 ICOL=1,1Ø
      COLSUM(ICOL)=Ø
    2 CONTINUE
      DO 3 IROW=1,5
      ROWSUM(IROW)=Ø
    3 CONTINUE
*-----AND NOW FOR THE ADDITIONS - FIRST THE ROW TOTALS:
      DO 4 IROW=1,5
      DO 4 ICOL=1,1Ø
      ROWSUM(IROW)=ROWSUM(IROW)+MAT(IROW,ICOL)
    4 CONTINUE
*-----AND NOW THE COLUMN TOTALS:
      DO 5 ICOL=1,1Ø
      DO 5 IROW=1,5
      COLSUM(ICOL)=COLSUM(ICOL)+MAT(IROW,ICOL)
    5 CONTINUE
*-----
      WRITE(6,6)ROWSUM
```

```
   6  FORMAT(/,' THE ROW TOTALS ARE:',//,'    ROW1   ROW2   ROW3',
     +'   ROW4   ROW5',/,1X,5I7)
      WRITE(6,7)COLSUM
   7  FORMAT(//,' THE COLUMN TOTALS ARE:',//,'   COL1  COL2  COL3',
     +'  COL4  COL5  COL6  COL7  COL8  COL9  COL1Ø',/,1X,9I6,I7)
*-----THIS SHOWS THE SUMS IN PERSPECTIVE:
      WRITE(6,9)((MAT(IROW,ICOL),ICOL=1,1Ø),ROWSUM(IROW),IROW=1,5)
   9  FORMAT(//,' IN PERSPECTIVE:',//,(1X,1ØI5,3X,'I',I6))
      WRITE(6,1Ø)COLSUM
  1Ø  FORMAT(1X,53('-'),'I',/,1X,1ØI5)
      END
```

```
THE ROW TOTALS ARE:

   ROW1   ROW2   ROW3   ROW4   ROW5
     -3     41    143    12Ø    165


THE COLUMN TOTALS ARE:

  COL1  COL2  COL3  COL4  COL5  COL6  COL7  COL8  COL9  COL1Ø
   129   -55    39    4Ø    35    87    69    29    61     32


IN PERSPECTIVE:

    3    3   -1    5   1Ø  -33    5    5    1   -1   I    -3
   45  -91    Ø    9   21   9Ø   12  -73   21    7   I    41
   1Ø    8   -6   22    1   34   87   34  -51    4   I   143
    Ø    5    3    1    3    3   -3    2   87   19   I   12Ø
   71   2Ø   43    3    Ø   -7  -32   61    3    3   I   165
-----------------------------------------------------I
  129  -55   39   4Ø   35   87   69   29   61   32
```

Example 11.11

Read the 5 × 10 matrix MAT from the file MATDATA and sort all the columns in numerically ascending order. Print the sorted matrix.

Solution The heart of the program consists of three nested DO-loops. The outer DO-loop acknowledges the fact that there are 10 columns to be sorted. The inner two DO-loops perform the brute-force sort, without either of the two optimization features discussed in Section 11.7. These could be introduced, of course, and this is left as an exercise. Note that the matrix-reading portion of the program is even simpler than in the previous two examples. You should be clear on why we still manage to read the array properly.

```
      DIMENSION MAT(5,1Ø)
      OPEN(7,FILE='MATDATA',STATUS='OLD')
      READ(7,*)((MAT(IROW,ICOL),ICOL=1,1Ø),IROW=1,5)
      CLOSE(7)
*-----
      DO 1 ICOL=1,1Ø
      DO 1 K=1,4
      DO 1 IROW=1,4
      IF(MAT(IROW,ICOL).GT.MAT(IROW+1,ICOL))THEN
          IHOLD=MAT(IROW,ICOL)
          MAT(IROW,ICOL)=MAT(IROW+1,ICOL)
          MAT(IROW+1,ICOL)=IHOLD
      END IF
    1 CONTINUE
*-----
      WRITE(6,2)((MAT(IROW,ICOL),ICOL=1,1Ø),IROW=1,5)
    2 FORMAT(/,' AFTER THE COLUMN SORT, THE MATRIX LOOKS LIKE THIS:',//,
     +(1X,1ØI5))
      END
```

```
AFTER THE COLUMN SORT, THE MATRIX LOOKS LIKE THIS:

    Ø  -91   -6    1    Ø  -33  -32  -73  -51   -1
    3    3   -1    3    1   -7   -3    2    1    3
   1Ø    5    Ø    5    3    3    5    5    3    4
   45    8    3    9   1Ø   34   12   34   21    7
   71   2Ø   43   22   21   9Ø   87   61   87   19
```

After performing the column sort, you could also perform a row sort. This would have the effect of shifting all the ''heavy'' elements to the bottom right corner, leaving the ''lightest'' elements in the top left corner.

11.9 THREE-DIMENSIONAL ARRAYS

A two-dimensional array, also known as a matrix, looks like a parking lot with rows and columns of cars. A three-dimensional array is readily viewed as a number of such parking lots stacked on top of each other to form a parking garage. The following specification statement declares such a three-dimensional structure with 25 floors, each floor with 80 rows and 140 columns:

```
DIMENSION GARAGE(8Ø,14Ø,25)
```

This is a mammoth array containing 280,000 elements, a typical one of which is

```
GARAGE(row,column,floor)
```

The first subscript still identifies the row, the second still points at the column, and the third subscript reveals the floor. If you remember that three-dimensional arrays have "real cute floors," you won't have trouble with the order of the subscripts.

You can probably guess how this structure is dismembered to be stored in the linear memory train. We start on the first floor, break it into its 140 columns, and load these aboard, one after the other. When the first floor is gone, we move to the second and break it into columns, and so on, right up to the 25th floor.

The following innocent looking program would prompt you for data and you would supply it, column by column, floor by floor, until it is satisfied with 280,000 data. That's when you would really learn to appreciate the virtues of file I/O, but it is to be hoped that you no longer need convincing.

```
DIMENSION GARAGE(80,140,25)
READ *,GARAGE
END
```

In the example, a lower dimension bound of 1 is implicit. You could, of course, define different lower dimension bounds for each of the three dimensions.

Example 11.12

Given the following 4 × 6 × 5 integer array M, write a program to read the array into memory in row order by floor, i.e., read the first floor row by row, then the second floor row by row, right up to the fifth floor. Then write the array to a file called GARAGEDATA in the same order. Also write the array to your screen to let you confirm that you entered it correctly. You will need the file for subsequent examples and problems. Write the file in unformatted form with a single write operation. If your system doesn't like such long records, you can switch to formatted output, generating 20 records.

Floor 1	18	56	68	6	19	60
	98	56	50	93	2	73
	83	55	79	78	58	38
	84	87	61	84	51	52
Floor 2	60	26	20	79	92	44
	50	95	18	53	49	16
	64	18	33	34	4	19
	13	33	76	59	71	91
Floor 3	1	47	70	97	51	36
	55	45	70	13	46	59
	17	49	39	95	18	50
	73	22	70	22	3	13
Floor 4	46	30	59	84	68	50
	28	48	30	50	24	98
	65	16	7	92	89	5
	97	52	37	56	95	68

Floor 5	39	3	67	76	51	15
	20	58	63	53	53	36
	71	4	84	68	46	66
	55	34	10	55	36	19

Solution

```
      DIMENSION M(4,6,5)
*-----READING THE DATA INTO MEMORY:
      READ*,(((M(IROW,ICOL,IFLOOR),ICOL=1,6),IROW=1,4),IFLOOR=1,5)
*-----OPENING THE FILE 'GARAGEDATA' FOR OUTPUT:
      OPEN(7,FILE='GARAGEDATA',FORM='UNFORMATTED',STATUS='NEW')
*-----WRITING THE ARRAY TO THE FILE IN UNFORMATTED MODE:
      WRITE(7)(((M(IROW,ICOL,IFLOOR),ICOL=1,6),IROW=1,4),IFLOOR=1,5)
      CLOSE(7)
*-----DISPLAYING THE ARRAY JUST READ:
      DO 1 IFLOOR=1,5
      WRITE(6,2)IFLOOR
    2 FORMAT(' THIS IS FLOOR',I2)
      DO 1 IROW=1,4
      WRITE(6,3)(M(IROW,ICOL,IFLOOR),ICOL=1,6)
    3 FORMAT(20X,6I4)
    1 CONTINUE
      END
```

```
?18 56 68 6 19 60 98 56 50 93 2 73 83 55 79 78 58 38 84 87 61 84 51 52
?60 26 20 79 92 44 50 95 18 53 49 16 64 18 33 34 4 19 13 33 76 59 71 91
?1 47 70 97 51 36 55 45 70 13 46 59 17 49 39 95 18 50 73 22 70 22 3 13
?46 30 59 84 68 50 28 48 30 50 24 98 65 16 7 92 89 5 97 52 37 56 95 68
?39 3 67 76 51 15 20 58 63 53 53 36 71 4 84 68 46 66 55 34 10 55 36 19

THIS IS FLOOR 1
                     18  56  68   6  19  60
                     98  56  50  93   2  73
                     83  55  79  78  58  38
                     84  87  61  84  51  52
THIS IS FLOOR 2
                     60  26  20  79  92  44
                     50  95  18  53  49  16
                     64  18  33  34   4  19
                     13  33  76  59  71  91
THIS IS FLOOR 3
                      1  47  70  97  51  36
                     55  45  70  13  46  59
                     17  49  39  95  18  50
                     73  22  70  22   3  13
```

```
THIS IS FLOOR 4
                    46  3Ø  59  84  68  5Ø
                    28  48  3Ø  5Ø  24  98
                    65  16   7  92  89   5
                    97  52  37  56  95  68
THIS IS FLOOR 5
                    39   3  67  76  51  15
                    2Ø  58  63  53  53  36
                    71   4  84  68  46  66
                    55  34  1Ø  55  36  19
```

Example 11.13

Fill a 4 × 6 × 5 integer array M from the file of the previous example. Compute and report the sum of the fourth row of each floor and of the sixth column of each floor.

Solution 1

```
      INTEGER M(4,6,5),ROW4,COL6
*-----READING THE DATA FROM THE FILE:
      OPEN(7,FILE='GARAGEDATA',FORM='UNFORMATTED',STATUS='OLD')
      READ(7)(((M(IROW,ICOL,IFLOOR),ICOL=1,6),IROW=1,4),IFLOOR=1,5)
      CLOSE(7)
*-----WE NOW INITIALIZE ROW4 AND COL6 TO ZERO ON EACH FLOOR.
      DO 1 IFLOOR=1,5
      ROW4=Ø
      COL6=Ø
*-----
      DO 2 IROW=1,4
      COL6=COL6+M(IROW,6,IFLOOR)
    2 CONTINUE
*-----
      DO 3 ICOL=1,6
      ROW4=ROW4+M(4,ICOL,IFLOOR)
    3 CONTINUE
*-----
      WRITE(6,4)IFLOOR,ROW4,COL6
    4 FORMAT(' ON FLOOR',I2,' ROW 4 SUMS TO',I4,', COLUMN 6 TO',I4)
    1 CONTINUE
      END

ON FLOOR 1 ROW 4 SUMS TO 419, COLUMN 6 TO 223
ON FLOOR 2 ROW 4 SUMS TO 343, COLUMN 6 TO 17Ø
ON FLOOR 3 ROW 4 SUMS TO 2Ø3, COLUMN 6 TO 158
ON FLOOR 4 ROW 4 SUMS TO 4Ø5, COLUMN 6 TO 221
ON FLOOR 5 ROW 4 SUMS TO 2Ø9, COLUMN 6 TO 136
```

Discussion The sums were computed and reported floor by floor. A different approach is to compute the five column sums and the five row sums before reporting these. The latter approach is presented as Solution 2. It requires the sums to be stored in arrays.

Solution 2

```
      INTEGER M(4,6,5),COL6(5),ROW4(5)
*-----READING THE DATA FROM THE FILE:
      OPEN(7,FILE='GARAGEDATA',FORM='UNFORMATTED',STATUS='OLD')
      READ(7)(((M(IROW,ICOL,IFLOOR),ICOL=1,6),IROW=1,4),IFLOOR=1,5)
      CLOSE(7)
*-----CLEARING OUT THE TWO SUM VECTORS
      DO 5 IFLOOR=1,5
      ROW4(IFLOOR)=Ø
      COL6(IFLOOR)=Ø
    5 CONTINUE
*-----
      DO 1 IFLOOR=1,5
      DO 2 IROW=1,4
      COL6(IFLOOR)=COL6(IFLOOR)+M(IROW,6,IFLOOR)
    2 CONTINUE
*-----
      DO 3 ICOL=1,6
      ROW4(IFLOOR)=ROW4(IFLOOR)+M(4,ICOL,IFLOOR)
    3 CONTINUE
    1 CONTINUE
*-----
      DO 6 IFLOOR=1,5
      WRITE(6,4)IFLOOR,ROW4(IFLOOR),COL6(IFLOOR)
    4 FORMAT(' ON FLOOR',I2,' ROW 4 SUMS TO',I4,', COLUMN 6 TO',I4)
    6 CONTINUE
      END
```

```
ON FLOOR 1 ROW 4 SUMS TO 419, COLUMN 6 TO 223
ON FLOOR 2 ROW 4 SUMS TO 343, COLUMN 6 TO 17Ø
ON FLOOR 3 ROW 4 SUMS TO 2Ø3, COLUMN 6 TO 158
ON FLOOR 4 ROW 4 SUMS TO 4Ø5, COLUMN 6 TO 221
ON FLOOR 5 ROW 4 SUMS TO 2Ø9, COLUMN 6 TO 136
```

Example 11.14

Still working with the array M of the previous example, you may think of each element on the first floor as the bottom of a pillar extending up to the fifth floor. Compute and report the sums of the pillars resting on elements M(1,1,1), M(1,6,1), M(3,5,1), M(4,6,1), and M(1,4,1).

Solution

```
      IMPLICIT INTEGER(S)
      DIMENSION M(4,6,5)
      OPEN(7,FILE='GARAGEDATA',FORM='UNFORMATTED',STATUS='OLD')
      READ(7)(((M(IROW,ICOL,IFLOOR),ICOL=1,6),IROW=1,4),IFLOOR=1,5)
      CLOSE(7)
*-----
      SUM111=Ø
      SUM161=Ø
      SUM351=Ø
      SUM461=Ø
      SUM141=Ø
*-----
      DO 1 IFLOOR=1,5
      SUM111=SUM111+M(1,1,IFLOOR)
      SUM161=SUM161+M(1,6,IFLOOR)
      SUM351=SUM351+M(3,5,IFLOOR)
      SUM461=SUM461+M(4,6,IFLOOR)
      SUM141=SUM141+M(1,4,IFLOOR)
    1 CONTINUE
*-----
      WRITE(6,2)SUM111,SUM161,SUM351,SUM461,SUM141
    2 FORMAT(' THE PILLAR RESTING ON M(1,1,1) SUMS TO',I4,/,
     +' THE PILLAR RESTING ON M(1,6,1) SUMS TO',I4,/,
     +' THE PILLAR RESTING ON M(3,5,1) SUMS TO',I4,/,
     +' THE PILLAR RESTING ON M(4,6,1) SUMS TO',I4,/,
     +' THE PILLAR RESTING ON M(1,4,1) SUMS TO',I4)
      END
```

```
THE PILLAR RESTING ON M(1,1,1) SUMS TO 164
THE PILLAR RESTING ON M(1,6,1) SUMS TO 2Ø5
THE PILLAR RESTING ON M(3,5,1) SUMS TO 215
THE PILLAR RESTING ON M(4,6,1) SUMS TO 243
THE PILLAR RESTING ON M(1,4,1) SUMS TO 342
```

Example 11.15

Still working with the 4 × 6 × 5 array M or the previous examples, write a program to (1) compute and report the sum of each floor, (2) compute and report the sum of all 120 elements of the array, (3) show the wall resting on the third row of the first floor and extending up to the fifth floor, and (4) show the wall resting on the fifth column of the first floor.

Solution

```
      INTEGER M(4,6,5),SUM(5),TOTAL
      OPEN(7,FILE='GARAGEDATA',FORM='UNFORMATTED',STATUS='OLD')
      READ(7)(((M(IROW,ICOL,IFLOOR),ICOL=1,6),IROW=1,4),IFLOOR=1,5)
      CLOSE(7)
*-----
      DO 1 IFLOOR=1,5
      SUM(IFLOOR)=Ø
    1 CONTINUE
*-----
      TOTAL=Ø
*-----
      DO 2 IFLOOR=1,5
      DO 2 IROW=1,4
      DO 2 ICOL=1,6
      SUM(IFLOOR)=SUM(IFLOOR)+M(IROW,ICOL,IFLOOR)
      TOTAL=TOTAL+M(IROW,ICOL,IFLOOR)
    2 CONTINUE
*-----
      WRITE(6,3)(IFLOOR,SUM(IFLOOR),IFLOOR=1,5)
    3 FORMAT(' THE ELEMENTS ON FLOOR',I2,' ADD UP TO',I5)
      WRITE(6,4)TOTAL
    4 FORMAT(/,' THE SUM OF ALL 12Ø ELEMENTS OF THE ARRAY IS',I5)
*-----
      WRITE(6,6)((M(3,ICOL,IFLOOR),ICOL=1,6),IFLOOR=5,1,-1)
    6 FORMAT(/,' THE WALL RESTING ON ROW 3 OF THE FIRST FLOOR IS',//,
     +(1X,6I4))
*-----
      WRITE(6,8)((M(IROW,5,IFLOOR),IROW=1,4),IFLOOR=5,1,-1)
    8 FORMAT(/,' THE WALL RESTING ON COLUMN 5 OF THE FIRST FLOOR IS',//,
     +(1X,4I4))
*-----
      END
```

```
THE ELEMENTS ON FLOOR 1 ADD UP TO 14Ø9
THE ELEMENTS ON FLOOR 2 ADD UP TO 1117
THE ELEMENTS ON FLOOR 3 ADD UP TO 1Ø61
THE ELEMENTS ON FLOOR 4 ADD UP TO 1294
THE ELEMENTS ON FLOOR 5 ADD UP TO 1Ø82

THE SUM OF ALL 12Ø ELEMENTS OF THE ARRAY IS 5963
```

```
THE WALL RESTING ON ROW 3 OF THE FIRST FLOOR IS

 71   4  84  68  46  66
 65  16   7  92  89   5
 17  49  39  95  18  5Ø
 64  18  33  34   4  19
 83  55  79  78  58  38

THE WALL RESTING ON COLUMN 5 OF THE FIRST FLOOR IS

 51  53  46  36
 68  24  89  95
 51  46  18   3
 92  49   4  71
 19   2  58  51
```

11.10 ARRAYS WITH MORE THAN THREE DIMENSIONS

FORTRAN allows arrays to have as many as seven dimensions, but some compilers accept more than that, provided you have enough memory.

A three-dimensional array is easily visualized as a parking garage and you can picture a four-dimensional array as a village composed of parking garages. The first subscript refers to the row, the second to the column, the third to the floor, and the fourth identifies the building. The following DIMENSION statement requests a village of 10 garages, each with 7 floors, each with 6 rows and 5 columns:

```
DIMENSION VILLAGE(6,5,7,1Ø)
```

This modest village can hold 2100 cars, and the address of a typical parking spot is

```
VILLAGE(row,column,floor,building)
```

As you could have predicted, this village is stored in memory column by column, floor by floor, building by building.

A five-dimensional array is a country composed of villages. The next DIMENSION statement defines a country with 33 villages, each with 10 garages, each with 7 floors, each with 6 rows and 5 columns:

```
DIMENSION COUNTRY(6,5,7,1Ø,33)
```

That country holds 69,300 cars, and a typical parking spot has the following address:

```
COUNTRY(row,column,floor,building,village)
```

You could go on and on, but you get the idea. Thinking in terms of arrays and subscripts becomes easier the more you do it. It is hoped that you worked through all the examples, and will now tackle the problems.

11.11 PROBLEMS

11.1. What is wrong with the following program? The problem is considered to be very serious.

```
READ(5,*)X
DIMENSION X(5)
WRITE(6,*)X
END
```

11.2. Each of the following twelve programs reads the number of records indicated below it. Justify that number.

```
  DIMENSION X(2Ø)
  READ(5,1)X
1 FORMAT(2ØF4.Ø)
  END
  (1)
```

```
  DIMENSION X(2Ø)
  READ(5,1)X
1 FORMAT(1ØF4.Ø)
  END
  (2)
```

```
  DIMENSION X(2Ø)
  READ(5,1)X
1 FORMAT(F4.Ø)
  END
  (2Ø)
```

```
  DIMENSION X(2Ø)
  READ(5,1)X(2Ø)
1 FORMAT(5F4.Ø)
  END
  (1)
```

```
  DIMENSION X(2Ø)
  READ(5,1)X(1),X(7)
1 FORMAT(5F4.Ø)
  END
  (1)
```

```
  DIMENSION X(2Ø)
  READ(5,1)(X(J),J=1,2Ø)
1 FORMAT(5F4.Ø)
  END
  (4)
```

```
  DIMENSION X(2Ø)
  READ(5,1)(X(J),J=1,2Ø,2)
1 FORMAT(F4.Ø)
  END
  (1Ø)
```

```
  DIMENSION X(2Ø)
  READ(5,1)(X(J),J=1,2Ø)
1 FORMAT(2ØF4.Ø)
  END
  (1)
```

```
  DIMENSION X(2Ø)
  READ(5,1)(X(J),J=2Ø,1)
1 FORMAT(F4.Ø)
  END
  (1)
```

```
  DIMENSION X(2Ø)
  DO 2 J=1,2Ø
  READ(5,1)X(J)
1 FORMAT(2ØF4.Ø)
2 CONTINUE
  END
  (2Ø)
```

```
  DIMENSION X(2Ø)
  DO 2 J=1,2Ø
  READ(5,1)X
1 FORMAT(1ØF4.Ø)
2 CONTINUE
  END
  (4Ø)
```

```
  DIMENSION X(2Ø)
  DO 2 J=1,2Ø
  READ(5,1)(X(K),K=2Ø,1)
1 FORMAT(2ØF4.Ø)
2 CONTINUE
  END
  (2Ø)
```

11.3. Show the output produced by each of the following programs. The horizontal spacing need only be approximate, but the number of records must be accurate. Confirm your predictions on the computer.

```
      DIMENSION M(10)
      DO 1 I=1,10
      M(I)=I
1     CONTINUE
      WRITE(6,2)M
2     FORMAT(1X,10I5)
      END
```

```
      DIMENSION M(10)
      DO 1 I=1,10
      M(I)=I
1     CONTINUE
      DO 3 K=9,1,-1
      WRITE(6,2)M(K)
2     FORMAT(1X,10I5)
3     CONTINUE
      END
```

```
      DIMENSION M(10)
      DO 1 I=1,10
      M(I)=I
1     CONTINUE
      WRITE(6,2)(M(K),K=9,1,-1)
2     FORMAT(1X,10I5)
      END
```

11.4. In the next nine programs, M is the following 3 × 4 matrix:

1	2	3	4
5	6	7	8
9	10	11	12

(a) In which order must the elements of this array be entered into the following program to have the array printed in proper row order? Confirm your prediction on the computer.

```
      DIMENSION M(3,4)
      READ(5,*)M
      DO 1 IROW=1,3
      WRITE(6,2)(M(IROW,ICOL),ICOL=1,4)
2     FORMAT(1X,4I5)
1     CONTINUE
      END
```

(b) Show the output produced by the following program if you were to enter the elements of the same array M in column order. Confirm your prediction on the computer.

```
      DIMENSION M(3,4)
      READ(5,*)M
      WRITE(6,2)M
2     FORMAT(1X,4I5)
      END
```

(c) Again the array M is entered in column order. Show and confirm the output produced by this program:

```
      DIMENSION M(3,4)
      READ(5,*)M
      WRITE(6,2)M
2     FORMAT(1X,3I5)
      END
```

(d) Reading the array M the same way, predict and then confirm the output generated by this program:

```
      DIMENSION M(3,4)
      READ(5,*)M
      WRITE(6,2)((M(IROW,ICOL),IROW=1,3),ICOL=1,4)
    2 FORMAT(1X,12I5)
      END
```

(e) Show and confirm the output, assuming the same array and the same reading order.

```
      DIMENSION M(3,4)
      READ(5,*)M
      WRITE(6,2)((M(IROW,ICOL),ICOL=1,4),IROW=1,3)
    2 FORMAT(1X,12I5)
      END
```

(f) Show and confirm the output, assuming the same array and the same reading order.

```
      DIMENSION M(3,4)
      READ(5,*)M
      WRITE(6,2)((M(IROW,ICOL),ICOL=1,4),IROW=1,3)
    2 FORMAT(1X,4I5)
      END
```

(g) Show and confirm the output, assuming the same array and the same reading order.

```
      DIMENSION M(3,4)
      READ(5,*)M
      DO 1 IROW=1,3
      DO 1 ICOL=1,4
      WRITE(6,2)M(IROW,ICOL)
    2 FORMAT(1X,4I5)
    1 CONTINUE
      END
```

(h) Show and confirm the output, assuming the same array and the same reading order.

```
      DIMENSION M(3,4)
      READ(5,*)M
      DO 1 IROW=1,3
      WRITE(6,2)(M(IROW,ICOL),ICOL=1,4)
    2 FORMAT(1X,4I5)
    1 CONTINUE
      END
```

(i) Show and confirm the output, assuming the same array and the same reading order.

```
      DIMENSION M(3,4)
      READ(5,*)M
      DO 1 ICOL=1,4
      WRITE(6,2)(M(IROW,ICOL),IROW=1,3)
    2 FORMAT(1X,4I5)
    1 CONTINUE
      END
```

11.5. Define the word *contiguous*. Are arrays stored contiguously in memory? In what order are the elements of a two-dimensional array stored in memory? A three-dimensional array?

```
      DO 1 I=1,2ØØØ
      M(I)=MOD(I**2,2*I+321)
    1 CONTINUE
```

11.6. Declare a 2000-element one-dimensional array M and fill it with data using the following DO-loop:

(a) Before entering the loop, write '. . . . STARTING TO FILL THE ARRAY'. After leaving the loop, write '. . . . ARRAY FILLED'. This will give you some feeling for the speed of your system once you execute the program.
(b) Print elements 1, 251, 501, 751, 1001, 1251, 1501, and 1751.
(c) Report the sum of the first 1600 elements.
(d) Now report the sum of all the odd-numbered elements, i.e., elements 1, 3, 5, 7, . . . , 1999. (Please be aware that we are not referring to the elements that contain odd numbers, but the elements in the odd-numbered positions in the array.)
(e) Compute and report the sum of all the elements that are odd numbers.
(f) Report the sum of all the even-numbered elements, i.e., elements 2, 4, 6, . . . , 2000.
(g) Compute and report the sum of all the elements that are even numbers.
(h) Compute and report the sum of all the elements in positions 1329 to 1871.
(i) Compute and report the average of the sum of the squares of the first 600 elements of the array.
(j) Compute and report the mean value of all 2000 elements. (The mean is the straight average.)
(k) Determine and report how many of the 2000 elements are smaller than 133.

Your output should look exactly like the output shown, although the two floating-point calculations might yield slightly different values on your system.

```
 .... STARTING TO FILL THE ARRAY
 .... ARRAY FILLED

ELEMENT    1 CONTAINS    1
ELEMENT  251 CONTAINS  453
ELEMENT  5Ø1 CONTAINS  954
ELEMENT  751 CONTAINS  694
ELEMENT 1ØØ1 CONTAINS  788
ELEMENT 1251 CONTAINS 1Ø59
ELEMENT 15Ø1 CONTAINS    7
ELEMENT 1751 CONTAINS 3778
```

```
THE SUM OF THE FIRST 16ØØ ELEMENTS IS 15243ØØ

THE SUM OF ALL THE ODD-NUMBERED ELEMENTS IS 1152175

THE SUM OF ALL THE ODD ELEMENTS IS 1165594

THE SUM OF ALL THE EVEN-NUMBERED ELEMENTS IS 1174657

THE SUM OF ALL THE EVEN ELEMENTS IS 1161238

THE SUM OF THE ELEMENTS IN POSITIONS 1329-1871 IS 949487

THE AVERAGE OF THE SUM OF THE SQUARES OF THE FIRST 6ØØ ELEMENTS IS 319729.8

THE MEAN VALUE OF ALL 2ØØØ ELEMENTS IS 1163.42

THE NUMBER OF ELEMENTS SMALLER THAN 133 IS 18Ø
```

11.7. Declare a 50 × 50 real matrix X and fill it with data using the following nested DO-loops:

```
      DO 1 IROW=1,5Ø
      DO 1 ICOL=1,5Ø
      X(IROW,ICOL) = MOD((IROW+ICOL)**3,IROW*ICOL+321)/1Ø.
    1 CONTINUE
```

(a) Before entering the loops, write '. . . . STARTING TO FILL THE MATRIX'. After leaving the loops, write '. . . . MATRIX FILLED'. Again, these messages are designed to give you some insight into the performance of your machine.
(b) Print elements X(19,24), X(27,42), X(33,1), X(39,37), and X(41,50).
(c) Compute all the column totals and store these in a 50-element vector called COLSUM.
(d) Report the column totals for columns 1, 11, 21, 31, and 41.
(e) Compute all the row totals and store these in a 50-element vector called ROWSUM.
(f) Report the row totals for rows 10, 20, 30, 40, and 50.
(g) Sum all the elements in all the rows to produce one grand total. Do not take the shortcut of simply adding the 50 elements of ROWSUM. That will be done later.
(h) Sum all the elements in all the columns to produce one grand total. Again, don't take the shortcut of adding all the elements of COLSUM. Don't be surprised if the two sums disagree slightly; floating-point arithmetic is the culprit. (There is no disagreement in the output shown, but you may be running on a different system.)
(i) Sum all 50 elements of ROWSUM. How does that sum compare with the previous sums? We are obviously dealing with *batch addition* here, and you would expect the total to be more accurate. (You may wish to review Problem 10.6 if batch addition isn't familiar.) Needless to say, if we were dealing with an integer array, the sum would always be the same no matter how we go about adding the elements.
(j) Sum all 50 elements of COLSUM. How does this sum compare with the previous sums?
(k) Report the sum of the elements of the diagonal running from the top left corner to the bottom right corner.
(l) Report the sum of the elements of the diagonal running from the top right corner to the bottom left corner.
(m) Show the 3 × 3 matrix cut out of the northwest corner of the 50 × 50 array X.
(n) Show the 3 × 3 matrix cut out of the northeast corner of the 50 × 50 array X.
(o) Show the 3 × 3 matrix cut out of the southeast corner of the 50 × 50 array X.

(p) Show the 3 × 3 matrix cut out of the southwest corner of the 50 × 50 array X.
(q) Compute and report the sum of all the elements on and below the diagonal running from the top left corner to the bottom right corner of the matrix.
(r) Compute and report the sum of all the elements on and below the diagonal running from the top right corner to the bottom left corner of the matrix.

Your output should look much like that shown. Some of your totals may differ slightly because different machines have different floating-point error accumulations.

```
.... STARTING TO FILL THE MATRIX
.... MATRIX FILLED

X(19,24)= 25.3     X(27,42)=113.4     X(33,1)=  1.0
X(39,37)=150.4     X(41,50)=196.4

     COL  1       COL 11       COL 21       COL 31       COL 41
     725.80      1549.90      2056.80      2638.10      3433.10

     ROW 10       ROW 20       ROW 30       ROW 40       ROW 50
    1313.90      2440.50      2337.30      2639.40      3896.50

ADDING ALL 2500 ELEMENTS ROW BY ROW PRODUCES THE SUM 120154.73

ADDING ALL 2500 ELEMENTS COLUMN BY COLUMN PRODUCES THE SUM 120154.73

THE SUM OF THE ROW TOTALS IS 120157.20

THE SUM OF THE COLUMN TOTALS IS 120157.20

THE SUM OF THE LEFT-RIGHT DIAGONAL ELEMENTS IS 3410.70

THE SUM OF THE RIGHT-LEFT DIAGONAL ELEMENTS IS 2127.80

                THE NORTH-WEST CORNER OF THE ARRAY:

                         .80     2.70     6.40
                        2.70     6.40    12.50
                        6.40    12.50    21.60

                THE NORTH-EAST CORNER OF THE ARRAY:

                       30.70    31.00    20.40
                       31.70    24.70    41.50
                       12.60    20.80     4.10

                THE SOUTH-EAST CORNER OF THE ARRAY:

                       11.10   118.00   244.70
                      118.00   210.20    44.90
                      244.70    44.90   136.60
```

```
                THE SOUTH-WEST CORNER OF THE ARRAY:

                     30.70    31.70    12.60
                     31.00    24.70    20.80
                     20.40    41.50     4.10

THE SUM ON AND BELOW THE LEFT-RIGHT DIAGONAL IS 61783.80

THE SUM ON AND BELOW THE RIGHT-LEFT DIAGONAL IS 85793.81
```

11.8. Declare a 50 × 50 real matrix X and fill it with data generated by the same nested DO loops:

```
      DO 1 IROW=1,50
      DO 1 ICOL=1,50
      X(IROW,ICOL) = MOD((IROW+ICOL)**3,IROW*ICOL+321)/10.
    1 CONTINUE
```

(a) Perform an ascending sort on all 50 columns of the array. Before launching into the sort, print '. . . . COLUMN SORT STARTS'. When the sort is finished, print '. . . . COLUMN SORT DONE'.
(b) Print elements X(1,1), X(1,21), and X(1,41).
(c) Print elements X(50,1), X(50,21), and X(50,41).
(d) Perform an ascending sort on all 50 rows of the array. Before the sort, print '. . . . ROW SORT STARTS'. When the sort is finished, print '. . . . ROW SORT DONE'.
(e) Print elements X(1,1), X(1,21), and X(1,41).
(f) Print elements X(50,1), X(50,21), and X(50,41).
(g) Compute and report the sum of all the elements of the array in row order, starting with element X(1,1) and concluding with element X(50,50).
(h) Compute and report the sum of all the elements of the array in row order, but this time starting with element X(50,50) and working back to element X(1,1).
(i) Show the two 3 × 3 matrices cut out of the northwest and southeast corners of the sorted 50 × 50 matrix.
(j) Your output should look something like the output shown, although your totals may differ if you are using a different system. If you are running DEC's VMS operating system on VAX hardware, for example, there will still be a difference, but it won't be nearly as significant. Explain why the two sums are different. Which of these two totals is more reliable and why?

```
.... COLUMN SORT STARTS
.... COLUMN SORT DONE

X(1 ,1)=     .70         X(1 ,21)=     .00        X(1 ,41)=     .00
X(50,1)=   34.60         X(50,21)=  102.60        X(50,41)=  224.60

.... ROW SORT STARTS
.... ROW SORT DONE

X(1 ,1)=     .00         X(1 ,21)=     .80        X(1 ,41)=    1.30
X(50,1)=   34.60         X(50,21)=  114.40        X(50,41)=  205.60
```

```
SUM OF ALL ELEMENTS FROM X(1,1) TO X(50,50) IS 120155.40

SUM OF ALL ELEMENTS FROM X(50,50) TO X(1,1) IS 120152.01

                    THE NORTH-WEST CORNER OF THE ARRAY:

                           .00       .00       .00
                           .30       .70       .80
                           .80      1.40      1.40

                    THE SOUTH-EAST CORNER OF THE ARRAY:

                        205.00    205.60    224.60
                        210.20    229.60    234.80
                        244.70    247.50    247.50
```

11.9. The following are the four floors of a 4 × 4 × 4 integer array M. Write a program to read this array in row order, starting with the first floor, then follow the steps indicated. The program will require a fair amount of testing, and you won't enjoy entering the data for each test run. It is therefore recommended that you create a data file and read from that file.

```
         FLOOR 1                             FLOOR 2

   1    4    2    1                   19    4   -3    1
   3   -7    5    9                    0    2    7   -7
   1    8   -1    0                    5    4    3    1
   6    3   -4   33                   71   -6   -4    3


         FLOOR 3                             FLOOR 4

   2    7    4    9                   18   -1    0    7
 -17    5   20    0                   -9    2    4    0
   1    2    4   -3                    3   32    1   18
  -2    7   17   22                   49   -3  -93   12
```

(a) Display all four floors of the array.
(b) Show the diagonal running from the top left to the bottom right on each floor.
(c) Compute and report the sum of all the positive elements.
(d) Compute and report the sum of all the negative elements.
(e) Compute and report the average of all the elements.
(f) Compute and report the sum of the diagonal elements located along the line joining elements M(1,1,1) and M(4,4,4).
(g) The diagonal plane contains the first column of the first floor, the second column of the second floor, the third column of the third floor, and the fourth column of the fourth floor. Show that diagonal plane.
(h) Interchange each element on the first floor with its counterpart on the third floor.
(i) Interchange each element on the second floor with its counterpart on the fourth floor.
(j) Display all four floors of the array.

Your output should be similar to that shown:

```
FLOOR 1                    1    4    2    1
                           3   -7    5    9
                           1    8   -1    Ø
                           6    3   -4   33

FLOOR 2                   19    4   -3    1
                           Ø    2    7   -7
                           5    4    3    1
                          71   -6   -4    3

FLOOR 3                    2    7    4    9
                         -17    5   2Ø    Ø
                           1    2    4   -3
                          -2    7   17   22

FLOOR 4                   18   -1    Ø    7
                          -9    2    4    Ø
                           3   32    1   18
                          49   -3  -93   12

FLOOR  1 DIAGONAL:         1   -7   -1   33

FLOOR  2 DIAGONAL:        19    2    3    3

FLOOR  3 DIAGONAL:         2    5    4   22

FLOOR  4 DIAGONAL:        18    2    1   12

THE SUM OF ALL THE POSITIVE ELEMENTS IS 442

THE SUM OF ALL THE NEGATIVE ELEMENTS IS -16Ø

THE AVERAGE OF ALL THE ELEMENTS IS 4.41

THE SUM OF THE 'DIAGONAL' ELEMENTS IS 19

THE DIAGONAL PLANE:        1    4    4    7
                           3    2   2Ø    Ø
                           1    4    4   18
                           6   -6   17   12

FLOOR 1                    2    7    4    9
                         -17    5   2Ø    Ø
                           1    2    4   -3
                          -2    7   17   22

FLOOR 2                   18   -1    Ø    7
                          -9    2    4    Ø
                           3   32    1   18
                          49   -3  -93   12

FLOOR 3                    1    4    2    1
                           3   -7    5    9
```

```
                        1     8    -1     Ø
                        6     3    -4    33

FLOOR 4                19     4    -3     1
                        Ø     2     7    -7
                        5     4     3     1
                       71    -6    -4     3
```

12

DOUBLE PRECISION

12.1 INTRODUCTION

The last three chapters were very important and quite intense, and you will therefore enjoy the brevity and simplicity of this one. To this point, especially in the problem section of the previous chapter, there have been numerous encounters with inaccuracies inherent in short floating-point (real) calculations, and it has been clear that the limited number of mantissa bits is the real culprit. On several occasions, it was mentioned that double-word floating-point storage, in which two words are linked, is also available. The first word still contains the exponent and the mantissa in the same form as in the case of short floating-point, but the second word is added to accommodate additional mantissa bits. The technical name for such double-word floating-point storage is long floating-point, and it is the subject of this chapter. To avoid potential confusion, we summarize the generic names and the equivalent FORTRAN names for the three storage modes. The generic and FORTRAN names are used interchangeably, depending on the context.

Generic name	FORTRAN name
Fixed-point	INTEGER
Short floating-point	REAL
Long floating-point	DOUBLE PRECISION

12.2 INTEGER, REAL, AND DOUBLE PRECISION VARIABLES AND CONSTANTS

In FORTRAN, numeric storage defaults implicitly to either integer or real, depending on the variable names chosen. If a variable begins with I, J, K, L, M, or N, integer storage is implied. If the variable name begins with one of the remaining twenty letters, real storage is chosen, but this implicit data typing can be overruled by using the REAL, INTEGER, or IMPLICIT specifications, as discussed in Chapter 6. Constants are also stored in fixed-point or in floating-point form, depending on whether or not they contain a decimal point. In the two assignment statements that follow, for example, KILO is an integer variable and 3 is an integer constant. Similarly, BETA is a real variable, and 5.78E−1 and 3.52 are real constants. Constants are stored in DOUBLE PRECISION mode when they contain a D. Examples are 1.3D+03, 1.3D03, 1.3D3, 5.0D0, 5D0, and 546.23D−4.

```
KILO = 3
BETA = 5.78E − 1 * 3.52
```

Double-precision variables must be specifically declared. Figure 12.1 shows a program in which the variable KILO is declared DOUBLE PRECISION. A double-precision constant is then assigned to it, and KILO is printed using both list-directed and formatted output. Note the double-precision constant in the second statement; the D identifies it as such.

```
      DOUBLE PRECISION KILO
      KILO=5.78D-1
      PRINT*,'KILO HAS THE VALUE',KILO
      WRITE(6,1)KILO
    1 FORMAT(/,' KILO HAS THE VALUE',D11.3)
      END

 KILO HAS THE VALUE .578ØØØØØØØØØØØØØØØ

 KILO HAS THE VALUE   .578D+ØØ
```

Figure 12.1 A double-precision variable and constant.

The program shows that formatted double-precision output requires Dw.d editing, where w is the total output field width, and d is the number of desired decimal places. The D is to be interpreted exactly like the E in Ew.d editing. Notice the D appearing in the output.

The opening statement in Fig. 12.1 is a data type-statement, specifying that KILO is to be stored in double-precision mode, and you now have three different data types to choose from. DOUBLE PRECISION specifications can also take the following two forms:

```
IMPLICIT DOUBLE PRECISION (A-K)
DOUBLE PRECISION KILO(10000)
```

The first informs the compiler that all variables with names beginning with any letter from A to K are to provide long floating-point storage, and the second is equivalent to the following two statements:

DIMENSION KILO(10000)
DOUBLE PRECISION KILO

The best way to learn how to use DOUBLE PRECISION is to see several examples. Figure 12.2 shows a program in which 0.1 is added 100,000 times to produce a sum. Only single-precision entities are involved, and the sum falls short of the expected 0.1000000000000E+05. You may wish to review Problem 10.6, where the two sources of error are discussed in considerable detail.

```
      FRAC=Ø.1
      SUM=Ø.
      DO 1 I=1,1ØØØØØ
      SUM=SUM+FRAC
    1 CONTINUE
      WRITE(6,2)SUM
    2 FORMAT(' THE ACCUMULATED SUM IS',E2Ø.13)
      END

 THE ACCUMULATED SUM IS  .9976ØØØØØØØØØE+Ø4
```

Figure 12.2 Short floating-point error accumulation.

In the next example, shown in Fig. 12.3, the accumulating variable SUM is declared DOUBLE PRECISION, but FRAC is left in single-precision mode and therefore contains the binary equivalent of 0.1 in truncated form, possibly rounded up, depending on the hardware. (You will recall from Prob. 10.6 that 0.1_{10} is a nonterminating fraction on the binary level.) The actual addition in Fig. 12.3 is performed in long floating-point mode, and bit dropping is greatly reduced when the exponents are adjusted, a mechanism explained in Problem 10.6. The resulting sum is very much improved, but the point is that although the addition is performed in long floating-point mode, the value stored in the single-precision variable FRAC

```
      DOUBLE PRECISION SUM
      FRAC=Ø.1
      SUM=Ø.
      DO 1 I=1,1ØØØØØ
      SUM=SUM+FRAC
    1 CONTINUE
      WRITE(6,2)SUM
    2 FORMAT(' THE ACCUMULATED SUM IS',D2Ø.13)
      END

 THE ACCUMULATED SUM IS  .1ØØØØØØØ149Ø1D+Ø5
```

Figure 12.3 The precision problem is addressed incompletely.

```
      DOUBLE PRECISION SUM,FRAC
      FRAC=Ø.1DØ
      SUM=Ø.DØ
      DO 1 I=1,1ØØØØØ
      SUM=SUM+FRAC
    1 CONTINUE
      WRITE(6,2)SUM
    2 FORMAT(' THE ACCUMULATED SUM IS',D2Ø.13)
      END

 THE ACCUMULATED SUM IS   .1ØØØØØØØØØØØØD+Ø5
```

Figure 12.4 Proper use of DOUBLE PRECISION.

is still inaccurate. As a matter of fact, you will notice that now the sum is greater than expected, suggesting that on the hardware on which this example was run, FRAC had been rounded up, but this may be different on your system.

In Fig. 12.4, FRAC is now also declared DOUBLE PRECISION, and the two constants are changed to double-precision form. Now the sum looks good, and the moral is that if you want double-precision results, all the contributing elements must be stored in double-precision mode.

12.3 INTRINSIC FUNCTIONS AVAILABLE FOR DOUBLE-PRECISION WORK

The FORTRAN 77 intrinsic functions were introduced in Section 4.12 and they are summarized in Appendix C. In general, any intrinsic function that accepts REAL arguments to produce a REAL result will also accept DOUBLE PRECISION arguments to produce a DOUBLE PRECISION result. The functions are

AINT(X)	ANINT(X)	NINT(X)	ABS(X)	MOD(X,Y)
SIGN(X,Y)	DIM(X,Y)	MAX(X,Y,..)	MIN(X,Y,..)	SQRT(X)
EXP(X)	LOG(X)	LOG10(X)	SIN(X)	COS(X)
TAN(X)	ASIN(X)	ACOS(X)	ATAN(X)	ATAN2(X,Y)
SINH(X)	COSH(X)	TANH(X)		

12.4 EXAMPLES

Example 12.1

The notation $n!$ represents the product $n(n-1)(n-2)(n-3)\ldots(3)(2)(1)$ and is referred to as *n factorial*. For example,

$$
\begin{aligned}
5! &= 5 \times 4 \times 3 \times 2 \times 1 = 120\\
4! &= 4 \times 3 \times 2 \times 1 \quad = 24\\
3! &= 3 \times 2 \times 1 \quad = 6\\
2! &= 2 \times 1 \quad = 2\\
1! &= 1\\
0! &= 1 \quad \text{(by definition)}
\end{aligned}
$$

Write a program to compute 1!, 2!, 3!, 4!, 5!, . . ., 95! Use real arithmetic.

Solution

```
      WRITE(6,1)
    1 FORMAT(3X,'N',18X,'N!',/,2X,'--',5X,'---------------')
*-----
      FAC=1.
*-----
      DO 2 I=1,95
      FAC=FAC*I
      IF(MOD(I,5).EQ.0)WRITE(6,3)I,FAC
    3 FORMAT(1X,I3,5X,E15.9E3)
    2 CONTINUE
*-----
      END
```

```
  N                    N!
 --      ---------------
  5      .120000000E+003
 10      .362880000E+007
 15      .130767428E+013
 20      .243290134E+019
 25      .155112052E+026
 30      .265252750E+033
 35      .103331426E+041
 40      .815914762E+048
 45      .119622132E+057
 50      .304140683E+065
 55      .126963926E+074
 60      .832097784E+082
 65      .824764085E+091
 70      .119785558E+101
 75      .248091055E+110
 80      .715693469E+119
 85      .281709951E+129
 90      .148571336E+139
 95      .103299593E+149
```

Discussion This problem doesn't appear to have much to do with double precision, but you need to understand how factorials are computed in order to feel comfortable with some of the subsequent examples and problems. This is also a golden opportunity to make several important general observations about factorials.

Only every fifth computation is printed to conserve space, but from the output you will notice that $n!$ grows rapidly as n increases. As a matter of fact, if we had performed the calculation in integer mode on a 32-bit machine, 12! would have been the ceiling, and 13! on a 36-bit computer. Excess-40, 32-bit floating-point arithmetic would not get past 55!, and the VAX's F-floating representation imposes the ceiling at 33!, although the same machine will reach 170! in G-floating mode. Factorial computations can easily encounter arithmetic overflow conditions on any machine, faster on some than on others, and you must be aware of this reality. Make the effort to understand the program; you will be rewarded.

Example 12.2

Compute 30! in single- and in double-precision modes and print both results to allow comparison.

Solution The required program follows. The two answers are slightly different, and this difference is highly hardware dependent.

```
      DOUBLE PRECISION DFAC
      FAC=1.
      DFAC=1DØ
*-----
      DO 1 I=1,3Ø
      FAC=FAC*I
      DFAC=DFAC*I
    1 CONTINUE
*-----
      WRITE(6,2)FAC,DFAC
    2 FORMAT(' 3Ø! COMPUTED IN SINGLE PRECISION =',E2Ø.12,/,
     +' 3Ø! COMPUTED IN DOUBLE PRECISION =',D2Ø.12)
      END
```

```
3Ø! COMPUTED IN SINGLE PRECISION =    .2652527500ØØE+33
3Ø! COMPUTED IN DOUBLE PRECISION =    .265252859812D+33
```

Example 12.3

2.718281828459045 is the accepted value of e, the base of the natural logarithms. The value of e can be computed with considerable accuracy by summing several terms of the following series:

$$e = 1 + \frac{1}{1!} + \frac{1}{2!} + \frac{1}{3!} + \frac{1}{4!} + \cdots + \frac{1}{n!}$$

Write a program to compute and report e for $n = 1$, $n = 2$, $n = 3$, . . . , $n = 20$ in single- and double-precision modes. The idea is to discover how many terms of the series are needed to produce a reasonable value of e and to discover how closely we can approximate the accepted value.

Solution

```
      DOUBLE PRECISION DE,DFAC
      WRITE(6,1)
    1 FORMAT(/,5X,'N',14X,'SINGLE PRECISION',14X,'DOUBLE PRECISION',/,
     +4X,'--',9X,21('-'),9X,21('-'))
*-----
```

```
      FAC=1.
      E=1.
      DFAC=1D0
      DE=1D0
*-----
      DO 2 I=1,20
      FAC=FAC*I
      E=E+1./FAC
      DFAC=DFAC*I
      DE=DE+1D0/DFAC
      WRITE(6,3)I,E,DE
    3 FORMAT(1X,I5,5X,1P,E25.15,5X,D25.15)
    2 CONTINUE
*-----
      END
```

```
  N          SINGLE PRECISION              DOUBLE PRECISION
 --       ---------------------        ---------------------
  1       2.000000000000000E+00        2.000000000000000D+00
  2       2.500000000000000E+00        2.500000000000000D+00
  3       2.666666630000000E+00        2.666666666666667D+00
  4       2.708333250000000E+00        2.708333333333333D+00
  5       2.716666580000000E+00        2.716666666666667D+00
  6       2.718055370000000E+00        2.718055555555556D+00
  7       2.718253730000000E+00        2.718253968253968D+00
  8       2.718278530000000E+00        2.718278769841270D+00
  9       2.718281270000000E+00        2.718281525573192D+00
 10       2.718281510000000E+00        2.718281801146384D+00
 11       2.718281510000000E+00        2.718281826198493D+00
 12       2.718281510000000E+00        2.718281828286169D+00
 13       2.718281510000000E+00        2.718281828446759D+00
 14       2.718281510000000E+00        2.718281828458230D+00
 15       2.718281510000000E+00        2.718281828458994D+00
 16       2.718281510000000E+00        2.718281828459042D+00
 17       2.718281510000000E+00        2.718281828459045D+00
 18       2.718281510000000E+00        2.718281828459045D+00
 19       2.718281510000000E+00        2.718281828459045D+00
 20       2.718281510000000E+00        2.718281828459045D+00
```

Discussion You will notice that the single-precision calculation of e reaches its terminal value at $n = 10$. Additional terms no longer contribute because their magnitudes are too small. In reality, the resulting value of e is quite good, the first seven digits agreeing with the accepted value. On the double-precision side, complete agreement occurs when $n = 17$, but remember that things may look a little different on your hardware.

Example 12.4

In the previous example we met e, the base of the natural system of logarithms. If this base is raised to the power of x, a new value results that is a function of x. The conventional symbol for this function is e^x, and the FORTRAN intrinsic function equivalent is EXP(X). The function can be approximated by summing sufficient terms of the following series:

$$e^x = 1 + \frac{x}{1!} + \frac{x^2}{2!} + \frac{x^3}{3!} + \frac{x^4}{4!} + \frac{x^5}{5!} + \cdots + \frac{x^n}{n!}$$

Write a program that prompts you to enter some x value. It then sums the first 31 terms of the series to compute e^x, and prints the result along with the value produced by the intrinsic function EXP(X) to permit comparison. The computations are all performed in the double-precision mode.

Solution The program loops to permit different X values to be entered, but we compute the factorials only once and store them in the array FAC(30). Only 31 terms of the series are added, making the last term $x^{30}/30!$. You will recall that 30! approaches overflow conditions on some machines. x^{30} also gets out of hand very rapidly, precipitating overflow on some machines as x approaches 19. The actual series summation occurs in the small DO-loop with the terminal statement labeled 3. The code in this loop is impressively compact and you may wish to dwell on it until you understand it clearly.

```
      DOUBLE PRECISION X,E,FAC(3Ø)
*-----
*-----COMPUTE 1! TO 3Ø! AND STORE THESE IN THE ARRAY FAC(3Ø)
      FAC(1)=1DØ
      DO 1 I=2,3Ø
      FAC(I)=FAC(I-1)*I
    1 CONTINUE
*-----
    2 PRINT*,'PLEASE ENTER SOME X VALUE'
      READ(5,*,END=99)X
*-----
*-----COMPUTING EXP(X) BY SUMMING THE FIRST 31 TERMS OF THE SERIES
      E=1DØ
      DO 3 I=1,3Ø
      E=E+X**I/FAC(I)
    3 CONTINUE
*-----
*-----REPORTING THE CALCULATED VALUE AND THE VALUE PRODUCED BY THE
*-----INTRINSIC FUNCTION
      WRITE(6,4)E,EXP(X)
    4 FORMAT(' THE FIRST 31 TERMS OF THE SERIES YIELD',1P,D23.15,/,
     +       ' THE INTRINSIC FUNCTION EXP(X) PRODUCES',D23.15)
      GO TO 2
   99 STOP 'USER REQUESTED EXIT'
      END
```

```
PLEASE ENTER SOME X VALUE
?0.01
THE FIRST 31 TERMS OF THE SERIES YIELD  1.0100501670841680D+00
THE INTRINSIC FUNCTION EXP(X) PRODUCES  1.0100501670841680D+00
PLEASE ENTER SOME X VALUE
?1
THE FIRST 31 TERMS OF THE SERIES YIELD  2.7182818284590450D+00
THE INTRINSIC FUNCTION EXP(X) PRODUCES  2.7182818284590450D+00
PLEASE ENTER SOME X VALUE
?9
THE FIRST 31 TERMS OF THE SERIES YIELD  8.1030838633053500D+03
THE INTRINSIC FUNCTION EXP(X) PRODUCES  8.1030839275753840D+03
PLEASE ENTER SOME X VALUE
?18
THE FIRST 31 TERMS OF THE SERIES YIELD  6.5441267165790020D+07
THE INTRINSIC FUNCTION EXP(X) PRODUCES  6.5659969137330510D+07
PLEASE ENTER SOME X VALUE
?(EOF CHARACTER SUPPLIED BY USER)
*STOP* USER REQUESTED EXIT
```

12.5 PROBLEMS

DOUBLE PRECISION is usually invoked when you need more than the standard seven- or eight-digit precision offered by short floating-point arithmetic. DOUBLE PRECISION is also used when it is necessary to add very small quantities to larger ones. You encountered both situations in the examples, specifically when we computed e. There we needed a result with approximately 16-digit precision, and the terms of the series became extremely small as n increased. A lot of computing involves iterations in which very small components are accumulated, and by now it is clear to you that such components no longer contribute as they get smaller. This is seen clearly in the single-precision column of Example 12.3. The following problems are similar to the examples. If your computing interests point in different directions, don't feel guilty about skipping them.

12.1. The series expansion for the *sine* function is shown. The expansion is considered valid for all values of x. Write a program similar to Example 12.4, allowing you to try different x values. Compute the sine in double-precision mode, and compare your result with the intrinsic SIN(X) function. (−1)**N provides an alternating sign as N steps along. If N increases two steps at a time, (−1)**(N/2) provides the necessary sign alternation.

$$\sin x = x - \frac{x^3}{3!} + \frac{x^5}{5!} - \frac{x^7}{7!} + \frac{x^9}{9!} - \cdots$$

12.2. Repeat Problem 12.1 for the *cosine* function. The series expansion for the cosine function is

$$\cos x = 1 - \frac{x^2}{2!} + \frac{x^4}{4!} - \frac{x^6}{6!} + \frac{x^8}{8!} - \cdots$$

12.3. Modify the previous program to compute the natural logarithm of x. Compare your computed value with that produced by the intrinsic function LOG(X). The appropriate series expansion is shown. It is obvious that n can be made quite large before overflow occurs. For that matter, you will need a fair number of terms because the series does not converge too rapidly. You might start with about 10 terms and test the program for x values close to 1. Then try x values as large as 100 and more. You should then increase the number of terms to several hundred and test the program with various x values. It's an instructive exercise, requiring only about 10 FORTRAN statements.

$$\ln x = 2\left[\frac{1}{1}\left(\frac{x-1}{x+1}\right)^1 + \frac{1}{3}\left(\frac{x-1}{x+1}\right)^3 + \frac{1}{5}\left(\frac{x-1}{x+1}\right)^5 + \frac{1}{7}\left(\frac{x-1}{x+1}\right)^7 + \cdots + \frac{1}{2n+1}\left(\frac{x-1}{x+1}\right)^{2n+1}\right]$$

13

The DATA and PARAMETER Statements

13.1 THE DATA STATEMENT

The DATA statement is a very special type of FORTRAN statement. It is not a specification statement (declarative) because it does not alter the environment, nor is it an executable statement (imperative). Instead, the DATA statement is directed at the compiler, asking it to assign data to variables at compile time, but has no further action at execution time. Figure 13.1 shows an interesting program, instructing the machine to print the contents of the variable X, even though no value has been assigned to it yet. Attempting to execute the program triggers one of three possible events, depending on the system. The machine will (1) inform you at compile or run time that X is unassigned, and quit; or (2) will have automatically initialized X to zero at compile time, in which case the program will print a zero; or (3) will faithfully print whatever was left behind by some previous user of that particular memory location. The machine on which the program in Fig. 13.1 was run obviously chose the third alternative, possibly serving up a different value each time the program is executed.

We can generalize and state that in the absence of instructions to the contrary, a compiler only arranges storage for variables, without necessarily sweeping out this memory by assigning zeros to it. The onus still falls on the programmer to move meaningful data into such locations when the program is executed.

The DATA statement, however, makes it possible for the programmer to communicate directly with the compiler, asking it to store specific data in specific variables.

```
PRINT *,X
END
```

```
.1180446E+47
```

Figure 13.1 An uninitialized variable.

```
DATA X/19.5/
PRINT *, X
END
```

```
19.50000
```

Figure 13.2 The DATA statement initializes a variable before the program is even executed.

Figure 13.2 shows a modified version of our earlier program. The first statement is the DATA statement instructing the compiler to store 19.5 in the variable X before turning the program over to us for execution. You can tell from the output that our instructions were obeyed.

The DATA statement must not be confused with an assignment statement. The assignment statement assigns data to a variable at execution time. The DATA statement, on the other hand, does it during the earlier compile phase. We say that the DATA statement *initializes* variables, in the sense of giving them a first, or initial, value. In Fig. 13.3, the DATA statement initializes the four variables in the list with zeros. The list, delimited by the slashes, is called the *list of constants* for obvious reasons.

The list of constants of the DATA statement in Fig. 13.3 contains four identical constants that can be lumped together, as shown in Fig. 13.4. The 4 is known as a *repeat factor*.

Arrays can also be initialized in a DATA statement, and this is probably one of its more popular applications. The program in Fig. 13.5 declares a 4 × 4 array M that is then printed in row order without initialization. Notice the random values picked up. Your system will either serve up different random values, or it will present you with a nicely swept out array in which all the elements were set to zero by the compiler.

In Fig. 13.6, the DATA statement is used to initialize the same array. It initializes each of the first eight elements with 5, and the remaining eight elements

```
DATA A,B,C,D /0.,0.,0.,0./
PRINT *, A,B,C,D
END
```

```
0.0000  0.0000  0.0000  0.0000
```

Figure 13.3 The list of variables and the list of constants in the DATA statement.

```
DATA A,B,C,D /4*0./
PRINT *, A,B,C,D
END
```

```
0.0000  0.0000  0.0000  0.0000
```

Figure 13.4 The repeat factor condenses a list of constants.

```
      DIMENSION M(4,4)
      DO 1 IROW = 1,4
    1 WRITE(6,2)(M(IROW,ICOL),ICOL=1,4)
    2 FORMAT(1X,4I12)
      END

     24Ø44Ø6  7272696897 1143Ø567424  8992587776
  7272696897  8744118272     2928694     3715126
 11Ø2398464Ø     24Ø44Ø6  72727ØØ499  7272694357
     24Ø44Ø6  72727ØØ481 11291371593 11295Ø47233
```

Figure 13.5 An uninitialized array.

with 17. Note that the array is simply mentioned by name in the list of variables of the DATA statement, causing it to be dealt with in column order, the natural FORTRAN order.

Figure 13.7 shows that even the implied-DO can be used in the DATA statement to control the order in which the elements of an array appear in the list of variables. This feature is useful whenever you wish to overrule the natural column-order initial-

```
      DIMENSION M(4,4)
      DATA M /8*5,8*17/
      DO 1 IROW = 1,4
    1 WRITE(6,2)(M(IROW,ICOL),ICOL=1,4)
    2 FORMAT(1X,4I12)
      END

            5           5          17          17
            5           5          17          17
            5           5          17          17
            5           5          17          17
```

Figure 13.6 The DATA statement initializes the elements of an array.

```
      DIMENSION M(4,4)
      DATA ((M(IROW,ICOL),ICOL=1,4),IROW=1,4) /8*5,8*17/
      DO 1 IROW = 1,4
    1 WRITE(6,2)(M(IROW,ICOL),ICOL=1,4)
    2 FORMAT(1X,4I12)
      END

            5           5           5           5
            5           5           5           5
           17          17          17          17
           17          17          17          17
```

Figure 13.7 The implied-DO can be used to control the list of variables.

ization. In that example, the DATA statement initializes the elements of the first two rows of the array with 5, and the elements of the last two rows with 17.

Some feel that once variables or arrays have been initialized in a DATA statement, the values are permanently frozen and cannot be reassigned in the same program. Figure 13.8 is designed to lay this erroneous notion to rest. The program is a simple extension of the preceding one. The same DATA statement is used to fill the same array and the array is printed. Zeros are then assigned to all the array elements, and the entire array is printed once again to convince you that the reassignment was successful:

```
      DIMENSION M(4,4)
      DATA ((M(IROW,ICOL),ICOL=1,4),IROW=1,4) /8*5,8*17/
      WRITE(6,2)((M(IROW,ICOL),ICOL=1,4),IROW=1,4)
    2 FORMAT(/,(1X,4I12))
      DO 3 IROW=1,4
      DO 3 ICOL=1,4
    3 M(IROW,ICOL)=Ø
      WRITE(6,2)((M(IROW,ICOL),ICOL=1,4),IROW=1,4)
      END

           5           5           5           5
           5           5           5           5
          17          17          17          17
          17          17          17          17

           Ø           Ø           Ø           Ø
           Ø           Ø           Ø           Ø
           Ø           Ø           Ø           Ø
           Ø           Ø           Ø           Ø
```

Figure 13.8 New values can be assigned to variables previously initialized in a DATA statement.

```
      REAL K
      INTEGER A(1Ø)
      DOUBLE PRECISION D(5)
      DATA K,A,D/122, 1Ø*Ø., 5*33.3333333333333333DØ/
      PRINT*,K
      PRINT*,D
      PRINT*,A
      END

122.ØØØØ
33.3333333333333333  33.3333333333333333  33.3333333333333333
33.3333333333333333  33.3333333333333333
Ø  Ø  Ø  Ø  Ø  Ø  Ø  Ø  Ø  Ø
```

Figure 13.9 Variables, arrays, and different data types appear in the same DATA statement.

Figure 13.9 shows a final illustration in which arrays and simple variables and various data types are dealt with together in a single DATA statement.

13.2 PLACEMENT OF THE DATA STATEMENT

In older versions of the language, the DATA statement also had to follow the specification statements, but it had to precede the executable imperatives. In FORTRAN 77, the DATA statement can appear *anywhere after* the specification statements.

13.3 THE PARAMETER STATEMENT

On the surface, the PARAMETER statement and the DATA statement look very similar, but the similarity is only superficial. The PARAMETER statement is a specification statement and has the following form:

PARAMETER (PI = 3.14159, E = 2.71828, PROD = PI*E)

This PARAMETER specification assigns the symbolic name PI to the constant 3.14159, the name E to 2.71828, and it assigns the symbolic name PROD to 3.14159 × 2.71828. Whenever you need any of these constants in your calculations, you can simply refer to them by name. The PARAMETER statement shown makes PI and 3.14159 synonymous. Similarly, E and 2.71828 can now be used interchangeably, and so can PROD and 3.14159 × 2.71828.

You are probably not overly impressed just yet because we could have handled PI and E quite nicely in a DATA statement, or even using two assignment statements. The DATA statement, however, would have choked on PROD, but an assignment statement would have looked after that one quite nicely. The real difference in using the PARAMETER specification lies in the fact that PI, E, and PROD are now not variables at all, and therefore cannot be reassigned, either deliberately or accidentally. The same cannot be said about variables initialized in a DATA statement, as was demonstrated convincingly in Fig. 13.8.

Because the PARAMETER statement is a specification statement, it must appear before any of the imperative statements. Figure 13.10 shows the PARAMETER statement in a program setting.

```
      PARAMETER (PI=3.14159, E=2.71828, PROD=PI*E)
      PRINT*, 2*PI
      PRINT*, E
      PRINT*, PROD
      END

 6.283180
 2.718280
 8.539721
```

Figure 13.10 The PARAMETER statement gives a symbolic name to a constant.

The point should be made once again that the PARAMETER statement provides very real protection because the symbolic constant names cannot be redefined, and therefore cannot be changed accidentally.

13.4 PROBLEMS

13.1. Modify the program of Fig. 11.11 by replacing the READ statement with the appropriate DATA statement. The output must be identical. You will have to continue the DATA statement over at least two lines, but that's easy enough, just don't lose a comma in the process.

13.2. Modify the program of Fig. 11.13 by replacing the READ statement with the appropriate DATA statement. The output must be identical.

13.3. In a PARAMETER statement, give 3.1415926536D0/180D0 the symbolic name CONFAC after first declaring CONFAC double precision. Rework Prob. 10.12 in double precision using the parameter CONFAC. You may wish to use the intrinsic function TAN(X) this time.

14

FORTRAN Character Manipulation

14.1 INTRODUCTION

To this point, we have worked with three data types, namely, INTEGER (fixed-point), REAL (short floating-point), and DOUBLE PRECISION (long floating-point). Each of these three has a specific internal storage mode, and each has its own form of *constant*. These three numeric data types are generally confined to a fixed number of storage bits, usually one word of memory for integers and reals, and two words for double precision, provided that the word size is adequate.

In Chapter 3, we investigated the internal representations of various data types, including CHARACTER data, and you may wish to review that section briefly before continuing. In the same chapter it was stressed that the basic unit of character storage is the byte, in which the character data are probably stored either in seven- or eight-bit ASCII, or possibly in the eight-bit EBCDIC code, depending on the hardware.

14.2 CHARACTER DATA

We are now ready to add this fourth data type, CHARACTER, and unlike numeric storage, which is word oriented, character storage is byte oriented. In your programs, you will have occasion to use character variables with a capacity as small as a single character, or possibly as large as a thousand or more. The former would require only a single byte of storage, whereas the latter needs a thousand or more bytes, or several hundred words. The machine deals with these varying size demands by simply linking a sufficient number of contiguous words of memory to provide the necessary storage. The storage required for numeric variables is of predictable size, but you can see that character variables can have extreme length variations from program to program, and possibly even within the same program. If the system reserved the maximum potential memory size for each character variable, a lot of memory would be wasted. To control this waste, FORTRAN gives the programmer full control over the size of character variables. You simply estimate the length requirements of each character variable and inform the compiler appropriately. If you don't specify the size of a character variable, the compiler gives it only a single byte.

We can summarize all this by stating that when you declare a variable to be of type CHARACTER, then you must also tell the machine how many characters the variable is to accommodate. Having to specify the size of a variable is probably new to you, but you can certainly appreciate the reasons.

As mentioned earlier, each data type has its own form of constant, and a character constant is simply a character string enclosed by single quotes. Similarly, each data type has its format edit descriptor, such as I for integers, F and E for reals, and D for double precision. For character data, the A edit descriptor is used, as you might have anticipated, because A is a good mnemonic for *alphabetic*. You may either be formal and specify Aw as the edit descriptor, where w is the width of the edit field, or you may omit the width specification.

All these points are summarized in Fig. 14.1. The first statement is a CHARACTER type-statement specifying that X is a character variable able to accommodate 26 characters. The character constant 'ABCDEFGHIJKLMNOPQRSTUVWXYZ' is assigned to the variable X in the second statement, after which X is printed three times, first using simple list-directed output and then the more formal formatted output using A editing and A26 editing. The differences between A and Aw editing will become clear after you see some of the subsequent examples.

```
      CHARACTER X*26
      X = 'ABCDEFGHIJKLMNOPQRSTUVWXYZ'
*-----
      PRINT*,X
*-----
      WRITE(6,1)X
    1 FORMAT(1X,A)
*-----
      WRITE(6,2)X
    2 FORMAT(1X,A26)
      END
```

```
ABCDEFGHIJKLMNOPQRSTUVWXYZ
ABCDEFGHIJKLMNOPQRSTUVWXYZ
ABCDEFGHIJKLMNOPQRSTUVWXYZ
```

Figure 14.1 A character variable and a character constant and the printing of character.

```
      CHARACTER KAR*15
      KAR='Ø123456789ABCDE'
*-----
      WRITE(6,1)KAR,KAR
    1 FORMAT(1X,2A15)
*-----
      WRITE(6,2)KAR,KAR
    2 FORMAT(1X,2A)
*-----
      WRITE(6,3)KAR,KAR
    3 FORMAT(1X,2A2Ø)
*-----
      WRITE(6,4)KAR
    4 FORMAT(1X,A1Ø)
      END

Ø123456789ABCDEØ123456789ABCDE
Ø123456789ABCDEØ123456789ABCDE
     Ø123456789ABCDE     Ø123456789ABCDE
Ø123456789
```

Figure 14.2 A and Aw output editing, and undersized output fields.

The program in Fig. 14.2 compares A and Aw output editing. KAR is a 15-byte character variable to which a 15-character constant is assigned. KAR is then written twice into two adjacent A15 fields and the output is exactly what you would expect. KAR is again written twice, but this time into two A fields that acted exactly like the two A15 fields. The machine obviously looked at the CHARACTER type-statement and concluded that the required output field width is 15 spaces. And so it would seem that if you use widthless-output A editing, the machine substitutes Aw editing, after deducing w from the CHARACTER type-statement. KAR is then again written twice, but this time into two adjacent A20 fields. You can see that the machine right-justified the output in the requested fields. The last experiment involves writing KAR into an undersized output field. The machine truncates the output from the right as you can see.

Figure 14.3 illustrates another important concept. The program is the same as Fig. 14.2. The character variable can still accommodate 15 characters, but the constant has been shortened to four characters. After looking at the output, it will be obvious that the constant occupies the leftmost four bytes in the variable KAR and that the remaining 11 bytes were filled with blanks; the blank, of course, is just another character. It is a general rule that when a short character string is assigned to a larger character variable, blank characters are added to the string to fill the entire variable. These padding blanks are indicated by the character ␣ in the example, although you would simply see blanks on your screen. Similarly, when a long character string is assigned to a smaller variable, the character string is truncated from the right until it fits, a fact you may wish to verify.

It is hoped that you won't ignore the seemingly trivial program shown in Fig. 14.4, but many feel that a blank is somehow different from other characters,

```
      CHARACTER KAR*15
      KAR='Ø123'
      WRITE(6,1)KAR,KAR
    1 FORMAT(1X,2A15)
      WRITE(6,2)KAR,KAR
    2 FORMAT(1X,2A)
      WRITE(6,3)KAR,KAR
    3 FORMAT(1X,2A2Ø)
      WRITE(6,4)KAR
    4 FORMAT(1X,A1Ø)
      END
```

```
Ø123␣␣␣␣␣␣␣␣␣␣␣Ø123␣␣␣␣␣␣␣␣␣␣␣
Ø123␣␣␣␣␣␣␣␣␣␣␣Ø123␣␣␣␣␣␣␣␣␣␣␣
     Ø123␣␣␣␣␣␣␣␣␣␣␣     Ø123␣␣␣␣␣␣␣␣␣␣␣
Ø123␣␣␣␣␣␣
```

Figure 14.3 A short character constant is assigned to a larger variable.

acting as some kind of delimiter. This is precisely what a blank does in the written world, separating a word from its neighbor, but inside the computer a blank is a character like all other characters, without any special significance. The example in Fig. 14.4 assigns a character constant to the variable L, but the constant contains embedded blanks. Unconsciously, you might view this constant as being several constants separated by blanks, but the computer treats the blank the same as all the other characters in the string, and for this reason sees only the single constant 'HI,␣THIS␣IS␣YOUR␣COMPUTER␣SPEAKING'.

```
CHARACTER L*6Ø
L='HI, THIS IS YOUR COMPUTER SPEAKING'
PRINT*,L
END
```

```
HI, THIS IS YOUR COMPUTER SPEAKING
```

Figure 14.4 Embedded blanks are no different from other characters.

14.3 A CLOSER LOOK AT THE CHARACTER TYPE-STATEMENT

The CHARACTER type-statement is a specification statement, and like all specification statements must precede the imperative statement. Its purpose is to declare variables to be of type CHARACTER, and to specify the length of such character variables. The CHARACTER type-statement can have various forms and we now look at these.

CHARACTER A*10,B*10,C*10,D*10,E*10

This statement declares A, B, C, D, and E to be variables of type character, each with a capacity to hold 10 characters. The 10 is known as the *length specification*.

In the example, each variable has the same length specification, permitting the following shortcut:

CHARACTER*10 A, B, C, D, E

The next CHARACTER type-statement declares A, B, C, D, and E to be character variables of differing lengths:

CHARACTER A*5, B*2, C*10, D*100, E*3

As implied earlier, when no length is specified, a length of a single character is implied. The next three CHARACTER type-statements declare A, B, C, D, and E to be character variables, each with a length of one character:

```
CHARACTER A,B,C,D,E
CHARACTER*1 A,B,C,D,E
CHARACTER A*1,B*1,C*1,D*1,E*1
```

In the next example, the character variables are assumed to have a length of 10, except B, which has a length of 25 characters:

CHARACTER*10 A, B*25, C, D, E

Character arrays can also be defined. The following CHARACTER type-statement declares an array LANG with seven elements, each of which is a character variable with a length of nine characters:

CHARACTER*9 LANG(7)

An alternative form of the same specification is

CHARACTER LANG(7)*9

14.4 EXAMPLES

Example 14.1

Write a simple program that reads a line of text from the keyboard and writes it to the screen. Assume the line can contain up to 70 characters.

Solution

```
      CHARACTER LINE*7Ø
*-----
      READ(5,1)LINE
    1 FORMAT(A)
      WRITE(6,2)LINE
    2 FORMAT(1X,A)
*-----
      END
```

```
?The middle years of the rule of Moctezuma were to be implicated ......
The middle years of the rule of Moctezuma were to be implicated ......
```

Discussion The A edit descriptor in both FORMAT statements obviously acts like A70. The first 70 characters coming from the keyboard are loaded into the character variable LINE and printed. Should your system reject lowercase character data, simply switch to uppercase.

Example 14.2

Repeat the previous problem using list-directed input/output.

Solution

```
      CHARACTER LINE*70
      READ*,LINE
      PRINT*,LINE
      END

?The middle years of the rule of Moctezuma were to be implicated ......
>>>> FORTRAN run-time error (I/O).  Expected delimiter not found <<<<
```

Discussion We got a run-time error. When the computer reads in list-directed mode, it interprets a blank as a separator between adjacent data—and yet we expect the computer to treat blanks embedded in character strings as any other character. The problem is resolved by enclosing the input character string in single quotes, or apostrophes, as X3.9–1978 refers to them. Blanks outside quotes are treated as normal data separators, but blanks inside quotes are treated as characters. While looking for the opening quote in the input stream, the computer found T, the first character of our input string, and hence the complaint. You are reminded that in addition to the blank, list-directed input also accepts the comma and the slash (/) as data separators. We'll run the above program again, but this time using the quote delimiters.

```
      CHARACTER LINE*70
      READ*,LINE
      PRINT*,LINE
      END

?'The middle years of the rule of Moctezuma were to be implicated ......'
The middle years of the rule of Moctezuma were to be implicated ......
```

Example 14.3

Declare a one-dimensional character array with 5 one-character elements. Read five character strings into this array, each string on a separate line, and print all five elements. Use formatted I/O.

Solution

```
      CHARACTER MAT(5)*1
      READ(5,1)MAT
    1 FORMAT(A)
      WRITE(6,2)MAT
    2 FORMAT(1X,A)
      END
```

```
?A
?B
?C
?D
?E
```

```
A
B
C
D
E
```

Discussion MAT is a one-dimensional array with five elements. Each element can hold a character string one character long. The FORMAT statement provides only a single A field, and must therefore be rescanned five times. The program reads one character string with each scan, and therefore prompts for input five times. The array is then printed, but again only a single A field is specified in the output FORMAT, and five output records result.

Example 14.4

Declare a one-dimensional character array with five 70-character elements. Read five character strings into this array, each string on a separate line, and print all five elements. Use formatted I/O.

Solution

```
      CHARACTER MAT(5)*7Ø
      READ(5,1)MAT
    1 FORMAT(A)
      WRITE(6,2)MAT
    2 FORMAT(1X,A)
      END
```

```
?The middle years of the rule of Moctezuma were to be implicated in a
?phenomenal series of natural disasters, each of which tested the
?resilience of the new state and the spirit of its rulers.  The Huaxtec
?War had just begun, and a glorious victory was anticipated when, in the
?summer of 145Ø, heavy rains began to fall and soon raised the surface ..
```

```
The middle years of the rule of Moctezuma were to be implicated in a
phenomenal series of natural disasters, each of which tested the
resilience of the new state and the spirit of its rulers.  The Huaxtec
War had just begun, and a glorious victory was anticipated when, in th
summer of 145Ø, heavy rains began to fall and soon raised the surface
```

Discussion This is obviously a repeat of the previous example, but each of the five elements can now accommodate 70 characters rather than just one. Notice that the fourth and the fifth strings were clipped because they were longer than 70 characters.

Examples 14.3 and 14.4 are clearly the same, and most would readily agree that the array MAT in Ex. 14.3 is one-dimensional. It is obvious when you look at the output and the input. But when it comes to Ex. 14.4, we are a little more hesitant about calling the array MAT one-dimensional, expecially when looking at the input and the output, which appear decidedly two-dimensional. It all depends how you view a character string, whether you are willing to view it as a scalar entity or whether you instinctively regard it as a one-dimensional array, in which case a one-dimensional array of one-dimensional arrays is certainly a two-dimensional structure.

In this context, FORTRAN views a character string as a scalar entity, and if you are willing to accept this approach, then you will also accept that the array MAT in Ex. 14.4 is one-dimensional, being nothing more than a set of five scalars. Another way of looking at it is that because each of the five character strings can be located with a single coordinate, the structure must be one-dimensional.

By now you are possibly wondering that if a one-dimensional character array looks suspiciously two-dimensional, then what does a two-dimensional character array look like? If you imagine a tile floor, with a character string sticking straight up out of each tile, then you have the picture. Yes, it does look three-dimensional, but because two coordinates are sufficient to pinpoint any one of the character strings, the structure is two-dimensional.

Example 14.5

Declare a one-dimensional array LANG with seven character elements, each with a 10-character capacity. Initialize this array in a DATA statement with the seven character constants 'ENGLISH', 'GERMAN', 'LATIN', 'GREEK', 'SPANISH', 'ITALIAN', and 'PORTUGUESE'. Print the array to confirm that the initializing worked.

Solution

```
      CHARACTER LANG(7)*1Ø
      DATA LANG/'ENGLISH','GERMAN','LATIN','GREEK','SPANISH',
     +          'ITALIAN','PORTUGUESE'/
      DO 1 I=1,7
      WRITE(6,2)I,LANG(I)
    2 FORMAT(1X,'LANGUAGE',I2,' IS ',A)
    1 CONTINUE
      END
```

```
LANGUAGE 1 IS ENGLISH
LANGUAGE 2 IS GERMAN
LANGUAGE 3 IS LATIN
LANGUAGE 4 IS GREEK
```

```
LANGUAGE 5 IS SPANISH
LANGUAGE 6 IS ITALIAN
LANGUAGE 7 IS PORTUGUESE
```

Example 14.6

Declare a 70-element one-dimensional character array LINE, in which the capacity of each element is one character. Fill this array by reading all 70 data from a single input record. Count the number of times the letter *e* appears in the input record.

Solution

```
      CHARACTER LINE(7Ø)*1
      READ(5,1)LINE
    1 FORMAT(7ØA)
      NUM=Ø
      DO 2 I=1,7Ø
      IF(LINE(I).EQ.'e')NUM=NUM+1
    2 CONTINUE
      WRITE(6,3)NUM
    3 FORMAT(' THE LETTER ''e'' APPEARS',I2,' TIMES')
      END
```

```
?The unpretentious houses of the poor were the first to melt away
THE LETTER 'e' APPEARS 9 TIMES
```

Discussion The input record looks as though we had read a single character string into the program. In reality, however, we read 70 different strings, each one a single character long. Notice the 70A in the input format statement. It acts like 70A1, dividing the input record into 70 one-character cells, causing each of the input characters to be stored in its private element of the array. We then run each element of LINE through the IF statement, where it is compared with the character string 'e'. Again, if your system rejects lowercase characters, do all your work in uppercase. If it does accept lowercase, however, use it freely.

14.5 THE OPEN STATEMENT REVISITED

We studied the OPEN statement extensively in Chapter 8. A typical OPEN statement has the following form:

```
OPEN(UNIT=5,FILE='TESTFILE',STATUS='OLD',FORM='FORMATTED')
```

You are now in a position to recognize the entities between quotes as character constants, and it will not come as a surprise that the following program segment works:

```
CHARACTER*10 C1,C2,C3
C1 = 'TESTFILE'
C2 = 'OLD'
C3 = 'FORMATTED'
OPEN(UNIT=5, FILE=C1, STATUS=C2, FORM=C3)
ETC.
```

This flexibility adds a whole new dimension to the OPEN statement because you can now assign items like the filename and the STATUS dynamically, under program control, and parachute them directly into the OPEN statement. A program might ask the user to provide the name of a file, for example. The user enters the filename from the keyboard and the OPEN statement goes after the specified file.

14.6 CHARACTER SUBSTRINGS

FORTRAN 77 provides the programmer with the ability to extract a substring from a character string. LINE(12:14), for example, is the substring of LINE, consisting of characters 12, 13, and 14. LINE(:14) is equivalent to LINE(1:14), and LINE(14:) is the same as LINE(14:N), where N is the declared length of LINE. Substrings are extracted in Fig. 14.5.

Figure 14.6 shows an interesting application of the substring function. The

```
      CHARACTER LINE*26
      LINE='ABCDEFGHIJKLMNOPQRSTUVWXYZ'
      WRITE(6,1) LINE(12:14), LINE(:14), LINE(14:)
    1 FORMAT(1X,3A16)
      END

             LMN  ABCDEFGHIJKLMN   NOPQRSTUVWXYZ
```

Figure 14.5 Character substrings.

```
      CHARACTER LINE*70
      READ(5,1)LINE
    1 FORMAT(A)
      NUM=0
      DO 2 I=1,70
      IF(LINE(I:I).EQ.'e')NUM=NUM+1
    2 CONTINUE
      WRITE(6,3)NUM
    3 FORMAT(' THE LETTER ''e'' APPEARS',I2,' TIMES')
      END
?The unpretentious houses of the poor were the first to melt away
THE LETTER 'e' APPEARS 9 TIMES
```

Figure 14.6 Substrings applied.

purpose of the program is the same as Ex. 14.6, where we took a sentence and broke it into 70 characters with the intention of counting the number of occurrences of the character string 'e'. This time, however, we feed the program with a single character string containing the same sentence. From it, we then extract 70 different substrings and compare these to 'e'. The program obviously works.

14.7 THE CONCATENATION OF CHARACTER STRINGS

The English words *catenate* and *concatenate* come from the Latin word *catena*, meaning *chain*, and to *concatenate* something means to *chain* it together. FORTRAN 77 provides the concatenation operator // to link character strings. This operator is demonstrated in Fig. 14.7, where we extract two substrings from the character string LINE and concatenate these into a new character string.

```
      CHARACTER LINE*26
      LINE='ABCDEFGHIJKLMNOPQRSTUVWXYZ'
      WRITE(6,1)LINE(12:14)//LINE(20:26)
    1 FORMAT(1X,A)
      END

 LMNTUVWXYZ
```

Figure 14.7 The concatenation of two substrings.

14.8 THE LEN FUNCTION

Another useful FORTRAN 77 character function is LEN. Its argument is a character string, and the function returns the length of that string as an integer. Study the example in Fig. 14.8 carefully to see just how the LEN function behaves. You might be surprised to see the length of the variable OTHER reported as 20 even

```
      CHARACTER LINE*26,OTHER*20
      LINE='ABCDEFGHIJKLMNOPQRSTUVWXYZ'
      OTHER='123456'
      PRINT*, LEN( LINE(12:14)//LINE(20:26) )
      PRINT*, LEN('ABCDEFG')
      PRINT*, LEN(LINE)
      PRINT*, LEN(OTHER)
      END

 10
  7
 26
 20
```

Figure 14.8 The LEN function is illustrated.

though we assigned the six-character string '123456' to it. You should not be surprised, though, because OTHER is declared with a length specification of 20 characters. Yes, we did assign a shorter constant to this variable, but that does not change the size of the variable. Blanks are added to the constant so that the variable ends up with '123456␣␣␣␣␣␣␣␣␣␣␣␣␣␣'. This isn't new, of course, but it is good to be reminded. The fourth line of the program brings together substrings, concatenation, and the LEN function. Take a moment to think about the length reported.

14.9 THE ICHAR FUNCTION

FORTRAN 77 also provides the ICHAR function, which is illustrated in Fig. 14.9. The function is designed to probe the internal representation of a particular character and to report that internal representation as an integer. The first statement in Fig. 14.9 instructs the machine to write the internal representation of the character A, which is reported as 65_{10}.

```
      WRITE(6,1)ICHAR('A')
    1 FORMAT(' THE INTERNAL REPRESENTATION OF ''A'' IS DECIMAL',I3)
      END

 THE INTERNAL REPRESENTATION OF 'A' IS DECIMAL 65
```

Figure 14.9 The ICHAR function produces the internal representation of a character numerically.

You are aware, of course, that each character sits in a byte of memory in the form of a pattern of bits. This bit pattern is a seven- or eight-bit binary number, and the ICHAR function reports the equivalent decimal value. The program in Fig. 14.9 reports that the internal representation of the character A is 65_{10}. The binary equivalent of 65_{10} is 01000001_2, and from the ASCII table in Appendix B, you will find that this is indeed the ASCII code for A. The program was obviously run on an ASCII machine, but had it produced $193_{10} = C1_{16}$, an EBCDIC machine would be indicated.

The ASCII and EBCDIC tables are arranged in numerically ascending order. The first cell of the seven-bit ASCII table is number 0, and the last cell is number 127. The character A sits in cell number 65, and this is precisely what the ICHAR function reported. The position in the code table and the internal representation of a character are the same, in other words. Similarly, the first cell of the EBCDIC table is number 0, and the last cell is number 255. The character A is located in cell number 193 of the EBCDIC table, as you can readily verify from Appendix A.

The ICHAR function decodes only a single character. If you feed it a character string longer than one character, it decodes only the first. ICHAR('ABCDEFGH'), therefore, produces the same value as ICHAR('A').

14.10 THE CHAR FUNCTION

The CHAR function is the mirror image of ICHAR. If you feed it the position number of a cell in the code table, it produces the character in that cell. In Fig. 14.10, we ask the computer to show us the character in cell number 77 and it prints the character M, and the ASCII table in Appendix B confirms that M is the correct character. The argument of the CHAR function must lie between 0 and 127 for seven-bit ASCII machines, and between 0 and 255 for EBCDIC systems.

In summary, the ICHAR function is supplied with a character, and it reports the position of that character in the code table. The CHAR function, on the other hand, is given a position in the code table, and it produces the character occupying that position.

```
      WRITE(6,1)CHAR(77)
    1 FORMAT(' SLOT 77 OF THE ASCII TABLE IS OCCUPIED BY ',A)
      END

 SLOT 77 OF THE ASCII TABLE IS OCCUPIED BY M
```

Figure 14.10 The CHAR function shows the character occupying a certain slot in the code table.

14.11 THE INDEX FUNCTION

Another intrinsic character-related function is INDEX. The function has two arguments, either character constants or character variables. If the second argument is a substring of the first, the function reports the point in the first argument from which the second matches. For example, INDEX('VVVVAAAAAVVVVV', 'AAA') reports 5, because if you lay the second argument on top of the first, the second argument finds a complete match in argument 1, starting at the fifth character position in argument 1. The function returns zero if a complete match does not occur. Study the output produced by the program in Fig. 14.11 and the behavior of the INDEX function will become very clear.

14.12 LEXICAL COMPARISONS: LGE, LGT, LLE, AND LLT

The six relational operators can be used to compare character data for sorting purposes. A character is said to be *less than* some other character if it precedes the latter in the character code table. This is very sensible, of course, because the characters

```
      CHARACTER ONE*14, TWO*6
*-----TEST 1
      ONE='THE IMPORTANCE'
      TWO='IMPORT'
      PRINT*, INDEX(ONE, TWO)
*-----TEST 2
      PRINT*, INDEX('IN THE EARLY PART OF HIS REIGN', 'LY')
*-----TEST 3
      PRINT*, INDEX(TWO, 'RT')
*-----TEST 4
      PRINT*, INDEX('HE DID NOT APPRECIATE THE IMPORTANCE', ONE)
*-----TEST 5
      PRINT*, INDEX(ONE, 'X')
      END
```

```
5
11
5
23
Ø
```

Figure 14.11 The INDEX function reports the leftmost position in the first argument from which complete agreement between the two arguments occurs.

are ordered in the code table in ascending numeric codes. Using the ASCII table in Appendix B, verify the truth values of the following logical expressions:

```
      ' ' .LT. '!'       = TRUE
      '1' .LT. '7'       = TRUE
      '&' .LT. '+'       = TRUE
      '1' .LT. 'A'       = TRUE
      'A' .LT. 'a'       = TRUE
    'AA ' .LT. 'AAA'     = TRUE
  'AAAA1' .LT. 'AAAAA'   = TRUE
'AAAAAAA' .LT. 'AAAAAAB' = TRUE
  'CURR1' .LT. 'CURR2'   = TRUE
    'aa ' .LT. 'aaa'     = TRUE
  'aaaaA' .LT. 'aaaaa'   = TRUE
'aaaaaaa' .LT. 'aaaaaab' = TRUE
  'curr1' .LT. 'curr2'   = TRUE
```

Now go to the EBCDIC table in Appendix A and perform the same comparisons, and you'll find major differences. These differences are due to the differences in the ASCII and EBCDIC collating sequences.

```
      ' ' .LT. '!'        = TRUE
      '1' .LT. '7'        = TRUE
      '&' .LT. '+'        = FALSE
      '1' .LT. 'A'        = FALSE
      'A' .LT. 'a'        = FALSE
    'AA ' .LT. 'AAA'      = TRUE
  'AAAA1' .LT. 'AAAAA'    = FALSE
'AAAAAAA' .LT. 'AAAAAAB'  = TRUE
  'CURR1' .LT. 'CURR2'    = TRUE
    'aa ' .LT. 'aaa'      = TRUE
  'aaaaA' .LT. 'aaaaa'    = FALSE
'aaaaaaa' .LT. 'aaaaaab'  = TRUE
  'curr1' .LT. 'curr2'    = TRUE
```

What this means is that programs performing character-data comparisons might produce one set of results on an EBCDIC machine and another set on an ASCII machine, an unacceptable situation. FORTRAN, therefore, provides the following four special *lexical comparsion functions*. C1 and C2 are either character variables or character constants.

LGE(C1,C2)	Lexically greater than or equal to
LGT(C1,C2)	Lexically greater than
LLE(C1,C2)	Lexically less than or equal to
LLT(C1,C2)	Lexically less than

These functions compare character data according to the ASCII collating sequence, even when running on an EBCDIC machine, guaranteeing consistency. The functions are supplied with two character arguments, and they compare the first with the second to produce the appropriate truth value. Figure 14.12 shows how the functions might be used in a program. The IF statement will make sense to you if you remember that the functions produce either true or false.

```
      CHARACTER*10 ONE,TWO
      ONE='CURR1'
      TWO='CURR2'
      PRINT*, LGT(ONE,TWO)
      IF(LLT(ONE,TWO))PRINT*,'THE FIRST IS ''LESS THAN'' THE SECOND'
      END
```

```
 F
THE FIRST IS 'LESS THAN' THE SECOND
```

Figure 14.12 Lexical comparison functions applied.

14.13 INTERNAL FILES

Still to come is a very simple and tremendously useful feature in the form of so-called *internal files*. A character variable, in effect, can be used as an internal blackboard from which data can be read, or to which data can be written, hence the term internal files. The startling simplicity is easily obscured by too many words, and examples are probably preferred. In Fig. 14.13, a character variable BBOARD is declared. We then write on this variable and print the resulting character string. Note the WRITE statement, where our blackboard variable takes the place of the unit number, and it's as simple as that.

In Fig. 14.14, we read from the blackboard to which a character constant is first assigned. Although the concept of internal files is easy to grasp, they do not seem all that useful at first. Example 14.15 in Section 14.15 demonstrates a good application.

```
      CHARACTER BBOARD*7Ø
      X=1234.567
*-----
*-----WE WRITE ON OUR INTERNAL 'BLACKBOARD'
*-----
      WRITE(BBOARD,1)X,SQRT(X)
    1 FORMAT('THE ROOT OF',F9.3,' IS',F7.3)
*-----
*-----AND NOW LET'S SEE WHAT'S ON THE 'BLACKBOARD'
*-----
      PRINT*,BBOARD
      END

THE ROOT OF 1234.567 IS 35.136
```

Figure 14.13 Writing to an internal file.

```
      CHARACTER BBOARD*7Ø
      BBOARD='MOCTEZUMA I WAS ELECTED IN THE YEAR 144Ø'
*-----
*-----'144Ø' IS NOW READ FROM THE BLACKBOARD AS A NUMBER
*-----EVEN THOUGH IT STARTED OUT AS A CHARACTER STRING
*-----
      READ(BBOARD,1)NUMBER
    1 FORMAT(35X,I5)
*-----
*-----IT'S A NUMBER ALL RIGHT - YOU CAN DO ARITHMETIC ON IT
      PRINT*,NUMBER,NUMBER*2,NUMBER*3,NUMBER*4
      END

 144Ø  288Ø  432Ø  576Ø
```

Figure 14.14 Reading from internal files.

14.14 SUMMARY

For practical purposes, the length of a character variable is unrestricted.

A or Aw editing is used for formatted character I/O. List-directed I/O can also be used.

The space is a legitimate character.

LINE(33:37), LINE(:12), LINE(43:) are substrings.

// is the concatenation operator.

LEN(C1) reports the length of the character variable (or character constant) C1 as an integer.

ICHAR(C1) reports the integer corresponding to the position of the character C1 in the code table, probably ASCII or EBCDIC, depending on the manufacturer.

CHAR(N) produces the character occupying cell N in the code table. The maximum value of N is one less than the number of cells in the table because the first cell is numbered 0. The maximum N value would thus be 127 for seven-bit codes and 255 for eight-bit codes.

INDEX(S1,S2) reports the starting point of the substring S2 within S1 as an integer. If S2 is not contained within S1, the function produces 0.

LGE, LGT, LLE, and LLT are the four lexical comparison functions. They compare character data as though the machine were based on the ASCII collating sequence, even if EBCDIC is used internally. The functions have two character arguments and return the truth values true or false. The logical expressions C1.LE.C2 and LLE(C1,C2) produce the same truth value in an ASCII environment, but not necessarily in the EBCDIC world.

Internal files are character variables on which it is possible to write, or from which you can read. A character variable appears in the READ and WRITE statements in place of the unit number.

14.15 EXAMPLES

Create a file called LONGLINE containing the following program. The program is faulty because two of the source lines extend beyond column 72. Don't attempt to run the program, but create it exactly as shown. You may have to adapt the name of the file to conform to your system's file-naming convention.

```
PRINT*,'LIST-DIRECTED INPUT AND OUTPUT ARE TREMENDOUSLY CONVENIENT'
PRINT*,'FOR THE PROGRAMMER.  IT IS ARGUED, HOWEVER, THAT FOR REALLY'
PRINT*,'FANCY OUTPUT, FORMATTED OUTPUT IS PREFERRED'
END
```

Example 14.7

An annoying problem encountered by FORTRAN programmers is a source line extending beyond column (space) 72. A right parenthesis, for example, might end up in column 73, where the compiler will not see it. The compiler will complain about the missing parenthesis, but the programmer, oblivious to the fact that the parenthesis is out of bounds, will see it and wonder what all the complaining is about. Write a program to check a FORTRAN source file for "beyond column 72" trespassing. The program asks you to enter the name of the file to be fumigated. It then opens the file and reads it record by record, reporting the locations of problem records and showing the actual spillover. Allow for a maximum spillover of 30 characters. Fumigate the file LONGLINE.

Solution

```
      CHARACTER SPILL*3Ø,NAME*2Ø
      PRINT*,'Please enter the name of the file to be fumigated '
      READ(5,1)NAME
    1 FORMAT(A)
      OPEN(7,FILE=NAME,STATUS='OLD',ERR=88,IOSTAT=IERR)
*-----
      NREC=Ø
      NUMBUG=Ø
    2 READ(7,3,END=99)SPILL
    3 FORMAT(72X,A)
      NREC=NREC+1
      IF(SPILL.NE.' ')THEN
         PRINT*,' Warning: Record',NREC,'too long.  Spillover: ',SPILL
         NUMBUG=NUMBUG+1
      END IF
      GO TO 2
*-----
   88 PRINT*,'Error:  Could not find a file called ',NAME
      STOP
   99 PRINT*,NREC,'records checked, ',NUMBUG,'problem records found.'
      END
```

```
Please enter the name of the file to be fumigated
?LONGLINE
 Warning: Record 1 too long.  Spillover: '
 Warning: Record 2 too long.  Spillover: Y'
 4 records checked,  2 problem records found.
```

Discussion The program is very simple and self-documenting. Read it and be sure to understand each statement. A short and a long character string are compared in the IF statement. Whenever such a comparison is made, the shorter string has enough blanks added to make the lengths equal. You will also notice that we are starting to use lowercase for the interactions. If your machine balks at this, simply switch back to uppercase. We allowed for a maximum filename length of 20 characters. If this is too many for your system, cut it back.

Example 14.8

Modify Ex. 14.7 to repair bad FORTRAN source programs by creating appropriate continuation lines with spillover from long lines. The system asks for the name of the file to be checked. The repaired version appears in a file with the name composed of FIX followed by the name of the input file. The fixed version of the file LONGLINE, for example, would appear under the name FIXLONGLINE. You will have to work within the framework of your system's file-naming conventions, of course.

Solution

```
      CHARACTER SPILL*66,NAME*20,BODY*72
      PRINT*,'Please enter the name of the file to be fixed '
      READ(5,1)NAME
    1 FORMAT(A)
      OPEN(7,FILE=NAME,STATUS='OLD',ERR=88,IOSTAT=IERR)
      OPEN(8,FILE='FIX'//NAME,STATUS='NEW',ERR=89,IOSTAT=IERR)
      PRINT*,' Creating file ','FIX'//NAME
      PRINT*,' It contains the repaired FORTRAN program.'
*-----
      NREC=0
      NUMFIX=0
    2 READ(7,3,END=99)BODY,SPILL
    3 FORMAT(2A)
      WRITE(8,3)BODY
      NREC=NREC+1
      IF(SPILL.NE.' ')THEN
         WRITE(8,4)'+'//SPILL
    4    FORMAT(5X,A)
         NUMFIX=NUMFIX+1
      END IF
      GO TO 2
*-----
   88 PRINT*,'Error:  Could not find a file called ',NAME
      STOP
   89 PRINT*,'Error:  Could not create file ','FIX'//NAME
      PRINT*,'Possibly it already exists - check your directory.'
      STOP
   99 PRINT*,NREC,'records were contained in source file ',NAME
      PRINT*,NUMFIX,'continuation lines were added to file ','FIX'//NAME
      CLOSE(8)
      END
```

```
Please enter the name of the file to be fixed
?LONGLINE
 Creating file FIXLONGLINE
 It contains the repaired FORTRAN program.
 4 records were contained in source file LONGLINE
 2 continuation lines were added to file FIXLONGLINE
```

Discussion Again the program is self-documenting, but a bit more involved. You should have little difficulty reading and understanding it. You will notice that the spillover-handling capacity has been increased to 66 characters. This program and the previous example are not only interesting, but also exceptionally useful. You may wish to retain them in your directory.

In order to continue with the examples, you will need a file containing several lines of text. The same file will also be required for some of the problems. Create a file called TEXTSAMPLE containing the following paragraph. The spacing and the number of words on a line must be exactly as shown here. Use uppercase only if your system insists on it.

```
The middle years of the rule of Moctezuma were to be implicated in a
phenomenal series of natural disasters, each of which tested the
resilience of the new state and the spirit of its rulers. The Huaxtec
War had just begun, and a glorious victory was anticipated in Mexico
when, in the summer of 1450, heavy rains began to fall that soon raised
the surface of the lake to alarming levels. The waters continued to
rise unabated until the streets and open patios of Tlatilulco and
Tenochtitlan were deep under the surface. The unpretentious houses of
the poor were the first to melt away, but finally even the artificial
terraces upon which the palaces and houses of the nobles were set became
undermined and were in their turn toppled into the floodwaters. This
damage to Mexico, however, was speedily repaired by a labor levy called
up from the subject cities of the lake side, though these communities
too had suffered heavily.
```

Example 14.9

Count the number of occurrences of each of the letters of the alphabet in the file TEXTSAMPLE. Count uppercase and lowercase versions of the same character together.

Solution

```
      CHARACTER LINE*80,LOWER*26,UPPER*26
      DIMENSION NUM(26)
      DATA NUM,LOWER,UPPER/26*0,'abcdefghijklmnopqrstuvwxyz',
     +'ABCDEFGHIJKLMNOPQRSTUVWXYZ'/
*-----
      OPEN(3,FILE='TEXTSAMPLE',STATUS='OLD')
    1 READ(3,2,END=99)LINE
    2 FORMAT(A)
*-----
      DO 3 IPOS=1,80
      DO 4 LET=1,26
      IF(LINE(IPOS:IPOS).EQ.LOWER(LET:LET))NUM(LET)=NUM(LET)+1
      IF(LINE(IPOS:IPOS).EQ.UPPER(LET:LET))NUM(LET)=NUM(LET)+1
    4 CONTINUE
    3 CONTINUE
      GO TO 1
```

```
*-----
  99 DO 5 LET=1,26
     WRITE(6,6)UPPER(LET:LET),LOWER(LET:LET),NUM(LET)
   6 FORMAT(' The letters ''',A,''' and ''',A,''' occur',I4,' times')
   5 CONTINUE
     END
```

```
The letters 'A' and 'a' occur  60 times
The letters 'B' and 'b' occur  10 times
The letters 'C' and 'c' occur  24 times
The letters 'D' and 'd' occur  29 times
The letters 'E' and 'e' occur 115 times
The letters 'F' and 'f' occur  22 times
The letters 'G' and 'g' occur   6 times
The letters 'H' and 'h' occur  43 times
The letters 'I' and 'i' occur  49 times
The letters 'J' and 'j' occur   2 times
The letters 'K' and 'k' occur   2 times
The letters 'L' and 'l' occur  34 times
The letters 'M' and 'm' occur  17 times
The letters 'N' and 'n' occur  41 times
The letters 'O' and 'o' occur  50 times
The letters 'P' and 'p' occur  16 times
The letters 'Q' and 'q' occur   0 times
The letters 'R' and 'r' occur  43 times
The letters 'S' and 's' occur  47 times
The letters 'T' and 't' occur  76 times
The letters 'U' and 'u' occur  29 times
The letters 'V' and 'v' occur   7 times
The letters 'W' and 'w' occur  16 times
The letters 'X' and 'x' occur   3 times
The letters 'Y' and 'y' occur   9 times
The letters 'Z' and 'z' occur   1 times
```

Discussion Three character variables are specified. One is LINE, with a capacity of 80 characters. It will be used to move the paragraph into the program, one line at a time. The purpose of LOWER and UPPER is to hold the lowercase and uppercase alphabets, respectively, both as single 26-character strings.

A 26-element integer array is then declared. Its purpose is to store the frequency of occurrence of each of the 26 letters of the alphabet. NUM(1), for example, will hold the number of times the letters "a" and "A" appear in the text, and NUM(26) stores the frequency of occurrence of "z" and "Z".

A DATA statement follows. In it, the 26 elements of NUM are initialized to zero, LOWER receives a character string composed of the 26 letters of the lowercase alphabet, and UPPER receives the uppercase equivalent.

The file TEXTSAMPLE is opened and the first line is picked up by the character variable LINE. It is assumed that no line in the paragraph is longer than 80 characters.

We then drop into the outer DO-loop, which steps along the 80 possible character positions of the input line. It stops at each position and runs the 26 lowercase and uppercase alphabetic characters past that position. Should a match occur on the nth letter, the nth bucket of the array NUM gets bumped up by one. Yes, the loop is wasteful because 52 comparisons are made for each character in the input line, but the program is clean and easy to understand. It would certainly be possible to halt the comparisons as soon as a match occurs. The following modification would accomplish that:

```
      DO 4 LET=1,26
      IF(LINE(IPOS:IPOS).EQ.LOWER(LET:LET)
     +    .OR. LINE(IPOS:IPOS).EQ.UPPER(LET:LET))THEN
             NUM(LET)=NUM(LET)+1
             GO TO 4
      END IF
    4 CONTINUE
```

With the modification, the program would run about twice as fast, but this becomes a problem only for longer text samples. If you were analyzing a book, for example, it would be a real issue.

The input lines and the two alphabets are character strings. Note that by extracting substrings, we can get at individual characters. The program is based on this, as you can readily see. The last DO-loop is an example of compact code. A lot of information is generated with very few lines. The program is simple, and if you take the trouble to understand each step in detail, you will learn a great deal.

Example 14.10

Modify the program in Ex. 14.9 to present the alphabetic spectrum in the form of a bar graph with 68 asterisks forming the longest bar.

Solution

```
      CHARACTER LINE*80,LOWER*26,UPPER*26
      DIMENSION NUM(26)
      DATA NUM,LOWER,UPPER/26*0,'abcdefghijklmnopqrstuvwxyz',
     +'ABCDEFGHIJKLMNOPQRSTUVWXYZ'/
*-----
      OPEN(3,FILE='TEXTSAMPLE',STATUS='OLD')
    1 READ(3,2,END=99)LINE
    2 FORMAT(A)
*-----
      DO 3 IPOS=1,80
      DO 4 LET=1,26
      IF(LINE(IPOS:IPOS).EQ.LOWER(LET:LET))NUM(LET)=NUM(LET)+1
      IF(LINE(IPOS:IPOS).EQ.UPPER(LET:LET))NUM(LET)=NUM(LET)+1
    4 CONTINUE
    3 CONTINUE
      GO TO 1
```

```
*-----
   99 LARGE=NUM(1)
      DO 7 I=2,26
      IF(NUM(I).GT.LARGE)LARGE=NUM(I)
    7 CONTINUE
*-----
      DO 8 I=1,26
      NUM(I)=NINT(NUM(I)*68./LARGE)
    8 CONTINUE
*-----
      DO 9 I=1,26
      WRITE(6,10)UPPER(I:I),('*',J=1,NUM(I))
   10 FORMAT(1X,A,1X,68A)
    9 CONTINUE
      END
```

```
A ***********************************
B ******
C **************
D *****************
E ********************************************************************
F *************
G ****
H *************************
I *****************************
J *
K *
L ********************
M **********
N ************************
O ******************************
P *********
Q
R *************************
S ****************************
T *********************************************
U *****************
V ****
W *********
X **
Y *****
Z *
```

Discussion The modification involves the final DO-loop of the previous program. By the time we reach that stage, the array NUM has been filled, and it is now only a matter of presenting the magnitude of each element graphically. We first step through the array to find the magnitude of the largest element. With the constraint of 68 characters for the longest line, we multiply each element of NUM by 68./LARGE. This scales the array appropriately. Don't forget the decimal point, because you don't want any integer division truncation. The NINT function rounds the result to the nearest integer. In the final WRITE statement, the asterisk is printed the required number of times. Note the 68 A fields in the FORMAT statement.

Each language has a characteristic spectrum, a fact that makes it possible to deduce the language behind some encoded texts. If you were to sort the bar graph in descending order, for example, a certain slope would emerge. If you then plot the sorted spectrum of some scrambled text and compare it to the sorted spectra of known language samples, the host language may be recognized. Needless to say, however, those who encode texts can get quite inventive as well.

Example 14.11

Extract and print the last word from each line of the paragraph in the file TEXTSAMPLE.

Discussion In the program, START is the character position at which the last word on the line starts. Once the last word on the line is located, it is transferred to the variable LAST. The file is opened, and the first record is read into the variable LINE. The outer DO-loop then begins at character position 80 and works backward along the input line until a nonblank is encountered, marking the end of the last word, including any punctuation. The inner DO-loop then takes over, searching for the beginning of the last word on the line by looking for a blank, indicating that the beginning of the last word has been passed. If the blank is found in position J, the word starts in position J + 1. It is possible, however, that there might be only a single word on the line and that this word begins in position 1. This situation is looked after by the ELSE IF.

Solution

```
      INTEGER START
      CHARACTER LINE*8Ø,LAST*2Ø
      OPEN(3,FILE='TEXTSAMPLE',STATUS='OLD')
    1 READ(3,2,END=99)LINE
    2 FORMAT(A)
*-----
      DO 3 I=8Ø,1,-1
      IF(LINE(I:I).NE.' ')THEN
*-----
         DO 4 J=I,1,-1
         IF(LINE(J:J).EQ.' ')THEN
            START=J+1
            GO TO 5
         ELSE IF(J.EQ.1)THEN
            START=1
            GO TO 5
         END IF
    4    CONTINUE
*-----
      END IF
    3 CONTINUE
```

```
*-----
      GO TO 1
    5 LAST=LINE(START:)
      WRITE(6,6)LAST
    6 FORMAT(1X,A)
      GO TO 1
   99 CONTINUE
      END
```

```
a
the
Huaxtec
Mexico
raised
to
and
of
artificial
became
This
called
communities
heavily.
```

Example 14.12

Scan the paragraph in the file TEXTSAMPLE and report which lines contain the character string 'ea'.

Solution

```
      CHARACTER LINE*8Ø
      OPEN(3,FILE='TEXTSAMPLE',STATUS='OLD')
      LOC=Ø
    1 READ(3,2,END=99)LINE
    2 FORMAT(A)
      LOC=LOC+1
*-----
      IF(INDEX(LINE,'ea').NE.Ø)WRITE(6,3)LOC
    3 FORMAT(' Line',I3,' contains the string ''ea''')
      GO TO 1
   99 CONTINUE
      END
```

```
Line  1 contains the string 'ea'
Line  2 contains the string 'ea'
Line  5 contains the string 'ea'
Line 14 contains the string 'ea'
```

Example 14.13

Print the paragraph in file TEXTSAMPLE after substituting '--' for each 'u'.

Solution

```
      CHARACTER LINE*80,LINOUT*90
      OPEN(3,FILE='TEXTSAMPLE',STATUS='OLD')
    1 READ(3,2,END=99)LINE
    2 FORMAT(A)
*-----
      LOC=1
      LINOUT=' '
      DO 3 I=1,80
      IF(LINE(I:I).EQ.'u')THEN
         LINOUT(LOC:LOC+1)='--'
         LOC=LOC+2
      ELSE
      LINOUT(LOC:LOC)=LINE(I:I)
      LOC=LOC+1
      END IF
    3 CONTINUE
*-----
      WRITE(6,4)LINOUT
    4 FORMAT(1X,A)
      GO TO 1
   99 CONTINUE
      END
```

```
The middle years of the r--le of Moctez--ma were to be implicated in a
phenomenal series of nat--ral disasters, each of which tested the
resilience of the new state and the spirit of its r--lers. The H--axtec
War had j--st beg--n, and a glorio--s victory was anticipated in Mexico
when, in the s--mmer of 1450, heavy rains began to fall that soon raised
the s--rface of the lake to alarming levels. The waters contin--ed to
rise --nabated --ntil the streets and open patios of Tlatil--lco and
Tenochtitlan were deep --nder the s--rface. The --npretentio--s ho--ses of
the poor were the first to melt away, b--t finally even the artificial
terraces --pon which the palaces and ho--ses of the nobles were set became
--ndermined and were in their t--rn toppled into the floodwaters. This
damage to Mexico, however, was speedily repaired by a labor levy called
--p from the s--bject cities of the lake side, tho--gh these comm--nities
too had s--ffered heavily.
```

Discussion The program reads a line from the file into the character variable LINE. The line is then copied to the new variable LINOUT character by character. Whenever a 'u' is found, '--' is copied into LINOUT. You will notice that the DO-variable I moves along LINE, character by character. The variable LOC points to the current position in LINOUT. Each time a character is moved to LINOUT, LOC is increased by 1, but whenever '--' is transferred, LOC is increased by 2. LINOUT = ' ' sweeps out LINOUT before the transfers begin.

Example 14.14

Right-justify the paragraph in file TEXTSAMPLE by stretching the lines to the length of the longest line. Extra blanks are inserted between words to stretch a line.

Solution

```
      CHARACTER LINE*80,LINOUT*80
      OPEN(3,FILE='TEXTSAMPLE',STATUS='OLD')
*-----'LONG' IS THE LENGTH OF THE LONGEST LINE
      LONG=0
    1 READ(3,2,END=4)LINE
    2 FORMAT(A)
*-----WE NOW CHECK THE LENGTH OF EACH LINE BY CHECKING FOR THE
*-----FIRST NON-BLANK CHARACTER, FROM THE BACK.  IF THE LINE IS
*-----LONGER THAN 'LONG', ITS LENGTH BECOMES THE NEW VALUE OF 'LONG'
      DO 3 I=80,1,-1
      IF(LINE(I:I).NE.' ')THEN
         IF(I.GT.LONG)LONG=I
      GO TO 1
      END IF
    3 CONTINUE
*-----WE NOW KNOW HOW LONG THE LONGEST LINE IS.  THE FILE IS REWOUND.
*-----EACH LINE IS READ AGAIN AND ITS LENGTH 'LENGTH' IS CHECKED
    4 REWIND(3)
    5 READ(3,2,END=99)LINE
      DO 6 I=80,1,-1
      IF(LINE(I:I).NE.' ')THEN
         LENGTH=I
         GO TO 7
      END IF
    6 CONTINUE
    7 NEED=LONG-LENGTH
*-----'NEED' IS THE NUMBER OF BLANKS NEEDED TO STRETCH THE LINE
*-----THE STRETCHED LINE IS WRITTEN TO 'LINOUT' WHICH IS FIRST CLEARED.
*-----THE ACTUAL STRETCHING IS BASED ON THE PREVIOUS EXAMPLE
      LINOUT=' '
      LOC=1
*-----SINCE THE LENGTH OF ANY GIVEN INPUT LINE IS 'LENGTH', WE
*-----COPY ONLY THE FIRST 'LENGTH' CHARACTERS.  THE REST IS BLANK
      DO 8 I=1,LENGTH
      LINOUT(LOC:LOC)=LINE(I:I)
      LOC=LOC+1
*-----IF A BLANK WAS JUST TRANSFERRED, AND IF WE STILL NEED TO
*-----STRETCH SOME MORE, AN EXTRA BLANK IS INJECTED INTO LINOUT,
```

```
*-----AND 'LOC' AND 'NEED' ARE UPDATED APPROPRIATELY
      IF(LINE(I:I).EQ.' '.AND.NEED.GT.0)THEN
         LINOUT(LOC:LOC)=' '
         LOC=LOC+1
         NEED=NEED-1
      END IF
    8 CONTINUE
      WRITE(6,9)LINOUT
    9 FORMAT(1X,A)
      GO TO 5
   99 CONTINUE
      END
```

```
The  middle  years  of  the rule of Moctezuma were to be implicated in a
phenomenal  series  of  natural  disasters,  each  of  which  tested the
resilience  of  the  new state and the spirit of its rulers. The Huaxtec
War  had  just  begun,  and a glorious victory was anticipated in Mexico
when,  in the summer of 1450, heavy rains began to fall that soon raised
the  surface  of  the  lake  to alarming levels. The waters continued to
rise  unabated  until  the  streets  and  open  patios of Tlatilulco and
Tenochtitlan  were  deep  under the surface. The unpretentious houses of
the  poor  were  the first to melt away, but finally even the artificial
terraces upon which the palaces and houses of the nobles were set became
undermined  and  were  in  their turn toppled into the floodwaters. This
damage  to Mexico, however, was speedily repaired by a labor levy called
up  from  the  subject cities of the lake side, though these communities
too  had  suffered  heavily.
```

Discussion The output looks impressive and the program is simple. It contains important comments explaining the various steps. Two passes are made through the file, the first to find the longest line, and the second to perform the actual stretching. The program has several shortcomings, such as the inability to cope with leading blanks in a line, as would be used to indent paragraphs. It also lacks the ability to move words between two consecutive lines to minimize the need to insert blanks. You will also notice that all the inserted blanks congregate in the left half of the paragraph, making it look lighter on the left than on the right. Another weakness is obvious in the last line, where some stretching did occur, but fortunately the computer stopped before spoiling the line by stretching the four words right across, with gaping spaces between them. It would have been better if no stretching had been attempted at all because the line was too short. Nevertheless, the program performed valiantly, and it will serve as a good starting point for greater efforts.

Example 14.15

Interactive programs often require a lot of numeric input. It is easy to enter invalid digits, such as the letter I in place of the digit 1, or the letter O instead of the digit 0, or a comma when a decimal point was intended. Without the ERR= branch, the program will choke on invalid input. With the error branch, the error is no longer fatal, but the resulting warning is rather general. Write a program that analyzes each input character and points out any offender.

Solution

```
      CHARACTER BBOARD*15,POINT*45
*-----Reading a CHARACTER string from the keyboard
    1 READ(5,2,END=99)BBOARD
    2 FORMAT(A)
*-----Checking for invalid input characters.
      DO 3 I = 1,15
      IF(.NOT.(BBOARD(I:I).EQ.' '.OR.BBOARD(I:I).EQ.'+'
     +.OR.BBOARD(I:I).EQ.'-'.OR.BBOARD(I:I).EQ.'.'.OR.
     +BBOARD(I:I).GE.'Ø' .AND. BBOARD(I:I).LE.'9') )THEN
*-----Creating a 'Peter-Pointer' error message
         POINT=' '
         POINT(I:I)='*'
         POINT(I+3:)='This character is invalid'
      WRITE(6,4)POINT
    4 FORMAT(2X,A)
         GO TO 1
      END IF
    3 CONTINUE
*-----Reading the fumigated input from the internal file.  The BN
*-----FORMAT switch treats trailing spaces in the input as NULLS
      READ(BBOARD,5)X
    5 FORMAT(BN,F15.Ø)
*-----
      PRINT*,'You entered',X
      GO TO 1
   99 CONTINUE
      END
```

```
?12
You entered 12.ØØØØØ

?432I.12
    *  This character is invalid

?+87.12
You entered 87.12ØØØ

?-87.12
You entered -87.12ØØØ

?=87.12
 *  This character is invalid

?-87,12
    *  This character is invalid
```

```
?Ø98765.432
You entered 98765.43

?Ø98765.432IØ
          *  This character is invalid

?Ø98765.432LØ
          *  This character is invalid

?Ø98765.Ø3
You entered 98765.Ø3

etc.
```

Discussion This is a useful program, the sort that you would probably want to add to a payroll system. You should study the interaction first to understand the exact purpose of the program. You will notice that an asterisk is placed directly underneath the offending input character. You will have to shift the error message to the left by one position if your machine does not prompt for input.

The program reads the "numeric input" into BBOARD as a character string. The DO-loop then steps along BBOARD, checking each of the 15 positions to make sure that no characters other than ' 0123456789.+ −' appear in the input. The IF statement deserves thoughtful attention, especially the AND condition, which works by virtue of the fact that the ten digits '0123456789' occupy ten contiguous slots in both the ASCII and EBCDIC tables. The AND condition states that an incoming character greater than or equal to the character 0 and at the same time less than or equal to 9 is acceptable. This encompasses all 10 digits. The condition could, of course, also have assumed the equivalent form

```
LGE(BBOARD(I:I),'Ø').AND.LLE(BBOARD(I:I),'9')
```

The error message is dynamic, with the ability to place the asterisk under bad input characters. Study how the message is assembled. Bad input causes the logic to return for more keyboard input.

Once the input has passed inspection, we treat BBOARD as an internal file and read the contents numerically. The BN format option frees us from having to right-justify the input when no decimal point is provided. You may wish to review the BN and BZ options near the end of Chapter 7 if you don't recall the details.

The program is impressively useful, but it does have some serious weaknesses. It cannot detect a double decimal point, for example, nor a sign in the middle of the number. Suitable modifications could be made, of course, and some of these will be suggested in the problem section.

14.16 PROBLEMS

14.1. In Ex. 14.4, a five-element character array was declared to hold five-character data. You would do well to review that example briefly. Now declare a similar array with fourteen 72-character elements. Fill this array with the 14 lines in file TEXTSAMPLE. Perform an ASCII sort, in ascending order, on the array. Print the sorted array. Recall that you will have to use *lexical* comparisons to be sure the program will produce the same output on ASCII and EBCDIC machines. After an ascending ASCII sort, you would expect the uppercase characters to appear first, in alphabetical order, followed by the lowercase characters, also in alphabetical order. An EBCDIC sort would produce the lowercase characters first, followed by uppercase. Your output should look as shown:

```
Tenochtitlan were deep under the surface. The unpretentious houses of
The middle years of the rule of Moctezuma were to be implicated in a
War had just begun, and a glorious victory was anticipated in Mexico
damage to Mexico, however, was speedily repaired by a labor levy called
phenomenal series of natural disasters, each of which tested the
resilience of the new state and the spirit of its rulers. The Huaxtec
rise unabated until the streets and open patios of Tlatilulco and
terraces upon which the palaces and houses of the nobles were set became
the poor were the first to melt away, but finally even the artificial
the surface of the lake to alarming levels. The waters continued to
too had suffered heavily.
undermined and were in their turn toppled into the floodwaters. This
up from the subject cities of the lake side, though these communities
when, in the summer of 1450, heavy rains began to fall that soon raised
```

14.2. Modify the previous problem to sort the lines from character position 14 to the end. LINE(3)(14:), incidentally, is the substring from character 14 to the end of element 3 of the array LINE. The expected output is shown. Note that in the first four lines, a blank appears in space 14, and blanks float to the top in a character sort.

```
the poor were the first to melt away, but finally even the artificial
resilience of the new state and the spirit of its rulers. The Huaxtec
rise unabated until the streets and open patios of Tlatilulco and
terraces upon which the palaces and houses of the nobles were set became
The middle years of the rule of Moctezuma were to be implicated in a
War had just begun, and a glorious victory was anticipated in Mexico
undermined and were in their turn toppled into the floodwaters. This
the surface of the lake to alarming levels. The waters continued to
damage to Mexico, however, was speedily repaired by a labor levy called
too had suffered heavily.
phenomenal series of natural disasters, each of which tested the
when, in the summer of 1450, heavy rains began to fall that soon raised
up from the subject cities of the lake side, though these communities
Tenochtitlan were deep under the surface. The unpretentious houses of
```

14.3. Write a program to count the number of words in the file TEXTSAMPLE. The simplest way involves reading the file line by line into an 80-character variable. Scan that variable from left to right, and assume you counted one word as soon as you encounter a blank. Then check the rest of the line. If it is blank, quit scanning and read the next line. *Answer*: 161 words.

14.4. Count the number of words in TEXTSAMPLE that begin with W or w. *Answer*: 12.

14.5. When text is composed from the keyboard, it is easy to type the same word twice, especially when editing or when meditating on style. It is even easier to use a certain word at the end of a line, and to repeat the same word at the beginning of the next line, a problem not readily caught when proofing. Create a new file called BADSAMPLE containing the paragraph from file TEXTSAMPLE. To the beginning of line 2 of BADSAMPLE, add the word "a", add "of" to the beginning of line 9, and add "communities" to the beginning of line 14. In the middle of line 11, change "in their turn" to "in in their turn". The file BADSAMPLE now contains the following paragraph:

```
The middle years of the rule of Moctezuma were to be implicated in a
a phenomenal series of natural disasters, each of which tested the
resilience of the new state and the spirit of its rulers. The Huaxtec
War had just begun, and a glorious victory was anticipated in Mexico
when, in the summer of 145Ø, heavy rains began to fall that soon raised
the surface of the lake to alarming levels. The waters continued to
rise unabated until the streets and open patios of Tlatilulco and
Tenochtitlan were deep under the surface. The unpretentious houses of
of the poor were the first to melt away, but finally even the artificial
terraces upon which the palaces and houses of the nobles were set became
undermined and were in in their turn toppled into the floodwaters. This
damage to Mexico, however, was speedily repaired by a labor levy called
up from the subject cities of the lake side, though these communities
communities too had suffered heavily.
```

Now write a program to detect cases of the last word of a line reappearing as the first word of the next line. Run the file BADSAMPLE through the program. The suggested output is

```
Warning:  The last word of line  1 is the same as the first word of line  2
Warning:  The last word of line  8 is the same as the first word of line  9
Warning:  The last word of line 13 is the same as the first word of line 14
```

14.6. Write a program to detect two identical successive words on a line. Run the file BADSAMPLE through the program to see whether you can catch the problem on line 11. Your output should look something like the following:

```
Warning: line 11

undermined and were in in their turn toppled into the floodwaters. This

Words 4 and 5 are the same
```

14.7. Write a program to show each character in the file TEXTSAMPLE shifted ahead by one position in the character table. You will recall that the CHAR function generates a character when given the numeric location in the table, and you will recall that the ICHAR function reports the table position of a particular character as an integer. To change "a" to "b", for example, replace "a" with CHAR(ICHAR('a')+1). The first four lines of the output are shown. You should have a good look at the code table for your system, found in either Appendix A or B.

```
Uif!njeemf!zfbst!pg!uif!svmf!pg!Npduf{vnb!xfsf!up!cf!jnqmjdbufe!jo!b!!!!
qifopnfobm!tfsjft!pg!obuvsbm!ejtbtufst-!fbdi!pg!xijdi!uftufe!uif!!!!!!!!
sftjmjfodf!pg!uif!ofx!tubuf!boe!uif!tqjsju!pg!jut!svmfst/!Uif!Ivbyufd!!!
Xbs!ibe!kvtu!cfhvo-!boe!b!hmpsjpvt!wjdupsz!xbt!boujdjqbufe!jo!Nfyjdp!!!!
```

14.8. Write a program in which you show each lowercase character in file TEXTSAMPLE changed to uppercase. You can determine the relationship between the lowercase and uppercase characters from the appropriate character table. Be sure to carry the punctuation and the numerics across. The first five lines of the output are shown:

```
THE MIDDLE YEARS OF THE RULE OF MOCTEZUMA WERE TO BE IMPLICATED IN A
PHENOMENAL SERIES OF NATURAL DISASTERS, EACH OF WHICH TESTED THE
RESILIENCE OF THE NEW STATE AND THE SPIRIT OF ITS RULERS. THE HUAXTEC
WAR HAD JUST BEGUN, AND A GLORIOUS VICTORY WAS ANTICIPATED IN MEXICO
WHEN, IN THE SUMMER OF 145Ø, HEAVY RAINS BEGAN TO FALL THAT SOON RAISED
```

14.9. In Ex. 14.11, the last word of each line of the file TEXTSAMPLE is printed. Modify the program to exclude punctuation marks. In this particular case, the period following the word "heavily" would be omitted.

14.10. In Ex. 14.14, lines were stretched to right-justify text, but it was pointed out that all the stretching occurred from the left, making the left side of the output look too light. Modify the program to alternate between left and right blank insertions. The first line, for example, would be stretched from the left, the second line from the right, the third line from the left, and the fourth from the right. The first four lines of the expected output are shown:

```
The  middle  years  of  the rule of Moctezuma were to be implicated in a
phenomenal series  of  natural  disasters,  each  of  which  tested  the
resilience  of  the  new state and the spirit of its rulers. The Huaxtec
War had just begun, and a glorious victory  was  anticipated  in  Mexico
```

14.11. The program in Ex. 14.14 has difficulties with leading blanks, such as might be encountered when paragraph indenting is used. In its current state, the program adds blanks to the indenting blanks, rather than between subsequent words. Modify the program to ignore leading blanks when stretching a line. Compose a small test input file on which to test your modification.

14.12. The program in Ex. 14.14 started to stretch the last line, but wasn't too successful because the line was too short. Add another modification to the program to prevent stretching lines shorter than half the longest line.

14.13. The program in Ex. 14.14 makes only a single space-insertion pass through a line when stretching it. This can lead to situations where a line cannot be stretched sufficiently. Modify the program to take another run at the stretched line, should further stretching be required.

14.14. In Ex. 14.7, a program was developed to detect overly long FORTRAN source lines. The way it stands, however, the program will also complain about long comment lines. Enhance the program so that it will ignore comment lines, whether they start with a C, or with an asterisk in column 1.

14.15. The program in Ex. 14.8 will also fix long comment lines. Comment lines cannot be continued, though, and the fix will lead to compile-time problems. Modify the program to turn lengthy comment lines into two separate comment lines.

14.16. A program has three types of numeric input. Type A input requires the computer to insert one decimal point between the last and second-to-last digits. Type B input requires a decimal point to be inserted two positions from the end, and type C input needs a decimal point three digits from the end. Typical input, and the computer's required interpretations, are shown:

The user enters	The computer interprets
A 451232	45123.200
B 121	1.210
C 15	0.015
B970091	9700.910
A1	0.100

Write a program that generates the following interaction. This is obviously a case for internal files. You may find it helpful to take another look at Ex. 14.15.

```
?A1
You entered      .100
?A 1
You entered      .100
?B1
You entered      .010
?B765
You entered     7.650
?C 987765
You entered   987.765
?C12321
You entered    12.321
```

14.17. Modify Ex. 14.15 to complain about multiple decimal points and about signs in the middle of the input.

14.18. In Ex. 14.10, the alphabetic spectrum of a sample of English text was presented in bar-graph form. It is interesting to produce similar spectra for other languages. Create files with samples of other languages, such as Spanish, German, French, Nahuatl, and some oriental languages, that can be written in romanized form. For many of the languages, you will have to ignore the diacritics such as the accents. The program should open the various files automatically to produce a series of spectra. This problem makes a good group project, with different individuals coming up with the various language samples. You will be surprised by the characteristic spectra displayed by the various language families. The Germanic and the Romance language families display distinct characteristics, but a language such as Nahuatl has a unique spectrum. Nahuatl is of considerable interest because it is one of North America's native languages that was widely understood.

14.19. Write a program to scramble the paragraph in TEXTSAMPLE. Write the scrambled version to a new file called SCRAMSAM. Accomplish the scrambling by interchanging character 1 with 37, 3 with 39, 5 with 41, 7 with 43, 9 with 45, . . . , 35 with 71 in each line of

TEXTSAMPLE. Assume each line, including trailing blanks, to be 72 characters long. The first five lines of the scrambled file SCRAMSAM are shown:

```
ehu aiwdre yoabs om lhc tudeio   o tTzemm dele te re ifptiearel  nfaM c
rh,nemcn lfswrieh tfsnet rhl d s s epse oaehao  ehics oe tadutae  i a t
seiiii nfeios rhl re. TtetH ant ch  rpsrlteoc  tf tueensw sha euaxdet e
iat ra  au tnbigina en  n Mlxrco s vWcrohydwjssa tecup,taddia geoiiou
ahnn  enat eosfmle  hft1s5o, haasydrwies,big nht  uamlrtoa  4o0n reive
```

14.20. Have someone scramble an unknown language sample, using the interchange algorithm of the previous problem. Perform a bar-graph spectrum analysis on the sample and deduce the source language. Unscramble the sample to verify your deduction.

15

User-Defined Functions

There is an infinite number of possible mathematical functions, but FORTRAN provides only a relatively small number. It is safe to say, however, that FORTRAN provides all the fundamental mathematical functions to permit the programmer to construct any mathematical expression that might be needed. If you require a special function, and if that function is not one of the intrinsic functions, FORTRAN allows you to define the function within your program. There are two ways of defining your own functions. One involves the so-called *statement function,* and the other involves a user-written program module called a *FUNCTION subprogram.*

15.1 THE STATEMENT FUNCTION

A simple example is the best way to introduce the statement function. Superficially, the first statement in Fig. 15.1 looks like an assignment statement until you notice that SUM(A,B,C) is not an array element because no array was declared. This is a signal to the compiler that we are not dealing with an assignment statement at all, but with the definition of a function. The first line serves as a pattern for the machine, instructing it what to do with the three arguments A, B, and C when it subsequently encounters SUM(A,B,C) in the program. In this particular case, it is required to add the three arguments and to return the total via SUM, the name of this new function. Study Fig. 15.1, justifying the output, and you will understand just how the function works.

```
      SUM(A,B,C) = A+B+C
*-----
      PRINT*, SUM(5.,10.,20.)
      PRINT*, 4.*SUM(100.,200.,55.)
      END

 35.000000
 1420.000
```

Figure 15.1 The statement function.

A function defined in this manner is known as a *statement function*. The name implies correctly that such a function definition is permitted to involve only a single FORTRAN statement, even if that statement is continued over the permissible 19 lines. Should the function definition require several statements, involving DO-loops, for example, then this simple approach no longer applies, and it becomes necessary to resort to the more elaborate *FUNCTION subprogram* to be discussed later.

The statement function definition must precede all executable statements, and it must follow all the specification statements. In other words, it is sandwiched between the specification statements and the executable statements.

The name of the statement function determines the data type. If the function name begins with I,J,K,L,M, or N, it returns an integer result, otherwise the result is real. This data typing can be overruled by including the name of the function in a data type-statement, or by including its first letter in an IMPLICIT declaration.

The statement function definition statement itself must be viewed as a template. The arguments appearing in the statement are called *dummy* arguments because they convey no value, but only information about how they are to be used, and information about the data type.

Have another look at Fig. 15.1, where the name of the function is SUM. The name tells us that the function returns a floating-point result, and this is confirmed by the output. All three dummy arguments are real in the function definition. If, when using the function, you fail to observe the data types implied in the definition, unpredictable behavior might result on many systems, without warning.

The statement function definition is allowed to invoke any of the intrinsic functions, such as the SQRT, SIN, MIN, MAX, etc. It can also use a statement function defined ahead of it in the same program module. You may, in other words, have as many statement functions as you like, each having access to previously defined statement functions and to all the intrinsic functions, provided you observe the placement rules, locating all the function definitions between the specification statements and the executable statements.

After this lengthy discussion, it is easy to lose sight of the simplicity of it all. We will bring that back into focus with specific examples, and deal with some of the remaining outstanding issues in the process.

One of these issues is the potential problem of a programmer unwittingly inventing a statement function name that coincides with the name of some obscure intrinsic function. Which one will win out, the intrinsic function or the statement function? There is only one way to find out. In Fig. 15.2, we define a function

```
      SQRT(M) = M**2
      PRINT*, SQRT(16)
      END

 256.0000
```

Figure 15.2 The statement function is the clear winner when its name conflicts with that of an intrinsic function.

```
      ROOT(X) = 2.*SQRT(X)+100.
      PRINT*, ROOT(16.)
      END

 108.0000
```

Figure 15.3 Statement functions are free to incorporate intrinsic functions.

called SQRT. Its purpose is to square its integer argument. It returns that square as a real number because of the function name.

The programmer is blithely unaware that there is an intrinsic function by the same name, requiring a real argument, and designed to compute the square root of its argument. The output reveals that the statment function is won.

The programmer is obviously the winner in Fig. 15.2. Now, if you were to remove the statement function definition, the machine would probably complain about a data-type conflict with the intrinsic function SQRT, and even if it ran, would certainly produce a different result. Figure 15.3 shows another example of a statement function, this one involving an intrinsic function in the definition.

15.2 EXAMPLES

Example 15.1

Define a function CUBERT(X) designed to compute the cube root of its argument X. The function is to report a real result. Test the function by computing the cube roots of the numbers from 1 to 10.

Solution The desired function can obviously be defined with a single statement and therefore is a "proper" statement function candidate. The name of the function guarantees a real result. What would happen if the brackets around the 1./3. were left off? If it's not obvious to you, run it without the brackets and compare the results.

```
      CUBERT(X)=X**(1./3.)
*-----
      DO 1 X=1.,10.
      WRITE(6,2)X,CUBERT(X)
    2 FORMAT(' The cube root of',F6.1,'  is',F8.4)
    1 CONTINUE
      END

 The cube root of   1.0  is  1.0000
 The cube root of   2.0  is  1.2599
 The cube root of   3.0  is  1.4422
```

```
The cube root of   4.Ø  is  1.5874
The cube root of   5.Ø  is  1.71ØØ
The cube root of   6.Ø  is  1.8171
The cube root of   7.Ø  is  1.9129
The cube root of   8.Ø  is  2.ØØØØ
The cube root of   9.Ø  is  2.Ø8Ø1
The cube root of  1Ø.Ø  is  2.1544
```

Example 15.2

Define a character function CAT(X) with a single character argument X. The function produces the argument concatenated to itself four times.

Solution This is another suitable statement function situation because the definition requires no more than a single FORTRAN statement. Because the function is expected to return a character result, it must be declared as type CHARACTER.

```
      CHARACTER CAT*6Ø,X*12
*-----
      CAT(X) = X//X//X//X
*-----
      X = ' HI YOU ALL'
      PRINT*, CAT(X)
      PRINT*, CAT(' =-=-=-=-=-')
      END
```

```
 HI YOU ALL  HI YOU ALL  HI YOU ALL  HI YOU ALL
 =-=-=-=-=-  =-=-=-=-=-  =-=-=-=-=-  =-=-=-=-=-
```

15.3 FUNCTION SUBPROGRAMS

The previous section explained and demonstrated how the statement function can be used to supplement FORTRAN's repertoire of intrinsic functions. The facility is tremendously useful and certainly simple, but it does suffer from the restriction that the definition of a new function is allowed to involve only a single FORTRAN statement, hence the name *statement function.* More complex function definitions frequently involve multistatement algorithms, however, and for these situations FORTRAN provides the so-called *FUNCTION subprogram,* a special program module attached to the program.

Lest too many words cloud the issue, an example is offered. It involves a simple function called MULT with a single integer argument. The function multiplies the argument by itself, and multiplies the resulting product by three. Requiring only a single FORTRAN statement, the function qualifies for the statement function approach, which is shown first:

```
      MULT(J) = J*J*3
      PRINT*, MULT(1Ø)
      END
```

```
      PRINT*, MULT(1Ø)
      END
*-----
      FUNCTION MULT(J)
      MULT=J*J*3
      RETURN
      END

 3ØØ
```

Figure 15.4 A FUNCTION subprogram is attached to the calling *main* program.

The same function is now defined within the more powerful and flexible framework of the FUNCTION subprogram, shown in Fig. 15.4. The first two lines constitute the so-called *main* program. It is a complete program unit, terminated by an END statement. The main program calls on a function MULT, and it would run quite nicely by itself if there were an intrinsic function by that name, but there isn't. There is, however, an attached FUNCTION subprogram in which the function MULT is defined.

FUNCTION subprograms are always introduced by the word FUNCTION, followed by the name of the function, along with the dummy arguments. In this case, there is only a single dummy argument, namely J. When the computer calls on this function, it brings with it a value for J, 10 in this particular case. The subprogram then proceeds to evaluate the function, see line 2 of the subprogram in Fig. 15.4, and returns to the calling program. The RETURN statement is optional because the END statement acts like a RETURN in a subprogram.

Actually Fig. 15.4 fails to do justice to the FUNCTION subprogram because this particular function definition is provided more easily by the statement-function approach, but Fig. 15.5 defines a more complex function that shares an array with

```
      DIMENSION W(3,4)
      READ(5,*)W
      WRITE(6,1)TOTSUM(W)
    1 FORMAT(' THE SUM OF ALL THE ELEMENTS OF W IS',F7.2)
      END
*-----
      FUNCTION TOTSUM(XX)
      DIMENSION XX(3,4)
      TOTSUM=0.
      DO 1 I = 1,3
      DO 1 J = 1,4
    1 TOTSUM=TOTSUM+XX(I,J)
      RETURN
      END

?3.2  1.2  5.4  3.2   9.0  6.5  2.1  12.2  32.1  45.3  1.2  1.1

THE SUM OF ALL THE ELEMENTS OF W IS 122.50
```

Figure 15.5 An array is shared between the main program and the subprogram.

its main program. In this particular case, the subprogram computes the sum of all the elements of the array, and that sum is then printed in the main program. Note the DIMENSION statement in the subprogram. No extra storage is required for the array declared in the FUNCTION subprogram because it occupies the same space in memory as the corresponding array in the main program. It is the same array by virtue of the dummy-array linkage between the main and subprograms. In the main program, the function TOTSUM is called with the argument W, the 3 × 4 array. In the subprogram header, we find the dummy argument XX. The difference in name is irrelevant because linking occurs by position in the argument list and not by name. The DIMENSION statement in the subprogram is essential, for without it the compiler would complain about syntax errors in the DO-loop, where subscripted array elements are used.

You probably noticed that the same statement label 1 is used in both program modules. This is allowed because label references do not cross from one program module to the next.

Figure 15.6 shows a very general function subprogram designed to go with any program containing a two-dimensional array. The function SUM, defined by the subprogram, is designed to compute the sum of any row of the array and it is designed to be used with any size two-dimensional array. The dimensions of the array are transmitted to the subprogram through the argument list.

There are four dummy arguments in the subprogram header. Values are transmitted to these dummy arguments by the calling program. Z is an array with NROW rows and NCOL columns. IROW is the row to be summed. This subprogram illustrates a very valuable FORTRAN feature, namely, arrays with *adjustable* dimensions, allowing the subprogram to adjust the size of its array to that in the calling program. Such adjustable DIMENSION statements are not permitted in main programs, only in subprograms.

Figure 15.7 shows how this powerful FUNCTION subprogram is used. The following 4 × 5 array is read into the array F in the main program, which then calls on the subprogram four times, asking it to sum each of the four rows.

4.5	1.2	2.3	12.3	10.2
10.2	13.9	0.3	9.3	11.4
3.1	4.9	2.6	1.1	9.7
1.2	4.3	1.2	7.6	0.8

In Fig. 15.7, the function SUM is invoked in line 5 of the main program with the argument list (F,4,5,I). This argument list is matched with the dummy arguments in the function header (Z,NROW,NCOL,IROW). The number of argu-

```
      FUNCTION SUM(Z,NROW,NCOL,IROW)
      DIMENSION Z(NROW,NCOL)
      SUM=0.
      DO 1 I = 1,NCOL
    1 SUM=SUM+Z(IROW,NCOL)
      RETURN
      END
```

Figure 15.6 A FUNCTION subprogram with adjustable array dimensions.

```
      DIMENSION F(4,5)
      DO 1 I = 1,4
    1 READ(5,*)(F(I,J),J=1,5)
      DO 2 I = 1,4
      WRITE(6,3)I,SUM(F,4,5,I)
    3 FORMAT(' THE SUM OF ROW ',I,' IS',F5.1)
    2 CONTINUE
      END
*-----
      FUNCTION SUM(Z,NROW,NCOL,IROW)
      DIMENSION Z(NROW,NCOL)
      SUM=0.
      DO 1 I = 1,NCOL
    1 SUM=SUM+Z(IROW,I)
      RETURN
      END

?    4.5   1.2   2.3  12.3  10.2
?   10.2  13.9   0.3   9.3  11.4
?    3.1   4.9   2.6   1.1   9.7
?    1.2   4.3   1.2   7.6   0.8

THE SUM OF ROW 1   IS 30.5
THE SUM OF ROW 2   IS 45.1
THE SUM OF ROW 3   IS 21.4
THE SUM OF ROW 4   IS 15.1
```

Figure 15.7 A function subprogram with adjustable dimensions.

ments matches, and the computer assumes that the entity called F in the main program coincides with the array Z in the subprogram. Similarly, it concludes that NROW=4, NCOL=5, and IROW=I. Because F and Z are the same, they refer to the same 20 words of memory. The subprogram performs admirably, as you can see from the output.

You will recall the concern expressed in connection with the statement function, about potential problems when the programmer inadvertently uses a function name already present among the intrinsic functions. You will also recall that experimentation showed that the user's statement function takes precedence over an intrinsic function of the same name, but it is not clear now whether the same is true when it comes to functions defined external to the main program in a FUNCTION subprogram. Again, experimentation is called for. In our experiment, shown in Fig. 15.8, the main program calls the ABS function. A FUNCTION subprogram definition of ABS is attached to the main program.

The program's output is somewhat startling—the computer ignored our definition of the function and instead resorted to the intrinsically defined version. You will recall that in a showdown between the statement function and the intrinsic function, it was the other way around.

```
      PRINT*, ABS(-4)
      END
*-----
      FUNCTION ABS(J)
      ABS=J**2
      RETURN
      END

ABS(-4) = 4
```

Figure 15.8 In case of conflict between an intrinsic function and a function defined in a FUNCTION subprogram, the computer chooses the intrinsic function.

```
      EXTERNAL ABS
      PRINT*, ABS(-4)
      END
*-----
      FUNCTION ABS(J)
      ABS=J**2
      RETURN
      END

16.ØØØØ
```

Figure 15.9 The EXTERNAL specification causes the computer to bypass the intrinsic function in case of conflict.

What happened should make us a bit uneasy because we may not know the names of all the intrinsic functions, and we could easily trip over one of these. The problem is readily overcome if we declare in our main program that we wish to use an external function called ABS. The EXTERNAL specification is used in Fig. 15.9 to instruct the computer to search *our* program for the function definition and not to invoke its intrinsic version. Our function is accepted, as you can tell from the output. Notice that even the data types of the outputs in these two examples are different.

15.4 FUNCTION NAMES AND DATA TYPES

A FUNCTION subprogram computes a result. This result is carried back to the calling program module via the name of the function. The computed result can be of any of the six available data types, namely, integer, real, double precision, character, logical, or complex. If, for example, the function is to compute a real result, its name must either conform to the variable-naming convention for real data, that is, its name must not begin with I, J, K, L. M, or N, or there must be an appropriate data-type specification, which must appear not only in the FUNCTION subprogram itself, but also in the program module calling on the function. If there is a data-type mismatch between these two modules, you can expect serious problems. Not all compilers have the ability to spot such mismatching and therefore cannot warn you. Data-type mismatches inevitably result in *wrong* data reaching the module calling on the function. If a FUNCTION subprogram returns a datum of type CHARACTER, the function name must be specified as type CHARACTER, both in the subprogram and in the module requesting the function. There must also be agreement on the length specification.

This discussion could make you somewhat uneasy when you think back to the intrinsic functions. There is, for example, the ABS function. The data type of the result is determined by the data type of the argument. It returns an integer when called with an integer argument, a real result when the argument is real, and a double precision result when you supply a double precision argument. The explanation is that in the library of intrinsic functions, there are four different versions of the ABS function, namely, ABS, IABS, DABS, and CABS, returning real, integer, double precision, and complex values, respectively. The compiler looks at the data type of the argument and provides communication with the appropriate version of the intrinsic function. The generic function name ABS, therefore, acts as a switch to one of four *specific* intrinsic functions. User-written FUNCTION subprograms cannot be front-ended with a general *generic* name and hence the need to watch for data-type matching. The three programs in Fig. 15.10 are properly type matched, and they are equivalent. Each produces the real result 9.00.

```
      PRINT*, TFUN(3.)
      END
*-----
      FUNCTION TFUN(X)
      TFUN=X+X+X
      RETURN
      END
```

```
      IMPLICIT REAL(A-Z)
      PRINT*, MFUN(3.)
      END
*-----
      REAL FUNCTION MFUN(X)
      MFUN=X+X+X
      RETURN
      END
```

```
      REAL MFUN
      PRINT*, MFUN(3.)
      END
*-----
      FUNCTION MFUN(X)
      REAL MFUN
      MFUN=X+X+X
      RETURN
      END
```

Figure 15.10 These three programs are equivalent and properly data-type matched.

15.5 EXAMPLES

Example 15.3

Write a FUNCTION subprogram SUM(X,N). The function adds the argument X N times to compute the total, SUM. Test this function by computing the sums of groups of 10,000 terms, where the terms range from 0.1 to 0.55 in steps of 0.11. This type of function can be used to probe the floating-point precision of a system.

Solution

```
      PROGRAM ADDER
      NUM=10000
      DO 1 TERM = 0.1, 0.55, 0.11
      WRITE(6,2) TERM, NUM, SUM(TERM,NUM)
2     FORMAT(1X,F6.2,'  added',I7,'  times sums to',2P,E17.9)
1     CONTINUE
      END
```

```
*-----
      FUNCTION SUM(X,N)
      SUM=Ø.
      DO 1 I=1,N
      SUM=SUM+X
    1 CONTINUE
      RETURN
      END
```

```
 .1Ø  added  1ØØØØ  times sums to  99.9814697ØE+Ø1
 .21  added  1ØØØØ  times sums to  2Ø.9992392ØE+Ø2
 .32  added  1ØØØØ  times sums to  31.9978641ØE+Ø2
 .43  added  1ØØØØ  times sums to  42.9978516ØE+Ø2
 .54  added  1ØØØØ  times sums to  53.9875879ØE+Ø2
```

Discussion The first thing you will notice is the PROGRAM statement at the beginning of the main program. This is an optional statement, but some feel that if a subprogram has a header statement, then so should the main program. It adds an attractive touch and reassures you that no statements evaporated from the top of the program. The name assigned in the PROGRAM statement follows the usual rules, such as no longer than six characters, letters and digits only, with a letter as the first character. The same name must not be given to a subsequent subprogram, nor can it be used as a variable name.

The function SUM is used inside the DO-loop and things obviously work. The resulting sums fall short of the expected results for reasons discussed in Probs. 10.6 and 10.7.

Example 15.4

Modify the function SUM of the previous example to double precision. Modify the main program appropriately.

Solution

```
      PROGRAM DADDER
      DOUBLE PRECISION SUM,TERM
      NUM=1ØØØØ
      DO 1 TERM = Ø.1DØ, Ø.55DØ, Ø.11DØ
      WRITE(6,2) TERM, NUM, SUM(TERM,NUM)
    2 FORMAT(1X,F6.2,'  added',I7,'  times sums to',2P,D17.9)
    1 CONTINUE
      END
*-----
      DOUBLE PRECISION FUNCTION SUM(X,N)
      DOUBLE PRECISION X
      SUM=ØDØ
      DO 1 I=1,N
      SUM=SUM+X
    1 CONTINUE
      RETURN
      END
```

```
.1Ø  added  1ØØØØ  times sums to  1Ø.ØØØØØØØØØD+Ø2
.21  added  1ØØØØ  times sums to  21.ØØØØØØØØØD+Ø2
.32  added  1ØØØØ  times sums to  32.ØØØØØØØØØD+Ø2
.43  added  1ØØØØ  times sums to  43.ØØØØØØØØØD+Ø2
.54  added  1ØØØØ  times sums to  54.ØØØØØØØØØD+Ø2
```

Example 15.5

The LEN function, as you saw in the previous chapter, has a single character argument. The function reports an integer result equal to the length of the argument. The following program, for example, reports a length of 80 because the trailing blanks are included in the count, and LINE is declared with a length of 80.

```
CHARACTER LINE*8Ø
LINE='ABCD'
PRINT*, LEN(LINE)
END
```

Develop and test a function LAST. The function has a single character argument. It reports an integer result equal to the position of the last nonblank character in the string. The function would report 4 in the above example.

Solution

```
      PROGRAM COUNT
      CHARACTER LINE*8Ø
      PRINT*,'Pls enter a line to be measured for information content'
      READ(5,2)LINE
    2 FORMAT(A)
      WRITE(6,1)LAST(LINE)
    1 FORMAT(1X,'There is no information beyond character',I3)
      END
*-----
      FUNCTION LAST(STRING)
      CHARACTER STRING*(*)
      DO 1 I=LEN(STRING),1,-1
      IF(STRING(I:I).NE.' ')THEN
         LAST=I
         RETURN
      END IF
    1 CONTINUE
      LAST=Ø
      RETURN
      END
```

```
Pls enter a line to be measured for information content
?TIHULI NAHUATL? SE TONALI CUALI IPAN FEBRERO, QUEMA YA TEMITOC METZTLI.
There is no information beyond character 71
```

Discussion The main program passes a character argument to the subprogram. That character string must be the same length in both program modules. If you specify a length of (*) in the subprogram, the lengths will match automatically, and the subprogram can be used with arguments of any length. An alternate form of this particular character type-statement is CHARACTER*(*) STRING.

Example 15.6

Develop and test a function LASTWD. The function accepts a character argument, such as a line of text, and returns the last word of the input. Assume that the last word will never be longer than 25 characters. The function can deal with lines containing only a single word, even if that word begins in space 1. It returns a blank string in case the input line is blank.

Solution

```
      PROGRAM COUNT
      CHARACTER LINE*80,LASTWD*25
    1 PRINT*,'Extract the last word from which line?'
      READ(5,2,END=99)LINE
    2 FORMAT(A)
      WRITE(6,3)LASTWD(LINE)
    3 FORMAT(1X,'The last word in the input line is: ',A)
      GO TO 1
   99 CONTINUE
      END
*-----
      FUNCTION LASTWD(STRING)
      CHARACTER*(*) STRING,LASTWD
*-----Searching for the first non-blank character from the back
      DO 1 I=LEN(STRING),1,-1
      IF(STRING(I:I).NE.' ')THEN
*-----Having found the end of the last word, searching for its beginning
         DO 2 J = I,1,-1
         IF(STRING(J:J).EQ.' ')THEN
*-----beginning of word found.  Transferring word to LASTWD
            LASTWD=STRING(J+1:)
            RETURN
         END IF
         IF(J.EQ.1)THEN
*-----Reached 1 without finding space.  Transferring STRING to LASTWD
            LASTWD=STRING
            RETURN
         END IF
    2    CONTINUE
      END IF
*-----If you get this far without finding non-blank, line is blank
      IF(I.EQ.1)LASTWD=' '
```

```
    1  CONTINUE
       RETURN
       END
```

```
Extract the last word from which line?
?CANQUE TITEQUITISE
The last word in the input line is: TITEQUITISE

Extract the last word from which line?
?TOPILE, PANOJ TOSAME NI MILA. TIJNEQUI TIQUINPAJTISE PARA MA MIQUICA?
The last word in the input line is: MIQUICA?

Extract the last word from which line?
?TLAXCALI
The last word in the input line is: TLAXCALI

Extract the last word from which line?
?       YOYOMITL
The last word in the input line is: YOYOMITL

Extract the last word from which line?
?(blank line entered here)
The last word in the input line is:  (blank)

Extract the last word from which line?
?  (EOF)
```

15.6 USER-CREATED LIBRARIES

You now have a clear idea how easy it is to write useful FUNCTION subprograms. Such subprograms can be compiled and collected in a file to serve as your private library. You can well imagine how useful such a library can be, and how greatly it can simplify programming. Instead of laboring to add a new feature to some program, you simply call on one of the treasures in the library, and the desired ability appears. The real advantage of subprograms lies in the fact that they make highly modular programming possible. Programming now frequently involves nothing more than tying together several well-developed, carefully tested and debugged modules. When a new feature is required, it can be developed and added to the library.

The actual mechanics of creating and maintaining a private library vary considerably from system to system, and you will have to refer to your computer's documentation. In general, however, it is true that subprograms can be compiled in isolation to be subsequently knit into a library. Once such a library exists, you no longer need to append the source versions of the subprograms to your main programs. Instead, you simply allow the library to be associated with your compiled main programs at run time.

In the following chapter, you will meet *subroutine subprograms*. These add the remaining dimension of flexibility to private libraries.

15.7 PROBLEMS

15.1. Write a FUNCTION subprogram SIND(X) that computes the sine of X, where X is expressed in degrees. You will recall that the intrinsic function SIN(X) expects the argument to be supplied in radians. To convert degrees to radians, multiply the degrees by 3.1415926/180. You may wish to review Prob. 10.12.

15.2. Write a FUNCTION subprogram COSD(X) to compute the cosine of X, where X is expressed in degrees. Also develop a function TAND(X) to compute the tangent of X, where X is expressed in degrees.

15.3. Develop and test the three double precision functions DSIND(X), DCOSD(X), and DTAND(X). The arguments are supplied in degrees, expressed in double precision mode, and they return a double precision result.

15.4. Write and test a character function FIRSTW(LINE). The function receives a character argument LINE. It returns the first word in LINE as a character string. Assume a maximum length of 25 characters. The function returns a blank FIRSTW when LINE contains only blanks.

15.5. Write and test a FUNCTION subprogram NUM(LINE,SUBSTR). LINE is a character variable of length 80, and SUBSTR is a character constant. A typical function reference is NUM(LINE, 'walls and doors'). The function reports the number of times the character string SUBSTR occurs in LINE. It reports that number as an integer, returning 0 if SUBSTR does not occur in LINE. The function also reports 0 if LINE and SUBSTR are both blank.

16

SUBROUTINE Subprograms and the COMMON Block

FORTRAN permits us to package logical units of code into subprograms. In the previous chapter, *FUNCTION subprograms* were introduced, and you saw how very useful that facility is. *SUBROUTINE subprograms* are closely related, and an example is the best way to introduce them.

Figure 16.1 shows a highly readable main program followed by four SUBROUTINE subprograms. The first subroutine reads an array. The second subroutine prints the array, and the third reports the sum of all the elements. The fourth does some fancy printing. Spend time looking at the program before you continue reading. In particular, notice how well-structured and readable the main program is. A detailed explanation follows.

16.1 WHAT TO NOTICE IN FIG. 16.1

1. A FUNCTION subprogram is invoked by simply using its name in an expression or an output list. SUBROUTINE subprograms, on the other hand, are invoked with *CALL subname*, where the *subname* is the name of the desired subroutine. Unlike a function name, the name of a subroutine carries no information. The CALL might or might not include an argument list. The argument list, when present, sets up two-way communication links between the subroutine and the calling program. In Fig. 16.1, two subroutines are called with a single argument, one is called with two arguments, and one is called without any.

```
      PROGRAM MODLAR
      DIMENSION W(3,4)
      CALL READER(W)
      CALL PRINTER(W)
      CALL ADDER(W,SUM)
      WRITE(6,1)SUM
    1 FORMAT(//,' THE SUM OF ALL THE ELEMENTS IS',F7.2,/)
      CALL PRETTY
      END
*-----
      SUBROUTINE READER(Z)
      DIMENSION Z(3,4)
      WRITE(6,1)
    1 FORMAT(' PLEASE ENTER THE 12 ELEMENTS OF THE ARRAY IN',
     +' COLUMN ORDER',/,' SEPARATED BY BLANKS OR COMMAS:',/)
      READ(5,*)Z
      RETURN
      END
*-----
      SUBROUTINE PRINTER(X)
      DIMENSION X(3,4)
      WRITE(6,1)
    1 FORMAT(//,' THE FOLLOWING ARRAY WAS READ:',/)
      DO 2 IROW = 1,3
      WRITE(6,3)(X(IROW,ICOL),ICOL=1,4)
    3 FORMAT(1X,4F10.1)
    2 CONTINUE
      RETURN
      END
*-----
      SUBROUTINE ADDER(W,SUM)
      DIMENSION W(3,4)
      SUM=0.
      DO 1 IROW = 1,3
      DO 1 ICOL = 1,4
      SUM=SUM+W(IROW,ICOL)
    1 CONTINUE
      RETURN
      END
*-----
      SUBROUTINE PRETTY
      WRITE(6,1)
```

Figure 16.1 A highly structured program, consisting of five modules, a main program and four SUBROUTINE subprograms.

```
1  FORMAT(1X,20'-->',/,1X,20'->-',/,1X,20'>--',/,1X,20'-->')
   RETURN
   END
```

```
PLEASE ENTER THE 12 ELEMENTS OF THE ARRAY IN COLUMN ORDER
SEPARATED BY BLANKS OR COMMAS:

? 3.2  1.2  5.4  3.2  9.0  6.5  2.1  12.2  32.1  45.3  1.2  1.1

THE FOLLOWING ARRAY WAS READ:
      3.2       3.2       2.1      45.3
      1.2       9.0      12.2       1.2
      5.4       6.5      32.1       1.1

THE SUM OF ALL THE ELEMENTS IS 122.50

-->-->-->-->-->-->-->-->-->-->-->-->-->-->-->-->-->-->-->-->
->-->-->-->-->-->-->-->-->-->-->-->-->-->-->-->-->-->-->-->-
>-->-->-->-->-->-->-->-->-->-->-->-->-->-->-->-->-->-->-->--
-->-->-->-->-->-->-->-->-->-->-->-->-->-->-->-->-->-->-->-->
```

Figure 16.1 *(continued)*

2. As in the case of FUNCTION subprograms, the arguments communicate by position and not by name. Note that the same array has various names in the different modules, although you could certainly use the same name in each.
3. Note the two-way communication between the main program and subroutine adder. The array W is sent into that subroutine and SUM is returned and printed in the main program.
4. Although not demonstrated here, subroutines can call each other, the only restriction being that a subroutine cannot call itself. Languages in which a subroutine can call itself are said to be *recursive*. FORTRAN is not a recursive language.
5. Each subroutine subprogram must be introduced by the SUBROUTINE statement and the last statement must be END. The proper way to leave a subroutine is through the RETURN statement. You will recall, however, that the END statement will act like RETURN in a FUNCTION subprogram. The same is true for SUBROUTINE subprograms.
6. The program in Fig. 16.1 is extremely readable, almost self-documenting.
7. To emphasize the similarities between SUBROUTINE subprograms and FUNCTION subprograms, we take SUBROUTINE ADDER from Fig. 16.1 and change it into a FUNCTION subprogram called SUM.

```
      SUBROUTINE ADDER(W,SUM)
      DIMENSION W(3,4)
      SUM=Ø.
      DO 1 IROW = 1,3
      DO 1 ICOL = 1,3
      SUM=SUM+W(IROW,ICOL)
    1 CONTINUE
      RETURN
      END
```

```
      FUNCTION SUM(W)
      DIMENSION W(3,4)
      SUM=Ø.
      DO 1 IROW = 1,3
      DO 1 ICOL = 1,3
      SUM=SUM+W(IROW,ICOL)
    1 CONTINUE
      RETURN
      END
```

On comparing the FUNCTION subprogram on the right with the SUBROUTINE subprogram on the left, you will notice that there are only three differences, two of which are in the header. The three differences are

1. The module on the right is called a function rather than a subroutine.
2. There is only one arugument in this particular function header whereas the corresponding SUBROUTINE header has two arguments. The reason is that the function name itself becomes the carrier of the result. The subroutine name does not convey a result, serving as nothing more than an entry point.
3. Functions are not CALLed. Instead they are automatically invoked when their names are used by the calling program. To use the above function in place of the subroutine in Fig. 16.1, we delete the statement CALL ADDER(W,SUM) and change the WRITE statement to WRITE(6,1)SUM(W).

16.2 THE COMMON STATEMENT

The *COMMON statement* is another very important and frequently used FORTRAN specification statement. Take the following as a typical COMMON declaration:

COMMON A,B,C,M(1000),D(3,4),W,X

This COMMON statement declares 1017 words, the three real words A, B, and C, followed by the one-dimensional integer array M with 1000 words, a real array with 12 words, and the two single real words W and X. These 1017 words constitute what is known as a *common block.* The common block has two unique properties to which it owes its usefulness. If the importance of these two properties is not fully understood, the common block will not be used properly.

1. The common block can be accessed by all the modules of a program.
2. The common block is contiguous.

All program modules, whether they be main programs, SUBROUTINE subprograms, or FUNCTION subprograms, can attach themselves to the common block for intermodule communication. Figure 16.2 is a repeat of Fig. 16.1, but this time

```
      PROGRAM MODCOM
      COMMON W(3,4),SUM
      CALL READER
      CALL PRINTER
      CALL ADDER
      WRITE(6,1)SUM
    1 FORMAT(//,' THE SUM OF ALL THE ELEMENTS IS',F7.2,/)
      CALL PRETTY
      END
*-----
      SUBROUTINE READER
      COMMON Z(3,4),SUM
      WRITE(6,1)
    1 FORMAT(' PLEASE ENTER THE 12 ELEMENTS OF THE ARRAY IN',
     +' COLUMN ORDER',/,' SEPARATED BY BLANKS OR COMMAS:',/)
      READ(5,*)Z
      RETURN
      END
*-----
      SUBROUTINE PRINTER
      COMMON X(3,4),SUM
      WRITE(6,1)
    1 FORMAT(//,' THE FOLLOWING ARRAY WAS READ:',/)
      DO 2 IROW = 1,3
      WRITE(6,3)(X(IROW,ICOL),ICOL=1,4)
    2 CONTINUE
    3 FORMAT(4F10.1)
      RETURN
      END
*-----
      SUBROUTINE ADDER
      COMMON W(3,4),SUM
      SUM=0.
      DO 1 IROW = 1,3
      DO 1 ICOL = 1,4
      SUM=SUM+W(IROW,ICOL)
    1 CONTINUE
      RETURN
      END
*-----
      SUBROUTINE PRETTY
      COMMON W(3,4),SUM
      WRITE(6,1)
```

Figure 16.2 The various modules of a program communicate through the common block.

```
    1  FORMAT(1X,20'-->',/,1X,20'->-',/,1X,20'>--',/,1X,20'-->')
       RETURN
       END
```

```
PLEASE ENTER THE 12 ELEMENTS OF THE ARRAY IN COLUMN ORDER
SEPARATED BY BLANKS OR COMMAS:

? 3.2  1.2  5.4  3.2  9.0  6.5  2.1  12.2  32.1  45.3  1.2  1.1

THE FOLLOWING ARRAY WAS READ:
        3.2        3.2         2.1       45.3
        1.2        9.0        12.2        1.2
        5.4        6.5        32.1        1.1

THE SUM OF ALL THE ELEMENTS IS 122.50

-->-->-->-->-->-->-->-->-->-->-->-->-->-->-->-->-->-->-->-->
->-->-->-->-->-->-->-->-->-->-->-->-->-->-->-->-->-->-->-->-
>-->-->-->-->-->-->-->-->-->-->-->-->-->-->-->-->-->-->-->--
-->-->-->-->-->-->-->-->-->-->-->-->-->-->-->-->-->-->-->-->
```

Figure 16.2 *(continued)*

the modules communicate through the common block. A complete explanation follows in the next section.

16.3 ANALYSIS

The program in Fig. 16.2 has five modules, a main program and four SUBROUTINE subprograms. Each module attaches itself to the first 13 words of the common block, as you can see from the COMMON declaration in each module. Scan the program to verify this. Each module thus has access to the same 13 words of memory, which are now common to all modules.

It makes no difference that the first 12 words are called W in three of the modules, Z in another, and X in yet another because we are dealing with the same 12 words. Items in the common block, in other words, communicate by position and not by variable name. By attaching each module to the common block, we have, in fact, run a *common data bus* past each module, which is now free to obtain data from it or to place data onto it. Subroutine READER, for example, reads data into the first 12 words of the common block, making these 12 data available to all the modules clipped onto the common block. Subroutine PRINTER then prints these 12 words. They are the same 12 words even though that subroutine calls them X. In subroutine ADDER, the same 12 are called W. This subroutine adds the 12 words and places the sum on the common data bus, where it occupies slot 13. The main program subsequently prints it.

Notice that subroutine PRETTY is also attached to the common block, even though it has no need to communicate with the other modules. Because it need not communicate, linking it to the common block is optional, and is done for the sake of uniformity.

It is clear that all intermodule communication is now accomplished via the common block and that the argument lists in CALL statements and in subprogram headers are no longer necessary, nor allowed for that matter, because items appearing in the common block cannot also appear in argument lists. This would constitute an attempt to establish double linkages.

Hybrid linking is permitted, though. It two modules need to exchange data, and no space was assigned in the common block for such data, a special communication link can be established through argument lists. Similarly, two modules may need to exchange data that are of no interest to any of the other modules in the program, in which case argument linkages are better than adding needless clutter to the common block.

In summary, we might say that common block linking is clean and simple, although it is often convenient to supplement this with argument linkages in many cases. Function linkages would still occur via the function names and argument lists, although the function subprograms can share additional data through the common block.

Subprogram modules using arrays with adjustable dimensions must still declare such arrays in dimension statements, and such arrays must still be passed back and forth through argument linkages. The reason is that once a program has been compiled, the common block is absolutely rigid as far as size is concerned, making dynamic array sizing within the common block impossible.

The COMMON statement in the main program in Fig. 16.2 is COMMON W(3,4),Z, which is equivalent to the following two statements:

```
DIMENSION W(3,4)
COMMON W,Z
```

Either form is acceptable, but the combined statement is obviously more economical.

Figure 16.3 shows an interesting program. In subroutine FILL, a one-dimensional array X is placed in the common block, where it occupies the first 60 words. In subroutine SPILL, a two-dimensional array Y also appears in the common block, and also occupies 60 words. Because the common block is contiguous, and because we are dealing with one common area in memory, the 60 words of array X in subroutine FILL are obviously the same 60 words occupied by the array Y in subroutine SPILL, and the output confirms this clearly. It also reminds us again that the elements of a two-dimensional array are stored in memory in column order.

Figure 16.4 shows a startling program where a one-dimensional array X(100) is declared in the common block and filled. The variable A sits next to the array in the common block and is assigned 99.99. We then "accidentally" assign 44.44 to the nonexistent element X(101), print A, and receive a surprise. This certainly drives home the meaning of *contiguity* within the common block. Note that there are no subprograms in Fig. 16.4. The common block can exist in a lone main program to provide contiguous storage.

```
      PROGRAM SPILFIL
      CALL FILL
      CALL SPILL
      END
*-----
      SUBROUTINE FILL
      COMMON X(6Ø)
      DO 1 I=1,6Ø
      X(I)=I
    1 CONTINUE
      RETURN
      END
*-----
      SUBROUTINE SPILL
      COMMON Y(6,1Ø)
      DO 1 IROW = 1,6
    1 WRITE(6,2)(Y(IROW,ICOL),ICOL=1,1Ø)
    2 FORMAT(1X,1ØF5.Ø)
      RETURN
      END
    1.   7.  13.  19.  25.  31.  37.  43.  49.  55.
    2.   8.  14.  2Ø.  26.  32.  38.  44.  5Ø.  56.
    3.   9.  15.  21.  27.  33.  39.  45.  51.  57.
    4.  1Ø.  16.  22.  28.  34.  4Ø.  46.  52.  58.
    5.  11.  17.  23.  29.  35.  41.  47.  53.  59.
    6.  12.  18.  24.  3Ø.  36.  42.  48.  54.  6Ø.
```

Figure 16.3 A one-dimensional array and a two-dimensional array are superimposed in the common block.

Figure 16.5 is also of considerable interest, and you will have no difficulty explaining the output. Z in the main program, Z in subroutine LOOK1, and M in subroutine LOOK2 are obviously the same word of memory. In the main program, a value is assigned to this word, where it is stored in floating-point form. The word is then printed in subroutine LOOK1, and all appears normal. In subroutine LOOK2, the same word of memory is viewed as an integer, and a very large

```
      PROGRAM SURPSE
      COMMON X(1ØØ),A
      DO 1 I = 1,1ØØ
    1 X(I)=I
      A=99.99
      X(1Ø1)=44.44
      PRINT*, 'A = ',A
      END
 A = 44.44ØØØ
```

Figure 16.4 Out-of-control subscripts will corrupt neighboring data.

```
      PROGRAM DBLTKE
      COMMON Z
      Z=3.1415926
      CALL LOOK1
      CALL LOOK2
      END
*-----
      SUBROUTINE LOOK1
      COMMON Z
      WRITE(6,1)Z
    1 FORMAT(' THE FIRST WORD OF THE COMMON BLOCK CONTAINS',F1Ø.6)
      RETURN
      END
*-----
      SUBROUTINE LOOK2
      COMMON M
      WRITE(6,1)M
    1 FORMAT(' THE FIRST WORD OF THE COMMON BLOCK CONTAINS',I1Ø)
      RETURN
      END

THE FIRST WORD OF THE COMMON BLOCK CONTAINS  3.141593
THE FIRST WORD OF THE COMMON BLOCK CONTAINS 294789Ø45
```

Figure 16.5 Two very different views of the same bit pattern in a word.

number results. The reason is that some of the bits near the left side of the word hold the exponent, and when this same word is regarded as an integer, a large number is seen. The exact magnitude of this number is hardware dependent, of course, because different manufacturers use different floating-point storage schemes.

Figure 16.6 shows a main program and a subroutine. The main program attaches itself to the first three data slots in the common block, of which the first slot occupies a double word because A is double precision. The subroutine also attaches itself to the first three data slots in the common block, but the common block as seen by the main program and by the subroutine is obviously out of alignment. The double precision variable A in the main program occupies the first two words, B gets the third word, and C the fourth. In the subroutine, A gets the first word of the common block, B the second, and C the third, and the output should not surprise you. You would, in fact, expect A in the subroutine to pick up something reasonable because the first word of a double precision datum is the same as its single-precision counterpart, with possibly the exception of the last bit. B in the subroutine sees the second half of the double precision datum and erroneously interprets it as a floating-point quantity. The interpretation, of course, will vary from system to system. Word C in the subroutine coincides with word B in the main program and picks up that value. The moral is that you have to take care not to misalign the common block.

```
      PROGRAM DBLSHK
      DOUBLE PRECISION A
      COMMON A,B,C
      A=3.1415926D0
      B=123.45678
      CALL SUB1
      END
*-----
      SUBROUTINE SUB1
      COMMON A,B,C
      PRINT*, 'A =',A,'   B =',B,'   AND C =',C
      RETURN
      END

 A = 3.141593     B = .9064301E-57     AND C = 123.4568
```

Figure 16.6 Two incompatible views of the common block because of careless use of double precision.

16.4 CHARACTER DATA AND THE COMMON BLOCK

You just saw how easily data can appear misaligned in the common block when it is viewed differently by different program modules, especially when one program module assumes a certain datum to occupy two words in the common block, while some other module assumes a single word for the same datum. Character data can occupy any number of words because of their varying lengths, and you can well imagine that chaos is probable when character data are placed in the common block. The added fact of character data not necessarily falling neatly between word boundaries compounds the problem. A six-character datum, for example, occupies six bytes, which is a word and a half on a typical machine. For this reason, ANSI X3.8–1978 states that if you insist on placing character data in the common block, then the entire common block must contain only character data; you cannot include any of the other five data types. The best way around this reasonable condition is not to place character data in the common block at all, but to use argument linkages for that data type, as required.

16.5 ADDITIONAL POINTS

For historical reasons, you must not use the DATA statement to initialize variables in the common block. The reasons, in part, go back to the days of small memories when programs had to be squeezed into memory to make them fit. While the loader loads a program, it too must sit in memory, because it is nothing more than a program itself. On systems with small memories, it can be advantageous to allow the loader, during the load phase, to remain in the same area of memory subsequently assigned to the common block of the program it is loading. Once the loader has loaded the program, it is no longer needed and data can then be moved into the common block. If you attempted to initialize data in the common block with a DATA statement at compile time, the loader on such systems would have to transfer these initial values into memory, and overwrite itself in the process.

You should also be aware that there is a secondary form of common block called *named common*. It has the form shown. The name appears between the slashes and must conform to the standard FORTRAN naming convention.

```
COMMON /FIRST/ A,B,C,D,E,F
```

Certain program modules may share this particular named common, and others might share a different named common. A named common, however, is subject to certain restrictions that make it less attractive. It is mentioned here only for the sake of completeness. Named common variables can be initialized in a DATA statement, but only if that DATA statement appears in a special program module called a *block data subprogram*, which is designed specifically for this purpose. The block data subprogram is rarely used and will not be discussed further. The common block with which we started has no name, and it is often called *blank common* for this reason. The following two blank common specifications are equivalent:

```
COMMON W(3,4),X(100),A,B,C
COMMON //W(3,4),X(100),A,B,C
```

16.6 EXAMPLES

Example 16.1

Write a program consisting of a main program UTILY1, a subroutine CREATE, and a subroutine CHECK. Subroutine CREATE creates a datafile DATA3 to which it writes a one-dimensional 100-word integer array with a single unformatted WRITE. The subroutine reports its progress along with any potential difficulties.

Subroutine CHECK verifies that the file was created properly. It too reports its various actions. The three modules are linked via the common block in which the array and the variable ISUM appear.

Discussion Because the program creates the file DATA3 that is required by other examples and by some of the problems, it is necessary for you to run it. The program is well-structured and you will profit from the exercise, especially if you take the trouble to read and to understand it. You will notice that the screen output is designed to let you follow the program's progress, so that, in the event of problems, you will know exactly how far it progressed and where it stopped. The algorithm in the DO-loop is designed to generate more or less random numbers. It's not a particularly elegant algorithm, but it's simple and serves the purpose. The program is somewhat more elaborate than necessary, but modular programming is so relatively simple that programmers often devote considerably more attention to polish.

Solution

```
      PROGRAM UTILY1
      COMMON M(1ØØ),ISUM
      CALL CREATE
      CALL CHECK
      IF(ISUM.EQ.2Ø544)THEN
         PRINT*,'...File DATA3 checks out all right'
      ELSE
         PRINT*,'...File DATA3 does not check out.  Delete the file,'
         PRINT*,'   check the program, and re-run.'
         PRINT*,'...Checksum was',ISUM,' but should have been 2Ø544'
      END IF
      END
*-----
      SUBROUTINE CREATE
      COMMON M(1ØØ),ISUM
      PRINT*,'...Arrived in CREATE.  Opening file DATA3 for output'
      OPEN(7,FILE='DATA3',STATUS='NEW',ERR=2,IOSTAT=KODE)
      PRINT*,'...Generating 1ØØ ''random'' numbers'
      K=1
      J=17
      DO 1 I=1,1ØØ
      K=MOD(K+J,9*I)
      M(I)=K
      J=J+97
    1 CONTINUE
      PRINT*,'...Dumping  array into DATA3 in single unformatted WRITE'
      WRITE(7)M
      PRINT*,'...Closing file DATA3 to permit proper test'
      CLOSE(7)
      PRINT*,'...Returning to MAIN program.'
      RETURN
    2 PRINT*,'...ERROR:  File problems.  Possibly DATA3 already exists'
      STOP
      END
*-----
      SUBROUTINE CHECK
      COMMON M(1ØØ),ISUM
      PRINT*,'...Arrived in Subroutine CHECK'
      PRINT*,'...Wiping out COMMON BLOCK before test reading of file'
      DO 1 I=1,1ØØ
      M(I)=Ø
    1 CONTINUE
      PRINT*,'...Just about to open file DATA3 for test reading'
      OPEN(7,FILE='DATA3',STATUS='OLD')
```

```
      PRINT*,'...Reading DATA3 into the array M in the COMMON BLOCK'
      READ(7)M
      PRINT*,'...Summing all the elements of DATA3'
      ISUM=Ø
      DO 2 I=1,1ØØ
      ISUM=ISUM+M(I)
    2 CONTINUE
      PRINT*,'...Returning to MAIN program to check result.'
      RETURN
      END
```

Example 16.2

The file DATA3 created in the previous example contains data to fill a 100-element integer vector with a single unformatted READ operation. Complete the following main program DATA3 by adding the required seven subroutine subprograms: READER, SHOW(N), SORTER, AVER, SQUARE, BAR(N), and CHSIGN. These routines are described.

```
PROGRAM DATA3
COMMON M(1ØØ)
CALL READER
CALL SHOW(1)
CALL SHOW(5)
CALL SHOW(15)
CALL SORTER
CALL SHOW(1)
CALL AVER
CALL SQUARE
CALL SHOW(1)
CALL AVER
CALL BAR(11)
CALL BAR(17)
CALL BAR(37)
CALL CHSIGN
CALL SORTER
CALL SHOW(1)
END
```

The array M is made available to all the modules through the common block. Argument list linking is also used where required.

Subroutine READER opens the file DATA3 and performs a single unformatted READ to fill the vector M in the common block. It closes the file and returns to the main program. This is the only time the program reads data.

Subroutine SHOW(N) shows the vector M. When called with N = 1, it shows every element. If called with N = 5, it shows only elements 5, 10, 15, 20, etc. When called with N = 12, it shows elements 12, 24, 26, 48, etc.

Subroutine SORTER sorts the 100 elements of the vector in numerically ascending order.

Subroutine AVER computes and reports the average of all 100 elements.

Subroutine SQUARE steps through the array, squaring each of the 100 elements.

Subroutine BAR(N) reports, in bar-graph form, the magnitudes of all the elements divisible by N. The graph is normalized to 65 asterisks. Normalization requires that you know the largest number in the array, and because you sorted the array, you can be confident that the largest number is element 100.

Subroutine CHSIGN changes the signs of elements 5, 10, 15, 20, 25, etc. by multiplying these elements by -1.

Solution The program and the output follow. It should be easy and instructive for you to work through it to understand the output in detail. The output from subroutine SHOW(1) is shown only partially to save space.

These seven subprograms may either be appended to the main program, or a library can be created with them, whichever is preferred on your system. The output is shown following the program.

```
      SUBROUTINE READER
      COMMON M(100)
      OPEN(7,FILE='DATA3',STATUS='OLD')
      READ(7)M
      CLOSE(7)
      RETURN
      END
*-----
      SUBROUTINE SHOW(N)
      COMMON M(100)
      WRITE(6,1)(J,J=N,5*N,N)
    1 FORMAT(/,' Elements ',5(I3,', '),'.....')
      WRITE(6,2)(M(J),J=N,100,N)
    2 FORMAT(1X,10I7)
      RETURN
      END
*-----
      SUBROUTINE SORTER
      COMMON M(100)
      WRITE(6,1)
    1 FORMAT(/,' Sorting the vector in ascending order....')
      DO 2 I=1,99
      DO 2 J=1,99
      IF(M(J).GT.M(J+1))THEN
         IHOLD=M(J)
         M(J)=M(J+1)
         M(J+1)=IHOLD
      END IF
    2 CONTINUE
      WRITE(6,3)
    3 FORMAT(' Sort finished....')
```

```
      RETURN
      END
*-----
      SUBROUTINE AVER
      COMMON M(100)
      ISUM=0
      DO 1 I=1,100
      ISUM=ISUM+M(I)
    1 CONTINUE
      WRITE(6,2)REAL(ISUM)/100.
    2 FORMAT(/,' The Average of the elements is',F10.2)
      RETURN
      END
*-----
      SUBROUTINE SQUARE
      COMMON M(100)
      DO 1 I=1,100
      M(I)=M(I)**2
    1 CONTINUE
      RETURN
      END
*-----
      SUBROUTINE BAR(N)
      COMMON M(100)
      WRITE(6,1)N
    1 FORMAT(/,' The following elements are divisible by',I3)
      DO 2 I=1,100
      IF(MOD(M(I),N).EQ.0)THEN
          ISTAR=NINT(REAL(M(I))*65./REAL(M(100)))
          WRITE(6,3)M(I),('*',J=1,ISTAR)
    3     FORMAT(1X,I7,1X,70A)
      END IF

    2 CONTINUE
      RETURN
      END
*-----
      SUBROUTINE CHSIGN
      COMMON M(100)
      DO 1 I=0,100,5
      M(I)=M(I)*(-1)
    1 CONTINUE
      RETURN
      END
```

```
Elements    1,   2,   3,   4,   5, .....
      0      6      1     21     21     37      6     54     37     27
     24     28     39     57     82    114      0     46     99    159
     37    111    192     64    159     27    136      0    123    253
    111    255    109    267    117    289    135    321    163      3
    210     46    267     99    334    162    411    235     57    327
    etc .  .  .  .  .  .  .....

Elements    5,  10,  15,  20,  25, .....
     21     27     82    159    159    253    117      3    334    327
    360    433    555     87    262    495     12    307    660    162


Elements   15,  30,  45,  60,  75, .....
     82    253    334    433    262    307


Sorting the vector in ascending order....
Sort finished....


Elements    1,   2,   3,   4,   5, .....
      0      0      0      1      3      6      6      9     12     15
     21     21     24     24     27     27     27     28     30     37
     37     37     39     45     46     46     54     54     55     57
     57     64     75     82     87     93     99     99    109    111
    etc .  .  .  .  .  .  .....


The Average of the elements is    205.44


Elements    1,   2,   3,   4,   5, .....
      0      0      0      1      9     36     36     81    144    225
    441    441    576    576    729    729    729    784    900   1369
   1369   1369   1521   2025   2116   2116   2916   2916   3025   3249
   3249   4096   5625   6724   7569   8649   9801   9801  11881  12321
    etc .  .  .  .  .  .  .....


The Average of the elements is  74569.20


The following elements are divisible by 11
      0
      0
      0
   3025
```

```
   9801 *
   9801 *
  53361 *******
  64009 ********
  64009 ********
  64009 ********
 184041 ***********************
 245025 *******************************
 435600 ******************************************************



The following elements are divisible by 17
      0
      0
      0
  18496 **
  65025 ********
  83521 **********
 195364 ************************
 260100 *********************************


The following elements are divisible by 37
      0
      0
      0
   1369
   1369
   1369
  12321 **
  12321 **
 308025 ***************************************


Sorting the vector in ascending order....
Sort finished....


Elements   1,   2,   3,   4,   5, .....
-518400-285156-242064-184041-117649 -94249 -78400 -65025 -55225 -28224
 -25281 -15129 -12321  -7569  -3249  -2116  -1369   -729   -225     -9
      0      0      0      1     36     36     81    144    441    441
    576    576    729    729    784    900   1369   1369   1521   2025
   2116   2916   2916   3025   3249   4096   5625   6724   8649   8901
    etc .   .   .  .  .  .....
```

Example 16.3

In Chapter 14, you created a file TEXTSAMPLE, containing a paragraph of text. If you no longer have the file in your directory, you should recreate it. Write a program that takes the paragraph in the file and reformats it with a maximum line length to be specified at run time. The program does not right-justify the text, but simply makes the lines as long as possible without exceeding the specified limit.

Discussion On the assumption that you will not attempt to run paragraphs of more than 2000 characters through the program, declare a character variable BUFF to act as the input buffer. Place the lines of the incoming text into this buffer, one after the other, with a single space between them. The 14 lines in the file TEXTSAMPLE, in other words, are turned into a single very long line. This line is then broken into chunks, none longer than the specified limit, and these chunks are written to produce the reformatted paragraph. It will mean more to you after you have seen the expected output. Shown are the outputs with maximum line lengths of 70, 55, and 35 characters.

```
Pls specify the maximum line length desired
?70

The middle years of the rule of Moctezuma were to be implicated in a
phenomenal series of natural disasters, each of which tested the
resilience of the new state and the spirit of its rulers. The Huaxtec
War had just begun, and a glorious victory was anticipated in Mexico
when, in the summer of 1450, heavy rains began to fall that soon
raised the surface of the lake to alarming levels. The waters
continued to rise unabated until the streets and open patios of
Tlatilulco and Tenochtitlan were deep under the surface. The
unpretentious houses of the poor were the first to melt away, but
finally even the artificial terraces upon which the palaces and houses
of the nobles were set became undermined and were in their turn
toppled into the floodwaters. This damage to Mexico, however, was
speedily repaired by a labor levy called up from the subject cities of
the lake side, though these communities too had suffered heavily.


Pls specify the maximum line length desired
?55

The middle years of the rule of Moctezuma were to be
implicated in a phenomenal series of natural disasters,
each of which tested the resilience of the new state
and the spirit of its rulers. The Huaxtec War had just
begun, and a glorious victory was anticipated in Mexico
when, in the summer of 1450, heavy rains began to fall
that soon raised the surface of the lake to alarming
levels. The waters continued to rise unabated until the
streets and open patios of Tlatilulco and Tenochtitlan
were deep under the surface. The unpretentious houses
```

```
of the poor were the first to melt away, but finally
even the artificial terraces upon which the palaces and
houses of the nobles were set became undermined and
were in their turn toppled into the floodwaters. This
damage to Mexico, however, was speedily repaired by a
labor levy called up from the subject cities of the
lake side, though these communities too had suffered
heavily.


Pls specify the maximum line length desired
?35

The middle years of the rule of
Moctezuma were to be implicated in
a phenomenal series of natural
disasters, each of which tested the
resilience of the new state and the
spirit of its rulers. The Huaxtec
War had just begun, and a glorious
victory was anticipated in Mexico
when, in the summer of 1450, heavy
rains began to fall that soon
raised the surface of the lake to
alarming levels. The waters
continued to rise unabated until
the streets and open patios of
Tlatilulco and Tenochtitlan were
deep under the surface. The
etc. . . . . ......
```

The program is composed of a main program, the function subprogram LAST borrowed from Ex. 15.5 in the previous chapter, a subroutine FILL to fill the 2000-character input buffer, and a subroutine WRITER to write the formatted output paragraph. You will recall that the function LAST reports the position of the last nonblank character of a character variable or character constant.

Look at the main program, which does nothing more than open the input file, receive information about the maximum output line length, and call the subroutines FILL and WRITER.

ISTART is the only variable in the common block. In the FILL routine, it always points at the next available character position in the input buffer. To start, it is set to 1 in the main program. The subroutine FILL is called with two arguments, the buffer BUFF and the character variable LINE, used to read the input paragraph line by line. Both of these character variables are specified in the character type-statement in the main program. Because they are also used in subroutine FILL, they are again specified there, but with adjustable lengths, indicated by (*). BUFF is then blanked out before it is filled. We next read the first line from the file into LINE and transfer LINE to BUFF, starting at ISTART, which, you will recall, was set to 1 in the main program. Notice that not all 80 characters are transferred, but only their information content, determined by the function LAST, plus one blank. The pointer ISTART is then updated to move it just beyond the high-water mark in the newly updated BUFF. The IF statement causes a warning to be issued when BUFF gets to within 79 or fewer spaces from the far end. The filling of BUFF continues until the paragraph has been read completely, or until we get too close to the end of the buffer BUFF.

The output routine works in reverse. It resets the pointer ISTART to 1, blanks out LINE, and dismantles and prints BUFF. It tries to get N characters from BUFF into LINE, but if it realizes that the Nth character falls in the middle of a word, it backs up until it finds the first blank, and takes fewer than N characters from BUFF. It then updates ISTART after searching forward in the buffer for the first nonblank character, and removes the next chunk for printing. The program follows. It is not difficult, and it deserves to be studied and understood.

```
      COMMON ISTART
      CHARACTER BUFF*2000,LINE*80
      OPEN(5,FILE='TEXTSAMPLE',STATUS='OLD')
      PRINT*,'Pls specify the maximum line length desired'
      READ*,N
      ISTART=1
      CALL FILL(BUFF,LINE)
      CALL WRITER(N,BUFF,LINE)
      END
*-----
      SUBROUTINE FILL(BUFF,LINE)
      COMMON ISTART
      CHARACTER BUFF*(*),LINE*(*)
      BUFF(ISTART:LEN(BUFF))=' '
    1 READ(5,2,END=99)LINE
    2 FORMAT(A)
      BUFF(ISTART:ISTART+LAST(LINE)+1)=LINE
      ISTART=ISTART+LAST(LINE)+1
      IF(ISTART.GT.LEN(BUFF)-80)THEN
         WRITE(6,3)
    3    FORMAT(' Warning:  Buffer full')
         RETURN
      END IF
      GO TO 1
   99 RETURN
      END
*-----
      FUNCTION LAST(LINE)
      CHARACTER LINE*(*)
      DO 1 I=LEN(LINE),1,-1
      IF(LINE(I:I).NE.' ')THEN
         LAST=I
         RETURN
```

```
      END IF
  1   CONTINUE
      LAST=0
      RETURN
      END
*-----
      SUBROUTINE WRITER(N,BUFF,LINE)
      COMMON ISTART
      CHARACTER BUFF*(*),LINE*(*)
      ISTART=1
  4   LINE=' '
      DO 1 I=ISTART+N,1,-1
      IF(BUFF(I:I).EQ.' ')THEN
         LINE=BUFF(ISTART:I)
         WRITE(6,2)LINE
  2      FORMAT(1X,A)
         DO 3 J=I,LEN(BUFF)
         IF(BUFF(J:J).NE.' ')THEN
            ISTART=J
            GO TO 4
         END IF
  3   CONTINUE
      RETURN
      END IF
  1   CONTINUE
      RETURN
      END
```

16.7 PROBLEMS

16.1 Example 11.1 in Chapter 11 is a simple 10-statement program. Logically, it consists of three distinct functions because it (1) fills an array, (2) writes the array to a file, and (3) dumps the same array to the screen. Restructure the program into a main program and the three subroutine subprograms GEN, FILEWR, and SCREEN. GEN generates the data, FILEWR writes the data to the file, and SCREEN writes the data to the screen. All four modules are linked through the common block. The main program is:

```
PROGRAM MKFILE
COMMON M(2Ø)
CALL GEN
CALL FILEWR
CALL SCREEN
END
```

Add the three required subroutines and run the program. The expected screen output is shown beside the program in Ex. 11.1. If the file ARRAYDATA still exists in your directory, you will have to delete it first.

16.2. Remove the common block linkages from each of the modules in Prob. 16.1 and implement argument-list linking. The modified main program is:

```
PROGRAM MKFILE
DIMENSION M(2Ø)
CALL GEN(M)
CALL FILEWR(M)
CALL SCREEN(M)
END
```

16.3. Restructure the program shown in Ex. 11.2 into a main program and the three subroutines FILL, FIND, and REPORT. FILL reads the file into the array, FIND searches for the largest element, and REPORT presents the largest element on the screen. Use common block linking. The common block contains the array M and the variable LARGE. The main program is shown. The expected output is the same as in Ex. 11.2, of course.

```
PROGRAM LRGFND
COMMON M(2Ø),LARGE
CALL FILL
CALL FIND
CALL REPORT
END
```

16.4. Remove the variable LARGE from the common block in Prob. 16.3, but keep the array there. Modify the program to pass LARGE through argument lists. The main program now has the form:

```
PROGRAM LRGFND
COMMON M(2Ø)
CALL FILL
CALL FIND(LARGE)
CALL REPORT(LARGE)
END
```

16.5. Break Ex. 11.3 into its logical units and restructure it into a main program and appropriate subroutines. Use common block linking, hybrid linking, or only argument-list linking, whichever you prefer.

16.6. Break Ex. 11.5 into its logical units and restructure it into a main program and appropriate subroutines. Use only common block linking.

16.7. Break Ex. 11.6 into its logical units and restructure it into a main program and appropriate subroutines. Use only argument-list linking.

16.8. Remove the two nested DO-loops from Ex. 11.7 and replace them with CALL SORTER(M,20), where M is the array being passed into the subroutine for sorting, and 20 conveys the size of the one-dimensional array to the subroutine. The subroutine is able to handle any size one-dimensional array by adjusting the size of its array dynamically. The first two lines of SORTER are shown:

```
SUBROUTINE SORTER(M,N)
DIMENSION M(N)
    etc. . ....
```

16.9. Break Ex. 11.10 into its natural logic blocks and restructure it into appropriate modules. Use common block linkages only. Don't forget to declare ROWSUM and COLSUM to be of type INTEGER. The following two statements will do the trick:

```
COMMON MAT(5,1Ø),ROWSUM(5),COLSUM(1Ø)
INTEGER ROWSUM,COLSUM
```

Because ROWSUM and COLSUM are already dimensioned in the COMMON statement, they must not be dimensioned again in the INTEGER type-statement. The following two statements arrange for identical storage:

```
INTEGER ROWSUM(5),COLSUM(1Ø)
COMMON MAT(5,1Ø),ROWSUM,COLSUM
```

16.10. Restructure Ex. 11.15 into a main program and appropriate subroutines. You will have developed good judgment by now about how the modules are best linked.

16.8 SUGGESTION

Example 16.3 shows FORTRANS's character abilities most impressively. Several desirable features could be added to the program to make it even more flexible. The lines could be stretched to get a right-justified margin, for example, and the input buffer could be made dynamic, so that when it is almost full, it allows itself to be drained to as low a point as possible so that it can be filled again. This would remove the 2000-character restriction on the input. It would be a demanding, but highly rewarding, project to enhance that program to turn it into a useful formatting system for essays, theses, and resumes. Anyone who tackles the project successfully will become an undisputed FORTRAN expert.

17

EQUIVALENCE

The EQUIVALENCE statement is another FORTRAN specification. EQUIVALENCE and COMMON are frequently confused. Whereas COMMON provides access to a mutual area of memory to various program modules for purposes of communication, EQUIVALENCE permits a word of memory to be given several different variable names within a given program module. EQUIVALENCE does not cross module boundaries. The concept of EQUIVALENCE is almost trivial, but there are those who sometimes consider it to be of dubious benefit and avoid it. A few illustrations follow to give you insight into the feature and to let you evaluate potential benefits. Figure 17.1 shows two programs. On the left, a value is assigned to word A, but word B is printed. As expected, a random value results because B was not previously assigned a value. The program on the right contains an EQUIVALENCE specification in which the machine is informed that A and B are to be considered equivalent within this program module, a main program in our particular case. In effect, A and B are now two different names for the same memory location and can be used interchangeably. They are equivalent, in other words, and this is confirmed by the program on the right.

Note the form of the EQUIVALENCE declaration, where the items to be equivalenced appear in parentheses. Figure 17.2 presents another simple illustration, demonstrating multiple equivalencing. To be specific, two sets of variable names are equivalenced. In the first set, five variable names are given to a single word of memory, and in the second set, a single word of memory goes under four different names. Study the program and the resulting output carefully.

```
      A=9.32                            EQUIVALENCE(A,B)
      PRINT*, 'B =',B                   A=9.32
      END                               PRINT*, 'B =',B
                                        END
```

```
 B = .1155178E+19                   B = 9.32ØØ
```

Figure 17.1 A and B are two separate variables on the left, but they are equivalent on the right, and can be used interchangeably in that program.

Return to Fig. 16.5 in the previous chapter. In that example, we used the common block and a subroutine to trick the machine into interpreting a floating-point word as an integer. The same can be accomplished by equivalencing a real and an integer variable name to a single word of memory, as is done in Fig. 17.3. In that program, a word of memory has the two names Z and M. A value is assigned to Z, where it is stored in floating-point form, but when we ask the machine to print M, it assumes that the word contains an integer. Compare the output with Figure 16.5; it is identical. If you don't recall how the large integer was justified, review the discussion associated with Fig. 16.5. If you run the program in Fig. 16.5 and the one in Fig. 17.3, you may well get a different integer because you may be using different hardware, but the two programs should also agree on your machine.

The elements comprising an array always occupy contiguous sections of memory, and you recall that memory is a linear entity, much like a long train. Because of the linear nature of memory, multidimensional arrays are broken into one-dimensional sections that are then stored contiguously. This understanding of array storage allows us to do some interesting things with equivalencing. As an example, consider

```
      EQUIVALENCE (HOUSE,HOSE,HOWSE,HOWS,HUSE),(BEE,BUMBLE,BUNGLE,STING)
      HOUSE=6.
      PRINT *,'HOUSE*HOSE = ',HOUSE*HOSE
      PRINT *,'HOWSE*HOWS = ',HOWSE*HOWS
      PRINT *,'HUSE*HOUSE = ',HUSE*HOUSE
      BEE=222.22
      PRINT *,'BUMBLE = ',BUMBLE
      PRINT *,'BUNGLE = ',BUNGLE
      PRINT *,'STING = ',STING
      END
```

```
HOUSE*HOSE = 36.Ø
HOWSE*HOWS = 36.Ø
HUSE*HOUSE = 36.Ø
BUMBLE = 222.22
BUNGLE = 222.22
STING = 222.22
```

Figure 17.2 Five different names are given to a single variable, and four names to another.

```
EQUIVALENCE(Z,M)
Z=3.1415926
PRINT*, Z,M
END

3.141593  294789Ø45
```

Figure 17.3 Two interpretations of the same word of memory.

the two programs of Fig. 17.4. In the one on the left, two arrays X and Y are declared in the DIMENSION statement. The DO-loop fills array X, but array Y is printed, and ten random values are produced. This program is obviously similar to the left side of Fig. 17.1. In the right program, we specify that element X(1) is equivalent to element Y(1), which makes each element in the array X equivalent to its counterpart in Y because the elements within any given array are contiguous. The output on the right confirms this clearly.

If we mention the arrays, to be equivalenced, by name only, without specifying particular elements, the first elements are assumed. The EQUIVALENCE specification in the right program could thus be changed to EQUIVALENCE(X,Y).

Figure 17.5 shows that arrays can be superimposed in an offset fashion. In the EQUIVALENCE specification, the first element of Y is aligned with the sixth element of X. The output shows that the first half of array Y overlaps the second half of X. The second half of Y extends beyond X into an undefined part of memory.

```
      DIMENSION X(1Ø),Y(1Ø)
      DO 1 I=1,1Ø
      X(I)=I
    1 CONTINUE
      WRITE(6,2)(Y(I),I=1,1Ø)
    2 FORMAT(6X,G12.4)
      END

       .8637E-99
      -8.593
       .8682E-99
      -8.815
       .8683E-99
      -8.671
       .1Ø73E+56
      -8.377
       .8685E-99
      -8.572
```

```
      DIMENSION X(1Ø),Y(1Ø)
      EQUIVALENCE(X(1),Y(1))
      DO 1 I=1,1Ø
      X(I)=I
    1 CONTINUE
      WRITE(6,2)(Y(I),I=1,1Ø)
    2 FORMAT(6X,G12.4)
      END

        1.ØØØ
        2.ØØØ
        3.ØØØ
        4.ØØØ
        5.ØØØ
        6.ØØØ
        7.ØØØ
        8.ØØØ
        9.ØØØ
        1Ø.ØØ
```

Figure 17.4 X and Y are two different arrays on the left, with Y undefined. On the right, X(1) and Y(1) are the same word of memory, and the rest of the elements fall in line because they are contiguous.

```
      DIMENSION X(10),Y(10)
      EQUIVALENCE(Y(1),X(6))
      DO 1 I = 1,10
      X(I)=I
    1 CONTINUE
      WRITE(6,2)(Y(I),I=1,10)
    2 FORMAT(6X,G12.4)
      END
```

```
        6.000
        7.000
        8.000
        9.000
        10.00
        .3433E-04
       -.2822E+27
        .2555E-02
        .1224E+77
        .2627E+76
```

Figure 17.5 Two arrays are superimposed in an offset fashion by equivalencing the first element of one to the sixth element of the other.

Figure 17.6 tells us that a one-dimensional array can be superimposed on a two-dimensional structure. The array X is filled, but Y is printed. The EQUIVALENCE specification is the same as EQUIVALENCE(X(1),Y(1,1)), and arranges for the 25 elements of Y to be superimposed on the 25 elements of X, column by column. The first five elements of X are obviously the same as the first column of array Y.

Figure 17.7 investigates what happens when attempts are made to equivalence items in the common block. The attempt must fail because items in the common block are stored contiguously but the EQUIVALENCE declaration tries to superimpose them. In order to comply, the compiler would either have to violate the structure

```
      DIMENSION X(25),Y(5,5)
      EQUIVALENCE (X,Y)
      DO 1 I=1,25
      X(I)=I
    1 CONTINUE
      DO 2 I = 1,5
      WRITE(6,3)(Y(I,J),J=1,5)
    3 FORMAT(1X,5I5)
    2 CONTINUE
      END
```

```
    1    6   11   16   21
    2    7   12   17   22
    3    8   13   18   23
    4    9   14   19   24
    5   10   15   20   25
```

Figure 17.6 A two-dimensional and a one-dimensional array are superimposed.

```
      COMMON A,B
      EQUIVALENCE (A,B)
      A=15.
      PRINT*, B
      END
```

```
*** ERROR:  EQUIVALENCE (A,B)
B in storage class COMMON cannot be equivalenced
to A of storage class COMMON.
```

Figure 17.7 Items in the common block cannot possibly be equivalenced.

of the common block or ignore the equivalence request. It will do neither, and rejects the contradictory request.

Figure 17.8 presents a final example in which a 10-element array is equivalenced to 10 individual items in the common block. The array is not specified in the COMMON declaration, but in a separate DIMENSION statement. The act of equivalencing X(1) to A, which is the first word in the common block, causes the array to be superimposed on all ten items in the common block. The program speaks for itself, and it certainly emphasizes the contiguous nature of the common block.

```
      COMMON A,B,C,D,E,F,G,H,P,Q
      DIMENSION X(1Ø)
      EQUIVALENCE(X(1),A)
*-----
      DO 1 I=1,1Ø
      X(I)=I
    1 CONTINUE
*-----
      PRINT*,A,B,C,D,E,F,G,H,P,Q
      END
```

```
 1.00   2.00   3.00   4.00   5.00   6.00   7.00   8.00   9.00   10.0
```

Figure 17.8 An array is superimposed on individual items in the common block. The array was not part of the common block before equivalencing.

18

COMPLEX Arithmetic

This chapter can be skipped by those who are unfamiliar with complex arithmetic. Complex arithmetic is tremendously useful in the area of applied mathematics, especially in fields such as electrical engineering and physics. It rests on a solid theoretical foundation, and the representation of a complex number as a point or as a vector in the complex plane has very great intuitive appeal. A significant family of physical phenomena is easily formulated in terms of complex arithmetic, and the solution to a problem often readily reduces to the evaluation of a complex expression.

Those who deal with complex calculations are well aware that the formulation of a problem is often easy, and that the reduction to the final complex expression is usually also straightforward, but that the evaluation of this final expression can at times, involve some very tedious algebraic manipulations. This is where FORTRAN comes to our aid because of its ability to perform complex arithmetic and its ability to evaluate the important complex functions.

18.1 COMPLEX NUMBERS

We are so accustomed to seeing complex numbers expressed in the form $x + iy$ that it is easy to forget the origins of this notation. In order to better appreciate FORTRAN's treatment of complex numbers, a brief review is valuable.

A *complex number* is defined as *an ordered pair of real numbers*. Examples of such pairs are (4,2), (−18,3), (5, −2.8), or in general (x,y), where x is referred to as the *real* part, and y is the *imaginary* part of the complex number. A complex number is usually referred to by a single symbol, but it is understood that this symbol represents an ordered pair of real numbers, ordered in the sense that the first position implies *real* and the second position implies *imaginary*. Because the order is important, the two complex numbers $z_1 = (3,9)$ and $z_2 = (9,3)$ are not the same. It is clear that two complex numbers are equal if and only if the *real* parts are equal and the *imaginary* parts are equal.

The fundamental operations of addition, subtraction, multiplication, and division of the two complex numbers $z_1 = (x_1, y_1)$ and $z_2 = (x_2, y_2)$ are defined as follows:

$$z_1 + z_2 = (x_1, y_1) + (x_2, y_2) = (x_1 + x_2, y_1 + y_2) \tag{18.1}$$

$$z_1 - z_2 = (x_1, y_1) - (x_2, y_2) = (x_1 - x_2, y_1 - y_2) \tag{18.2}$$

$$z_1 z_2 = (x_1, y_1)(x_2, y_2) = (x_1 x_2 - y_1 y_2, x_1 y_2 + x_2 y_1) \tag{18.3}$$

$$\frac{(x_1, y_1)}{(x_2, y_2)} = \left(\frac{x_1 x_2 + y_1 y_2}{x_2^2 + y_2^2}, \frac{x_2 y_1 - x_1 y_2}{x_2^2 + y_2^2}\right) \tag{18.4}$$

We next define a new entity i, where $i = (0,1)$. Obviously $i^2 = (i)(i) = (0,1)(0,1)$, and from Eq. (18.3), the multiplication definition, $(0,1)(0,1) = (-1,0)$, or $i^2 = -1$. From this definition of i, and from the definitions of Eqs. (18.1) and (18.3), we now show that $(x,y) = x + iy$. We will show, in other words, that these two notations are equivalent, provided we accept the above definition of i.

$$\begin{aligned}(x,y) &= (x + 0, y + 0)\\ &= (x,0) + (0,y)\\ &= (x,0) + (0,1)(y,0)\\ &= (x,0) + iy\\ &= x + iy\end{aligned}$$

Because, as we have just shown, $(x,y) = x + iy$, Eqs. (18.5) to (18.8) follow from Eqs. (18.1) to (18.4).

$$z_1 + z_2 = (x_1 + iy_1) + (x_2 + iy_2) = (x_1 + x_2) + i(y_1 + y_2) \tag{18.5}$$

$$z_1 - z_2 = (x_1 + iy_1) - (x_2 + iy_2) = (x_1 - x_2) + i(y_1 - y_2) \tag{18.6}$$

$$z_1 z_2 = (x_1 + iy_1)(x_2 + iy_2) = (x_1 x_2 - y_1 y_2) + i(x_1 y_2 + x_2 y_1) \tag{18.7}$$

$$\frac{(x_1 + iy_1)}{(x_2 + iy_2)} = \frac{x_1 x_2 + y_1 y_2}{x_2^2 + y_2^2} + i\frac{x_2 y_1 - x_1 y_2}{x_2^2 + y_2^2} \tag{18.8}$$

18.2 FORTRAN COMPLEX VARIABLES, COMPLEX CONSTANTS, AND LIST-DIRECTED I/O

FORTRAN does not adopt the $x + iy$ notation, but instead prefers the alternate approach of regarding complex numbers as ordered pairs of real numbers. Whenever you declare a certain datum to be of type COMPLEX, the machine simply reserves

```
      COMPLEX Z
      Z=(5.51,-21.7)
      PRINT*,'THE COMPLEX NUMBER Z IS',Z
      END

 THE COMPLEX NUMBER Z IS (5.5100,-21.700)
```

Figure 18.1 Assigning a complex constant to a complex variable.

two contiguous storage locations for that datum, the first location to hold the *real* component, and the second stores the *imaginary* component. The two components are stored in floating-point form, that is, as real numbers, but don't confuse the technical FORTRAN term real with the mathematical concept of *real*. You are reminded that FORTRAN refers to data stored in floating-point form as real, but mathematicians refer to the *real* component of a complex number.

Figure 18.1 shows a very simple program in which a variable Z is declared to be of type COMPLEX. In the second statement, a complex constant is assigned to Z. Note the form of this complex constant, consisting of a pair of numbers separated by a comma, and enclosed by parentheses. The third statement is a list-directed output statement instructing the machine to print Z, and you can see that the computer supplies the parentheses and comma.

Figure 18.2 illustrates list-directed input of a complex number. The program emphasizes some very important points and it deserves your careful attention. You will note that a datum is entered four times, each time in a different form. The first datum is entered complete with parentheses and comma, and the computer plays it back faithfully.

The second attempt omits the parentheses, and the computer assumes that you entered two *real* numbers, which is the same as two complex numbers with

```
      COMPLEX Z
      DO 1 I=1,4
      READ*, Z
      PRINT*,'ATTEMPT',I,'- YOU ENTERED THE COMPLEX NUMBER',Z
    1 CONTINUE
      END

?(1.2,-8.3)
ATTEMPT 1 - YOU ENTERED THE COMPLEX NUMBER (1.2000,-8.3000)
?1.2,8.3
ATTEMPT 2 - YOU ENTERED THE COMPLEX NUMBER (1.2000,0.0000)
?1.2
ATTEMPT 3 - YOU ENTERED THE COMPLEX NUMBER (1.2000,0.0000)
?(1.2 -8.3)
FORTRAN run-time error:  expected comma not found .....
```

Figure 18.2 List-directed input of complex data.

no *imaginary* components, but the machine only needs one datum, and ignores the 8.3. The output is precisely as expected, and this is confirmed by the third attempt. On the fourth attempt, the comma is omitted, and a run-time error results. The moral is that when using list-directed input of complex data, each complex datum must be enclosed by parentheses and the *real* and *imaginary* components must be separated by a comma. In the special case of a complex datum with a zero *imaginary* component, which is nothing more than a *real* number anyway, the *real* component can be entered alone, but without parentheses.

18.3 EDITED I/O OF COMPLEX DATA

List-directed input and output are simple enough and you will probably use them extensively. But what about edited input and output? It turns out that FORTRAN has no special edit descriptors for complex data, but because a complex datum is stored in floating-point form in two adjacent memory locations, it can be printed into two F, E, or G fields, or read under this type of editing from two fields. Figure 18.3 is basically the same program as Fig. 18.1, but output editing is used. Note that the output appears without the parentheses and without the comma.

Figure 18.4 shows what happens when you forget that a complex number requires two output fields. The example is the same as Fig. 18.3 with the exception that one of the output fields was removed. You should have no difficulty explaining the appearance of the output.

Figure 18.5 shows F-edited input of a complex number. Note that the number is read from two adjacent fields. The two components are entered without parentheses and without a comma. The ruler below the input allows you to check the horizontal

```
      COMPLEX Z
      Z=(5.51,-21.7)
      WRITE(6,1)Z
    1 FORMAT(' THE COMPLEX NUMBER Z IS',2F7.2)
      END

 THE COMPLEX NUMBER Z IS   5.51 -21.70
```

Figure 18.3 Output editing of complex numbers.

```
      COMPLEX Z
      Z=(5.51,-21.7)
      WRITE(6,1)Z
    1 FORMAT(' THE COMPLEX NUMBER Z IS',F7.2)
      END

 THE COMPLEX NUMBER Z IS   5.51
 THE COMPLEX NUMBER Z IS -21.70
```

Figure 18.4 Careless output editing.

```
      COMPLEX Z
      READ(5,2)Z
    2 FORMAT(2F10.0)
      WRITE(6,1)Z
    1 FORMAT(' THE COMPLEX NUMBER Z IS',2F7.2)
      END

?5.51␣␣␣␣␣␣-21.7␣␣␣␣␣
 ----+----+----+----+----+----+

THE COMPLEX NUMBER Z IS   5.51 -21.70
```

Figure 18.5 Run-time edited input of complex data.

spacing, and the blanks in the input are indicated in a manner familiar from Chapter 7.

18.4 ILLUSTRATING THE FOUR FUNDAMENTAL OPERATIONS WITH COMPLEX NUMBERS

In Section 18.1, we defined addition, subtraction, multiplication, and division of complex numbers, and we saw that Eqs. (18.1) to (18.4) were equivalent to Eqs. (18.5) to (18.8). These four operations are demonstrated in Fig. 18.6.

```
      COMPLEX Z1,Z2,Z3
      PRINT*,'PLS ENTER TWO COMPLEX NUMBERS Z1 AND Z2'
      READ*,Z1,Z2
      PRINT*,'YOU ENTERED',Z1,'AND',Z2
      Z3=Z1+Z2
      PRINT*,'THE SUM Z1+Z2 IS',Z3
      Z3=Z1-Z2
      PRINT*,'THE DIFFERENCE Z1-Z2 IS',Z3
*-----THE REMAINING CALCULATIONS ARE DONE IN THE PRINT STATEMENTS
      PRINT*,'THE PRODUCT Z1*Z2 IS',Z1*Z2
      PRINT*,'THE QUOTIENT Z1/Z2 IS',Z1/Z2
      END

PLS ENTER TWO COMPLEX NUMBERS Z1 AND Z2
?(-13.21,5.79),(4.121,-6.7)

YOU ENTERED (-13.21000,5.790000) AND (4.121000,-6.700000)
THE SUM Z1+Z2 IS (-9.089000,-.9100001)
THE DIFFERENCE Z1-Z2 IS (-17.33100,12.49000)
THE PRODUCT Z1*Z2 IS (-15.64541,112.3676)
THE QUOTIENT Z1/Z2 IS (-1.506828,-1.044830)
```

Figure 18.6 The four fundamental operations with complex numbers.

```
      DOUBLE COMPLEX Z1,Z2,Z3
      PRINT*,'PLS ENTER TWO COMPLEX NUMBERS Z1 AND Z2'
      READ*,Z1,Z2
      PRINT*,'YOU ENTERED',Z1,'AND',Z2
      Z3=Z1+Z2
      PRINT*,'THE SUM Z1+Z2 IS',Z3
      Z3=Z1-Z2
      PRINT*,'THE DIFFERENCE Z1-Z2 IS',Z3
*-----THE REMAINING CALCULATIONS ARE DONE IN THE PRINT STATEMENTS
      PRINT*,'THE PRODUCT Z1*Z2 IS',Z1*Z2
      PRINT*,'THE QUOTIENT Z1/Z2 IS',Z1/Z2
      END
```

```
PLS ENTER TWO COMPLEX NUMBERS Z1 AND Z2
?(-13.21,5.79),(4.121,-6.7)

YOU ENTERED (-13.2100000000000000,5.7900000000000000) AND
 (4.1210000000000000,-6.7000000000000000)
THE SUM Z1+Z2 IS (-9.0890000000000000,-.9100000000000000)
THE DIFFERENCE Z1-Z2 IS (-17.3310000000000000,12.4900000000000000)
THE PRODUCT Z1*Z2 IS (-15.6454100000000000,112.3675900000000000)
THE QUOTIENT Z1/Z2 IS (-1.5Ø68277Ø81324943,-1.Ø4483Ø299Ø6546255)
```

Figure 18.7 DOUBLE COMPLEX is not defined in FORTRAN 77, but it is offered by several compilers.

In studying the output in Fig. 18.6, you notice the slight inaccuracies inherent in single-precision floating-point calculations. The variables were declared COMPLEX to be sure, but the single-precision floating-point arithmetic unit operated behind the scenes. Some systems provide the additional data type DOUBLE COMPLEX, which is not defined by ANSI X3.9–1978. If your machine provides it, you may find occasion to use it, but potential problems could arise with the use of complex functions. It is best to research the appropriate documentation accompanying your compiler before venturing into this area. Figure 18.7 is a rerun of the program in Fig. 18.6, but this time the complex variables are declared DOUBLE COMPLEX. The accuracy is better, and it was safe to run this program because it does not involve any of the intrinsic complex functions.

18.5 THE TWELVE INTRINSIC FORTRAN FUNCTIONS FOR COMPLEX ARITHMETIC

FORTRAN provides several intrinsic functions for complex computations. Most of these were already encountered in Chapter 4 within the framework of real and integer data types. There was a second encounter with most of these functions in Chapter 12 in connection with double precision data, and now several of the functions appear for a third time, along with two new ones. They are discussed in the order in which they appear in the ANSI X3.9–1978 document. Appendix C, incidentally, provides a summary of all the intrinsic functions and their interactions with the various data types.

INT(Z) This function accepts a single complex argument. It removes any fractional part from the *real* component, and reports this truncated *real* component as an integer. For example, INT((3.983,23.1)) = 3.

REAL(Z) The REAL function accepts a single complex argument and produces its *real* component as a single-precision real (floating-point) quantity. For example, REAL((7.12,−6.32)) = 7.12.

DBLE(Z) This function also accepts a single complex argument and produces its *real* component as a double precision quantity. For example, DBLE((7.12,−6.32)) = 7.12D0.

CMPLX(X) This function has a single argument that can be integer, real, double precision, or even complex. It always generates a complex number. If the argument is complex, it produces a complex value identical to the argument. If the argument is real, integer, or double precision, the function produces a complex number with a zero *imaginary* component and a *real* component equivalent to its argument when that argument is changed to single-precision floating-point. The following four examples illustrate the CMPLX function.

```
CMPLX((3.1,1.8)) = (3.1,1.8)
CMPLX(4) = (4.ØØ,Ø.ØØ)
CMPLX(14.3) = (14.3Ø,Ø.ØØ)
CMPLX(3.1DØ) = (3.1Ø,Ø.ØØ)
```

ABS(Z) The ABS function accepts a complex argument and computes the length of the vector representing the argument in the *complex* plane. For example, ABS((3.0,4.0)) = 5.00.

AIMAG(Z) This function produces a single-precision floating-point number corresponding to the *imaginary* component of the argument. The function is peculiar to complex data and was not encountered previously. For example, AIMAG((4.5,7.1)) = 7.10.

CONJG(Z) The CONJG function produces the *complex conjugate* of its argument by changing the sign of the *imaginary* component. This function, like the previous one, is also peculiar to complex arithmetic. For example, CONJG((3.6,0.38)) = (3.6,−0.38).

SQRT(Z) The SQRT function computes the *complex* square root of its argument. It is assumed that you are familiar with the theory of the functions of a *complex variable* for this and for the remaining functions. Their uses are demonstrated in Fig. 18.8.

EXP(Z) The argument and the result are complex. *e* is raised to a *complex* power. See Fig. 18.8.

LOG(Z) The argument and the result are complex. See Fig. 18.8.

SIN(Z) The argument and the result are complex. See Fig. 18.8.

COS(Z) The argument and the result are complex. See Fig. 18.8.

Example 18.1

This example is similar to Ex. 12.4, and you might find it rewarding to review it briefly. In Ex. 12.4, we computed e^x. The complex function e^z also exists, and FORTRAN provides it in the form EXP(Z). e^z is defined by the following series expansion:

$$e^z = 1 + \frac{z}{1!} + \frac{z^2}{2!} + \frac{z^3}{3!} + \frac{z^4}{4!} + \frac{z^5}{5!} + \cdots + \frac{z^n}{n!}$$

```
      PRINT*,'INT((1.72,2.91)) =',INT((1.72,2.91))
      PRINT*,'REAL((1.72,2.91)) =',REAL((1.72,2.91))
      PRINT*,'DBLE((1.72,2.91)) =',DBLE((1.72,2.91))
      PRINT*,'CMPLX(3) =',CMPLX(3)
      PRINT*,'CMPLX(3.) =',CMPLX(3.)
      PRINT*,'CMPLX(3.DØ) =',CMPLX(3.DØ)
      PRINT*,'CMPLX((1.72,2.91)) =',CMPLX((1.72,2.91))
      PRINT*,'ABS((1.72,2.91)) =',ABS((1.72,2.91))
      PRINT*,'AIMAG((1.72,2.91)) =',AIMAG((1.72,2.91))
      PRINT*,'CONJG((1.72,2.91)) =',CONJG((1.72,2.91))
      PRINT*,'SQRT((1.72,2.91)) =',SQRT((1.72,2.91))
      PRINT*,'EXP((1.72,2.91)) =',EXP((1.72,2.91))
      PRINT*,'LOG((1.72,2.91)) =',LOG((1.72,2.91))
      PRINT*,'SIN((1.72,2.91)) =',SIN((1.72,2.91))
      PRINT*,'COS((1.72,2.91)) =',COS((1.72,2.91))
      END
```

```
INT((1.72,2.91)) = 1
REAL((1.72,2.91)) = 1.72ØØØØ
DBLE((1.72,2.91)) = 1.72ØØØØØØØØØØØØØØØØ
CMPLX(3) = (3.ØØØØØØ,Ø.ØØØØØØ)
CMPLX(3.) = (3.ØØØØØØ,Ø.ØØØØØØ)
CMPLX(3.DØ) = (3.ØØØØØØ,Ø.ØØØØØØ)
CMPLX((1.72,2.91)) = (1.72ØØØØ,2.91ØØØØ)
ABS((1.72,2.91)) = 3.38Ø311
AIMAG((1.72,2.91)) = 2.91ØØØØ
CONJG((1.72,2.91)) = (1.72ØØØØ,-2.91ØØØØ)
SQRT((1.72,2.91)) = (1.596921,.9111286)
EXP((1.72,2.91)) = (-5.435433,1.2818Ø6)
LOG((1.72,2.91)) = (1.217968,1.Ø36972)
SIN((1.72,2.91)) = (9.1Ø336Ø,-1.36Ø327)
COS((1.72,2.91)) = (-1.368424,-9.Ø4949Ø)
```

Figure 18.8 Illustrating the twelve intrinsic functions for complex calculations.

Write a program that prompts you to enter some complex z value. It then sums the first 31 terms of the series to compute e^z, and prints the result along with the value produced by the intrinsic function EXP(Z) to permit comparison.

Solution

```
      COMPLEX Z,E
      DIMENSION FAC(3Ø)
*-----
*-----COMPUTE 1! TO 3Ø! AND STORE THESE IN THE ARRAY FAC(3Ø)
      FAC(1)=1.
      DO 1 I=2,3Ø
      FAC(I)=FAC(I-1)*I
```

```
    1  CONTINUE
*-----
    2  PRINT*,'PLEASE ENTER SOME COMPLEX NUMBER Z'
       READ(5,*,END=99)Z
*-----COMPUTING EXP(Z) BY SUMMING THE FIRST 31 TERMS OF THE SERIES
       E=(1,Ø)
       DO 3 I=1,3Ø
       E=E+Z**I/FAC(I)
    3  CONTINUE
*-----
*-----REPORTING THE CALCULATED VALUE AND THE VALUE PRODUCED BY THE
*-----INTRINSIC FUNCTION
       PRINT*,'THE FIRST 31 TERMS OF THE SERIES YIELD',E
       PRINT*,'THE INTRINSIC FUNCTION EXP(Z) PRODUCES',EXP(Z)
       GO TO 2
   99  STOP 'USER REQUESTED EXIT'
       END
```

```
PLEASE ENTER SOME COMPLEX NUMBER Z
?(1,-5)
THE FIRST 31 TERMS OF THE SERIES YIELD (.771Ø735,2.6Ø6626)
THE INTRINSIC FUNCTION EXP(Z) PRODUCES (.771Ø738,2.6Ø6626)

PLEASE ENTER SOME COMPLEX NUMBER Z
?(3.65,Ø.33)
THE FIRST 31 TERMS OF THE SERIES YIELD (36.39862,12.46745)
THE INTRINSIC FUNCTION EXP(Z) PRODUCES (36.39866,12.46745)

PLEASE ENTER SOME COMPLEX NUMBER Z
?(3,3)
THE FIRST 31 TERMS OF THE SERIES YIELD (-19.88455,2.83447Ø)
THE INTRINSIC FUNCTION EXP(Z) PRODUCES (-19.88453,2.834471)

PLEASE ENTER SOME COMPLEX NUMBER Z
?(EOF CHARACTER SUPPLIED BY USER)
*STOP* USER REQUESTED EXIT
```

18.6 USER-DEFINED COMPLEX FUNCTIONS

In Chapter 15, we learned about statement functions and FUNCTION subprograms. The basic principles encountered in that chapter apply to complex functions as well, and Ex. 18.2 provides a comprehensive summary. The example and its output deserve thoughtful attention.

Example 18.2

Write a program in which you use the statement function approach to define and test a function TANY(Z), where TANY(Z) = SIN(Z)/COS(Z).

Also append and test a FUNCTION subprogram in which you define a function ABS(Z) that produces a complex number equal to the argument Z multipled by 10. Because this function name conflicts with the intrinsic function of the same name, declare it to be EXTERNAL.

Finally, define and test a function MYFUN(Z). If the real part of the argument is greater than 1 and if the imaginary part is greater than 0, MYFUN(Z) returns Z*1000. If the imaginary part is negative, MYFUN(Z) returns Z*1000000.

Solution

```
      EXTERNAL ABS
      COMPLEX ABS,TANY,MYFUN,Z
*-----
*-----A STATEMENT FUNCTION FOLLOWS:
      TANY(Z)=SIN(Z)/COS(Z)
*-----
      Z=(2.Ø3,-Ø.225)
      PRINT*,'Z =',Z
      PRINT*,'TANY(Z)=',TANY(Z)
      PRINT*,'ABS(Z)=',ABS(Z)
      PRINT*,'MYFUN(Z)=',MYFUN(Z)
      END
*
      COMPLEX FUNCTION ABS(Z)
      COMPLEX Z
*-----A PERVERTED DEFINITION OF THE ABS FUNCTION FOLLOWS
      ABS=1Ø.*Z
      RETURN
      END
*
      COMPLEX FUNCTION MYFUN(Z)
      COMPLEX Z
      IF(REAL(Z).GT.1.AND.AIMAG(Z).GT.Ø.)MYFUN=Z*1ØØØ.
      IF(AIMAG(Z).LT.Ø.)MYFUN=Z*1ØØØØØØ.
      RETURN
      END
```

```
Z = (2.Ø3ØØØØ,-.225ØØØØ)
TANY(Z)= (-1.6Ø2464,-.9384Ø96)
ABS(Z)= (2Ø.3ØØØØ,-2.25ØØØØ)
MYFUN(Z)= (2Ø3ØØØØ.,-225ØØØ.Ø)
```

18.7 PROBLEMS

18.1. Using Eq. (18.3) in Section 18.1, show on paper that (3,2)(5, −3) = (21, 1), or you may prefer to adopt the alternate i notation along with Eq. (18.7) to show that $(3 + 2i)(5 - 3i) = 21 + i$. Then write and execute a small FORTRAN program to perform the same multiplication.

18.2. Using Eq. (18.4) or (18.8) in Section 18.1, show on paper that the complex division that follows was perfomed correctly. Then write a small FORTRAN program to perform the same division.

$$\frac{(3 + 2i)}{(5 - 3i)} = (0.2647 + 0.5588i)$$

18.3. If you ask the machine to compute $(36)^{1/2}$, it reports 6, but you also know that there is another root, namely, −6. Similarly, should you be asked for the square root of 25, you would probably report 5 rather than offering the more rigorous ±5 answer, because 5 could be regarded as the principal root of $(25)^{1/2}$. The concept of the square root of a complex number also exists and you would again expect to find two roots, one of which may be called the principal root. If, for example, this principal root were $x + iy$, then the other root would be $-(x + iy)$. When FORTRAN computes the square root of a complex number, it reports only the principal root, but the other root is readily deduced. Write a FORTRAN program to verify that the principal square root of $192 - 79i$ is approximately equal to $14.14 - 2.79i$ by simply computing and reporting SQRT((192, −79)). Now verify that the other root is $-14.14 + 2.79i$ by computing and reporting (−14.14,2.79)**2.

In general, a complex number has n nth roots. For example, there are five 5th roots. For (4, −12)**(1./5.) the machine reports (1.61, −0.41), but this is only one of five roots, namely, the principal root. There are standard procedures for deducing the remaining roots, but this isn't really a chapter on the theory of complex variables.

18.4. The conjugate of the complex number $x + iy$ is $x - iy$. It is customary to indicate the conjugate of z by $\bar{z}$ or by z^*, where the asterisk notation is preferred by those who use the bar over the variable name to denote its average value. Thus, $\overline{12 + 1.2i} = (12 + 1.2i)^* = 12 - 1.2i$. Write a two-line test program to convince yourself that the FORTRAN function CONJG((3,12)) does indeed produce (3, −12).

18.5. It can be shown that in general $\overline{z_1 z_2 z_3 z_4 \ldots z_n} = \bar{z}_1 \bar{z}_2 \bar{z}_3 \bar{z}_4 \ldots \bar{z}_n$. Write a small program to test this claim for $n = 3$ by computing $\overline{(4 - 2i) \times (-12 + 7i) \times (3 + 19i)}$ and $\overline{(4 - 2i)} \times \overline{(-12 + 7i)} \times \overline{(3 + 19i)}$. The two computed values should be the same. You may also wish to attack this one by hand to enhance your appreciation of FORTRAN. The conjugate of a complex number is easily visualized as the reflection, in the *real* axis, of the vector representing the complex number in the complex plane.

18.6. The absolute value $|x + iy|$ of the complex number $x + iy$ is defined as $(x^2 + y^2)^{1/2}$. Use the computer to evaluate $|742.12 - 9878.43i|$. The FORTRAN equivalent is ABS((742.12, −9878.43)), and your computed result should be approximately 9906.27. The absolute value of a complex number, incidentally, can be pictured as the length of the vector representing the complex number in the complex plane.

18.7. It can be shown that $|z_1/z_2| = |z_1|/|z_2|$ provided that $|z_2| \neq 0$. Verify this claim by testing both sides of the equation in a FORTRAN program, using a random pair of complex numbers.

18.8. The complex number $z = x + iy$ is composed of a *real* part x and an *imaginary* part y. It is customary to denote the *real* part of z by $Re\{z\}$ and the *imaginary* part by $Im\{z\}$. You will recall that FORTRAN provides the two functions REAL and AIMAG for extracting the *real* and *imaginary* components of a complex number. For $z_1 = 4 - 3i$ and $z_2 = -5 + 2.9i$, write a FORTRAN program to test the following two identities:

$$Re\{z_1 z_2\} = Re\{z_1\}Re\{z_2\} - Im\{z_1\}\,Im\{z_2\}$$
$$Im\{z_1 z_2\} = Re\{z_1\}Im\{z_2\} + Im\{z_1\}Re\{z_2\}$$

18.9. The series expansion for the complex sine function is shown, and is considered valid for all values of z. Write a program similar to Ex. 18.1, allowing you to enter different z values. Compute the sine by summing a reasonable number of terms, and compare your result with the intrinsic SIN(Z) function. You will recall from Prob. 12.1 that (−1)**N provides an alternating sign as N steps along. If N increase two steps at a time, (−1)**(N/2) provides the necessary sign alternation.

$$\sin z = z - \frac{z^3}{3!} + \frac{z^5}{5!} - \frac{z^7}{7!} + \frac{z^9}{9!} - \cdots$$

19

LOGICAL Data

In Section 9.9, logical data were encountered indirectly, and logical expressions, the logical operators, and the relational operators were discussed in detail. This chapter builds on the same concepts, but views them from a different perspective.

The six FORTRAN data types are integer, real, double precision, character, complex, and logical. In general, a desired data type is requested explicitly for each variable in a so-called type-statement, or implicit data typing is possible through the use of the IMPLICIT declaration. In the absence of any data typing on the part of the programmer, the machine automatically considers all variables to be either of type integer or real, depending on the initial letter of a particular variable name. Associated with each one of these six data types are the concepts of *constants*, and *expressions*, and each data type has its peculiar I/O (input/output) characteristics.

19.1 LOGICAL DATA, LOGICAL CONSTANTS, AND OUTPUT OF LOGICAL DATA

Figure 19.1 shows a program demonstrating the LOGICAL type-statement, in which VAR1 and VAR2 are declared logical. This is followed by two assignment statements in which the logical constants .TRUE. and .FALSE. are assigned to VAR1 and VAR2, respectively, and, as you would expect, these are the only two possible values a logical constant can assume. Note the periods surrounding .TRUE. and .FALSE.

```
      LOGICAL VAR1,VAR2
      VAR1=.TRUE.
      VAR2=.FALSE.
      PRINT*,'VAR1 =',VAR1,'      VAR2 =',VAR2
      WRITE(6,1)VAR1,VAR2
    1 FORMAT(1X,'VAR1 = ',L1,5X,'VAR2 = ',L1)
      END
```

```
 VAR1 = T      VAR2 = F
 VAR1 = T      VAR2 = F
```

Figure 19.1 Logical constants, assignment statements, and logical output.

The assignment statements are followed by a list-directed PRINT statement to generate the first line of the output. Note that the machine reports the truth values of a logical variable simply as T or F. A formatted WRITE statement follows, and looks familiar, with the exception of the new edit descriptor Lw. The L implies logical, and the w specifies the width of the output field. The machine again produces T or F, and right-justifies these within the output field of width w. In this particular case, an output width of one space is chosen.

19.2 READING LOGICAL DATA AT RUN TIME

Figure 19.2 shows that when reading logical data, the machine accepts anything beginning with .T, .F, T, or F, but most users confine themselves to T or F.

In Fig. 19.3, input editing is used to extract logical data from very specific positions in an input string. In the FORMAT statement, the machine is instructed to look for a logical datum in the first space, where it finds T. It is then told to skip five spaces to find a logical datum in space seven, and there it finds another T. You should follow the remaining FORMAT specifications to confirm the output.

```
      LOGICAL V1,V2,V3,V4,V5,V6,V7,V8,V9,V1Ø
      READ*,V1,V2,V3,V4,V5,V6,V7,V8,V9,V1Ø
      PRINT*,'YOU JUST READ',V1,V2,V3,V4,V5,V6,V7,V8,V9,V1Ø
      END
```

```
? T  .T  TRUE  .TRUE.  F  .F  FALSE  .FALSE.  TXXXXXXX  FXXXXXX
YOU JUST READ T  T  T  T  F  F  F  F  T  F
```

Figure 19.2 Entering logical data at run time.

19.3 EVALUATING LOGICAL EXPRESSIONS

In Section 9.9, considerable attention was devoted to logical expressions and you will recall that such expressions produce a value of either TRUE or FALSE. Figure 19.4 shows how you can use the computer to evaluate such expressions.

```
      LOGICAL V1,V2,V3,V4,V5
      READ(5,1)V1,V2,V3,V4,V5
    1 FORMAT(L1,5X,L1,16X,L1,6X,L1,6X,L1)
      WRITE(6,2)V1,V2,V3,V4,V5
    2 FORMAT(' THE INPUT STRING CONTAINS',5L5)
      END

?THE GATHERING DARKNESS FILLED THEM WITH APPREHENSION
THE INPUT STRING CONTAINS    T    T    F    T    T
```

Figure 19.3 Edited input of logical data.

```
      LOGICAL V1
      V1 = .TRUE. .AND. .FALSE. .OR. .NOT. .TRUE.
      PRINT*,'THE EXPRESSION HAS THE TRUTH VALUE',V1
      END

 THE EXPRESSION HAS THE TRUTH VALUE F
```

Figure 19.4 Using FORTRAN to evaluate complex logical expressions.

19.4 THE LOGICAL IF STATEMENT REVISITED

Figure 19.5 represents the bridge between the logical IF statement and logical data. In retrospect, it is obvious that we already encountered logical data in Chapter 9, but it was important at that time not to stress the existence of a new data type at the expense of the issue at hand. You will enjoy stepping through this simple program because it ties things together nicely.

19.5 SIMPLE STATEMENTS, CONNECTIVES, AND COMPOUND STATEMENTS

Statements such as, "Cats purr," or "Dogs bark," or "The sun's heat is derived from diesel fuel" are called *simple statements* because each asserts one basic fact that is either true or false. So-called *connectives* can be used to combine simple statements into *compound statements*, which are also either true or false. "Cats purr *and* dogs bark" is an example of an obviously true compound statement, tied together by the connective *and*. Two other important connectives are *or* and *not*, but more on this later.

Human language has different cultural overtones for different people, causing occasional disagreement or confusion about the truth values of simple statements, not to mention those of compound statements. It is, however, possible to disengage the study of logic from potential linguistic encumbrances by viewing it symbolically, and this is shown in the following section.

```
      LOGICAL V1
*-----
      V1=.TRUE.
      IF(V1)PRINT*,'V1 WAS TRUE WHEN THIS WAS PRINTED'
*-----
      IF(.FALSE.)PRINT*,'OH, OH - THIS SHOULD NOT PRINT'
*-----
      V1=5.GT.3
      IF(V1)PRINT*,'LOOKS LIKE 5 IS GREATER THAN 3'
*-----
      IF(.NOT.V1)THEN
         PRINT*,'EITHER THE UNIVERSE IS OUT OF JOINT'
         PRINT*,'OR ELSE MY FORTRAN COMPILER IS BUGGY'
      ELSE
         PRINT*,'HUMANS NEED A CONSISTENT UNIVERSE'
      END IF
*-----
      END
```

```
V1 WAS TRUE WHEN THIS WAS PRINTED
LOOKS LIKE 5 IS GREATER THAN 3
HUMANS NEED A CONSISTENT UNIVERSE
```

Figure 19.5 The logical IF statement is based on logical data.

19.6 LOGIC GATES AND LOGICAL OPERATORS

Instead of using verbal statements, we let a and b represent simple logical assertions that are either true or false. The connectives are now called *logical operators* and perform in small boxes called *logic gates*. The truth value resulting from the compounding process leaves the logic gate through a single output pipe x. This symbolic approach is simplified further by referring to the truth values *true* and *false* as *logic states 1* and *0*, or as *logic levels 1* and *0*. Figure 19.6 shows a generalized two-input *logic gate* with inputs a and b, and output x. The incoming assertions a and b can appear in four different true/false combinations, namely, (F,F), (F,T), (T,F), or (T,T). In our new terminology, we say that a and b can assume the four logic-level combinations (0,0), (0,1), (1,0) and (1,1). For each of these input combinations, the logic gate produces an output that is either true or false, depending on the design of the gate. A so-called *truth table* appears beside the logic gate, showing the particular output x_n resulting from each of the four possible input combinations.

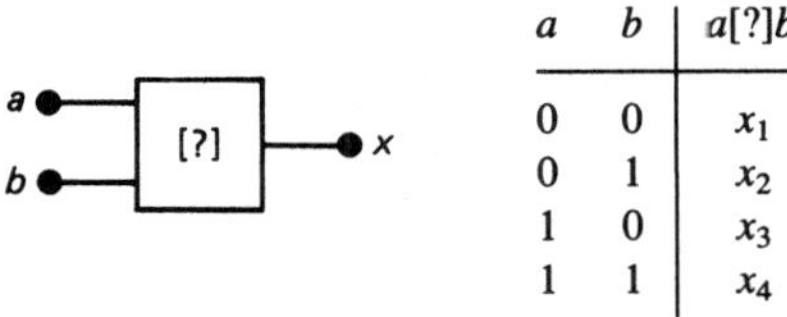

a	b	a[?]b
0	0	x_1
0	1	x_2
1	0	x_3
1	1	x_4

Figure 19.6 A generalized logic gate and its truth table.

In Fig. 19.6, the general logical operation of the gate is represented by [?], and the table tells us that 0[?]0 = x_1, 0[?]1 = x_2, 1[?]0 = x_3, and 1[?]1 = x_4.

19.7 HOW MANY DIFFERENT TWO-INPUT LOGIC GATES, OR LOGICAL OPERATORS, CAN EXIST?

The various logic gates with two inputs differ from each other by generating different sequences of truth values as the four true/false assertions appear at the input leads, and this means that only 16 different two-input logic gates can exist. The truth tables corresponding to these sixteen gates are shown in Fig. 19.7, where the logical operator represented by truth table *n* is called [*n*]. A detailed discussion of each logical operator follows in the next section.

The truth tables in Fig. 19.7 are arranged such that the output column forms a four-digit binary number that increases by 1 each time you move to the next table. Table [1], for example, has the output column 0001, [2] has outputs 0010, [3] has 0011, and so on. This order was chosen to convince you that all possible gates are included, and to give you a more instinctive feeling for the underlying simplicity. The order in which we discuss the gates in the next section will be different, however.

a	*b*	*a* [1] *b*
0	0	0
0	1	0
1	0	0
1	1	1

a	*b*	*a* [2] *b*
0	0	0
0	1	0
1	0	1
1	1	0

a	*b*	*a* [3] *b*
0	0	0
0	1	0
1	0	1
1	1	1

a	*b*	*a* [4] *b*
0	0	0
0	1	1
1	0	0
1	1	0

a	*b*	*a* [5] *b*
0	0	0
0	1	1
1	0	0
1	1	1

a	*b*	*a* [6] *b*
0	0	0
0	1	1
1	0	1
1	1	0

a	*b*	*a* [7] *b*
0	0	0
0	1	1
1	0	1
1	1	1

a	*b*	*a* [8] *b*
0	0	1
0	1	0
1	0	0
1	1	0

a	*b*	*a* [9] *b*
0	0	1
0	1	0
1	0	0
1	1	1

a	*b*	*a* [10] *b*
0	0	1
0	1	0
1	0	1
1	1	0

a	*b*	*a* [11] *b*
0	0	1
0	1	0
1	0	1
1	1	1

a	*b*	*a* [12] *b*
0	0	1
0	1	1
1	0	0
1	1	0

a	*b*	*a* [13] *b*
0	0	1
0	1	1
1	0	0
1	1	1

a	*b*	*a* [14] *b*
0	0	1
0	1	1
1	0	1
1	1	0

a	*b*	*a* [15] *b*
0	0	1
0	1	1
1	0	1
1	1	1

a	*b*	*a* [16] *b*
0	0	0
0	1	0
1	0	0
1	1	0

Figure 19.7 The truth tables of all 16 two-input logic gates.

19.8 A CLOSER LOOK AT THE 16 LOGICAL OPERATORS AND LOGIC GATES

[1]

a	b	$a \wedge b$
0	0	0
0	1	0
1	0	0
1	1	1

The truth table for *logical conjunction* $a \wedge b$, also known as the AND operation.

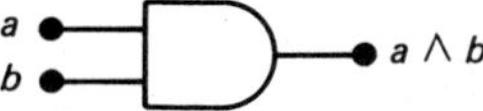

The conventional symbol for the AND gate.

AND (logical conjunction $\wedge$)

The action of the logical operator $\wedge$ is defined by its truth table, which states that the compound statement $a \wedge b$ is true only if a and b are both true. The operation $\wedge$ is known as *conjunction*, and the operator $\wedge$ is usually called *AND*. The symbol for the AND gate is also shown. It is easily remembered because its shape is like the letter D of AND. The output of this gate remains at the low logic level unless both inputs a and b are high, in which case the output $a \wedge b$ also shifts to the high logic state. The FORTRAN version of this logical operator is .AND., and the logical expression (M.GT.5.AND.X.GT.Y) is false unless M is greater than 5, and at the same time X is greater than Y.

[7]

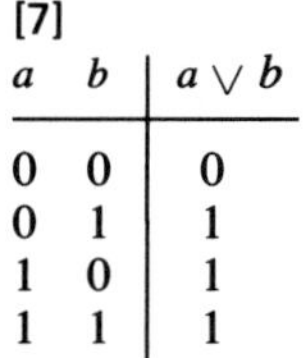

a	b	$a \vee b$
0	0	0
0	1	1
1	0	1
1	1	1

The truth table for *logical inclusive disjunction* $a \vee b$, also known as the OR operation.

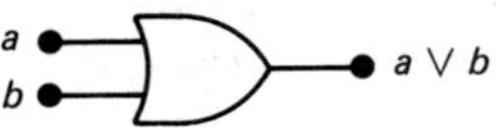

The conventional symbol for the OR gate.

OR (logical inclusive disjunction $\vee$)

The logical operator $\vee$ is defined by its truth table. $\vee$ connects two simple statements a and b in such a manner that the resulting compound statement is true when either a or b is true. This operation is known as *disjunction*. Because $a \vee b$ is also true when both a and b are true at the same time, the operation is more properly called *inclusive disjunction*. The operator $\vee$ is generally called *OR*, although *INCLUSIVE OR* would be more accurate. The symbol for the OR gate is also shown. Its output becomes high when either a or b is raised, or when both go high simultaneously. The corresponding FORTRAN logical operator is .OR. and the logical expression (M.GT.5.OR.X.GT.Y) is true when M is greater than 5, or when X is greater than Y, or if both are true.

[6]

a	b	$a \veebar b$
0	0	0
0	1	1
1	0	1
1	1	0

The truth table for *logical exclusive disjunction* $a \veebar b$, also called the EXCLUSIVE OR operation.

a, b → $a \veebar b$

The conventional symbol for the EXCLUSIVE OR gate.

EXCLUSIVE OR, also called EOR and XOR (logical exclusive disjunction $\veebar$)

The truth table defines the logical operator $\veebar$. The compound statement $a \veebar b$ is true when one of a or b is true, but when both are true, the compound statement is false. $\veebar$ is known as *exclusive disjunction*, and the operator $\veebar$ is usually called *EOR* or *XOR*. The symbol for the corresponding logic gate is also shown. The output of this gate remains at the low logic level unless one of a or b is high, in which case the output is also high, but when both inputs are high, the output is low. ANSI X3.9–1978 does not include the EXCLUSIVE OR, but many compilers do offer it, and usually call it either EOR or XOR, or both.

[6]

a	b	$a \not\Leftrightarrow b$
0	0	0
0	1	1
1	0	1
1	1	0

The table for *logical nonequivalence* $a \not\Leftrightarrow b$. The statement T $\not\Leftrightarrow$ F is true because it is true that T and F are not equivalent. Note that $\veebar$ and $\not\Leftrightarrow$ share the same truth table.

NEQV (logical nonequivalence $\not\Leftrightarrow$)

The truth table defines the action of the logical nonequivalence operator $\not\Leftrightarrow$. FORTRAN provides the nonequivalence operator in the form .NEQV. You have probably noticed that the truth tables for $\not\Leftrightarrow$ and $\veebar$ are the same. This is no mistake but simply two different aspects of the same logic pattern. And so you see that although FORTRAN 77 does not provide an EOR operator, you can always use .NEQV. to the same end.

[9]

a	b	$a \Leftrightarrow b$
0	0	1
0	1	0
1	0	0
1	1	1

The table for *logical equivalence* $a \Leftrightarrow b$. The statement T $\Leftrightarrow$ T is true because it is true that T and T are equivalent.

EQV (logical equivalence $\Leftrightarrow$)

The truth table defines the action of the logical equivalence operator $\Leftrightarrow$. The corresponding FORTRAN operator is .EQV.

[10]

a	b	$a[10]b$
0	0	1
0	1	0
1	0	1
1	1	0

The truth table [10] from Fig. 19.7 shows that $a[10]b$ is the negation of b. The logic state of a is ignored.

[12]

a	b	$a[12]b$
0	0	1
0	1	1
1	0	0
1	1	0

The truth table [12] from Fig. 19.7 shows that $a[12]b$ is simply the negation of a. The logic state of b is ignored.

NOT (logical negation $\sim$)

Operators [10] and [12], defined in Fig. 19.7, appear to be binary in the sense of connecting two simple statements. In fact, they are not binary, because each ignores one of its operands, acting only on the other, thus making them *unary* operators. It turns out that both operators do the same thing, namely, invert the truth value of the operand, and thus we are dealing with only a single unary operator, called the *NOT* operator, and its action is called *logical negation*. The operator is usually represented by $\sim$, where it is understood that $\sim$T = F, and $\sim$F = T. Negation is also often indicated by placing a bar over a truth value, thus, $\overline{\text{T}}$ = F and $\overline{\text{F}}$ = T. FORTRAN's negation operator is .NOT.

The NOT logic gate is shown. The actual negation symbol is the small open circle, and the wedge shape tags along to provide a place to hang the circle. When the input or the output of some logic gate needs to be inverted, the circle is usually moved right up to the gate, and shown without the wedge shape. When referring to logic gates, negation is frequently called *inversion*.

d	$\sim d$
0	1
1	0

The essence of truth tables [10] and [12] is represented by the truth table for *logical negation* $\sim$, where $\sim$T = F, and $\sim$F = T.

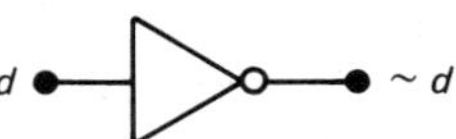

The conventional symbol for the NOT gate. The open circle symbolizes the negation.

[8]

a	b	$\sim(a \vee b)$
0	0	1
0	1	0
1	0	0
1	1	0

Table [8] of Fig. 19.7 is a negation of the OR defined by table [7]. Table [8], therefore, defines $\sim (a \vee b)$

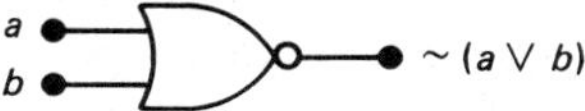

The NOR gate symbol shows an OR gate with its output inverted.

[14]

a	b	$\sim(a \wedge b)$
0	0	1
0	1	1
1	0	1
1	1	0

Table [14] of Fig. 19.7 is a negation of the AND defined by table [1]. Table [14], therefore, defines $\sim(a \wedge b)$

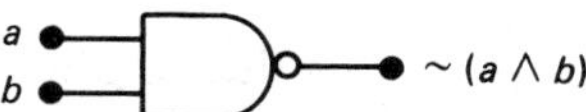

The NAND gate symbol consists of an AND gate with its output inverted.

When dealing with symbolic logic, it is understood that the various logic operators act with a certain *precedence* in the sense that when a complex logical expression is evaluated, the operators act in the following well-defined order:

Operation	Precedence
$\sim$	First
$\wedge$	Second
$\vee$	Third
$\veebar$, $\not\Leftrightarrow$, $\Leftrightarrow$	Fourth

This precedence permits complex logical expressions to be written with fewer brackets than would otherwise be required. FORTRAN adheres to this precedence.

NOR $\sim(a \vee b)$

Some feel that although there are 16 possible diadic (two-input, binary) logical operators, only NOT, AND, and OR are fundamental, because any of the remaining 13 operators can be constructed from these three. The *NOR* operation is an example, being a combination of NOT and OR. The gate shows the nature of this combination clearly. The FORTRAN equivalent of NOR is .NOT.(A.OR.B), where the brackets are important to prevent the NOT from acting before the OR, as would otherwise happen because of the precedence among the operations.

NAND $\sim(a \wedge b)$

This operation is a combination of *NOT* and *AND*. The gate shows the NOT placed at the output of the AND. The FORTRAN equivalent of NAND is .NOT.(A.AND.B), where again the brackets are important to prevent the NOT from acting before the AND.

[13]

a	b	$a \rightarrow b$
0	0	1
0	1	1
1	0	0
1	1	1

Table [13] of Fig. 19.7 defines the *logical implication* "if a then b; symbolized by $a \rightarrow b$.

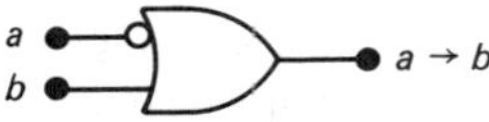

The $a \rightarrow b$ logic gate is an OR gate with the a input inverted, i.e., $\sim a \vee b$.

If a then b (implication $a \rightarrow b$)

$a \rightarrow b$ is usually read "if a then b" or as "a implies b," but it is probably most easily understood in the form "b is true if a is true." Let's keep this latter form in mind as we look at the truth table. The last line of the table has both a and b true, so that the statement "b is true if a is true" is obviously true. The second-to-last entry in the table has a true and b false, and "b is true if a is true" is clearly false. The first and second lines of the truth table cannot be tested because a is false in both, and our test can be applied only if a is true. And so the arbitrary decision is made to define $a \rightarrow b$ as being true whenever a is false. The corresponding logic gate is an OR gate with input a inverted, and it is very easy to see how this gate generates the truth table. The FORTRAN equivalent expression is (.NOT.A.OR.B). Because of the precedence among the operators, a is inverted before the OR is performed. The position of the inverter makes this gate very different from the NOR gate.

[2]

a	b	$\sim(a \rightarrow b)$
0	0	0
0	1	0
1	0	1
1	1	0

Table [2] of Fig. 19.7 is the negation of the implication $a \rightarrow b$ defined by table [13]. It, therefore, represents $\sim(a \rightarrow b)$

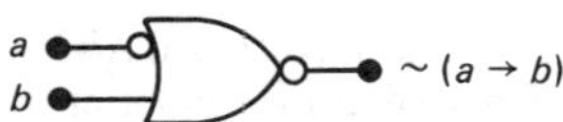

An OR gate with input a inverted, and with its output inverted, i.e., $\sim(\sim a \vee b)$

$\sim$(If a then b) ($\sim(a \rightarrow b)$)

The logic gate generates the truth table for the operation $\sim(a \rightarrow b)$. The equivalent FORTRAN statement is (.NOT.(.NOT.A.OR.B)). The logic gate shown has the same truth table, as you can easily verify. This provides the alternative FORTRAN statement (A.AND..NOT.B).

There are six operators, or logic gates, left. Truth table [11] in Fig. 19.6 describes $b \rightarrow a$, as you can easily verify, and the complementary $\sim (b \rightarrow a)$ is defined by table [4].

The operation defined by table [3] always reproduces the truth value of input a, ignoring input b. This means that should $a[3]b$ appear in a logical expression, it can be replaced by a. The equivalent logic gate would have a wire connecting the output terminal to the input terminal a. Similarly, $a[5]b$ always produces a truth value the same as b. The equivalent logic gate would be a piece of wire connecting input terminal b to the output terminal.

The operator defined by table [15] always produces a logic value of true no matter what input combination is presented. The equivalent logic gate is one in which the output is locked into a permanently high state. Similarly, [16] corresponds to a logic gate with the output permanently false.

19.9 DISCUSSION

The study of elementary symbolic logic is so interesting and stimulating on its own that it is easy to lose sight of the FORTRAN connection, but you are reminded that logical expressions are the essence of IF statements. You have now seen all 16 possible logical operators, some of them indispensable, and some of them trivial, and you have come to understand that all 16 are available through various combinations of the basic operators $\sim$, $\wedge$, and $\vee$. The FORTRAN equivalents are .NOT., .AND., and .OR., in addition to which .EQV. and .NEQV. are provided, although these could be generated from a combination of the basic three.

In the discussion of the possible logical operators, we used operands with names such as *a* and *b*. These can be the logical constants .TRUE. and .FALSE., or they can be relational expressions, such as X.GT.Y, or they can be other, more complex, logical expressions. All of these are logical entities with truth values that are either true or false. This is illustrated by showing the logical operator .AND. operating first on constants, then on relational expressions, and finally on more complex logical expressions.

```
        .TRUE.    .AND.   .FALSE.
     M .LE. L     .AND.   M**2 .GT. MAX(N,K,J)
.OR. W.GT.5.2)    .AND.   .NOT. (M.EQ.3 .OR. X.EQ.Y .OR. K.EQ.M)
```

The point is easily belabored, but its importance must be appreciated. Several examples follow. They are straightforward, but may look a little strange at first. Any effort you invest in understanding them will benefit you considerably.

19.10 EXAMPLES

Example 19.1

In order to study the behavior of some of the binary logical operators, you must use the four possible true/false combinations. Write a program to test the .AND. operator. Feed the true/false combinations at run time.

Solution

```
      LOGICAL A,B
      WRITE(6,1)
    1 FORMAT(20X,'A',3X,'B',4X,'A.AND.B',/,19X,18('-'))
      DO 2 I=1,4
      READ(5,3)A,B
    3 FORMAT(2L1)
      WRITE(6,4)A, B, A.AND.B
```

```
    4  FORMAT(2ØX,L1,3X,L1,7X,L1)
    2  CONTINUE
       END
                           A   B     A.AND.B
                          ------------------
?FF
                           F   F        F
?FT
                           F   T        F
?TF
                           T   F        F
?TT
                           T   T        T
```

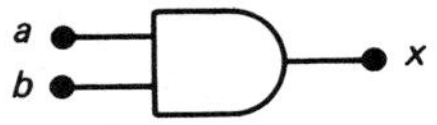

Example 19.2

Automate the program in Ex. 19.1 to make it generate its own test data.

Solution

```
       LOGICAL A,B
       WRITE(6,1)
    1  FORMAT(2ØX,'A',3X,'B',4X,'A.AND.B',/,19X,18('-'))
*------
       DO 2 I=Ø,1
       A=.FALSE.
       IF(I.EQ.1)A=.TRUE.
*------
           DO 3 J=Ø,1
           B=.FALSE.
           IF(J.EQ.1)B=.TRUE.
           WRITE(6,4)A, B, A.AND.B
    4      FORMAT(2ØX,L1,3X,L1,7X,L1)
    3      CONTINUE
*------
    2  CONTINUE
       END
                           A   B     A.AND.B
                          ------------------
                           F   F        F
                           F   T        F
                           T   F        F
                           T   T        T
```

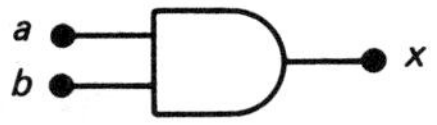

Discussion The heart of the program is a pair of nested DO-loops, each executing two cycles. DO-variables must be numeric, but we require logical data to compute the value of the logical expression. You will notice how the logical constants are assigned to A and B. By default they are both assigned .FALSE., but when the DO-variable becomes 1, the value .TRUE. is assigned to the variables. This is a general pattern followed in some of the subsequent examples, and you will find it valuable for several of the problems.

Example 19.3

Derive the logical expression describing the structure of Fig. 19.8. The structure might be a logic circuit.

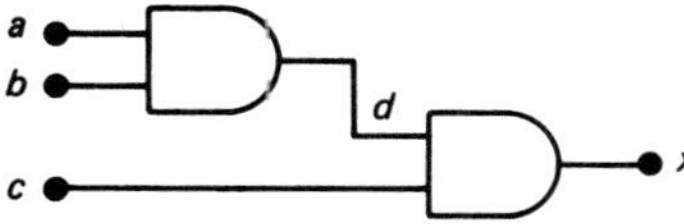

Figure 19.8 Structure for Ex. 19.3.

Solution Start with the output and describe its composition. In this particular case, x is the output from an AND gate with inputs d and c, and this is reflected by Eq. (19.1).

$$x = d \wedge c \tag{19.1}$$

d, however, is the output of another AND gate with inputs a and b; thus,

$$d = (a \wedge b) \tag{19.2}$$

In general, the parentheses are recommended to avoid potential precedence problems, but these can be cleaned up in the final expression, if desired. Substituting Eq. (19.2) into (19.1), we end up with the required logical expression. The FORTRAN equivalent is also shown.

$$\begin{aligned} x &= (a \wedge b) \wedge c \\ &= a \wedge b \wedge c \end{aligned}$$

or

```
X=A.AND.B.AND.C
```

Example 19.4

Derive the logical expression describing the logic circuit of Fig. 19.9.

Solution

$$x = e \vee f$$

$$e = (\sim(a \wedge b))$$

$$f = (\sim(c \wedge d))$$

$$\begin{aligned} x &= (\sim(a \wedge b)) \vee (\sim (c \wedge d)) \\ &= \sim(a \wedge b) \vee \sim(c \wedge d) \end{aligned}$$

or

```
X=.NOT.(A.AND.B).OR..NOT.(C.AND.D)
```

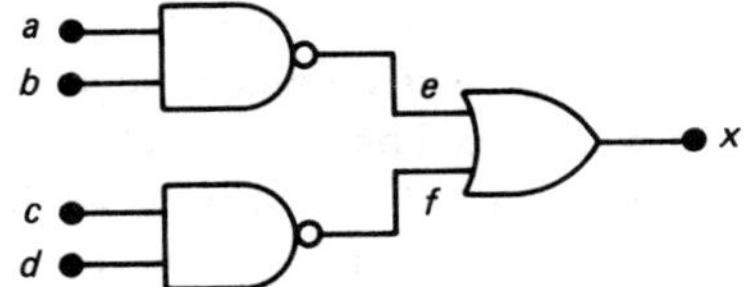

Figure 19.9 Logic circuit for Ex. 19.4.

Example 19.5

Derive the logical expression for the circuit of Fig. 19.10.

Solution

$$
\begin{aligned}
x &= n \wedge p \\
n &= (j \wedge k) \\
j &= (\sim(a \vee b)) \\
k &= (c \wedge d) \\
p &= (l \vee m) \\
l &= (e \wedge f) \\
m &= (g \wedge h) \\
\text{Thus, } x &= ((j \wedge k) \wedge (l \vee m)) \\
&= (((\sim(a \vee b)) \wedge (c \wedge d)) \wedge ((e \wedge f) \vee (g \wedge h))) \\
&= \sim(a \vee b) \wedge c \wedge d \wedge (e \wedge f \vee g \wedge h)
\end{aligned}
$$

or

```
X=.NOT.(A.OR.B).AND.C.AND.D.AND.(E.AND.F.OR.G.AND.H)
```

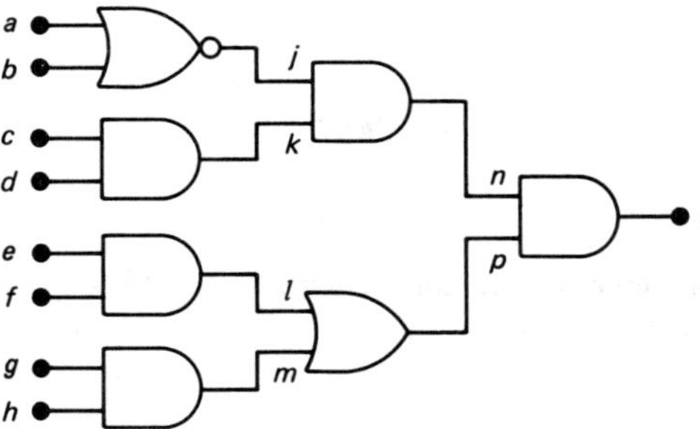

Figure 19.10 Logic circuit for Ex. 19.5.

Example 19.6

A three-input AND gate is composed of 2 two-input AND gates connected as shown in Fig. 19.11. The equivalent FORTRAN logical expression is (A.AND.B).AND.C, where the brackets can be omitted because there is no precedence conflict. Write a program to generate the truth table for this three-input AND gate.

Solution

```
      LOGICAL A,B,C
      WRITE(6,1)
1     FORMAT(1ØX,'A',3X,'B',3X,'C',4X,'A.AND.B.AND.C',/,9X,28('-'))
      DO 2 I=Ø,1
      A=.FALSE.
      IF(I.EQ.1)A=.TRUE.
          DO 3 J=Ø,1
          B=.FALSE.
          IF(J.EQ.1)B=.TRUE.
              DO 5 K=Ø,1
              C=.FALSE.
              IF(K.EQ.1)C=.TRUE.
              WRITE(6,4)A, B, C, A.AND.B.AND.C
4             FORMAT(1ØX,L1,3X,L1,3X,L1,1ØX,L1)
5             CONTINUE
3         CONTINUE
2     CONTINUE
      END
```

```
A   B   C    A.AND.B.AND.C
----------------------------
F   F   F          F
F   F   T          F
F   T   F          F
F   T   T          F
T   F   F          F
T   F   T          F
T   T   F          F
T   T   T          T
```

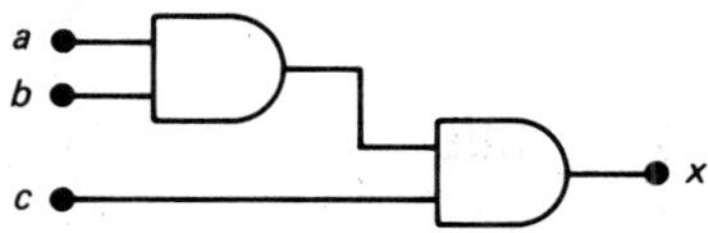

Figure 19.11 Logic circuit for Ex. 19.6.

$$x = a \wedge b \wedge c$$

or

```
X=A.AND.B.AND.C
```

Example 19.7

The circuit of Fig. 19.12 consists of five gates. The circuit has six inputs and one output. Because there are six inputs, a total of 64 input combinations is possible, nine of which cause the output to go high. Write a program to determine and to report these nine input combinations.

Solution

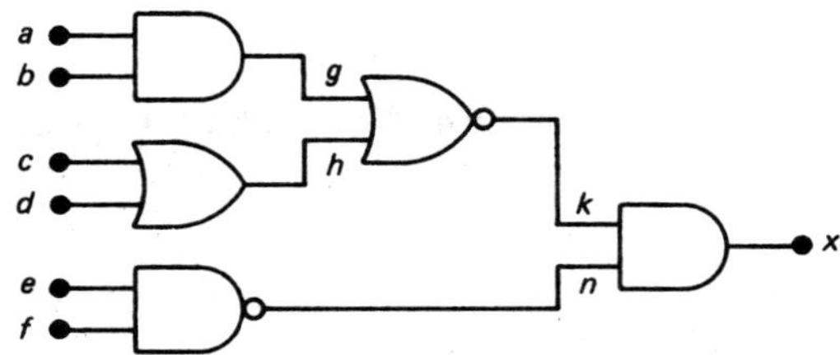

Figure 19.12 Logic circuit for Ex. 19.7.

```
      LOGICAL A,B,C,D,E,F,GATE
      WRITE(6,8)
    8 FORMAT(1X,' A B C D E F  GATE',/,1X,18('-'))
      DO 1 I=Ø,1
      A=.FALSE.
      IF(I.EQ.1)A=.TRUE.
         DO 2 J=Ø,1
         B=.FALSE.
         IF(J.EQ.1)B=.TRUE.
            DO 3 K=Ø,1


            C=.FALSE.
            IF(K.EQ.1)C=.TRUE.
               DO 4 L=Ø,1
               D=.FALSE.
               IF(L.EQ.1)D=.TRUE.
                  DO 5 M=Ø,1
                  E=.FALSE.
                  IF(M.EQ.1)E=.TRUE.
                     DO 6 N=Ø,1
                     F=.FALSE.
                     IF(N.EQ.1)F=.TRUE.
*-----
                     GATE = .NOT.(A.AND.B.OR.C.OR.D).AND..NOT.(E.AND.F)
                     IF(GATE)WRITE(3,7)A,B,C,D,E,F,GATE
*-----
    7                FORMAT(1X,6L2,L5)
    6                CONTINUE
    5             CONTINUE
    4          CONTINUE
    3       CONTINUE
    2    CONTINUE
    1 CONTINUE
      END
```

```
A B C D E F  GATE
------------------
F F F F F F   T
F F F F F T   T
F F F F T F   T
F T F F F F   T
F T F F F T   T
F T F F T F   T
T F F F F F   T
T F F F F T   T
T F F F T F   T
```

Example 19.8

The logic circuit of Fig. 19.13 has 10 inputs. With 10 inputs, $2^{10} = 1024$ distinct input combinations are possible. Of these 1024 input combinations, only a small number should produce a logical high at the output x. Write a program to display all the input combinations for which the output is high, and report how many such combinations exist. Some of the gates, in this and subsequent circuits, are not brilliant from a circuit-design perspective. The first gate in this circuit, for example, could be replaced by a simple OR gate, but it does generate an interesting logical expression.

Solution The circuit is so big now that it is no longer realistic to attempt to boil it down to a logical expression in a single step. The process of reducing a circuit to a single

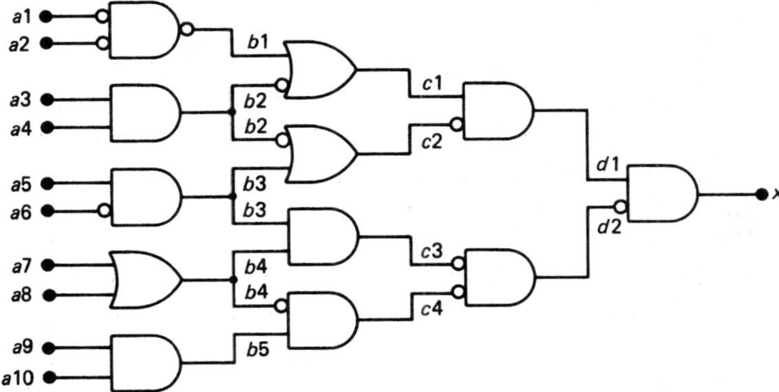

Figure 19.13 Logic circuit for Ex. 19.8.

expression is highly error prone because of all the substitutions, and because the parentheses are easily confused. It is, therefore, much easier to let the computer look after the substitutions. The program is somewhat lengthy because 30 statements are required just to generate the test data, but we took a shortcut by letting all the DO loops share a common terminus. The program may be lengthy, but it is remarkably simple, and it only takes a fraction of a second to execute on a midsize machine. The circuit is described between the two comment lines, and you should be able to follow each step without the slightest difficulty.

```
      IMPLICIT LOGICAL (A-D)
      LOGICAL X
      WRITE(6,3)
    3 FORMAT(1X,' A1  A2  A3  A4  A5  A6  A7  A8  A9  A10    X',
     +/,3X,44('-'))
      NUMHIT=0
      DO 1 I1=0,1
      A1=.FALSE.
      IF(I1.EQ.1)A1=.TRUE.
      DO 1 I2=0,1
      A2=.FALSE.
      IF(I2.EQ.1)A2=.TRUE.
      DO 1 I3=0,1
      A3=.FALSE.
      IF(I3.EQ.1)A3=.TRUE.
      DO 1 I4=0,1
      A4=.FALSE.
      IF(I4.EQ.1)A4=.TRUE.
      DO 1 I5=0,1
      A5=.FALSE.
      IF(I5.EQ.1)A5=.TRUE.
      DO 1 I6=0,1
      A6=.FALSE.
      IF(I6.EQ.1)A6=.TRUE.
      DO 1 I7=0,1
      A7=.FALSE.
      IF(I7.EQ.1)A7=.TRUE.
      DO 1 I8=0,1
      A8=.FALSE.
      IF(I8.EQ.1)A8=.TRUE.
      DO 1 I9=0,1
      A9=.FALSE.
      IF(I9.EQ.1)A9=.TRUE.
      DO 1 I10=0,1
      A10=.FALSE.
      IF(I10.EQ.1)A10=.TRUE.
*-----
      B1 = .NOT.(.NOT.A1.AND..NOT.A2)
      B2 = A3.AND.A4
      B3 = A5.AND..NOT.A6
      B4 = A7.OR.A8
      B5 = A9.AND.A10
      C1 = B1.OR..NOT.B2
      C2 = .NOT.B2.OR.B3
      C3 = B3.AND.B4
      C4 = .NOT.B4.AND.B5
```

```
      D1 = C1.AND..NOT.C2
      D2 = .NOT.C3.AND..NOT.C4
      X  = D1.AND..NOT.D2
*-----
      IF(X)THEN
          WRITE(6,2)A1,A2,A3,A4,A5,A6,A7,A8,A8,A10,X
          NUMHIT=NUMHIT+1
          END IF
    2 FORMAT(1X,10L4,L6)
    1 CONTINUE
      PRINT*,' '
      PRINT*,'    THERE WERE',NUMHIT,'HITS OUT OF A POSSIBLE 1024'
      END
```

A1	A2	A3	A4	A5	A6	A7	A8	A9	A10	X
F	T	T	T	F	F	F	F	F	T	T
F	T	T	T	F	T	F	F	F	T	T
F	T	T	T	T	T	F	F	F	T	T
T	F	T	T	F	F	F	F	F	T	T
T	F	T	T	F	T	F	F	F	T	T
T	F	T	T	T	T	F	F	F	T	T
T	T	T	T	F	F	F	F	F	T	T
T	T	T	T	F	T	F	F	F	T	T
T	T	T	T	T	T	F	F	F	T	T

19.11 PROBLEMS

19.1. Six circuit diagrams are shown in Fig. 19.14. Write FORTRAN programs to compute the truth table of each, basing the programs on Ex. 19.2. Although the circuits are quite simple, the substitutions, in some cases, are error prone, especially for the circuit using all NAND gates, and for the one using all NOR gates. For this reason, let the computer perform the substitutions, following the step-by-step approach illustrated by Ex. 19.8. It will require that you label the inputs to each gate.

You should find that each circuit has the same truth table, namely, that of the EXCLUSIVE OR gate. This problem highlights the fact that there are many ways to construct a circuit with a specific truth table. The ultimate choice depends on available components, on costs, power consumption, and speed. It may be assumed that the more components a circuit involves, the slower it gets, the more power it consumes, and the more it costs, but sometimes the availability of components becomes the overriding criterion.

19.2. The Boolean Algebra distributive law states that

$$a \wedge (b \vee c) = a \wedge b \vee a \wedge c,$$

asserting that the two circuits shown in Fig. 19.15 are equivalent. Write a program to test both sides for equivalence, using the logical operator .EQV. provided by FORTRAN. The expression

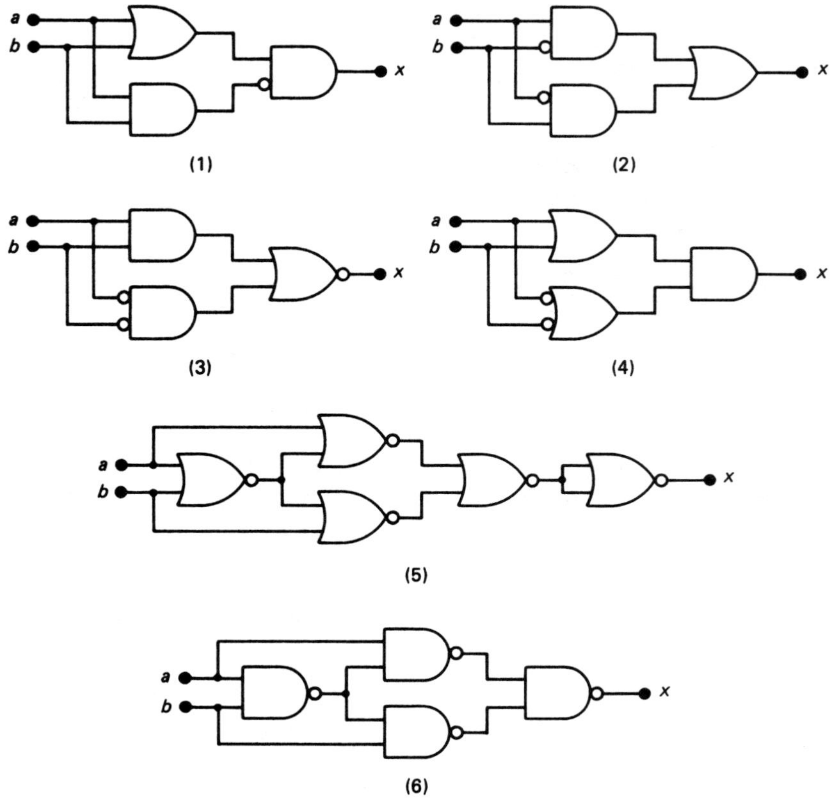

Figure 19.14 Logic circuits for Prob. 19.1.

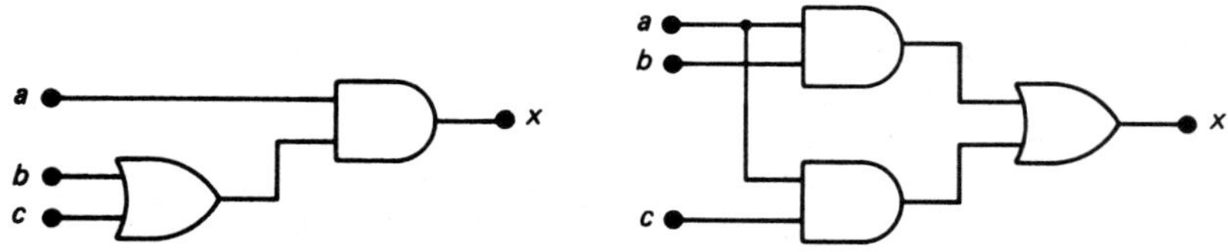

Figure 19.15 Logic circuits for Prob. 19.2.

```
A.AND.(B.OR.C) .EQV. A.AND.B.OR.A.AND.C
```

should be true for all eight input combinations of A, B, and C.

The distributive law has considerable implications, not only for circuit designers, but also for programmers. For example, if you ever came across a compound logical expression such as

```
A.AND.B.OR.A.AND.C.OR.A.AND.D.OR.A.AND.E.OR.A.AND.F.OR.A.AND.G,
```

you could simply replace it with

```
A.AND.(B.OR.C.OR.D.OR.E.OR.F.OR.G),
```

and life would become more enjoyable.

19.3. De Morgan's Law states that

$$a \wedge b \wedge c \wedge d \cdot \cdot \cdot = \sim(\sim a \vee \sim b \vee \sim c \vee \sim d \cdot \cdot \cdot)$$

The left side is true if all the inputs are true, but if only a single input is false, the left side is false. On the right side, if all the inputs are true, the expression in parentheses is false, but the negation preceding the opening parenthesis makes the right side true. You can easily see that the right side becomes false as soon as one of the inputs becomes false. The two sides are, therefore, obviously equivalent. De Morgan's Law thus implies that the two gates in Fig. 19.16, for example, are equivalent. Write a program to test these two gates for equivalence. If you are disturbed by an AND gate with three inputs, you should review Exs. 19.3 and 19.6. For that matter, you can picture AND gates with N inputs, which are logically equivalent to N − 1 two-input interconnected AND gates. Similarly, N-input OR gates can be constructed, and De Morgan's Law defines the relationship between such AND and OR gates.

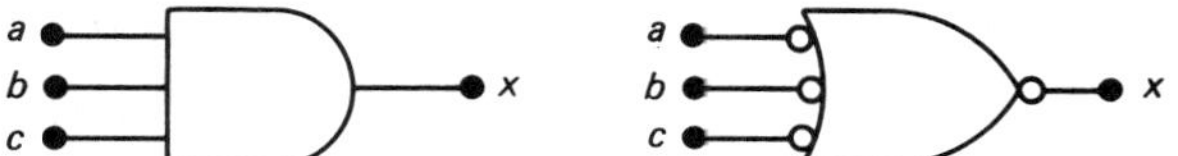

Figure 19.16 Logic gates for Prob. 9.3.

19.4. The circuit of Fig. 19.17 has 14 inputs. This means that 16,384 input combinations are possible. Determine how many of these input combinations produce an output of true. You should find 192.

19.5. Verify that the first logic gate in Fig. 19.13 of Ex. 19.8 can indeed be replaced by a simple OR gate. The gate has inputs $a1$ and $a2$, and output $b1$.

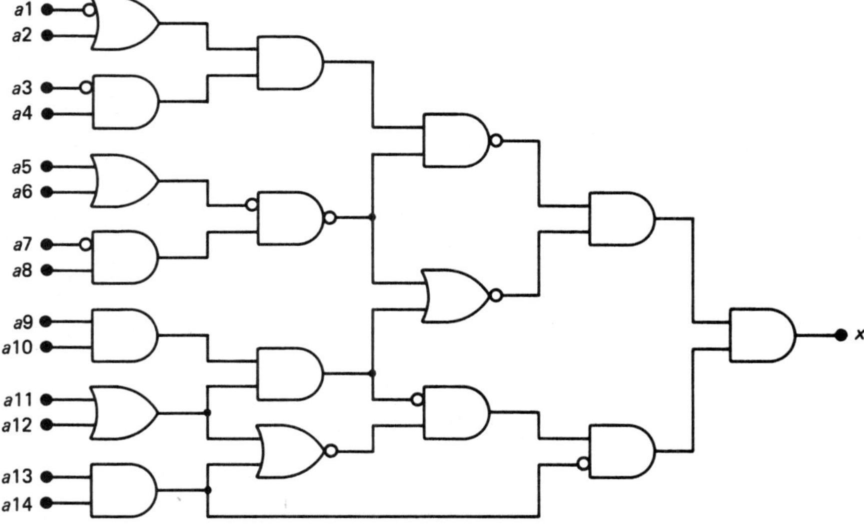

Figure 19.17 Logic circuit for Prob. 19.4.

Appendix A
The EBCDIC Table

		0000	0001	0010	0011	0100	0101	0110	0111	1000	1001	1010	1011	1100	1101	1110	1111
		0	1	2	3	4	5	6	7	8	9	A	B	C	D	E	F
0000	0	NUL	DLE	DS		SP	&	–									0
0001	1	SOH	DC1	SOS				/		a	j			A	J		1
0010	2	STX	DC2	FS	SYN					b	k	s		B	K	S	2
0011	3	ETX	TM							c	l	t		C	L	T	3
0100	4	PF	RES	BYP	PN					d	m	u		D	M	U	4
0101	5	HT	NL	LF	RS					e	n	v		E	N	V	5
0110	6	LC	BS	ETB	UC					f	o	w		F	O	W	6
0111	7	DEL	IL	ESC	EOT					g	p	x		G	P	X	7
1000	8		CAN							h	q	y		H	Q	Y	8
1001	9		EM							i	r	z		I	R	Z	9
1010	A	SMM	CC	SM		¢	!		:								
1011	B	VT	CU1	CU2	CU3	.	$	,	#								
1100	C	FF	IFS		DC4	<	*	%	@								
1101	D	CR	IGS	ENQ	NAK	(	)	_	'								
1110	E	SO	IRS	ACK		+	;	>	=								
1111	F	SI	IUS	BEL	SUB	|	~	?	"								

The EBCDIC code for a given character is readily deduced from the table. You will notice that each character defines a unique row and column intersection. The four bits at the top of the column are the first four EBCDIC bits, and the four bits shown to the left of each row are the trailing bits of the code. The hex abbreviations are shown next to each group of four bits.

To find the EBCDIC code for the character H, for example, simply locate H in the table. Combining the four bits at the head of the column with the four bits to the left of the row gives you the EBCDIC code 11001000, or C8 in hex-condensed form.

As another example, the code for g is obviously 10000111, or hex 87, and the code for the character ? is 01101111, or hex 6F.

The first four columns of the EBCDIC table contain special control characters. The remaining 12 columns define the so-called graphic characters. You will notice that there are many unassigned positions left in the table for potential future use.

The control characters are used to control printer tabbing, transmission flow, transmission monitoring and verification, etc.

Appendix B
The Seven-Bit ASCII Table

		0000	0001	0010	0011	0100	0101	0110	0111
		0	1	2	3	4	5	6	7
0000	0	NUL	DLE	SP	0	@	P	`	p
0001	1	SOH	DC1	!	1	A	Q	a	q
0010	2	STX	DC2	’’	2	B	R	b	r
0011	3	ETX	DC3	#	3	C	S	c	s
0100	4	EOT	DC4	$	4	D	T	d	t
0101	5	ENQ	NAK	%	5	E	U	e	u
0110	6	ACK	SYN	&	6	F	V	f	v
0111	7	BEL	ETB	′	7	G	W	g	w
1000	8	BS	CAN	(	8	H	X	h	x
1001	9	HT	EM	)	9	I	Y	i	y
1010	A	LF	SUB	*	:	J	Z	j	z
1011	B	VT	ESC	+	;	K	[	k	{
1100	C	FF	FS	,	<	L	\	l	¦
1101	D	CR	GS	–	=	M	]	m	}
1110	E	SO	RS	.	>	N	^	n	˜
1111	F	SI	US	/	?	O	—	o	DEL

The ASCII code corresponding to a given character is readily deduced from the table. You will notice that each character defines a unique row and column intersection. The four bits at the top of the column are the first four ASCII bits, and the four bits shown to the left of each row are the trailing bits of the code. The hex abbreviations are shown next to each group of bits.

To find the ASCII code for the character H, for example, simply locate H in the table. Combining the four bits at the head of the column with the four bits to the left of the row gives you the ASCII code 01001000, or 48 in hex-condensed form.

As another example, the code for g is obviously 01100111, or hex 67, and the code for the character ? is 00111111, or hex 3F.

Yes, it is true that the table reports eight bits for each ASCII character, but you will notice that the first bit is always a zero. Eight-bit ASCII uses this additional bit position. NISO Z39.47–1985, discussed in Section 3.11, is an example.

The first two columns of the seven-bit ASCII table contain 32 special control characters. Some of these have their own keys, and others are generated by holding down the control key while striking some character key. The symbol X^c, for example, means CONTROL-X. It is generated by striking the X while the control key is held down. The 32 control characters are now listed:

Character	Generation	Function
SOH	A^c	Start Of Header—communication control
STX	B^c	Start of TeXt—communication control
ETX	C^c	End of TeXt—communication control
EOT	D^c	End Of Transmission—communication control
ENQ	E^c	ENQuiry—"who are you"—communication control
ACK	F^c	ACKnowledge—communication control
BEL	G^c	BELl
BS	H^c	BackSpace—often has its own key
HT	I^c	Horizontal Tabulation—format control
LF	J^c, LF	Line Feed—format control. Often has its own key
VT	K^c	Vertical Tabulation—format control
FF	L^c	Form Feed—format control
CR	M^c, CR	Carriage Return—usually has its own key
SO	N^c	Shift Out—special communication code
SI	O^c	Shift In—special communication control
DLE	P^c	Data Link Escape—communication control
DC1	Q^c	Device Control 1
DC2	R^c	Device Control 2
DC3	S^c	Device Control 3
DC4	T^c	Device Control 4
NAK	U^c	Negative AcKnowledge—communication control
SYN	V^c	SYNchronous Idle—communication control
ETB	W^c	End of Transmission Block—communication control
CAN	X^c	CANcel
EM	Y^c	End of Medium
SUB	Z^c	SUBstitute
ESC	^{c}, ESC	Function is highly system dependent
FS	$\backslash^c$	File Separator—software control
GS	^{c}	Group Separator—software control
RS	^{c}	Record Separator—software control
US	$-^c$	Unit Separator—software control
NUL	$@^c$	Causes delays of one character time per NUL

Appendix C
The Intrinsic Functions

The following is a list of the intrinsic functions, essentially as it appears in X3.9–1978. Please note that the use of the generic names is recommended. The concept of a generic name has meaning only in cases where the function operates in the realms of several data types. In each of these realms, the function has a specific name, but the generic name is its universal name. Before FORTRAN 77, a programmer had to know all the specific names of the functions, and had to be careful to use the right version of a function with a particular data type. But now, only the much smaller number of generic names need to known, and data types are accommodated automatically. FORTRAN 77 still accepts the specific names for the sake of compatibility with older programs, but these names are already receding into obscurity.

Data Type Conversion Functions

Definition	Number of arguments	Generic name	Specific name	Type of argument	Type of function
Conversion to in-	1	**INT**	—	Integer	Integer
teger			INT	Real	Integer
See Note 1			IFIX	Real	Integer
			IDINT	Double	Integer
			—	Complex	Integer

Definition	Number of arguments	Generic name	Specific name	Type of argument	Type of function
Conversion to real See Note 2	1	**REAL**	REAL	Integer	Real
			FLOAT	Integer	Real
			—	Real	Real
			SNGL	Double	Real
			—	Complex	Real
Conversion to double See Note 3	1	**DBLE**	—	Integer	Double
			—	Real	Double
			—	Double	Double
			—	Complex	Double
Conversion to complex See Note 4	1 or 2	**CMPLX**	—	Integer	Complex
			—	Real	Complex
			—	Double	Complex
				Complex	Complex
Conversion to integer See Note 5	1		ICHAR	Character	Integer
Conversion to character See Note 5	1		CHAR	Integer	Character

Truncation

Definition	Number of arguments	Generic name	Specific name	Type of argument	Type of function
int(*a*) See Note 1	1	**AINT**	AINT	Real	Real
			DINT	Double	Double

Nearest Whole Number

Definition	Number of arguments	Generic name	Specific name	Type of argument	Type of function
$int(a + 0.5), a \geq 0$	1	**ANINT**	ANINT	Real	Real
$int(a - 0.5), a < 0$			DNINT	Double	Double

Nearest Integer

Definition	Number of arguments	Generic name	Specific name	Type of argument	Type of function
$int(a + 0.5), a \geq 0$	1	**NINT**	NINT	Real	Integer
$int(a - 0.5), a < 0$			IDNINT	Double	Integer

Absolute Value

Definition	Number of arguments	Generic name	Specific name	Type of argument	Type of function
$\|a\|$	1	**ABS**	IABS	Integer	Integer
			ABS	Real	Real
See Note 6			DABS	Double	Double
$(ar^2 + ai^2)^{1/2}$			CABS	Complex	Real

Remaindering

Definition	Number of arguments	Generic name	Specific name	Type of argument	Type of function
$a_1 - int(a_1/a_2)*a_2$ See Note 1	2	**MOD**	MOD	Integer	Integer
			AMOD	Real	Real
			DMOD	Double	Double

Definition	Number of arguments	Generic name	Specific name	Type of argument	Type of function
Transfer of Sign					
$\lvert a_1 \rvert, a_2 \geq 0$ $-\lvert a_1 \rvert, a_2 < 0$	2	**SIGN**	ISIGN	Integer	Integer
			SIGN	Real	Real
			DSIGN	Double	Double
Positive Difference					
$a_1 - a_2, a_1 > a_2$ 0 if $a_1 \leq a_2$	2	**DIM**	IDIM	Integer	Integer
			DIM	Real	Real
			DDIM	Double	Double
Double-Precision Product					
$a_1 * a_2$	2		DPROD	Real	Double
Choosing the Largest Value					
$max(a_1, a_2, \ldots)$	≥2	**MAX**	MAX0	Integer	Integer
			AMAX1	Real	Real
			DMAX1	Double	Double
			AMAX0	Integer	Real
			MAX1	Real	Integer
Choosing the Smallest Value					
$min(a_1, a_2, \ldots)$	≥2	**MIN**	MIN0	Integer	Integer
			AMIN1	Real	Real
			DMIN1	Double	Double
			AMIN0	Integer	Real
			MIN1	Real	Integer
Length of a Character Entity					
Length of character entity	1		LEN	Character	Integer
Index of a Substring					
Location of substring a_2 in string a_1. See Note 10	2		INDEX	Character	Integer
The Imaginary Part of a Complex Argument					
ai. See Note 6	1		AIMAG	Complex	Real

Definition	Number of arguments	Generic name	Specific name	Type of argument	Type of function
The Conjugate of a Complex Argument					
$(ar, -ai)$ See Note 6	1		CONJG	Complex	Complex
The Square Root					
$(a)^{1/2}$	1	**SQRT**	SQRT	Real	Real
			DSQRT	Double	Double
			CSQRT	Complex	Complex
Exponential					
e^a	1	**EXP**	EXP	Real	Real
			DEXP	Double	Double
			CEXP	Complex	Complex
Natural Logarithm					
$\ln(a)$	1	**LOG**	ALOG	Real	Real
			DLOG	Double	Double
			CLOG	Complex	Complex
Common Logarithm					
$\log_{10}(a)$	1	**LOG10**	ALOG10	Real	Real
			DLOG10	Double	Double
Sine					
$\sin(a)$	1	**SIN**	SIN	Real	Real
			DSIN	Double	Double
			CSIN	Complex	Complex
Cosine					
$\cos(a)$	1	**COS**	COS	Real	Real
			DCOS	Double	Double
			CCOS	Complex	Complex
Tangent					
$\tan(a)$	1	**TAN**	TAN	Real	Real
			DTAN	Double	Double
Arcsine					
$\arcsin(a)$	1	**ASIN**	ASIN	Real	Real
			DASIN	Double	Double

Definition	Number of arguments	Generic name	Specific name	Type of argument	Type of function
Arccosine					
arccos (a)	1	**ACOS**	ACOS DACOS	Real Double	Real Double
Arctangent					
arctan (a)	1	**ATAN**	ATAN DATAN	Real Double	Real Double
arctan (a_1/a_2)	2	**ATAN2**	ATAN2 DATAN2	Real Double	Real Double
Hyperbolic Sine					
sinh (a)	1	**SINH**	SINH DSINH	Real Double	Real Double
Hyperbolic Cosine					
cosh (a)	1	**COSH**	COSH DCOSH	Real Double	Real Double
Hyperbolic Tangent					
tanh (a)	1	**TANH**	TANH DTANH	Real Double	Real Double
Lexically Greater Than or Equal					
$a_1 \geq a_2$ See Note 12	2		LGE	Character	Logical
Lexically Greater Than					
$a_1 > a_2$ See Note 12	2		LGT	Character	Logical
Lexically Less Than or Equal					
$a_1 \leq a_2$ See Note 12	2		LLE	Character	Logical
Lexically Less Than					
$a_1 < a_2$. See Note 12	2		LLT	Character	Logical

Note 1: When the argument a is real or double precision, if $|a| < 1$, INT(a) = 0. If $|a| \geq 1$, INT(a) is the integer obtained by removing the fractional part of a. The sign is not affected. When the argument a is complex, the above rule is applied only to the real part of the argument. The imaginary part is ignored.

Note 2: REAL(a) always produces a single-precision real value, regardless of the data type of the argument a. When the argument is complex, the function produces the real part of the argument, ignoring the imaginary component.

Note 3: DBLE(a) always produces a double-precision result for arguments of all numeric data types. When the argument is complex, the function ignores the imaginary component and produces the value of the real component in double-precision mode.

Note 4: CMPLX(a) always produces a complex result. If the argument a is integer, real, or double precision, CMPLX(a) produces a complex number with the real component equal to the argument when that argument is converted to single-precision real mode, and the imaginary component equal to zero. When the argument is complex, the function produces a value equal to the argument.

The function CMPLX can also have two arguments of any of the numeric data types, but both arguments must be of the same type. CMPLX(a_1, a_2) produces a complex value $a_1 + ia_2$ when a_1 and a_2 are integer, real, or double precision, and it produces $Rea_1 + iRea_2$ when the arguments are complex.

Note 5: See Sections 14.9 and 14.10 in Chapter 14.

Note 6: (ar, ai) is a complex quantity $ar + ai$, where ar is the real component, and ai is the imaginary component.

Note 7: All functions with arguments that are angles expect the angles to be expressed in radians.

Note 8: A complex function returns the *principal value*. See Prob. 18.3 for a discussion of principal value.

Note 9: Whenever an intrinsic function has more than one argument, all arguments must be of the same data type. Also see the second part of Note 4, above.

Note 10: See Section 14.11 in Chapter 14.

Note 11: When LEN(a) is called, the value of the character argument a need not be defined.

Note 12: See Section 14.12 in Chapter 14.

Additional Notes:

MOD (a_1,a_2) is undefined when a_2 zero.

If $a_1 = 0$, SIGN(a_1,a_2) produces a value of zero, which is neither positive nor negative.

The SQRT function cannot operate on negative arguments.

The logarithmic functions must have positive arguments. A zero argument is not allowed. When the argument is complex, it must not be (0.,0.)

The trigonometric functions SIN, COS, and TAN can have arguments larger than 2π.

ASIN and ACOS must have arguments less than or equal to 1.

Index

E

F

L